FE   D0314350

Richard Askwith has been a journalist since 1980. He lives in Northamptonshire. This is his first book.

Shortlisted for the William Hill Sports Book of the Year, the Boardman-Tasker Award and awarded Best New Writer at the British Sports Book Publishing Awards 2005.

'This book is one of the most effervescent books about anything – never mind fell-running – that I have ever read. It is an explosion of enthusiasm about the sport which whips along in a most compelling fashion and, once started, proves very difficult to put down... He has obviously steeped himself in the history, traditions and personalities of the sport and has researched his material most assiduously to produce a work which is both stimulating and informative . . . The book is a very rich and tasty stew with an amazing number of very piquant ingredients spiced with not a little controversy here and there and what forms its base is the sheer quality of the writing coupled with the constant sense of freshness and enthusiasm' Dave Jones, *The Fellrunner*

'In this excellent book, Richard Askwith somehow manages to convey some of the charm of fell-running and the indomitable willpower of those who excel at it. It is an indispensable part of the life of some rural communities, with colourful protagonists that the author brings to life with a vivid pen . . . Great book, but you will never catch me doing it' Matthew Syed, *The Times*

'Wonderfully well-written' Rob Bagchi, *Guardian*

'[A] rousingly readable chronicle of his life as a fell-runner . . . The book wants for nothing in terms of rhythm and drama and tug. And, like all the best heroes, Askwith comes to understand something of himself during his narrative trajectory. Whichever

way his story had turned out, it would have been a good read'
Christopher Bray, *Sunday Times*

'A sharp yet moving tale of a sporting journey that results in a very personal conquest' *Observer*

'A beautifully told and at times very personal story of fell-running' *Scotland on Sunday*

'Bracing and inspiring' Mike Higgins, *Independent on Sunday*

'A truly superb book . . . An inspirational as well as an engrossing exploration into one of the last genuinely amateur sports' *Westmorland Gazette*

'As a champion of the sport, Askwith would be hard to beat, since he appears to have left very few stones unturned in his thirst for knowledge and his desire to do a proper job in writing about a sport and the people who make it so special. *Craven Herald and Pioneer*

'Richard Askwith's book will be judged by most readers to be the best ever devoted to fell-running, its people and its background' *Keswick Reminder*

'A fascinating insight into a sport that for the most part is never witnessed by spectators, save the odd diehard, and will hardly be considered for prime-time TV. It is an opportunity to experience a different world . . . A book you don't want to put down' *Conserving Lakeland*

'A wonderful, funny and surprisingly moving tale' *Daily Telegraph*

'A book to stir the spirit' *Independent*

FEET IN THE
CLOUDS

A tale of fell-running
and obsession

RICHARD ASKWITH

First published in Great Britain 2004 by Aurum Press Ltd
The Old Brewery, 6 Blundell Street, London N7 9BH

Copyright © Richard Askwith 2004, 2013, 2021
Introduction copyright © Rob Macfarlane 2013
This updated paperback edition first published 2021

Parts of Chapters 6 and 25 originally appeared in
the *Daily Telegraph*
Parts of Chapter 27 originally appeared in the
Independent on Sunday
Parts of Chapter 34 originally appeared in the
Countryman Companion

All rights reserved. No part of this book may be
reproduced or utilised in any form or by any means,
electronic or mechanical, including photocopying,
recording or by any information storage and retrieval
system, without permission in writing from Aurum.

Every effort has been made to trace the copyright
holders of material used in this book. The publisher
apologises for any omission, and will be happy to
rectify them in future editions.

A catalogue record for this book is available
from the British Library.

ISBN 978 1 78131 056 4
eBook ISBN 978 1 84513 649 9

13

Design by Roger Hammond
Maps by Reg Piggott
Typeset in Simoncini Garamond by M Rules
Printed and bound by CPI Group (UK) Ltd, Croydon, CR0 4YY

For Clare, Isobel and Edward

WARNING:
The activities described in this book are dangerous
and may result in injury or death.
Don't try them. Go to a gym instead,
or stay at home and watch television.

CONTENTS

Introduction by Robert Macfarlane

Whenever I press yet another copy of *Feet in the Clouds* upon yet another friend, I try to explain why they should read it, even if they are as likely to take up fell-running themselves as they are to become cave-divers, Classical Mandarin scholars or astronauts. But explanation often proves difficult, because *Feet in the Clouds* is, like most great books, far too many things to be easily summarised. It is a wonderful evocation of the joys of 'running with like-minded friends in wildernesses'; it is a detailed social history of a niche sport; it is a smartly told memoir of obsession and ageing; it is a personal story about how a 'pathetic, sybaritic yuppie' set out to refine himself to whipcord, steel and grit; it is an exploration of pain and endurance, and how these keenly private experiences might be conveyed in language; it is an investigation of two major fault-lines of Britishness (between north and south, rural and urban). It is also frequently very funny, and sometimes beautiful, and several times moving. Above all – and perhaps unexpectedly – it is a study of heroes and heroism, which is why when I find that I have failed to explain to the person upon whom I am pressing the book all the reasons why they should read it, I tell them to imagine it as a cross between the Greek Myths, *The Loneliness of the Long-Distance Runner* and the Marvel Superhero comics.

For what gods populate these pages! The fell-runners we meet here are near-mythical in their stamina and their skills. There is Kenny Stuart, who 'could run on scree and the stones didn't even move'; there is Ernest Dalzell, who flew down nine-tenths of a mile of hillside in under three minutes; there is Joss Naylor, who had half his back removed in an operation and twelve years later ran seventy-two peaks in twenty-four hours; there is John Atkinson, who could descend sixteen-foot precipices at a single bound, and once did a mid-air somersault, landed on his feet and just kept running. Not that these men give themselves the airs of gods, or lounge be-laurelled in their pantheon, of course. No, they are the most down-to-earth divinities you could imagine. When Bob Graham made his legendary round of the Lake District tops in 1932, he did so 'wearing a pyjama top and plimsolls and eating mainly boiled eggs'.

There is something especially superhuman in their tolerance for pain. Reading *Feet in the Clouds*, you realise that fell-running has produced not only some of Britain's most extraordinary athletes, but also some of its toughest individuals. Up on the fells, whingeing is unacceptable and fortitude indispensable. Askwith tells us of Peter Livesey, who broke both ankles in the course of a race, but still completed it; of Chris Gravina, who ran three-quarters of a Mountain Trial with a broken leg; of how, when Joss Naylor did all the Wainwrights (those 214 Lakeland peaks included in Alfred Wainwright's guides to the region) in a continuous push during one summer week at the age of fifty, he covered the distance of almost fifteen marathons laid end to end, he ascended and descended the equivalent of four Everests, he became so dehydrated that his tongue and mouth swelled until he could not eat or talk, and his ankles were rubbed clean through to the ligaments by his ill-fitting shoes. 'Few people have ever conquered themselves so completely,' observes Askwith, 'or so utterly subdued the weaknesses of the flesh to the will of the spirit.'

A book of heroes, then – and a book of hero-worship, too. Askwith's admiration for the great fell-runners shines charmingly out of its pages. Bill Teasdale is 'one of Britain's greatest-ever athletes'; Billy Bland's Bob Graham round time of 13 hours and 53 minutes is 'arguably the most extraordinary record in this or any other sport'; Joss Naylor 'as hard a man as ever had a go at anything'; Kenny Stuart is 'one of the very greatest of British athletes'. Like all true sports fans, Askwith has a passion for stats – feet climbed, miles covered, seconds and minutes shaved from records – but like all true sports writers he also knows that stats are sawdust in the mouth of readers, and that what is needed to prove the extraordinariness of his subject is evocation rather than documentation.

So, of course, the experiences of his own fell-running years – especially his attempts to complete the Bob Graham Round – become the means by which he conveys his love of the sport and its people, and his body becomes the surface on which the mountains and their stories are scored, stored, scribed and harrowed. Literally, in fact: among the numerous injuries and mishaps he suffers is a bottom-slide while coming down Ben Nevis that 'earns me a set of gouges such as I haven't seen since I was beaten at boarding school'. Ha! As that 'earns' suggests, these are the stripes of promotion rather than of punishment. They are tribal scars of belonging; evidence of his commitment to the sport, as well as to a broader ethos of living. For you need, he writes near the book's end, to 'feel . . . nature, to interact with it; to be in it, not just looking from the outside. You need to lose yourself – for it is then that you are most human.'

And how well he writes about that 'interaction', and that sense of 'losing yourself'. He conveys the thrill of moving fluently, at speed and length over remote country (dreams of the Spartans, dreams of the Masai); he catches at the exhilaration of honing one's motor-skills of balance and impact-control, the feel of tilt and push-off, slope and counter-slope; he captures the hurly-burly of wild weather at altitude; the serene beauties of evening runs, with 'the white moon glowing icily out of the deepening blue ahead' and a 'sea of ancient Cumbrian twilight' at his feet; he recalls the profound strangeness of a night run on Skiddaw, with shooting stars floating across the sky every few minutes, such that he seems to be racing through a dream. 'Joy' is a word that recurs in this joyful book: 'the joy of being totally absorbed, as our ancestors were, in wild environments; the joy of throwing off the straitjackets of caution and civilisation; the joy of finding and pushing back limits; and, occasionally, the joy of doing things that one had thought impossible'. The elite runners with whom Askwith meets in the book's course are prodigious inspirations and generous teachers, for by its end he has acquired a fraction of their powers: 'down I fly ... leaping and bouncing, joyfully, madly, hanging in the air longer than nature intended, my whole being singing with physical alertness'.

Such high-flown writing can't be sustained for too long, of course, and Askwith is always quick to ground epiphany with bathos, and to freight passion with self-mockery. An intense aside about upland beauty is followed a few paragraphs later with advice about how to lance blackened toenails with a red-hot paper clip, resulting 'in a spectacular fountain of pus'. 'That's what a mountain is for: stretching your limits on, not pussy-footing around,' he writes shortly after another discourse on beauty. A fascinating tussle emerges over the book's course, in fact, between his instinct for beauty and his appetite for challenge and reward. The tension results most often in humour: 'You can enthuse all you like about the Lake District's fresh air, its awe-inspiring views, its wildness. But I doubt that any of these things is ever really so uplifting to a man's spirits as the smell of a fresh Keswick pub at opening time.' I'm not sure he believes that, but it's a good line nevertheless.

The book is ingeniously structured such that two contrasting time-schemes run concurrently. There is the calendrical telling of the 'fell-running year' as it unfolds month by month. And there is a longer-term telling of Askwith's own fell-running years, driven forwards by the will-he/won't-he challenge of the arduous Bob Graham Round. This clever dual structure allows him to explore the various weathers and territories of fell-running, and to feature many of the classic annual races: the Hill Forts and Headaches Race, the Morning After Race, the Dragon's Back, the Three Peaks (each sounding like a malicious invention from Willy Wonka's Discomfort Factory).

It also allows him to cut away into the sport's history, from the 'anarchic' and unrecorded years before 1850, into its formalisation in the early 1900s, through the pioneering decades of the 1950s to the 1970s, 'when peace and the freedom to roam Britain's wild places were still recently won luxuries', through the internecine wars between professionals and amateurs, 'incomers' and locals, and up to the recent rise of ultra-distance running. A complex social picture emerges of a sport that was born of old landscapes but has been inevitably infiltrated by modernity. 'No modern fell-running club can conform to the clichéd stereotype of a tight-knit band of shepherds and gamekeepers,' he writes, 'deeply rooted in their unchanging rural community . . . we are all new Britons now.' The whole book rises towards its tremendous apex, when Askwith sets off for his fourth and final attempt on the Bob Graham Round with the spirit of Joss in his joints, and a headful of hard-won wisdom about what endurance really means.

I've read *Feet in the Clouds* four or five times now. I tend to reach for it when I'm feeling lax or weak or glum. I always end it rallied, inspired, cheered. And I also always end it thinking that if I could convert my body by means of a magic trick into the physique of any kind of elite athlete, I wouldn't choose the gymnast's chiselled perfection, certainly not the mahogany pneumatics of a bodybuilder or weightlifter, and not even the honed sinews of the rower. No, I'd want the body of a fell-runner; and more than that, I'd want the mind of a fell-runner, too, because as one of Askwith's friends tells him early on: 'Anyone can be fit. It's being hard that's hard.'

There are aspects of the elegy present here. Askwith writes of 'the passing-away of an old way of thinking' about people and place. He speaks of the 'vanished world' in which runners like Bill Teasdale won their glories, and of legends like Joss Naylor slipping into 'isolated obscurity . . . fading away like old soldiers, unheard and irrelevant'. But as I write this introduction, nearly a decade on from the first publication of his book, fell-running feels – to me at least – far from a dying sport. Unlikely high-profile participants have emerged: Boff Whalley, the rock-star anarchist, has just written a book about his own obsession with fell-running. Strange re-expressions of the fell-running impulse are emerging: I recently met an artist called Tim Brennan who was beginning a six-year project to run the frontiers of the Roman Empire at its zenith – he had started with Hadrian's Wall: a 98-mile non-stop run through wild country. And most hopefully of all, the sport seems to be rejuvenating itself at the grass-roots level.

Late this summer I was in the North-West Lakes, due to take part in a small fell race from Keswick up into the Skiddaw valley. But I'd torn both calves while training, and could barely hobble to the start line (no Livesey-style heroics for me). So I successfully looked after everyone's bags, while my parents (aged in their early sixties), my sister-in-law (aged thirty-two), my children (aged six and eight), and my niece (aged two and half) all took part in fell races, over distances ranging from 500 yards to 10 miles. There was nothing elite about the occasion, but the atmosphere was buzzingly happy and the race-lists were full, from junior to senior. A samba band drummed and crashed to warm up the runners, sunlight flared on the brackened slopes of Skiddaw, and kids galloped past in their Walshes with the glow of fanaticism in their eyes.

The next day I was at another fell race, this time at the Loweswater Show. It was a simple brute of a run, from a field in the valley to a marshal halfway up a scree-sided peak called Whiteside, then back down to the field again. I watched the runners leave, watched them reappear as ants on the hillside, watched the fastest of them float impossibly quickly back over the screes, watched the winner glide back into the field preposterously soon after leaving and barely out of breath. Later, a big man jogged over the line, his skin covered in tattoos, his singlet and shorts covered in blood. He'd fallen on the descent, cut himself up and broken at least one rib, but had kept going anyway. I saw him later getting bandaged up by the first-aid team, his arms held in the air as they strapped his ribs, and his young daughter at his side, looking up at him like he was a god or a superhero.

Robert Macfarlane, 2012

1

A hard place

THIS IS HOW DEATH MUST FEEL. Not the pain, although I imagine most deaths must be painful, but the fear. Fear of what? I hardly dare say.

Something has happened to me. For more hours than I can remember, a storm has been screaming around me. For more hours than I can remember, I have been running – or trying to run – in the mountains. Now I am lost, utterly. Every muscle in my body is shaking, both feet are blistered raw, every joint aches, and my last reserves of warmth and strength are gushing away like steam.

A cloud of icy fog clings thickly to everything, smothering the afternoon into twilight. Winds whip it, randomly, like a loose sail in a wild sea. Obscure horrors gust through it: hailstones, dark shapes, hints of lightning, great explosions of rain. Yet I cannot actually see more than a few yards around me – except on two brief occasions when the storm rips the curtain apart to reveal ghastly cliffs in all directions. My map and my local knowledge insist that such cliffs cannot possibly be there. The rip closes too quickly for me to make sense of this.

So now I have stopped; or, at least, I am hobbling so pathetically and aimlessly that it cannot reasonably be classified as movement. I have no idea what to do. I am a big, strong, fit young man, with a deep voice, broad shoulders and a hairy chest. At home, I am father of a family; London is full of successful journalists who consider me or have considered me their boss. And I want to cry.

This is not despair. This is the raw animal distress of the wounded and the terrified; the kind that combines self-pity with panic. Something has gone badly wrong.

It doesn't help that my compass is malfunctioning, showing north in diametrically the wrong direction. Nor, I suppose, does my sprained ankle. Yet the pain is almost a comfort. If I focus on the agonies shooting from my mangled joint, or on the splinters of glass that slice through my clothes, masquerading as rain, it reminds me of how things were an hour or so ago. Then, I was miserable but still myself. Now I have been unmanned: a poor, bare, forked animal cowering helplessly on the rocks.

Perhaps this is what wounded soldiers feel, as they call with their dying breath for their mothers: the same sense of losing one's integrity as a functioning adult; the same sense that one can do no more. Except that I am not yet dying. Not yet, if I could just think what to do.

I cannot.

I feel sleepy. I have been at this for eight hours or more. I have, I repeat, no idea what to do. I am starting to feel strangely warm. I think I might lie down.

But not quite yet. Somehow, I can still think – with just enough coherence to see that thinking is my best hope. There is an answer to this problem. With sufficient thought, I will find it.

Think, then. This is not the worst. I could be clinging to a cliff by my fingertips. I could have broken a leg – two legs. I could be lost in the Himalayas. I could have been lost for days. Countless billions of men have faced worse challenges than this, not just through adventuring but in such routine tests as war and natural disaster. Many have abandoned hope and life. Many haven't.

Better men than me have whimpered and cowered; but plenty of others – also better than me – have hardened in the challenge. Think of them. Think of Shackleton, lost without hope in the Antarctic night. Think of Joe Simpson, starving with broken limbs in a lost Andean valley. Think of all those generations of men, before my self-indulgent cohort of baby-boomers, who lived hard lives without complaining and would have scorned to pity themselves in the face of catastrophe. Think of my father, and all those other fathers who fought with him in the Second World War.

Think of the men who have lived whole lives in these mountains. Think of Joss Naylor.

Joss Naylor! A flush of shame restores my alertness. What kind of pathetic, sybaritic yuppie am I, whingeing to myself and dreaming of hot baths, just because of a sore ankle, a broken compass and a few million drops of horizontal hail? This is England, for God's sake; the nearest road can't be more than 5 or 6 miles away. The temperature can't be that many degrees below zero. I could crawl 5 miles on my hands and knees and still be back by Monday. Anyway, they'd send the mountain rescue team out before I had time to die. And, more to the point, I'm supposed to be a fell-runner.

That means I'm a member of the same breed as Joss Naylor and Billy Bland and Kenny Stuart and Bill Teasdale; the same as Ian Holmes and Helene Diamantides. I'm finding it tough, am I? Well, it's supposed to be tough. If I can't handle it, I should bugger off back to London where I came from.

Self-respect drags an impulse for survival from my depths. Somehow I must get moving – anywhere. Almost anywhere. Not down the frightful cliffs. But somewhere.

Time for the option of last resort: trust the compass. In which case, if it's right, and if my estimate of my position is accurate to within even half a mile, then all I need to do is head that way – what the compass calls 'south' – and sooner or later I'll have to intersect the path I was on half an hour ago.

I stagger off: limp, whimper, limp, whimper. Or rather: limp, whimper, chatter-chatter-chatter; limp, whimper, chatter-chatter-chatter. I'm going downhill, when it ought to be up, but who cares? If I can just keep in a straight line then at least I'll be getting somewhere.

The wind bites through me, from behind now, but I shrug it off. No more whingeing. Think of Eddie Campbell, trotting through Glencoe snowstorms in his plimsolls, with just a handful of boiled sweets in his anorak pocket to stave off hypothermia. Think of the hard men – and women, too – who run on these rocks every day.

Sure enough, a path appears. It bears no resemblance to the

path I was on before, but let's ignore that. All paths lead somewhere. Follow it round to the west and I'll either end up somewhere I recognise or . . . well, who knows, maybe bump into that great big river on the next map-square across, or perhaps another human being.

I force myself to run, although my legs are so shaky that I keep tripping on loose rocks. I cannot describe the pain: every step lands on sharp, slimy stones, which either bite like teeth or slide from under me, or, in some cases, both. My thighs protest each time I lift a leg; my whole body screams each time I put a foot down. Very well: don't listen. Feelings are for girls. My mind is full of thoughts of toughness: the sheer brute willpower by which hostile mountains are sometimes tamed. Think of Simon Bolivar's starving, half-naked peasant army, stumbling blindly across the most lethal summits in the Andes. Think of George Brass, hobbling through a blizzard with one shoe, not just to win the toughest mountain race of the 1960s but to be its only finisher. Limp, whimper; limp, whimper. At least it's keeping me warm.

Some time later – I cannot say how much later – I realise that I am on the right path. Not the right part of it – I passed this narrow rock cleft hours ago – but on it, nonetheless. I must have been in a vast circle, or perhaps a figure of eight. Never mind: at least now, if I double-check with map and compass, I can fix my position with certainty. I do so; and, as if as a sign from heaven, two shadows appear in the fog ahead. People, walking towards me, gradually emerging as two red-faced men, tightly wrapped in sodden, flapping cagoules. Now I can treble-check.

'Sorry, mate,' shouts one, 'can you tell us where we are?'

I point them in what I imagine to be the right direction, then resume my painful trot. I feel confident now. If I take my time, and avoid any further navigational disasters, I'm now within two or three hours of my hot bath. (*Two or three hours? Holy Jesus.*) But I'm not thinking about it any more. Hot baths are for babies. I am a fell-runner. I am, if it comes to that, a big strong man again: big enough and strong enough to have brought a glow of reassurance into the day of two panicking walkers. I am also in possession of a map and, it now seems, a working compass. I am master of this mountain.

And I think of Joss Naylor, charging like a mad animal over peak after peak through the most atrocious storm of 1972, in the middle of the night; and of Bill Teasdale, skipping through the hail and mist of the 1953 Mountain Trial, while the official runners who deemed him unworthy to race against them struggled and shivered miles behind; of Helene Diamantides leaving a trail of battered paratroopers snivelling in her wake in the 1992 Dragon's Back race; of Martin Stone screaming defiance at Pen Llithrig-Y-Wrach, the final peak in his record-breaking Paddy Buckley Round of 1985; of Kenny Stuart flying up and down Ben Nevis in 1984, light-footed as a ballet-dancer; of 'Dalzell's race' in 1910. All those miracles of human endeavour; all those heroes, lost in the hill-mists of time. Great things are done when men and mountains meet; and, though not one Briton in a hundred has any inkling that the great kings of their fells ever existed, the heroics of the greatest are as glorious as anything in sport's history.

In some bizarre way, I can feel their spirit in me now; and by the time I have begun the long, long descent towards the lake by which I have left my car, there is adrenalin pumping through my body. THUMP-thump-THUMP-thump-THUMP-thump. I am scarcely even limping. Sweat splashes from me as if the sun were blazing. I shake the drops from my face with rhythmic tosses of the head, driving myself with the beat. I am a boxer, pummelling a speedball, skipping, dancing. Keep the speed up, keep the reflexes moving. Above all, keep on top. For the one immutable rule when men and mountains meet is this: that either man or mountain must be in charge. They cannot both be master.

By the time I reach the bottom, half an hour later, the mountain has pretty much wrested back control. My rhythmic jog has slowed again to an agonised shuffle, and the tosses of my head smack less of aggression than of desperation. Never mind: I am down now, and have only to limp a few hundred yards along the tarmac to reach the car. I will force myself to cover those yards at a jog, and only when I have done so I will think about hot baths.

I cover those yards at a walk. Thoughts of hot baths sap my every slack-legged stride. Finally, I fumble my way into my car, collapse on to the passenger seat, half-change into the dry clothes I have left there, close the door, and fall asleep.

This, I should add, is what I do for fun.

2

Scenes from a fell-running year: January

New Year's Day dawns damp and chill, as if the sky were hungover. Across the United Kingdom, people go about their bank-holiday business according to the approved traditions of the twenty-first century: tottering nauseously to pubs, slumping in front of screens, shopping, doing DIY. In at least ten counties, however, small bands of hardy eccentrics – no more than two or three hundred, all told – are marking the fresh year through more primitive rituals.

In the south Pennines, at Ogden Reservoir, thirty-one scantily clad runners race up and down the peaty sides of Ovenden Moor to the Giant's Tooth monument and back, a journey of 3 steep miles in heavy drizzle. In east Cumbria, there are nearer sixty runners who brave rain, snow and icy winds to contest the Nine Standards fell race: an 8-mile circuit of the mountains, or fells, above Kirkby Stephen. In North Yorkshire, near Whitby, 157 people splash up slimy tracks to Captain Cook's monument and back; on Snowdon, more than forty runners struggle through cold winds and swollen rivers for a 5-mile race from Pen-y-Pass; in Grampian, only twenty-four people complete the Tap o' Noth race; in Northumberland, fierce rain and snow add to the rigours of the uphill-only Hill Forts and Headaches race at Rothbury; on the Isle of Man, the Rass Valley Keein Eoin race is rerouted because of an impassably torrential river; in Shropshire, several competitors in the Morning After race above Church Stretton show unmistakable signs of an overenthusiastic night before.

You could watch any one of these events and form much the same impression: pale, hollow-faced runners, many in thermal hats and gloves, moving at a wide range of speeds but all heading for the cold mountaintops with apparent indifference to the gradient and the elements. If you had some experience of running or of mountains, you might be impressed by the relentlessness with which they maintain their uphill momentum. You would almost certainly be struck by the abandon of their subsequent downhill gallops: thundering down the wet slopes like ponies, drips of sweat bouncing from them into the drizzle, a faint trail of steam lingering in the air behind them. But your overall verdict, had you never seen such a sight before, would be more likely to dwell on its strangeness than on its beauty. Most people, after all, would consider themselves wildly adventurous and energetic if they so much as walked up a mountain on New Year's Day; the idea of running up one – or more than one – seems preposterous. A fat man in the car park at Ogden Reservoir speaks for many when, glowering from his car as the finished runners hastily half-change into warmer clothing, obstructing his exit, he growls: 'Bloody weirdos. Weirdos and masochists.'

Yet to dismiss these people as freaks would be a mistake. There are more of them than you might think: when the season gets going they can be counted in thousands. And they are more normal than they seem. Look more closely at some of the people involved in those New Year's Day events, and in the dozen or so that succeed them as January unfolds, and you'll find a perfectly ordinary range of respectable citizens, holding down a perfectly ordinary range of responsible jobs.

Take a few examples. Tim Austin, winner of the Giant's Tooth race, is a twenty-seven-year-old chartered surveyor from Sheffield. Wendy Dodds, fourth woman home in the Nine Standards, is a fifty-one-year-old rheumatologist from Milnthorpe in Cumbria. Ian Holmes, winner of both the Boulsworth Hill race in Lancashire and the Stanbury Splash in West Yorkshire (the former in deep snow and the latter in a screaming gale), is a thirty-seven-year-old Jacuzzi fitter from Keighley. Mark Hartell, placed third in the White Nancy fell race in Cheshire, is a thirty-nine-year-old IT project manager from Leek in Staffordshire. Louise Sharp, first female finisher in the Howgill fell race near Tebay in Cumbria, is a thirty-one-year-old junior-school teacher from Keswick. All look young for their age: Austin crop-haired and muscular; Dodds handsome and severe; Holmes miniature and alert; Hartell strong-jawed and restless; Sharp pretty and laid-back. But none would strike you as strange if you met them. As Allan Greenwood, the forty-one-year-old printer who organises the Giant's Tooth race, puts it: 'They're just an easy-going bunch of people who love running and love the hills.'

Yet they are, to be fair to the man in the car park, not exactly standard-issue human beings. Holmes, for example, is one of the most gifted athletes alive. A little, unassuming man who subsists largely on baked beans on toast, he combines the aerobic gifts of an elite distance runner with the hardiness of a polar explorer. In a decade or so at the top of his sport, he's been British fell-running champion four times and English fell-running champion four times. He holds more than twenty records, and there's not a major mountain race in Britain that he hasn't won at least once; in fact, there's a growing number of races in West Yorkshire that he's won ten years on the trot. (In Borneo – where he won the famous Mount Kinabalu race three years running – he's a celebrity.) Lou Sharp, similarly, is – though she's too modest to mention it – the reigning British women's fell-running champion. She only took up running seven years ago, when her mountain-bike was stolen on holiday, and drifted into fell-running when she married a fell-runner; now she has her eye on a place in the England team for the World Mountain Running Trophy. She's also captain of Keswick, Britain's leading women's fell-running team. Wendy Dodds is the English over-50s champion; she's also a former international swimmer and orienteer and British Olympic team doctor, and knows Britain's mountains as intimately as anyone alive. Mark Hartell – who follows the White Nancy race with a 16-mile run back to his home – has run races of 100 miles or more in places as far afield as Alaska and the Sahara, and holds the prestigious Lake District twenty-four-hour record for the most peaks run up and down in a single day. Tim Austin came to the sport less than four years ago and is already pushing for a place in the England team.

Over the next twelve months, their talent and passion will take these people all over the mountainous parts of Britain, on a largely informal circuit that encompasses some of the most beautiful and romantic sporting events imaginable. Some of these will relate to the quest for titles; other races they'll be running simply because they're there. In the process, they'll rub shoulders both with championship rivals (perhaps a couple of dozen serious contenders for the men's title and a few hundred more who are vying to be champions in other categories – women's, Over-40s, Over-50s, etc); and with several thousand others who have quite different agendas.

Some of this last group will aspire merely to perform well in certain local events; others are concentrating on some recognised big race, such as the Three Peaks in April or the Ben Nevis in September. A few have their eyes on one of the great ultra-distance solo challenges. Most – including me – don't really have any plans at all, beyond trying to run a good range of races, preferably without coming last, and to have some fun in the process. We run in the mountains in the same way that ordinary people play football or tennis: for pleasure and companionship – and simply because it is what we do. But we're still committed, like the champions, to hundreds of miles of reckless mountain endeavour.

For all the average British sports fan knows about such activities, they might as well take place on a different planet. It's a fair bet that not one fell race from the coming season will rate a column inch on the sports pages of the national newspapers. Which is a pity, because, between them, the sport's champions and also-rans know some things that are well worth knowing: about sport, about themselves, and about Britain.

3

The basics

THERE IS NOTHING OBVIOUSLY COMPLICATED
ABOUT FELL-RUNNING. You run up the fell; you run down
again. Sometimes, by way of variation, you then run up and down
another – perhaps many others. That's about all there is to it.

Apart from the complications.

Try it for yourself and you can't miss them. The surface, for a
start, is wrong. What's normally meant by 'running' is rarely done
on anything bumpier than a pavement or running track, or, at
worst, mown grass. Your feet do the running and your mind
focuses on other things. The fell-runner has to contend with mud,
boulders, pebbles, loose scree, wet grass, bog, slabs of greasy rock,
bumps, holes, loose tussocks, streams and more, much of it
concealed by heather or bracken (or, in extreme cases, darkness).
With every step, your foot lands at a different angle, which is rarely
the kind of angle nature intended. Every footfall – if you're not
concentrating on it – can potentially lead to a sprain, fracture or
fall. And even without mishaps, the incessant sliding-about within
your shoes will almost certainly lacerate you with blisters.

Then there's the slope. Again, normal running is generally done
on the flat. Road-runners moan if they're confronted with a few
hundred metres of mild uphill gradient. Most other people never
run uphill at all (with good reason: it's difficult). Fell-runners face
steep climbs that continue for miles at a time, climbing hundreds
or sometimes thousands of feet, at gradients that many people
would hesitate to walk up. This isn't quite as hard as it sounds,
once you've done it a few times and worked out how to change
down to a sufficiently low gear. But it is hard to keep going; and

the further – or faster – you go, the harder it gets. Sooner or later, your calves run out of fuel, after which every step burns with pain, each one more fiercely than the last.

And then, of course, there's what you find at the top: rocks, grass, the odd sheep; and, most importantly, the weather. Other athletes give little thought to weather, unless they're the kind who see rain as a reason for cancelling their activities altogether. Fell-runners spend half their time being lashed by the peculiarly icy varieties of wind and rain that blow at the top of mountains, and, worse, being engulfed in cloud. I say 'worse' because, while no one likes being cold or wet, such experiences are usually tolerable if brought to a swift conclusion. Get lost – as easily happens when visibility is severely reduced in a featureless wasteland of rocks, grass and sheep – and you could be looking at hours of unplanned coldness and wetness, exacerbated by exhaustion. Such hazards are remote to those whose sporting exertions are performed in stadia, gyms, courts or playing fields (or, for that matter, in memory or imagination). But for fell-runners they are real and potentially fatal; as is, of course, the risk that the lost, disoriented, hypothermic runner will plunge off an unseen cliff.

But even that isn't the worst of it. In fact, it's the good bit. The main trouble with fell-running lies in the fact that, having run up a mountainside, you have to run down. This is where the pain starts.

The problem is gravity. Going up, it's a brake; going down, an accelerator. Yes, but isn't acceleration what runners want? In a sense, it is. Tommy Metcalfe, a famous fell-runner of the early 1900s, in later life ran a pub in Bradford, where he would occasionally boost his income by betting customers that he could sprint 100 yards in ten seconds – an improbable feat for a middle-aged man, but one that he accomplished with ease by performing it down the steep side of a slag heap.

With enough gravity on my side, even I, a moderate, recreational runner in my mid-forties, can run faster than Linford Christie. On the whole, though, I'd rather not. Even on the smoothest surface (try it on a steep road), it takes intense concentration to run at such a speed without getting your feet tangled up; on a bumpy, slippery fellside, foot-tangling is the least of your worries – every stone is a potential leg-breaker.

But the real hazard is not the treachery of the surface so much as the fact that, on a long, steep hill, your speed and momentum grow almost instantaneously to unmanageable levels. I wouldn't mind risking the occasional mad downhill dash at Olympic sprinting speed if there were any assurance that having reached that speed – about 22 miles per hour – I could then stop accelerating. On a big hill, you can't. Even if you're not making any effort at all to run fast, gravity keeps on sucking you down, inexorably, faster and faster, until – well, the ground's the limit, really. I don't suppose a fell-runner's terminal velocity is anything like the 160 miles per hour a human body can achieve in freefall, but I see no theoretical reason why a totally committed runner with no sense of self-preservation at all shouldn't reach, say, 60 miles per hour on a really steep, long, flat-out, downhill sprint.

Except, of course, that it would be suicidal to do so.

So: you slow down – only to find that that, too, is harder than it sounds. As anyone who has ever walked down a mountain knows, coming downhill in a controlled way places a dreadful strain on your thighs and, if you're heavily laden, your knees and ankles. Running downhill in a controlled way has a similar effect, except that the added momentum doubles or trebles the impact. Doing so on a treacherous surface doubles or trebles the risk that something will snap under the strain – at which point a violent fall will almost certainly multiply your injuries.

In one sense, the more cautiously you run, the greater your risk of injury, because in attempting to bring your weight under control you are putting greater pressure both on your tendons and on the loose ground that your feet are trying to grip; whereas while you are accelerating – and thus pushing *with* your momentum rather than against it – the impact of any individual step is relatively slight. The trouble is that while you are accelerating you are multiplying the forces that you will ultimately have to bring under control.

Essentially, then – despite the paradox that you seem to

increase your risk of injury both by running more cautiously and by running less cautiously – the choice facing every fell-runner is a simple one: which do I value more – safety or speed? Or, to put it more simply still: how fast do I dare go?

For many, the answer is: very fast indeed.

Go to Grasmere for the Lake District's most famous summer sports show, and if you watch the Senior Guides Race (as the main fell race is known) from the end of the field furthest from the mountain, you'll probably assume that the fellside is smooth and springy and soft, for the runners come down it as freely as children rushing across a gently sloping playground. Go a bit closer – or, better, actually walk up the hill yourself – and you'll see the slope for what it is: a wildly uneven slice of raw mountain, on which boulders, stones, crevasses, lumps, holes and wet turf are largely concealed by knee-high bracken – except towards the top, where the greenery gives way to bare rock and scree that most people would fear to negotiate without using hands as well as feet. A normal walker would walk down this hill with extreme caution. The runners all but fly down it.

'When you turn at the top, disengage the brain,' is one former champion's tip. 'Brakes off, brain off,' says another. 'Just run it flat out,' advises a third, 'and the feet take care of themselves.' It's a lot easier to say than to do, but that doesn't mean that some people don't do it. Fell-running lore is full of tales of crazy, reckless descents, in which the boundaries between running, leaping and plummeting all but disappear. One early twentieth-century report speaks of a runner in the Grasmere Guides Race forging ahead, 'with great leaps, throwing himself through the air, crashing down the bracken and heather, skimming over rocks'. Disasters are frequent, though not invariably catastrophic. Tommy Garside fell three times in the Grasmere Guides Race in 1968, but still won (though he collapsed at the line). Reg Harrison famously fell six times while winning the same race in 1962; a report at the time described him as 'shaken but not stirred'. But to say that it isn't dangerous is to miss the point. It is. It just doesn't necessarily kill you.

Tommy Sedgwick, the great fell-running champion of the 1970s whose victories were invariably achieved by descending more recklessly than his rivals, once told me proudly that he 'didn't finish many seasons' – he was always injured. His most spectacular prang was at Grasmere in 1967, when he fell down a well. Among other injuries, he burst a blood vessel in his right thigh, which has never entirely regained its natural shape. He sprained his ankles so often they ended up twice as thick as those of a normal man. But that didn't stop him winning the British Hill Running Championship – on the notoriously steep course at Alva in Scotland – twelve times in a row. On the twelfth occasion, he 'tripped and rolled from halfway down to virtually the bottom'. His wife 'was still pulling black bits of gorse out of my shoulder in October, and Alva was in July'. But he still won. And, though the state of his knees leaves something to be desired, he still leads a fit and hearty life as a farmer in his fifties.

Trawl the libraries of the north for reports of fell races past and you'll find any number of accounts of descents celebrated for their recklessness: runners leaping rather than running, or falling, rolling and righting themselves, or simply propelling themselves with such abandon that they might reasonably have been described as flying.

Here's the great Bill Teasdale in full downhill flight in the *Craven Herald* in 1953, 'bounding and springing over knee-deep heather, huge boulders and high walls . . .'. Here's W. C. Skelton's 1921 description of the Three Gullies Race at Coniston, with runners 'leaping over precipitous crags on to beds of bracken'. Skelton enthuses particularly about 'a thrilling leap down Coniston fell – something like 16 feet sheer drop taken at top speed . . .'. Here's Canon Rawnsley's report of R. Lancaster's winning Grasmere run in 1887: 'The way in which he throws himself rather than leaps down, his hands above his head as he steadies himself in the downward plunge, fairly startles one . . .'. Here's Gurkha Karkabir Tharpa, descending Glamaig in 1899: 'He came down,' according to his superior officer, 'in a series of jumps, and each time his foot landed he slid for some distance as the scree moved under him.' Here's Sir Percy Hope, master of Blencathra

Foxhounds, on the descending technique of the great Ernest Dalzell: 'To see him take a flying leap over a stone wall and roll over in the bracken to his feet on the other side was unforgettable.' And here's John Atkinson, champion guides-racer of the late 1980s and early 1990s, on a moment in the Hawkswick Dash when, leaping from the steep summit, he found himself doing a somersault in mid-air: 'I somehow landed back on my feet without any other part of my body hitting the ground. All of this was totally unintentional and frightened the life out of me.'

To say that such strategies constituted the *best* way of running down a mountainside is debatable, but they were certainly the fastest. It was Dalzell, an Ormathwaite gamekeeper, who in 1910 won the Burnsall race, in North Yorkshire, with a descent so spectacular and swift that the race starter, the local vicar, refused to accept the verdict of the official time-keeper's watch, insisting (and reporting in his parish magazine) that Dalzell's winning time was a whole minute slower than had been recorded. Most others present disagreed, and the record – and the controversy – stood for the next sixty-seven years. Even today, a few old people survive who claim that they, or someone they knew, actually watched 'Dalzell's race', in the same way that others will tell you that they saw 'Obolensky's try' or 'Botham at Headingley'. According to my calculations, Dalzell must have run the downhill section – a distance of nine-tenths of a mile, over grass, heather, mud, rock, bracken and loose stones – at an average speed of 21 miles per hour. That's equivalent to a 10.65-second 100 metres.

'It is impossible to describe the terrific pace with which Dalzell flung himself down the slope,' reported the *Craven Herald* of that race. 'Dalzell's descent was hair-raising in the extreme,' wrote H. Mortimer Batten, who witnessed it, in a subsequent race programme. 'Never would one have credited that legs other than those of a deer could perform the terrific leaps and bounds over hollows and boulders which carried Dalzell to victory.'

'It was something inhuman,' an anonymous observer was quoted as saying, 'for the man stayed in the air longer than nature intended.' 'He was not running merely, or leaping, or sliding over the treacherous ground,' wrote Halliwell Sutcliffe, a local author. 'He was doing all three at once, in some astounding way, and his gait suggested the antelope's, slim, carefree – swift as the footless wind.'

Described like this, it sounds like Formula One. And, indeed, when you consider the demands that the sport makes on strength, stamina, speed and nerve, together with the constant risk of catastrophic injury, it's curious that fell-running has never shown signs of evolving into a multimillion-pound sport with a global audience and sponsorship from tobacco companies. In fact, hardly anyone outside the fell-running counties has heard of the sport, let alone its stars. There's more money in bowls.

The reason is simple: fell-running is inconvenient to watch. Even for the dedicated hundreds who turn up to fell races to spectate (and most modern sports fans would consider even that an act of ill-advised hardiness), there isn't often much to look at. Yes, the action is incomparably more exciting than running around in circles on a flat track, but most of it takes place out of sight, high in the crags – and clouds – above. Energetic spectators can find vantage points further up than the road-level start and finish, but there's no guarantee that they'll choose the right bit of the mountainside to see the most thrilling moments. This is particularly true of the longer-distance events, some of which carry on all day (or, in a few cases, longer).

The same inconveniences – coupled with the impossibility of conveying the scale of the mountains, the difficulty of the ground and the violence of the runners' movements in the same shot – limit the capacity of photographers and television cameramen to capture the drama of the sport, especially in an age in which armchair sports audiences expect multiple camera angles, facial expressions, close-ups, replays, overviews. (You could throw helicopters at the problem; but the cost is enormous, and the resulting noise rather spoils the wild, idyllic environment that is part of the sport's charm.) And if a sport cannot be experienced through television, it's hard for the modern mind to comprehend it at all.

Yet fell-running deserves comprehension. If greatness in sport is defined by drama, courage and sheer athletic excellence, I see no objective reason why Dalzell's 1910 Burnsall race, or Kenny Stuart's 1984 Ben Nevis race, or George Brass's 1962 Mountain Trial, or Joss Naylor's 1986 Wainwrights round, or Mark Hartell's 1997 Lakeland twenty-four-hour record (all of which we'll return to later) should be considered less outstanding or sublime than the better-documented exploits of Botham, Bannister and Beckham. But whereas the latter have a permanent place in folk memory, the supreme achievements of fell-running have left scarcely a trace on the nation's consciousness. And although Ian Holmes, for one, has an infinitely better claim to sporting immortality than most of today's super-rich British Olympians, neither his name nor his face has the slightest resonance beyond the boundaries of his minority sport.

Perhaps that is what drew me into the sport, and what spurs me now to write about it. The heroes of fell-running have not been men – or women – prone to bragging; without a historian, there will soon be no more trace of their achievements than of the mists in which they were performed.

In fact, there are records in various libraries, if you know what to look for, and a few useful volumes in second-hand bookshops (although you'll be lucky to track down a copy of *Stud Marks on the Summits*, Bill Smith's magnificent 1985 history of amateur fell-running, from which much of my historical information is drawn). But most of these are written for those inside the sport, with a reliance on stark statistics ('He reached the summit in a time of 3:21.35, with 8.38 to spare over the next arrival') which means little to those not already in the know.

What I want to find out about – and, if possible, to preserve – are the stories behind these statistics. Who were these people? What kind of lives did they lead? What did the mountains mean to them? Where did they find the strength to master them? And what drives their modern successors to attempt to emulate them?

My quest for answers to these questions has been more successful in some cases than in others. But, in the course of it, I have encountered an overwhelming consensus about the answer to another, simpler question: what makes a good fell-runner?

Answer: you need four things. A good heart and lungs. A light frame, preferably well under 10 stone, with no excess fat. The kind of sure-footedness that comes from lifelong familiarity with the hills. And a disregard for pain and danger that verges on lunacy.

As a 13-stone Southerner with weak ankles who spent the best years of his life smoking and is terrified of heights, I'm a less-than-perfect fit for this profile.

I wish someone had told me that fifteen years ago.

4

Scenes from a fell-running year: February

Wendy Dodds (the Milnthorpe rheumatologist) spends February 'resting' a freak foot injury; that is, restricting her training to gym, bicycle and swimming pool. A few days after the Nine Standards race, she landed awkwardly when jumping a ditch on a training run and completely ruptured the plantar fascia in her right foot – the major tendon that runs along the bottom. It will never heal: she'll be lucky to walk normally again. She's back at work the next day ('I'd have to be dead to miss a day's work') and plans to be racing again within three months. But she's not, for the time being, running.

Lou Sharp (the Keswick teacher) has her first 'real' fell race of the season in Midlothian, where 460 runners, including many of the travelling elite, contest the 6-mile Carnethy 5 Hill Race under a brilliant blue sky. The race commemorates the Scottish victory over the English in the Battle of Roslin in 1303: hence the battle re-enactment before the start, and the fact that several competitors – including the ladies' winner, Angela Mudge – wear kilts or similar battledress.

Lou, who comes second, has an impressively relaxed running style, suggestive less of speed than of strength and confidence. She is, however, at pains to point out that Mudge, a multiple former champion, is a far better runner than she is. 'I only won the title last year because Angela was too busy competing abroad to run in the championship races. I'm not exactly up there with the real elite.' We can judge the accuracy of that statement for ourselves as, from time to time in the course of this book, we follow Lou's fortunes – and those of various other runners, including her husband Nick – through the course of a fell-running season.

The crucial thing to remember, when reading these occasional monthly snapshots, is that the races described are not simply athletic contests: they are events involving mountains – steep, cold, dangerous things on which it isn't sensible to race. This is well demonstrated in South Yorkshire, where Tim Austin (the Sheffield surveyor) wins the 12.5-mile Mickleden Straddle in a vicious blizzard that causes seventeen mid-race retirements and at least two cases of hypothermia. One of the victims is saved by a heroic marshal on Howden Clough who first lends him her gloves and coat, then procures him a survival bag from a passing cyclist and then, for his benefit and hers, gets into the bag with him. Two other passers-by are then persuaded to take it in turns to wrap their arms around the bag until help arrives. Afterwards, there's a brief panic when one runner is still unaccounted for nearly two hours after the finish. A major rescue operation is about to be launched; then she is found in the shower. She retired from the race hours ago but neglected to inform the organisers.

Elsewhere, Ian Holmes (the Keighley Jacuzzi-fitter) claims his third victory of the year on Haworth Moor, West Yorkshire, beating more than 330 rivals to win 'John's Race' – a new event commemorating the late John Taylor. John was a popular and hugely talented young international runner who died suddenly from hypertrophic cardiomyopathy the previous autumn at the age of thirty-three and is still sadly missed. Holmes's victory is somehow reassuring – he's won more than fifty races on Haworth Moor in the past decade. The event raises £2,700 for the John Taylor Foundation for Young Athletes Trust.

Mark Hartell (the Staffordshire IT project manager) fails narrowly to win the High Peak Marathon, a notoriously hard event centred on Edale in Derbyshire. Unlike a conventional marathon, which is a mere 26.2 miles (usually on the flat), this one continues for 42 unmarked miles, over some of the roughest, steepest and boggiest terrain in England. It's also run at night. Hartell is better equipped than most to deal with such rigours: most of the clutch of records he holds have been set in events that involve running all night as well as all day. Nonetheless, his four-man team comes only second out of twenty-eight, in a time of just over ten-and-a-half hours.

Finally, there is some spectacular action down in Shropshire, where two classic events – the 2.5-mile Titterstone Clee and the 10.5-mile Long Mynd Valleys – take place on a single weekend. Most people associate Shropshire with hills rather than fells. But, as countless top-level northern fell-runners have learnt to their cost, the grassy slopes around Church Stretton are as cruel as any in Britain.

'This one's a bastard,' a grim-looking man in a yellow Mercia Fellrunners vest tells me as I line up on the rabbit-trimmed grass of Carding Mill Valley for the start of the Long Mynd. 'I've done everything in fell-running – Snowdon, the Three Peaks, Ben Nevis, the Bob Graham, the Karrimor. And I tell you, none of them's as hard as this.' It's not immediately obvious why. The first 5 or 6 miles are more like cross-country than fell: a round, rolling course over turf and heather, with larks singing in a wide, empty sky and, later on, streams glittering in idyllic valleys, with little oak trees clinging to the hillsides in groves. Then, insidiously, the killer slopes begin: nothing too spectacular at first, and never more than a few hundred feet at a time, but all ludicrously steep. Going up, you can pull on the turf with your hands without even leaning forward; going down, you need all your strength – on every step – to stop yourself sliding flat on your back. Bit by bit, the stuffing is knocked out of us, until even the smallest climb seems like a monstrous peak. Finally, after more than two hours, we reach what I take to be the final slope. The people in front of me are swaying and staggering like delirious desert explorers – and no matter how hard I push I can't gain on them. Down the other side, our legs are so jellied that we descend in wild, involuntary zigzags. And then, just as we are ready to collapse at the finishing line, we realise that there is yet another vicious climb to go. Tim Davies, generally reckoned to be the best fell-runner in Wales, has long since finished by then; his winning time – 1 hour 26 minutes 36 seconds – is the second-fastest ever for the 10.5-mile course. Tim Austin comes seventh, after challenging for the lead at one point but then getting lost. I finally lurch across the finishing line about forty minutes later – in something like eighty-eighth position out of 130 – and it's all I can do to crawl a few yards out of the way before collapsing into a moaning heap. No one remarks on this. There are moaning heaps all around me.

Half an hour later, I'm back in the car park trying to get my tracksuit on. I've stiffened up severely, and it's a struggle to bend my leg enough to get it through the relevant hole. A skeletal young man in Mercia Fellrunners colours is having a similar problem in a car nearby. We commiserate with one another. Then, hearing my Home Counties accent, he says: 'If you think that was hard, you should try some proper fell-running. There's a lot tougher things you can do than that.'

I'm tempted to tell him that it's less than three hours since his clubmate told me the opposite. Instead, I just say: 'I know.'

Because I do know.

5

A long day's journey into folly

IT BEGAN FOR ME ON A GREY, BLOOD-CHILLING SATURDAY – the kind of day with which, oddly, many a love affair between man and mountain has begun.

I can feel it now. About 9 a.m., still punch-drunk from a six-hour drive up from London the night before, the car scattered with empty crisp packets and inexplicably purchased cassettes. Above us: Steel Fell, dank and precipitous, weighed down by rolls of battleship-grey cloud. Behind, the brutal howling of the A591. In the air, a faint whiff of wet exhaust, giving way, as we started up the slope, to the fresher, wilder scent of damp, cold mountain.

There were four of us, all middle-class Southerners. Gawain, a super-fit London stockbroker and one of my oldest friends; Charlie, a Manchester-based museum curator; Matt, a skeletal marathon-runner I'd not met before, who did something financial that I couldn't quite understand; and me. Yomping yuppies, you would have called us; ignorant intruders, even (if you were of a certain cast of mind), because our collective experience of fell-running's heritage was minimal. But at least three of us were serious athletes. Gawain had won many prizes for boxing and karate; Matt had a marathon best of two hours something; and Charlie, despite a thickening waistline, had not long ago been a distinguished amateur jockey.

As for me: I must (like them) have been in my early thirties. Just married, not yet a father, working in London as deputy editor of the *Observer* magazine, and with fewer pretensions to athletic excellence than at any previous point in my adult life. Some relevant details of that life: at fourteen, after showing flashes of spectacular promise as a schoolboy cross-country runner, I discovered smoking, drinking, gambling and girls. At twenty-three, feeling the premature onset of middle age, I resumed running – informally, on London parks and pavements – and for the rest of my twenties fitness vied with my other addictions for a share of my then-plentiful time and energy. Around thirty, I cleaned up my act properly, only for my ungrateful body to break down in protest. Nothing dramatic: just a year or so of continual flu, colds, coughs and overwhelming exhaustion. Whether it was ME or post-viral fatigue or something else was something no one – least of all my doctor – could say; but the irrefutable fact was that whenever I tried to shrug it off and start running again, the illness returned like a bout of malaria. I eventually put it down to my endless gulping in of great lungfuls of polluted urban air, at which point I decided to forget the whole idea of running. Instead, I began to get my exercise from regular long weekend walks in the countryside – an enthusiasm I shared with, among other friends, my future wife, Clare. Some time after that, perhaps eighteen months after my first illness, I found myself able to try occasional, gentle jogs. A month or two later, Gawain asked me to try my luck on the fells.

On the day of my first fell run, therefore, I was in a condition that could be described as, at best, good general fitness. I'd agreed to come along because Gawain had told me that on this occasion there would be almost as much fast walking as running, especially on the steep uphills, and that seemed to fit into the target range of fitness that I had now set myself: that is, general hardiness rather than spectacular athletic excellence.

Any doubts I felt were intensified by the wet breeze that made my bones ache as we strode up Steel Fell. God, it felt steep – steep and slippery. God, I felt cold – cold and weak. And the higher we got, the bleaker it all seemed.

Yet the odd thing was that, although I was puffing a bit, I seemed to be progressing faster than the others. Charlie and Gawain, who had done it before, were plodding leadenly, without any spring in their steps. 'Take your time,' said Charlie more than once. 'We'll be doing this all day.' But by the time we had crossed Steel Fell and begun to run across the grassy, undulating track towards Calf Crag, it seemed impossible to go any slower. This was ridiculously easy and enjoyable: not too much up, not too much down, the turf soft and springy but firm enough for my newly purchased rubber studs to grip on. I was flying, holding myself back only by conscious thought. I had no idea where I was going, but the clouds seemed to be rising, and Charlie and Gawain were navigating confidently. Before long Calf Crag was behind us, and we had begun the long, slow trudge – over ever steeper, boggier turf – up to High Raise.

We passed the time chatting about the purpose of our visit: Charlie and Gawain's preparations for the Bob Graham round. This is one of the great fell-running challenges: a 66-mile course, over a particular sequence of forty-two Lake District peaks, with 27,000 feet of ascent and descent, which runners aim to complete within twenty-four hours. It's not a race: the challenge is simply to do it. Charlie and Gawain had been training for it for months and were proposing to attempt it a few weeks later, around midsummer's day, on a weekend chosen for its full moon. Matt and I had been recruited as support runners. The idea is that the runner does the complete round, while various supporters take it in turns to accompany him, carrying supplies, helping with navigation and witnessing that each peak is indeed reached.

The course starts and finishes at the Moot Hall in Keswick, and, with four road-crossing points, divides naturally into five sections. Our route today was the big central section, from Dunmail Raise to Wasdale Head, covering about 18 miles and fifteen peaks, including Scafell Pike. Runners doing the whole course aim to complete this section in five hours and thirty-eight minutes. But, warned Charlie, it could easily take a lot longer.

I remember looking at my watch at this stage and noting (a) that we had been going for about an hour-and-a-quarter, and (b) that we still seemed to be going up the same broad, featureless slope we had been going up half an hour earlier. Simultaneously, I noticed

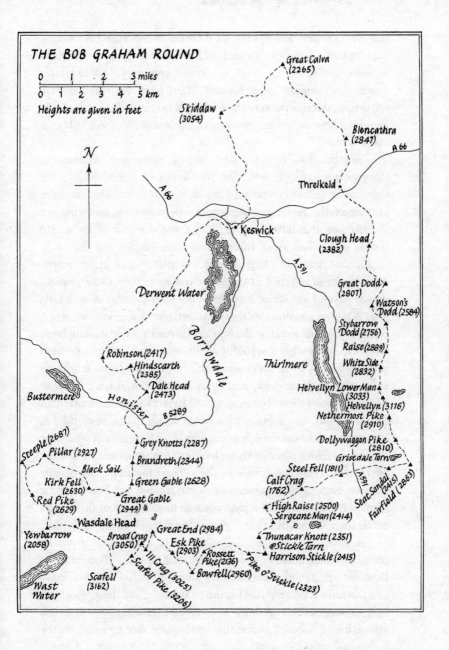

THE BOB GRAHAM ROUND

0   1   2   3 miles
0   1   2   3   4   5 km

Heights are given in feet

N

Great Calva
(2265)

Skiddaw
(3054)

Blencathra
(2847)

A 66

Threlkeld

A 66

Keswick

A 591

Clough Head
(2382)

Derwent Water

Great Dodd
(2807)

Watson's
Dodd (2584)

Stybarrow
Dodd (2756)

Raise (2889)

Borrowdale

Thirlmere

White Side
(2832)

Robinson (2417)

Hindscarth
(2385)

Helvellyn Lower Man
(3033)

Dale Head
(2473)

Helvellyn (3116)

Buttermere

Honister

B 5289

Nethermost Pike
(2910)

Dollywaggon Pike
(2810)

Grisedale Tarn

Grey Knotts (2287)

Steel Fell (1811)

Pillar (2927)

Steeple (2687)

Brandreth (2344)

Calf Crag
(1762)

Seat Sandal
(2415)

Fairfield (2863)

Black Sail

Green Gable (2628)

Kirk Fell
(2630)

Red Pike
(2629)

High Raise (2500)

Sergeant Man (2414)

Great Gable
(2949)

Thunacar Knott (2351)

Wasdale Head

Great End (2984)

Stickle Tarn

Yewbarrow
(2058)

Broad Crag
(3050)

Esk Pike
(2903)

Harrison Stickle (2415)

Ill Crag (3025)

Rossett
Pike (2136)

Pike o'Stickle (2323)

Scafell
(3162)

Scafell Pike (3206)

Bowfell (2960)

Wast
Water

that my legs were losing some of their bounce. Somewhere ahead, Charlie insisted, was the summit of High Raise, though it was hard to believe that an expanse so curved and dumpy could have anything so angular as a summit. Ages later, we reached it: a miserable concrete pillar in the middle of nowhere. (On a clear day, the views here would be spectacular, but today there was only turf and cloud.)

The story of the next two hours was, in essence, the same as the story of any difficult run. The first aches of apprehension; the debilitating sense of punctured morale – of '*Do I not like this?*'; the gritting of the teeth; the digging-in; the desperate plodding-on. What made this different was that, come the end of those two hours, we still had about three hours – and 7 miles – to go.

I'm not, generally, a great one for giving up, but my recent experiences of illness had made me less keen than usual to push myself beyond my limits. I began to toy with the idea of chucking it in. A moment's contemplation revealed the idea's flaws. We were, by now, three-quarters of the way up Bowfell – a particularly long, steep ascent on what is arguably a path and arguably just a random arrangement of loose rocks and heather. I seemed to be stumbling every two or three steps, and every time I looked up I had lost ground to the others. Nothing would have pleased me more than to call it a day. But if I did, what next? A huge bank of cloud was descending as fast as we ascended, and I had little idea of where we were – I had long since given up looking at the map, conserving my energy for following grimly in the others' footsteps. Yet it was obvious even to me that the nearest bus, taxi or hot bath must be many miles away; and that the only way to get to any of these must be on foot. Which didn't really sound much like giving up.

On I staggered, therefore, because there was no alternative: up on to the rocky plateau – the highest in England – that connects Bowfell to Scafell Pike via Esk Pike, Great End, Ill Crag and Broad Crag. Nearly every step had become a stumble, and the ground was now so uneven that running – as opposed to hobbling – was all but impossible. I hobbled heroically, upping my pace to a trot on the occasional stretch of relatively empty grass. At some point, Charlie gave me a fun-sized Mars bar ('It would be a lot more fun,' he observed, 'if it was three times the size') and a little life returned to my legs as the glucose flowed into my blood.

Then, better still, Charlie sprained his ankle. This is an occupational hazard for fell-runners, and I was disappointed to find that no one considered it serious enough to warrant calling the whole thing off. But a certain amount of first aid was deemed necessary, and every second of fiddling with shoes and bandages was a heavenly relief.

Thereafter, Charlie's limp helped slow the rest of the party down to something nearer my pace; but an unprejudiced observer would probably have concluded that I was the one with the injury, for I was by now not so much stumbling as lurching. There was no point seeking sympathy. We all knew what the matter was, and the only available solution – to this and to any other problem – was to keep going.

Somehow I made it through the ever rockier moonscape, the general heaviness of my legs giving way in my consciousness to specific, burning pains: in my ankles, in the soles of my feet, in my knees – until eventually uniform burning pain suffused both legs in their entirety.

I hobbled on and up to Scafell Pike, then down to Mickeldore, where all that remained – all! – was to cross over to the Pike's semi-detached cousin, Scafell, via the short climb known as Broad Stand, and then begin the long downhill run to Wasdale.

I was unaware of it at the time, but this is one of the great route dilemmas of the British fells. Alfred Wainwright describes it best, in volume four of his *Pictorial Guide to the Lakeland Fells*: 'Obstacles met on other ridges can be overcome or easily bypassed; not so Broad Stand. It is an infuriating place, making a man angry with himself for his inability to climb the 30 feet of rock that bar his way to the simple rising slope beyond. From a distance it looks nothing; close at hand it still looks not much to worry about; but with the first platform underfoot, while still not seeming impossible, the awkward movement to the left, plus an uneasy sense of worse hazards above and as yet unseen, influences sensible walkers to retreat from the scene and gain access to Scafell's top by using one or other of the two orthodox pedestrian routes . . . each of which entails a long detour and, unfortunately, a considerable descent . . . . Mere pedestrians . . . should return . . . resolving, as is customary, to do the climb next time. The author first made this resolve in 1930 and has repeated it a score of times since then; his continuing disappointment is amply compensated by the pleasure of going on living.'

In years to come, the bitterness of this dilemma would return to torment me many times, but for now I was too done-in to be very conscious either of my hopeless terror of heights or of the fact that this was a place where such terror might reasonably be expected to kick in. By the time I had realised what was going on, and that somewhere in Wainwright's '30 feet of rock' is a point where, for the length of a single swing from one grip to another, you are exposed to a 1,000-foot drop, I had already been coaxed halfway through the dangerous bit and had no choice but to keep going, comforting myself with the semi-security of a rope – left there by who knows whom? – clasped loosely in one hand. Ten minutes later I was on the 'simple rising slope above', shivering with fear, exhaustion and cold as I crouched pathetically towards the rocks in front as if to protect myself from the great void of sky behind me.

From here on the route was simple. Straight on across the gradually flattening top to the summit, then back and down on the other side, and on down until the very bottom. Six hours earlier, I would have regarded such a prospect with relish. But I had now understood the nature of fell-running enough to realise that a long, long downhill stretch might not be quite the unmitigated relief it sounded.

I was right. The others stretched out and soon left me far behind, although Charlie hung back until we had reached and returned from the summit of Scafell, so that he could show me the beginning of the downward path. Then he too flung himself down it, limp notwithstanding, and a couple of minutes later was just a scurrying midget far below. I hobbled feebly after – and was brought to a halt within seconds by pains shooting from my feet, ankles and knees. This was the steepest descent we had tried yet, on a path of loose stones and sharp boulders. Every normal instinct dictated keeping one's momentum under control. But to do so made every step torture.

I tried walking. Ten minutes later, I had made no perceptible progress towards the first brow – which I took to be the beginning of the bottom of the hill – and my legs were turning to water. I tried running again, and the stabs of pain made me cry out. More worryingly, my legs were so wobbly that they had taken on a life of their own. Every few minutes I'd fall over; the effect was often quite painful, but at least it was a relief from the alternate miseries of walking and running. Somehow I kept going and, after about half an hour, reached the longed-for brow. Wasdale valley came into view, unimaginably far below. The descent so far, I realised, had effectively all been summit – the bit where, if you were looking at the mountain from the far side of the valley, you would see the steep sides levelling off towards the top. Now the real descent began: thousands of feet of it, on slippery grass and treacherous scree, all so steep that a single step crucified the knees – and so long that one could spend the rest of the day hobbling downwards and still not reach the bottom.

Even now, more than a decade later, I remember the bitterness of my disappointment. Someone – fate – had betrayed me. I gave up.

Then, after five minutes of exquisite relaxation, I remembered the drawbacks of giving up and hauled myself back to my feet. And then . . . well, it would take a whole book to do justice to the next hour. I remember sliding large stretches on my bottom, and wriggling, hobbling, even crawling. From time to time I would walk or run for a few minutes, but my legs always gave out before I had made any noticeable impact on the remaining distance.

At some point, somehow, I must have reached the bottom. Trying not to whimper, I hobbled the last 100 metres or so to the campsite and car park. Charlie, Clare and Charlie's wife Lulu were waiting anxiously. I hobbled straight past them to be sick behind a red Volvo.

Then the real joy began. An hour or so in a warm car back to our bed-and-breakfast in Keswick, half dozing, half savouring the bliss of having no more mountainsides to negotiate. Half an hour in a hot bath. Half an hour dozing on a soft bed. And then – after a brief, painful interlude involving getting dressed, hobbling down the stairs and limping 50 yards along the pavement – the climactic ecstasy of settling down in an empty pub with a pint of bitter and a packet of crisps.

Gawain and Matt were still on the fells, doing a further nine peaks on the section from Wasdale to Honister Pass. Clare and Lulu had kindly volunteered to fetch them afterwards, at the end of an excursion of their own. That left Charlie and me with an hour or more to luxuriate in what is arguably the greatest of all the joys of fell-running: the fact that, every now and then, it is over.

You can enthuse all you like about the Lake District's fresh air, its awe-inspiring views, its wildness. But I doubt that any of these things is ever really so uplifting to a man's spirits as the smell of a fresh Keswick pub at opening time: that curious shandy-like scent in the air, with the evening sun gleaming off polished tables – and the warm restorative flush as the first sip of beer rushes through the veins of the exhausted, dehydrated fell-runner.

'You may find this makes you rather drunk,' said Charlie, emptying his glass as if it were water. The same thought had occurred to me – too late.

I nodded at his ankle, which was raised on the chair beside me with a packet of frozen peas strapped to it. 'How's it feeling?'

'Fine.'

He temporarily removed the peas and we examined the tennis-ball-sized bulge.

'Do you think it will be better in time?'

'Perhaps. But I might just take the morning off to be on the safe side.'

I realised that he was talking about tomorrow. I had meant for his Bob Graham attempt in a month's time. But fell-runners, I was learning, see sports injuries in a different way to other athletes. I had noticed this earlier on, out on the mountains, when I'd asked

Gawain how his chronic Achilles tendon problem was bearing up. He told me that it was giving him pain, but that he felt that 'all this scree-running is doing it a power of good'. Subsequent experience taught me that such idiocy was not unique to Gawain; pig-headed refusal to face the medical facts is a central tenet of fell-running dogma. According to Fred Rogerson, founding father of the Bob Graham 24 Hour Club, 'Hard men put the pain to the back of their minds, get their heads down and have a go.' According to Joss Naylor, as hard a man as ever had a go at anything: 'If you ever want to do anything on the fells, then if you're suffering with some ailment, you've just got to shrug it off.' Martin Stone, another hallowed name in ultra-distance fell-running, calls it 'the time-honoured fell-runners' treatment of carrying on regardless'. ('COR' is the medical shorthand.) Oddly enough, it often works.

But fell-runners' enthusiasm for the treatment may have less to do with its efficacy than with the fact that most of them see demonstrable indifference to health-threatening agonies as a necessary badge of honour, without which you cannot really claim to be a paid-up member of the sport.

This theme began to emerge as Charlie and I moved on to our second pint and he began to regale me with tales of the fells. The names he cited meant nothing to me – Joss Naylor? Billy Bland? Fred Rogerson? – and nor did most of their feats. How could I know if 'doing all the Wainwrights in less than a week' was a particularly commendable achievement? I didn't even know what 'all the Wainwrights' were, let alone how long a normal person might expect to take to 'do' them. But there was a heroic flavour to the tales that attracted me, with their recurring themes of courage in the face of grotesque adversity. The beer may have muddled some of the details, or my memory of them, but, given what I know now, I doubt it has exaggerated anything.

'Joss had half his back removed and was told he could never run again,' said Charlie. 'Twelve years later he ran seventy-two peaks in twenty-four hours. And did a day's work with his sheep straight afterwards . . . Pete Livesey once broke both ankles in the

Kilnsey Crag race but still finished . . . Chris Gravina ran three-quarters of a Mountain Trial with a broken bone in his leg . . . Duncan MacIntyre collapsed 100 yards from the line in the Ben Nevis race. Just like Devon Loch in the Grand National. But he came back and won the next year. Only had one eye.'

Any discomfort was deemed worthy of respect; the greater the physical difficulties faced, the greater the implied honour. 'Joss Naylor finished one round with the flesh on both feet cut through to the nerve . . . When Carol Greenwood set her Snowdon record she heard a loud "pop" on the descent – turned out it was the skin on her left heel bursting open . . . Eric Beard had a blister so big there was four inches of skin dangling off his foot – he went straight from the finish to hospital . . . Stanley Bradshaw. Now that's a really hard man. Did the Bob Graham when he was sixty-five, I think. Didn't go up a proper mountain till he was forty, because he worked seven days a week in a tripe factory. Anyway, he first tried the BG when he was forty-eight, and he got lost. Lost his torch, too, and broke his thumb. Had cramp for most of the day, too. And he was suffering from a painful carbuncle. He still did it, though. Well, he didn't actually finish in twenty-four hours that time. But he came back two weeks later and did it again. Which is even better, in a way.'

The tales about the Bob Graham round were the ones that made most sense. For a start, I could at least begin to comprehend its difficulty. And, because this was his particular obsession, Charlie could recount its legends with the poetry of a true believer. As the beer slipped down and our promise to rejoin the rest of our party promptly at 8 p.m. drifted from our minds, that is precisely what he did.

'Bob Graham ran a bed-and-breakfast in the 1930s. In Keswick. Lake Road, I think it was, although later on he moved to what's now the youth hostel, on the road out to Borrowdale. Fit sort of bloke – used to be a guide as well, and a gardener, I think. On his forty-second birthday, he decided to celebrate by running forty-two peaks in twenty-four hours.'

'Any particular reason?'

'Because they were there, I suppose.'

'But so were lots of things. Couldn't he have climbed forty-two trees? Or gone to forty-two pubs?'

'Well, there was a bit of a tradition, I think, of a Lakeland twenty-four-hour record, going back to the Victorians. Fred Rogerson, who keeps all the records relating to the BG, wrote a book about it. There was a Dr A. Wakefield, a notable mountaineer, who set a record in 1903: about twenty-one peaks, all 2,000-footers, in just over twenty-two hours. And then there was Eustace Thomas – the man who invented the Thomas stretcher that's still used by mountain rescue teams – he did about twenty-eight peaks in 1920. But what Bob Graham set out to do was of a completely different order to anything that had been attempted before. The others had just been walkers. This was only possible with a lot of fast running.

'Anyway, he did it. He was wearing a pyjama top and plimsolls and ate mainly boiled eggs. I don't think he even had a map. Afterwards a lot of people refused to believe he'd done it. But he had, and he'd had witnesses with him throughout.

'Over the years, other people tried to match him, following the same route, but no one could get near it. That was 1932, and twenty-eight years later people were still trying. It was like Everest, or the four-minute mile: an impossible target. In fact, sometimes the same people were involved, like Dr Wakefield, who was on the 1922 Everest expedition, or Eustace Thomas, who designed the shoes in which Roger Bannister broke the four-minute mile; or Chris Brasher, who paced Bannister and also tried the BG a couple of times – *and* was a reserve for the 1953 Everest expedition. Anyway, in the late 1950s – after they'd done the mile and Everest – some people began to get really serious about it. A group of them planned an attempt, for months, right down to the last detail – you know, the best bearings, a peak-by-peak schedule – and eventually, in 1960 I think, a chap called Alan Heaton did it. And then over the next ten years three or four others got round, all supported by the same people, and so they started a club. And, ever since, anyone who wants to can join, as long as they've done the round. I think there's six or seven hundred members now, but it's still bloody hard.

'It's great, really. A typically British thing. You've got this incredibly exclusive club that anyone can join, free of charge. The only catch is that, to get in, you have to run forty-two peaks in twenty-four hours.

'I tried it last year, but I only got as far as Wasdale. That's about thirty peaks. The weather was terrible and I just wasn't fit enough. We were two hours down on the schedule when we got there. But my friend Rob, who was doing it with me, had a bite to eat and then decided he was going to carry on. It was unbelievable – it was just so exciting. Off he went, and by the time he'd got to Honister – that's the next road crossing – he'd made back about forty minutes. So it was still theoretically possible, but only if he ran flat out all the way over the last three mountains and then on the road section back to Keswick, which is about another 6 or 7 miles. So he just shoots past us without stopping and disappears into the darkness up Dale Head.'

This reminded me of something. 'How the hell does anyone run on the fells in the dark?'

'Oh, you manage.' He was too wrapped up in his narrative to be bothered with such trivia; I never did get a better answer. 'The excitement,' he continued, 'was simply unbearable. His brother's girlfriend had gone up on the fells to cheer him on, and in the excitement everyone forgot about her. They just roared off in the car to the point where they come down on to the road again, and it was hours before anyone noticed she was missing.

'Anyway, Rob got there with five minutes to spare, but, God, you should have seen the state of him. He'd pissed himself, shat himself, puked all over himself. I thought he was going to die.'

There wasn't the slightest suggestion of disgust in his voice; just awe and respect, with perhaps a trace of envy.

'I really wish I'd kept going myself,' he added quietly. 'It's not a physical thing. It's just mental.'

Oh yes? I thought. I could still feel burning in my knees, and had to shake my legs every few minutes to relieve the pain.

But in the months to come – during which I joined Charlie and Gawain on the fells again and again, with growing confidence – I realised that he was right. Charlie himself, for example, had a solid, distinctly unathletic build, and a prodigious appetite for beer and food. (I once saw him eat a steak so huge that the restaurant in question offered it on a free-to-anyone-who-can-finish-it basis.) But there was a deep diamond-hard core of inner toughness to him: an indomitable will power that kept him going when it was no longer reasonable to do so, to shrug off pains that would cause lesser men to give up.

As Gawain once put it: 'Anyone can be fit. It's being *hard* that's hard.'

If I'd been a little wiser, I would have taken that message to heart. Instead, by the end of that first evening's commiseration in the pub, I had allowed a small idea to gain a bridgehead in my mind: I was going to do the Bob Graham myself.

6

Rocks around the clock

THE FULL STORY OF MY OBSESSION WITH THE BOB GRAHAM ROUND would need a book of its own. It dominated five years of my life.

Sometimes I look back on the period as a second childhood; at other times, as a kind of madness, especially that first year. Weekend after weekend – and sometimes for whole weeks or fortnights of annual holiday – we would drag ourselves up to the Lake District from the south: sometimes by car, sometimes by train; sometimes just me and my fellow runners; sometimes just me and Clare; sometimes whole gangs of running and non-running enthusiasts – Gawain, Charlie, Matt, Rupert, Ada, Jo, Rob, Baer, Charles, Titch, Tim, Matthew, Pete, Sarah, Lulu, Alice, David, J, Nick, Carolyn, Alan, Lou, Jon, Lida . . . I had always associated mountain activities with solitude, but this seemed wildly sociable.

Unfamiliar joys repeatedly surprised us: the scenery, the air, the history, the people. Above all, the running: the intoxicating discovery that, just because running flat out down a rocky slope isn't *sensible*, that doesn't mean you can't do it. Our first tentative descents gave way to more daring ones; which, because they also turned out to hurt less, spurred us on to still greater daring the next time. Our confidence grew, and I, at any rate, began to realise that, for most of my adult life, I had been encased in an imperceptible but increasingly constricting shell of physical caution.

Oh, the joy of throwing such caution to the winds! It reminded me of one of my earliest mountain experiences: a school trip to the Yorkshire Dales when I was nine or ten, which culminated with a group of us racing headlong down the side of Ingleborough. From above, the master in charge shouted vainly to us not to be so bloody stupid; but, in more senses than one, we couldn't stop ourselves. Every so often one of us would fall, roll and tumble back to his feet. None of us was seriously hurt. It is, of course, easier at that age and size. But that doesn't mean that such pleasures should be out of bounds to adults. The whoops of excitement with which my friends and I now hurled ourselves down the Lake District's craziest descents suggested that reclaiming such pleasures can be deeply liberating.

There were other, secondary joys as well. For example, the discovery that, if you travel across the hills at speed (and a fairly relaxed fell-running pace is about three times as fast as brisk hill-walking), vast tracts of wonderful mountain country open up to you that were previously beyond your reach. We roamed across mile upon mile of hitherto unimagined Lake District: deserted green slopes, empty valleys, wild bog and moorland, spectacular rockscapes, picturesque becks and nameless tarns – all scarcely touched by man, and far beyond the range of the walkers who queue patiently on the tourist paths up Helvellyn and Scafell Pike.

Then there was our rediscovery of the particularly delightful tiredness that is the reward of extended outdoor physical exertion: not exhaustion as stressed adults know it, but the sensual, limb-dissolving, bedtime tiredness that we knew as children after a long day's play.

There were pains too: sprains, blisters, bruises; coldness, wetness, exhaustion; the agonies of stiffening up in southbound traffic jams on Sunday afternoons; thighs so tenderised by battering descents that we'd be waddling rather than walking for a week afterwards. But most of the drawbacks provided as much laughter as distress – navigational errors so outrageous that we buried them in solemn vows of eternal secrecy; ludicrously tiresome and complicated arrangements for getting the right cars in the right places for non-circular expeditions (one of which ended, after an hour's overconfident shuffling, with the cars back in their original position); last-minute diversions to kit shops (for there is no item of equipment so essential that at least one intelligent fell-runner will not forget to bring it on any given day); grotesque injuries (glistening sores, giant blisters, lost toenails), displayed with competitive pride; bed-and-breakfasts that ran out of hot water just as we returned, shivering, aching and pining for baths; pubs that stopped serving food ten minutes before we arrived, faint with hunger.

Even getting hopelessly lost in the mountains, in weather so foul that there was an element of serious danger in the situation, could be a source of amusement. I was disappointed, when I subsequently immersed myself in the history and folklore of the sport, to discover that Jo (a former Outward Bound instructor whom I had recruited to my cause) wasn't the first fell-runner to have uttered the words: 'Why don't we sit down and have a good cry?'

If it hadn't been for the sheer scale of the challenge that was the pretext for all this, it would have been unadulterated joy. In fact, for those of us who had committed ourselves to attempting the entire round, the fun was really just a welcome distraction from a task so extreme and intimidating that its presence in our lives sometimes felt more like a shadow than a pleasure.

The first time I tried it was the year after Gawain and Charlie's attempt, which (thwarted by a combination of Gawain's tendon, Charlie's ankle and impenetrable weather) had ended in failure. I was convinced that, with proper planning and focus, anything ought to be possible, especially something so essentially straightforward as forcing myself to put one foot in front of the other for twenty-four hours. So I made my plan – and trained like an Olympian for six unbroken months, seven days a week, often twice a day, until there was nothing on my body but lean, honed muscle. (You need to have known me in my early twenties to realise how improbable this was.) All memory of my earlier illness evaporated. The friendly physiotherapists who were treating my various niggling injuries told me that my lung capacity and leg power defied belief for a non-professional athlete. My pulse rate dropped to forty-four beats a minute.

But it wasn't the same as being 'fell-hard'. I was based in

London then, and each time I went up to train on the fells I found myself struggling to translate my fitness into speed, and to absorb the battering my body seemed to take each time I tried to do more than 15 miles or so at a stretch. I also struggled to find my way without assistance, over measureless miles of featureless terrain, despite hours spent poring over maps in London, memorising bearings and learning the relevant passages of Wainwright by heart. I was becoming an athlete again; but I was a long way from being a proper fell-runner.

Nonetheless, I devoted every minute of my free time to training, reconnoitring, planning and – no less important – coaxing a dozen or so of my hardier friends into joining my support team and briefing them in their duties.

I also spent an alarming amount of time and money on what might loosely be called scientific preparations. My work as a journalist had over the previous decade brought me into contact with many of the country's top coaches and sports scientists, and it was with the confidence that comes of thorough research that I assembled my optimum outfit – a high-tech mixture of lightweight Gore-Tex and Lycra, with a high-ankled version of the traditional rubber-studded fell-running shoe. I also soaked my feet in formalin to toughen them up; dosed myself up on arnica and cod liver oil as a prophylactic against bruising; built up my lung power with agonising but low-impact interval sessions in a London gym (three forty-minute bursts, with a five-minute rest in between, on exercise bikes and step machines turned up to maximum resistance); drank and sweated a gallon of water a day; and fine-tuned my diet to maximise carbohydrate uptake and energy conservation. For the day itself I developed a vile but easy-to-digest mixture of liquidised banana, honey and Lucozade that could be swigged straight from a bottle, supplemented with energy bars and isotonic fluid-replacement drinks.

'You're cheating,' said Charlie.

But when I studied the colour-coded training schedule in my kitchen – or the giant, annotated Ordnance Survey map on my bathroom wall – I knew that the extravagance of my preparations was matched only by the magnitude of the task I had set myself. I could do it, God willing; but only if I stuck religiously to my plan.

God wasn't willing. Ten days before the attempt, in my last practice session on the fells, I sprained my ankle, catastrophically. It took me three hours to hop and crawl from Rossett Pike down to Seathwaite. By then it had swollen up like a rotten melon, and for a week I thought it was broken.

It was obvious that I would have to pull out, but the thought was so horrifying that I couldn't bring myself to do so. How would I tell all the friends I had cajoled into supporting me? How would I tell all the people who had sponsored me? How would I tell myself that all my efforts for the past six months had been wasted?

Then my physiotherapist friends, reassured by an X-ray, proposed a gung-ho plan to strap up the ankle with a padded fibreglass brace, which, while it looked ridiculous, would make further sprains physically impossible. It seemed worth a try. And so it was that, shortly after 1 a.m. on a foul midsummer night, I found myself heading hopefully up the dark, wooded lower slopes of Skiddaw – the first of Bob Graham's forty-two peaks.

The first few miles felt like flying. I had never known my legs and lungs so strong. Then things started going wrong. The cloud and darkness on top of Skiddaw were so dense, flinging our torchlight back in our faces from just a few feet away, that we were reduced to a walk – except for the moments when the monstrous wind in our faces blew us to a standstill. By the time we left the rocky summit, Charlie – my pacer for the first section – was having difficulty keeping up. The descent, in the blackest part of the night, passed, to my surprise, without accident, our feet somehow feeling their way down the grassy slope in the dim light of our head-torches. But by the bottom we were badly off course, and had to take an unscheduled, strength-sapping short cut through knee-high heather to get back on track. Worse, the shooting pains from my ankle had begun.

Memory can never quite retain the full horror of a bad long-distance fell-running experience. Looking back now, I can say that the pain continued to get worse over a period of about fifteen or sixteen hours, especially on the downhill stretches. But how trivial that sounds: a minor mishap, contained within the bounds of a single sentence. If I force myself to remember more clearly, I can say that I surrendered to despair on the stony descent from Blencathra – the third peak, at the end of the first section. I was already behind schedule, by about ten minutes, and it was all I could do to keep thumping my ankle towards the ground just to the bottom of that long, twenty-minute descent. How long those twenty minutes lasted – and yet even the next day I had forgotten quite how long. How horrified I felt at the prospect of continuing like that for another twenty hours – and yet within a week I was struggling to remember how I could possibly have wanted to give up at such an early stage.

I didn't give up; not straightaway. I forced myself through the next section – each of whose ten peaks felt like an interminable epic of endurance in its own right – and towards the end of it, on the particularly steep and treacherous descent from Fairfield, the hammering of my weight on my ankle was drawing involuntary yelps from me with every other downward step. I had given up all hope of finishing the round by that stage, and was nearly half an hour behind schedule. But with the rest of my supporters waiting to help me through the next section, I could hardly let them down.

My twenty-minute rest at Dunmail Raise seemed to flash by in a minute. Pig-headedness dragged me back on to my feet, and a slow trudge up Steel Fell began what must have been the longest six hours of my life. How odd that, today, I can piece together only enough memories to account for about twenty minutes of it. I remember Alice and Alan meeting us near Pike o' Stickle with a Thermos of something. I remember getting hopelessly lost with Rob in the fog between Bowfell and Scafell Pike, and the screaming hail that battered us to the point of bruising as we struggled to make sense of the flapping map. I remember Jo – who had agreed against his better judgment to guide me up Broad Stand before running the fourth section with me – clipping me on to a rope and guiding me up a rockface which had been transformed into a raging waterfall. I remember looking at my watch as I hobbled down Scafell and realising with relief that I was now so far behind – more than two hours off schedule – that no one could possibly be expecting me to continue any further.

And I remember Clare meeting me at the bottom, and the almost tearful gratitude I felt as she somehow manoeuvred me into warm, dry clothes, and the exquisite delicacy of the ham sandwich that someone thrust into my hand, and the heavenly, soporific comfort of the back seat of the car.

As for the other five-and-a-half hours, I can only speculate. It's reasonable to assume that they were agonising, but somehow my brain has censored the awful detail. I'm told that this often happens with fell-runners. It's nature's way of keeping the sport going. If you could remember, you wouldn't do it again.

As it was, my failure taught me three things.

First: fitness alone isn't enough to get you through this kind of thing. Mastery of the mountains – fell-hardness, as Charlie called it – is the key.

Second: science can only do so much, if that. One of my most vivid memories of that day is of lying under a foil insulation blanket during my twenty-minute break at Dunmail Raise, trying to meditate my way into a state of deep relaxation while Clare poured isotonic drinks and banana-and-honey mix down my throat and someone else unlaced my boot to adjust my fibreglass splint. Ten metres away, another runner – attempting the same feat in the opposite direction – was taking a similar break. He sat on an old deckchair, wrapped only in a red anorak, and refreshed himself with sweet tea and bacon and eggs fried on a camping stove. He finished; I didn't.

And third: if I thought I was weird, I'd seen nothing yet.

Over the subsequent decade, I have met many strange people in the world of fell-running, and learnt many strange things. One of the strangest was the discovery that, whereas my London friends considered me howling mad even to have contemplated running 66 miles over England's highest mountains with a sprained ankle, there were plenty of people in the world of fell-running who would struggle to comprehend the notion that I might have done anything else – and who would consider my attempt remarkable only in the sense that I was too pathetic to carry on further than I did.

That's not to say that BG failures are unusual. On the contrary, two attempts in three fail (and most people, of course, don't get as far as trying). But among the elite who have tried and succeeded, there is a smaller, stronger elite for whom the Bob Graham round, far from being the ultimate test of stamina and mountain hardiness, is merely a test for beginners.

This first came home to me years later, when I was lucky enough to attend the biennial dinner of the Bob Graham 24 Hour Club. It was held – as it usually is – in a large, institutional hotel in the little town of Shap, on the bleak eastern edge of the Lake District. Two hundred men and a couple of dozen women squeezed into the main dining room. Some wore ties and jackets; others wore sweaters or even T-shirts. Some were staying in the hotel; others were camping nearby; a few seemed to have run there. Many were obviously among old friends, drinking uproariously; others, like me, were among strangers. Yet no one was stuck for an opening conversational gambit. You could ask anyone 'When did you do it?' and be confident that they would be glad you had asked.

In most cases, people spoke of the day they did their BG as a high point in their lives – in some cases, an almost sacred high point. 'The best thing I'd ever done,' was how Selwyn Wright, a social worker from Barrow, described it to me. 'It became a central part of what confidence I've got – not just in running, but in terms of your daily life. You think, if I've done the Bob Graham, I can do anything.' But for others it seemed more of a base camp than a summit: memorable enough, but not so thrilling as the more ambitious challenges to which they had subsequently turned. Some spoke of the Paddy Buckley round and Ramsay's round, respectively the Welsh and Scottish equivalents of the BG, both designed by members of the club to satisfy their need for fresh heights to conquer. (Opinions vary as to which is hardest; but many feel that the BG's route secrets are now so widely known, with so much expert support available from club members, that the other rounds, though not necessarily harder in purely physical terms, constitute greater tests of resilience and mountaincraft. The Ramsay, which is the remotest, has been done by fewest people.) Others talked of doing a winter round (something first achieved, incidentally, by Selwyn Wright), or an unsupported round; of high-speed rounds; of doing the Pennine Way or the Coast-to-Coast in ludicrously brief times; or of seeking fresh challenges overseas, in the Himalayas, America, even the Sahara.

Later on, new club members were awarded their certificates, to hearty applause. But the heartiest applause was reserved for the 'Long Distance Achievement of the Year', awarded on this occasion to a man called Ronald Turnbull who had traversed all the 2,000-foot Scottish peaks outside the Highlands in a continuous 390-mile run lasting 9 days 14 hours 25 minutes. Other winners, I subsequently learnt, have included Mike Hartley (the Pennine Way in 2 days 17 hours 20 minutes, 1990), Joss Naylor (all the Wainwright tops in 7 days 1 hour 25 minutes, 1987), Martin Stone (all the Lochaber Munros in 23 hours 24 minutes, 1988) and Mark Hartell (seventy-seven Lakeland peaks in 24 hours, 1997), while any number of other equally extreme – and pointless – achievements have failed to win prizes but nonetheless presumably tested those who achieved them to their limits. Examples include Roger Baumeister's double Bob Graham round in 1979 (achieved in 46 hours 34 minutes 30 seconds), Billy Bland's incomprehensibly fast 1982 Bob Graham in 13 hours 53 minutes, and Leo Pollard's 1981 linking – in 35 hours 30 minutes – of all twenty-six lakes, meres and waters in the Lake District.

From the conversational point of view, none of this made much difference: 'We were twelve minutes up at Honister . . .' 'Got lost coming down Carn Mor Dearg . . .' 'Gary twisted his knee on Glyder Fach . . .' 'You couldn't see further than the end of this table . . .' 'Half his foot peeled off . . .' 'Came off the scree a bit too far south . . .' 'Tried some dried apricots but they went straight through me . . .' 'Swelled up like grapefruit . . .' 'Got confused in the dark . . .' 'Thought I was going to be sick . . .' 'Thought I was going to pass out . . .' The dynamics and dramas of long-distance mountain endurance challenges are much the same wherever you undertake them. But it was interesting to realise that in this room there must be quite a few people who had run forty-two peaks in twenty-four hours and yet still felt – in fell-running terms – inadequate.

Or perhaps 'inadequate' is too harsh a word. 'Humble' might be better. For you rarely find at the Bob Graham club the kind of egotistical ambition that is endemic in most modern sport. Members compete against themselves and the mountains, not each other. Indeed, it is a point of honour among members that, if someone else is making an attempt on the round, or even on a record that you've set, you'll go out and support as required, at any hour of the day or night.

To understand this fully, you need to meet the man who, more even than Bob Graham, created this curious fellowship. Fred Rogerson is an old man now, a widower in his eighties. Apart from a brief spell of National Service in the Far East, he has rarely left Cumbria. Yet he has a charisma and an adoring fan club that many a celebrity would kill for.

He was born in Lindeth, near Bowness, in 1921. He still lives there, in a house he built himself forty-five years ago. He didn't witness Bob Graham's original run, which took place when he was eleven, and, having a weak chest, was never much of a fell-runner himself. But he knew and loved his local hills, and when, in 1960, he read an article in the *Lancashire Evening Post* by the author and climber A. Harry Griffin, calling for some new Hillary or Bannister to rise to the challenge of the Bob Graham round, he knew that he had found his vocation. Then thirty-nine, Rogerson was an important member of the band of friends who helped to plan, prepare and support Alan Heaton's successful attempt in 1960. But that, in Rogerson's view, was only a beginning. He wanted to spread the word. 'I felt that there were other people out there who could do what Bob Graham and Alan Heaton had done, and I wanted to encourage them.'

He duly did so, 'managing' a succession of attempts in the 1960s involving some of the hardest mountain men then living: Stanley Bradshaw, Maurice Collett, Frank Caradus, Ted Dance, Kenneth Heaton (Alan's brother), Eric Beard. Bradshaw succeeded at his second attempt in 1960, Heaton at his second in

1961, and Beard at his first in 1963. But by 1966, when Bob Graham died, there had been no other successful rounds; and nor had there, despite numerous attempts, by the end of 1970. Then, in January 1971, four days before Fred's fiftieth birthday, at a reunion dinner for all those associated with the attempts of the previous decade, the Bob Graham 24 Hour Club was formed, with Rogerson as its chairman. Full membership was open only to those who had completed the round (something Rogerson never achieved). Its aims were stated as being: to specify and define the forty-two summits traversed by Bob Graham during his twenty-four-hour round; to provide would-be members with all relevant information; to encourage and advise such potential members before and during attempts; and to record in detail all registered attempts.

The subsequent success of the club has surpassed the wildest imaginings of those who gathered for that dinner. By the time of Rogerson's retirement, twenty-eight years later, the Bob Graham round had been achieved by more than 1,000 people. At the time of writing (more than a decade after my painful initiation), the total has passed 1,200.

This is partly because, among the fit, standards of fitness have increased. It also reflects improvements in clothing and footwear; the fact that people now come from all over the world to try it; the fact that so many people now know the route intimately and are prepared to share their expertise; and the fact that, as with Everest and the four-minute mile, once one person has shown that a psychological barrier can be broken, it somehow becomes easier for everyone else to break it.

Above all, however, it is because of Rogerson. Since the club was formed, he has developed and disseminated an encyclopedic expertise on the Bob Graham round. He's advised hundreds of runners, drawing on their shared experience, on the minutest details of route, timing and preparation. On many hundreds of occasions, in all weathers and at all hours of the day and night, he has waited, usually with his wife, Margaret, in bleak places like Wasdale Head and Dunmail Raise to watch those attempting the round as they pass and encourage them with food, drink, blankets and well-chosen words. And he has rewarded well over 1,000 successful runners with a handshake, a certificate and a 'Well done' that they will remember for the rest of their lives.

'It's been an enormous personal commitment for him simply in terms of sheer hours,' says Mark Hartell, who is honorary president of the Bob Graham 24 Hour Club. 'But it makes an enormous difference. Fred's incredibly supportive, but in a quiet, rock-solid way. He's of the old school – "You'll be all right, lad," that sort of thing. When I did my twenty-four-hour record, it was my third attempt, and on each of those three occasions I had a 5 a.m. start at Braithwaite, and each time Fred was there to see me off. And Fred lives an hour's drive away.'

The late Christopher Brasher, an Olympic gold medallist who twice tried and failed to do what he called the 'desperately difficult' Bob Graham, was one of Rogerson's most fervent admirers. 'You have to plan these things, and to have people there,' he told me once, 'and Fred's support has been absolutely matchless. The hours, weeks, months, years he's put in, encouraging people and making sure it's all done properly – it's a desperately hard thing to do, but it's the high point of many people's lives.'

Selwyn Wright, who took over from Rogerson as chairman of the club when Rogerson retired in 1998, makes a similar point: 'I'm sure that, without Fred, Alan Heaton would maybe still have done the second round, and maybe a few more over the years. But it wouldn't have had the effect it's had on all those thousand-plus people who've done it, and for them, he's a central part of their lives. Without Fred, it wouldn't have happened. And I think that's what Fred gets out of it.'

I first met Fred on another of those blood-chilling Saturdays, with mountain ranges of clouds once again crushing the fells and the A591 once again howling in the background. We were halfway through a practice run, crossing the road westwards as we passed from Seat Sandal to Steel Fell. He was standing with his binoculars by the roadside stile, a white-skinned, bespectacled, anoraked man, waiting to offer tea and encouragement to a runner who was actually making a BG attempt that morning. He recognised us as BG enthusiasts and offered some of the encouragement to us. For some reason, the subject of more advanced challenges came up. 'No one knows what they're capable of until they try it,' he said. 'Some people do this and they're quite content. Others find that it becomes a kicking-off point for some greater challenge. But no one gets round the Bob Graham if they go into it thinking it will be easy. There's a lot more to it than meets the eye.' In my ignorance, I wondered what such a sedentary-looking old man could possibly know about such matters.

Many months later, I telephoned him (as club rules required) to register my own BG attempt. I mentioned in passing that I was thinking of writing an article on the subject. He raised no objection, but gently suggested that I might have more than enough on my plate already when the day came, without the added psychological burden of thinking about writing. 'This is as much about mental stamina as physical stamina,' he warned me, 'and I wouldn't advise giving yourself too much to do.

'We've had things written about us in the past,' he added, 'and it's led to an influx of people attempting the round who were ill-equipped to do it. People who've done a couple of marathons and a couple of walks on Dartmoor think, oh, no problem, I'll try that. But there's much more to it than that. You've really got to know and love every inch of the ground. A lot of people don't appreciate it, but what Bob Graham did in 1932 was one of the epic achievements of the century. If you don't go into it deeply enough, you won't do it.'

Over the years, I have seen the truth of this remark demonstrated many times. I have seen many fine athletes pit themselves against the challenge of the Bob Graham without sufficient humility, and come off worse. I have been humbled myself, repeatedly, by the enormity of this mountainous challenge. And I have gone into it deeply, too, more deeply than I had imagined possible: both into the Bob Graham and into the wider heritage of fell-running.

In the process, I have learnt many surprising things. I have learnt that fell-runners have a special way of taping up their ankles with sticking plaster to reduce the risk of sprains; a special word ('bonking') to describe the kind of total leg failure that I experienced on, among other occasions, my first attempt at the sport; and a special way of doing up their shoelaces (too complicated to explain here) to prevent them from coming undone. I have learnt that successful ultra-distance fell-running can have as much to do with what you eat and drink as anything else; and that, while most people struggle to keep down sufficiently large quantities of food and drink on the run, there are usually a few particular foodstuffs (as personal to you as cravings in pregnancy) that you will be be able to tolerate – in my case, banana, Lucozade and cherry cake. I have learnt that, if you (or, at least, I) try too enthusiastically to load up with carbohydrates in advance using drinks specially developed for that purpose, it can cause violent sickness – and that, if you try to mix Carbobooster in the bath, it leaves a nasty purple stain that no amount of scrubbing will remove. (God knows what my insides now look like.)

I have learnt, too, that, if I underestimated the difficulty of doing the BG, I also underestimated my ignorance of one of the most exhilarating sports known to man. I have learnt that there are other, quite separate traditions of fell-running, some with more in common with athletics than mountaincraft, others closer to hiking, which are no less awesome, in their way, than the Bob Graham tradition. I have learnt that there are many ordinary-looking people in Britain who are far, far tougher than they seem. I have learnt that even the superheroes I met at that reunion dinner – the BG-and-more brigade – would not necessarily be considered, by those who understand fell-running, the ultimate high achievers of the sport. And I have learnt that the story of fell-running is interwoven with a series of undeservedly forgotten chapters of British social history.

Above all, I have learnt that, in my ignorance of these things, I have missed out on a whole layer of my country's heritage: a particularly inspiring layer, what's more, with which no one who loves green hills and fresh air and traditional British virtues such as hardiness and stoicism should wish to remain unfamiliar.

7

Scenes from a fell-running year: March

The month begins with a flood of obituaries for Christopher Brasher, creator of the London Marathon, pioneering orienteer and one of the founding fathers of amateur long-distance fell-running. He witnessed some of the sport's defining moments, and in his writings – notably in the *Observer* in the 1970s and 1980s – he articulated the romance of the sport as few others have before or since.

But his passing is overshadowed, even for fell-runners, by world affairs. The newspapers are full of rumours of impending war with Iraq, bolstered by warnings of suicide bombings and hair-raising dossiers on weapons of mass destruction. Perhaps Brasher picked a good time to die. For thirty-eight-year-old Mark Croasdale, the implications are more complicated. A former British and English fell-running champion from Lancaster, he's also a corporal in the Royal Marines. Since January, he's been posted in the Gulf, attempting to keep fit on a treadmill in the bowels of his ship. Now he's preparing to go into action. He's as apprehensive as you'd expect a soldier to be who's being sent into battle on the grounds that his enemy both has and intends to use chemical and biological weapons. But what bothers him scarcely any less is the hole that war will blow in his training plans. Croasdale's big target for the year – as it has been for several years now – is to beat the leading horse in the Man vs Horse marathon in Powys in June. He's been taking part in the challenge – an annual race of 22 miles over Welsh mountains in which runners, riders and mountain-bikers compete over the same rugged course – for nearly a decade. There's a £24,000 prize on offer for the first human to win the race outright. No one has ever claimed it, but Croasdale once got within a minute and a half of the horse. And he's convinced that victory is attainable: 'All it takes is a bit of luck. That year when I got within 90 seconds, for example, there was only the one horse that beat me. So: what if that horse had lost a shoe, say?' This time, though, it looks as though luck may be against him – even a 2-hour-16-minute marathon-runner won't be at his best if he can't train properly. Croasdale's age – it's a decade since he won his championships – lends urgency to the problem: 'I reckon I might have two more chances at it,' he says. So he's still planning to give it his best shot this June – Saddam Hussein permitting.

Meanwhile, the fell-running season goes onward the same, with champions and plodders alike turning out for some of the classics of the calendar. For the initiated, even the names sound magical: the Trunce in South Yorkshire; the Noon Stone in the South Pennines; the Holyhead Mountain Race in Anglesey; Causey Pike in the northern Lake District; the Raas Ving Vradda in the Isle of Man; and the Edale Skyline, a breathtaking 21-mile circuit to the south of Kinder Scout. But for others it's the quantity and ubiquity of the events that's striking. There's even a fell race in Cornwall: the 11-mile Five Tors Moorland Run, near Liskeard, which attracts around 100 runners; and another in Surrey: the 7.5-mile Box Hill Fell Race, completed this year by 162 people.

Whether Box Hill – or even Bodmin Moor – really constitutes a fell is debatable. What's beyond debate is the arduous nature of the terrain covered by the 31-mile Wuthering Hike – also known as the Haworth Hobble. The mountains aren't tall or steep by Lake District or Scottish standards, but they're big enough to be punishing, plentiful enough to be agonising, and frequently boggy enough to sap every last drop of strength from over-confident legs. For Mark Hartell, it's another disappointment: once again, he comes a close second. He's almost certainly the only person there who finds the distance a bit on the short side.

Meanwhile, all four 'regional' championships (that is, the English, the Scottish, the Welsh and the Northern Irish) are finally getting underway. Altogether, around 650 runners compete in the year's first title races: Lad's Leap (in Derbyshire), Chapelgill (in the Scottish Borders), Ras Pen-Cerrig-Calch (in Glamorgan) and Slieve Gullion (near Killeavy). At Lad's Leap, on a busy day for the first-aid team (with several bad sprains and one broken ankle), John Brown of Salford, better known as a cross-country man, holds off more than 340 challengers to win the men's race. Ian Holmes is third, with his friend and clubmate Rob Jebb, a BT telephone engineer from Bingley, one place behind.

Lou Sharp is disappointed to come second in the separate ladies' race, beaten in the final half-mile on an unseasonably hot day by a pregnant Christine Howard. 'Second again – always second,' she laughs afterwards. 'I've been trying to practise my sprint finishes, but it hasn't worked.' If she's seriously disappointed, she hides it well.

But Wendy Dodds, fifty-two places further back, is anxiously hoping that she hasn't done further damage to her foot. It's her first attempt at racing since sustaining the injury barely ten weeks ago, and she readily concedes that it would have been prudent to leave it longer. 'No, it wasn't a sensible thing to do. But I wanted to help my team [Clayton-le-Moors Harriers], although as it turned out none of us ran well.' She was also hoping to start getting back a bit of racing fitness in time for next month's Three Peaks race. She's run the famous Yorkshire race a remarkable nineteen times before, 'and I want to run my twenty-first in the fiftieth-anniversary race next year. So I can't afford to miss it this year.'

There's a brisk confidence about Wendy's manner that makes one wary of arguing with her – let alone suggesting that there might be something foolish about letting such numerical coincidences weigh against the long-term well-being of her foot. In any case, as a former Olympic doctor, she's in a better position than most to judge her best course of rehabilitation. As for the logic of her priorities, there are scores of people in the sport who plan their lives around similar statistical targets. Fell-runners have a strong sense of history. And with a history like theirs, who can blame them?

8

The mists of time

THE FIRST BRITISH FELL-RUNNERS RAN NAKED. Well, perhaps not quite the first. The earliest fell race of which records survive was organised by King Malcolm Canmore of Scotland in 1064 as a talent contest for would-be messengers. The race up Creag Choinnich, near Braemar, was won by a local youth named Dennisbell McGregor of Ballochbuie, who was kilted.

But in the immediate prehistory of the modern era – just before formal contests began to be established and recorded in the nineteenth century – there's good reason to believe that, when men raced one another on the mountains, clothes were rarely worn. One of the most celebrated modern fell races, the Burnsall, began around 1865 after a certain Thomas Young ran naked to the cairn on the village skyline and back following a closing-time bet in the Red Lion. And several contemporary accounts – one from the seventeenth century – describe 'foote races', in Yorkshire, Lancashire and Derbyshire, in which the competitors were 'stark naked'. Given the absence of accounts in which anyone was clothed, it's logical to assume that this was the norm.

Why? You could put it down to machismo. A more likely explanation is that it never occurred to anyone to do otherwise. Most people only had one set of clothes – especially the poor shepherds and labourers who lived among the mountains. Who but a fool would risk damaging them on some reckless hillside chase? The only reason we believe that young McGregor did so is that one of his rivals, his brother, is reported to have tried to hold him back by grabbing at his kilt – which duly fell off. But other early fell-runners – including Pheidippides, who ran through the

Greek fells from Marathon in 490BC – should probably be assumed naked until proven otherwise.

For similar reasons, few early fell-runners wore anything on their feet. Their modern counterparts wince at the very thought of the discomfort this must have involved – it's scarcely tolerable *with* shoes, for pity's sake. Yet the human body is tougher than we imagine. The Zulus used to run barefoot for 50 miles or more a day through the thorn-carpeted South African mountains, often rounding it all off with a battle. (Originally they wore rawhide sandals, but Shaka, the psychotic warrior-king of the early nineteenth century, forebade these as an effeminate, morale-sapping luxury.) And if we imagine that many early guides racers could afford to risk damaging whatever footwear they possessed in the cause of sport, we have forgotten what life used to be like.

It's not much of an exaggeration to say that running barefoot up and down mountains was once something that a man was expected to be able to do – like mending a roof or lighting a fire or killing people in battle. Bob Graham prepared for his 1932 round by reconnoitring each peak barefoot – partly to toughen up his feet and partly to avoid wear to the plimsolls in which he eventually completed his circuit. From a historical perspective, modern fell-runners are wimps.

Yet it's hard to blame them, for our historical perspective of the sport is pitifully flat. Apart from those passing references to 'foote races', no record survives of any organised fell-running between 1064 and the mid-nineteenth century. That's not to say that no races took place; they probably did. Legend has it, for example, that Cromwell's troops organised a fell race in Lothersdale while besieging Skipton Castle in the Civil War. But no one considered it worth recording. So it was with most sports. Before the Victorians, few people had room in their lives for formalised rituals of competitive exertion. The rich were too busy hunting and fighting, the poor too busy surviving and being oppressed. And while heroic feats were no doubt accomplished from time to time by runners in the hills, they were the wrong kind of feats – tied up with work, or war, or cattle-thieving – accomplished by the wrong kind of people. The sport of fell-running as we know it is scarcely a century old.

Its modern roots can be traced perhaps a hundred years further, to the early nineteenth century, when the right kind of people discovered the fells. Following in the footsteps of Wordsworth, Coleridge, Turner, Keats and Scott, leisured, literate, wealthy visitors began to arrive in Cumbria and Scotland, bringing with them an articulated sense of the romance of the mountains. These moneyed tourists and second-homers knew what they wanted – 'sublime' scenic adventure – but had little idea how to find it. They were, however, anxious to avoid the fate of Charles Gough, the 'unfortunate tourist' who in 1805 got lost and died on Helvellyn (where he was allegedly watched over for three months by his faithful dog, Foxey, as described in Wordsworth's 'Fidelity'). So a new category of local employment was created: guiding.

Any local man with enough courage, energy and local knowledge could become a guide. The only real requirement was a patron wishing to be guided. It's likely that the earliest guides were simply shepherds who knew the fells, for whom long days moving through the mountains were all part of the daily struggle for survival. Reliability was what mattered, not speed.

Except that, for some people, then as now, something else mattered more: status. It wasn't enough that your guide should be adequate for your needs – he also needed to be 'better' than anyone else's. So races were organised, and wagers were struck, and, in due course, men with a talent for running were sought and wooed, and kept on retainers, and persuaded to undergo training regimes, with the prime or even sole purpose of winning such races.

In due course, these private contests began to coalesce into something resembling a sport. Most villages had a summer festival of some kind; Wordsworth and Dickens both attended them, at Ambleside and Windermere respectively. Many of these included sporting contests, such as wrestling and hound trails, or the 'foot race' recorded by an Ambleside governess, Miss Weeton, in around 1811, in which one of the four contestants wore 'only drawers, very thin calico', which burst in mid-race, 'and the man cried out as he ran: "O Lord! O Lord! I cannot keep my tackle in, G–d d–n it! I cannot keep my tackle in!" ... The ladies, disgusted, every one left the ground . . .'. It's reasonable to infer that this was a track race, but at some point around that time the first 'guides races' on the fells must have started. In due course, records began to be kept.

The Lothersdale race traces its ancestry back to 1847, Grasmere to 1868, the Braemar Gathering hill race (over the same course used by young McGregor in 1064) to 1842, Hallam Chase to 1863, Burnsall to about 1870, Rivington Pike to 1893, Ben Nevis to 1895, and so on.

This was, of course, precisely the period when railways were being built and newspapers were being founded and tourist industries were being developed, and so the fame of particular races could spread beyond their particular valleys – and both contestants and spectators began to arrive from further afield. Queen Victoria watched her ghillie, Duncan, win the Braemar race in 1850; unfortunately, she recorded in her journal, 'like many others, he spit blood after running up that steep hill in this short space of time and has never been so well since'. The race was suspended in deference to the queen's distress and was only reinstated (with the present queen's permission) in 1979. By 1850, I should add, clothing was *de rigueur*, although it was rarely designed for running.

Similar stories were unfolding with football, rugby, boxing and several other sports. The anarchic, anonymous prehistory of the pre-1850 era, in which games were contested locally under locally agreed rules for local renown, had given way by the end of the nineteenth century to a recognisably modern world of sport, with national governing bodies and nationally accepted rules, and competitors who measured themselves against national – or international – standards.

But the process of evolution hurt. In 1880, two years after John Greenop of Langdale had offered in the *Sporting Life* to race 'any man in the world on Grasmere Sports day for £100 a side', the

Amateur Athletic Association was founded. Its mission, whose benefits were more obvious to its moneyed committee members than to many of the athletes it sought to govern, was to ensure that all athletic contests in Britain were conducted under the same rules, and that they were not conducted for financial reward. Unfortunately, this coincided with the boom years of professional running in Britain. Races revolving around cash prizes – put up by promoters or wagered as 'purses' by competitors' backers – drew crowds of tens of thousands in the latter decades of the nineteenth century, especially in the cities of the industrial North. Even relatively unimportant, rural contests could draw four-figure crowds; there wasn't, after all, much else in the way of public entertainment. And, in town or country, track or fell, the betting was spectacular. That was what the amateurs hated most about it, because gambling brought with it corruption, cheating, intimidation and race-throwing. According to the AAA zealots, a man who raced for money could not be trusted to run true. Often they were right.

For most ordinary people the issues were less clear cut. Amateurs often received prizes – cups, medals, clocks, cutlery – which it wouldn't take much imagination to convert into cash. Betting, the source of most of the corruption, was still possible in amateur races, even if it was discouraged. (At the amateur Hallam Chase, for example, bookies were reported to employ 'nobblers' to cause obstructions at gates and stiles 'if the right man were not winning', while Rivington Pike, also amateur, was said to be impossible to win unless you were 'well in' with the locals.) And, as with other sports, poor people who needed extra cash didn't always like being lectured on the evils of professionalism by rich 'Corinthians' who didn't.

For guides racers, meanwhile, the idea of amateurism was absurd. The only reason they were running the races in the first place was because wealthy patrons were paying them. Without that inducement, the sport would have evaporated overnight.

It didn't. Instead, thanks to the patronage of aristocratic enthusiasts such as Lord Lonsdale, the insatiable gambler whose personal marquee dominated Grasmere Sports in the early decades of the twentieth century (and whose passions for motoring and the colour yellow were responsible for the colour of AA vans), professional guides racing took root and flourished in the culture of the North-West and the Scottish Borders, while amateurism didn't. Other Northern and Scottish runners, notably sprinters, competed on the same professional circuit, usually in handicap races, for much of the twentieth century. The prizes – anything from £2 to £20 on the eve of the Second World War – were not huge, but were big enough to be a significant incentive. And if competing for them debarred runners from taking part in the Olympics, well, this was still the pre-television age, when what happened in one's backyard was infinitely more real than most events on the world stage. Who cared about the Olympics? Fame and fortune came from the local show.

Amateurism did win some converts, even in guides-racing country; but most of its successes involved track and cross-country rather than fell-racing. Between the wars, the Northern Counties branch of the AAA (which was actually a year older than the AAA itself) revived a handful of defunct or moribund fell races under amateur rules – the Rivington Pike in 1929, the Burnsall race in 1932 and the Ben Nevis in 1937. But the number of amateur competitors involved was small, and the mainstream tradition of guides racing continued unhindered. Britain was a bigger place then. The resumption of sporting activities after the Second World War attracted unprecedented crowds both for the 1948 London Olympics and for the guides races at Ambleside and Grasmere Sports.

The days of peaceful coexistence were numbered. While professional guides racing was enjoying its golden age – from about 1900 to about 1960 – a rival, amateur tradition of the sport was developing, unnoticed, from quite separate roots, but in the same mountains. This had nothing to do with the AAA or the 'amateurisation' of existing races. Rather, it came from the non-athletic traditions of mountaineering, rambling and pedestrianism. From the late nineteenth century onwards, the relentless evolution of leisure, fuelled by bank holidays, better wages, buses, railways and mass communication, brought forth a growing stream of idealistic young men from the cities in search of fresh air and open spaces; as the twentieth century unfolded, successive victories in the struggle for public access to the mountains gradually expanded the territory available for them to explore. At first they came to climb or to walk, encouraged by such organisations as the Yorkshire Rambling Club (founded 1892), the Manchester Rucksack Club (founded 1902), the British Workers' Sports Federation (founded 1922), the British Youth Hostel Association (1930) and the Ramblers Association (founded 1935). But as time and experience tamed the mountains, so the lines between mountaineering and pedestrianism blurred. By the early 1950s, a whole generation of fit young men – many fresh from the armed services – had fallen in love with the outdoor life. The idea of 'peak-bagging' – climbing as many mountains as possible as quickly as possible – began to spread. Eventually, and inevitably, races followed.

The first of these new races was the Lake District Mountain Trial, designed as a test for Youth Hostel Assocation members and inaugurated in 1952 to mark the twenty-first anniversary of the YHA's Lakeland Regional Group. This began as a fixed course of about 16 miles over six peaks, but by 1956 had evolved into a 'blind' orienteering contest, copied from the Norwegians under the guidance of the local Outward Bound schools, in which contestants had not only to race but also to find their own route with the help of a few grid references. Forty-two people took part in the 1956 event; thirty-two finished.

By then, the Three Peaks race was underway as well: a 24-mile course taking in the West Yorkshire peaks of Whernside, Ingleborough and Pen-y-Ghent. The first Three Peaks was held in 1954, with six runners, three finishers and a winning time of 3 hours 48 minutes. (The current record, set in 1996 on a slightly different course, is 2 hours 46 minutes 3 seconds.) The winner and organiser, Fred Bagley of Preston, came second in that year's Mountain Trial.

Contestants in these early events ran – and walked – in sturdy mountain boots (which were specifically required by YHA rules). An early Mountain Trial winner, Joe Hands, representing Carlisle Holiday Fellowship Rambling Club, described his equipment thus: 'a hat, two long-sleeved vests, corduroy shorts, pair of scree socks, climbing stockings, and a pair of lightweight climbing boots. In the pockets were a compass, gloves, bottle of "sustenance" and two sandwiches. All were used except the gloves and the sandwiches.' The qualities required for such events were different from those required in guides races: the latter tested speed, daring, balance and co-ordination; these new events placed a greater premium on stamina and mountaincraft. Nonetheless, Hands and Bagley and their fellow competitors were mostly running rather than walking; and in succeeding years they ran faster.

The 1950s and 1960s saw a steady growth in this new kind of fell-running, which overlapped naturally with the quest for the Bob Graham round. Some of the greatest practitioners were mountaineers – men such as Ted Dance of the Rucksack Club, or Eric Beard, the itinerant, jam-buttie-addicted Yorkshireman who in 1963 not only became the fourth person to complete the Bob Graham but in the process raised the twenty-four-hour record to fifty-six peaks. Others – such as Chris Brasher, Derek Ibbotson, Gordon Pirie and Bruce Tulloh – were primarily athletes. Brasher, gold medallist in the 3,000-metre steeplechase at the 1956 Olympics, proved more successful at writing about this new sport than at competing in it, but success wasn't really the point. This was the age of outdoor idealism, of post-war optimism, in which vigorous, self-disciplined New Elizabethans set themselves impossible challenge after impossible challenge (Everest, the four-minute mile, the Bob Graham), and in conquering them more often than not forewent personal glory for the sake of supporting a friend through selfless teamwork.

Many of these idealists were quite sympathetic to the professionals they discovered in the mountains. Brasher wrote generously of the guides-racers in his journalism. Others used subterfuge to test themselves on the professional circuit. Bill

Smith, who in addition to writing *Stud Marks on the Summits* was an amateur runner of considerable distinction, used to run in the Grasmere Guides Race under the pseudonym 'W. Wilson of Chorley'. Conversely, professionals were occasionally allowed to 'run along' with the amateur races, as long as they kept well away from the real competitors. (They were not, however, allowed to win.)

But as the popularity of amateur fell-racing grew, so it became harder for the administrators charged with upholding the amateur ideal not to draw some kind of line in the bracken where professional fell-racing was concerned. The 1970s brought this problem to a head. That decade saw an even younger generation of mountain-lovers – many of them employed by the YHA or the Outward Bound Trust – push back the frontiers both of their own fitness and of the sport. Most of the classic races in the amateur calendar date from this period: brutal long-distance tests of endurance and mountaincraft such as the Ennerdale (1968), the Wasdale (1972), the Borrowdale (1974), and the Kentmere (1975), as well as simpler – but no less severe – challenges such as Snowdon (1976). These counted their fields in dozens at their first runnings, but in hundreds by the end of the decade.

In 1970, meanwhile, the Fellrunners' Assocation was formed, under the chairmanship of Alf Case, organiser of the Three Peaks race. Some felt that any kind of administrative body was against the free spirit of mountain-running, but most of these races had to be run under AAA rules anyway – otherwise competitors would have been banned from running in other AAA events. Forming the FRA allowed amateurs to shape their sport in accordance with its own particular needs and priorities (such as safety). One member, Pete Walkington, memorably argued that 'the rules of fell-running should be capable of being written on the back of a postage stamp', which was true to the wishes of most of his fellow members but also unrealistic. The Association in due course spawned as much small print and as many subcommittees as any other governing body, as well as countless arguments – none of which I propose to discuss – about its degree of affiliation to the AAA (subsequently repeatedly reborn, most recently as an offshoot of UK Athletics). All that need concern us here is that, from 1970 onwards, amateur fell-running was subject to the ultimate control of the AAA.

The result of this administrative convenience was a feud so nasty that it requires a chapter of its own.

9

What price tradition?

AMATEUR FELL-RUNNING THRIVED IN THE 1970s, despite having started out as little more than a private eccentricity indulged in by a like-minded gang of friends and friends-of-friends. By 1972, the FRA had nearly 300 members. By 1985, it had more than 2,000. Intentionally or not, fell-running had become a sport.

Professional fell-running, by contrast, struggled. The communities that had sustained the tradition of local sport were fragmenting. People acquired televisions and cars; there were football matches to watch, shops to visit, foreign holidays to go on. The appeal of standing around in a damp field watching a few men run up to a cloud-smothered peak and back was beginning to fade – which was bad news for a sport whose twin *raisons d'être* were to draw crowds and bookmakers.

Nor were the inducements to take part as attractive as before. In 1930, the first prize for the Grasmere Guides Race – the blue-riband event of the professional circuit – was £12 and a silver cup. In 1970, it was £20 and a silver cup. Even in 1930, the prize was hardly a fortune. Four decades later, it barely covered transport costs. And this was the biggest prize of the season. Nine out of ten 'professional' guides weren't going to win it. Or anything else, apart from a lifetime ban from amateur athletics.

So guides racing withered. Fields shrank to single figures, with the crowds not a great deal bigger. Those who persisted as competitors did so because they had always done so, or for love of their local heritage, or simply for the joy of running on the fells. Those who cared about money and prestige took to the roads and became amateurs.

For this was also a time when, away from the fells, money was pouring into athletics – from television and kit manufacturers and anyone else who wanted to cash in on the running boom. Even British amateur runners, not a wildly distinguished bunch in the 1970s, were getting a share. In a few cases this was surreptitious – 'boot money', as the wads of notes handed over on the quiet as appearance money used to be called. More often it came respectably through the back door, in expenses; or, later, through trust funds.

The ironies were obvious. Tommy Sedgwick, one of the leading professional guides racers of the period, remembers watching a leading track runner of the day in an amateur road race in Barrow which was sponsored by a local businessman. 'They picked him up from his home in a taxi and took him to a heliport, and brought him over to Barrow in a helicopter, and then picked him up from the heliport in the mayor's Rolls, or whatever it was, and took him to the race, which he duly won. And then they paid him expenses of about ten grand, I think. And we said: hang on, where the hell has he incurred any expenses?

'Good luck to him, though, because he had the talent and deserved a reward. But when I went up to Scotland to race, you paid your own bed-and-breakfast and your own fuel and bought your own gear, and if you were lucky enough to win, you picked twenty quid up. I think the most I picked up in a season was £167. And I was the professional and he was the amateur.'

Sedgwick is now a genial, pink-faced, prosperous, middle-aged farmer, with several hundred sheep, a herd of pedigree Limousin cattle and a small caravan park under his charge. Life has treated him well, and there is no bitterness in his reminiscences. But it is hard not to feel bitterness on his behalf at the way the amateurs shunned him.

For a further irony, which largely passed the general public by, was that the athletes who were getting rich from running during that period (the amateurs) were arguably lesser talents than the best of those who weren't (the professionals). The 1972 and 1976 Olympics brought Britain a total of three medals, all bronze, in the individual men's track events. Meanwhile, some of the best athletes

Britain has ever produced were running in professional obscurity. One obvious example, who doesn't come into this story, was the Scottish professional sprinter George McNeill, whose 100-yards times put him on a par with the world-record-holders of the day, at a time when Britain's best amateur sprinters were struggling to qualify for Olympic heats. Two others, who do, were Sedgwick and his great rival, Fred Reeves.

Few people outside the fell-racing counties have heard of them, but Sedgwick and Reeves were, in their day, a local sensation: Coe and Ovett with studs on. Reeves, a draughtsman from Barrow, was a distinguished former track athlete; Sedgwick, a farmer's son from New Hutton in the southern Lakes who crammed his training between a morning milk round and afternoons labouring in the fields, was an out-and-out fellsman. Reeves excelled at going up; Sedgwick was an unmatched descender. Each found in the other a rival to draw out the last drop of his talent.

Between 1969 and 1980 there was scarcely an event in the professional calendar that one or other of them did not win, or a record that they did not smash. It is hard to make objective comparisons with track athletics, but attempts that have been made suggest that they were at least on a par with that of their Olympian contemporaries. Their training was no less intense – Reeves trained twice a day, seven days a week – and their electrifying performances began to inject traces of life back into their moribund sport. As word spread of their dramatic duels – with Reeves carving out spectacular leads on the ascent, only for Sedgwick to carve them back with his insane descents – so crowds and runners began to return to the events: not in huge numbers, but enough to stop the sport dying. Reeves was generally felt to be the better athlete: he won the professional championship every year from 1970 to 1979, and eventually even beat Dalzell's legendary 1910 Burnsall record (see Chapter 24). But Sedgwick's courage and commitment were arguably more inspiring, especially on the most rugged courses; and, as previously mentioned, he won an unprecedented twelve British Hill Running Championships on the steep Scottish hillside at Alva.

Could Reeves or Sedgwick have transferred this excellence to the international track? Dr J. H. L. Humphreys, who performed extensive tests on Reeves at Leeds University in 1981, certainly thought so, as did the then national marathon coach, who witnessed the tests and tried to persuade Reeves to forsake the fells for the roads. Reeves, recorded Humphreys, had 'the potential to run a sub-4 minute mile and a sub-2 hours 15 minute marathon', although comparisons with the physiques of previous Olympic competitors suggested that 'Fred's measurements most nearly approximate to the mean measurements of the steeplechasers'. For those who are interested in such figures, Reeves was recorded as having a body-fat ratio of just 6.64 per cent, a resting pulse rate of 42 beats per minute, and a VO^2 max (maximum rate of oxygen uptake) of 79 millilitres/minute/kilogram. (An average sedentary person would typically score 25, 70 and 40 on such tests; an average fit person perhaps 15, 55 and 55.)

It's impossible to say if this high-grade physiological raw material could have been successfully converted into Olympic medals. Any switch in disciplines would have involved extensive retraining, because different techniques and muscles are involved in running on the flat. But no one can dispute that Sedgwick and Reeves were sensationally talented athletes at a time when Britain was desperately short of such creatures. They fitted their training around day jobs, while growing numbers of amateurs could afford to be full-time athletes. And yet, as far as the amateur establishment was concerned, they were pariahs.

Tommy Sedgwick used to like to tag along with some of the amateur fell races, by way of varying his training and testing himself against new, longer challenges. 'I used to sort of stand at back, starting off, and then when you hit a checkpoint you used to bear off and shout "non-competitor", and once we got within half a mile of the finish I used to branch out, so that you didn't create any problems. And it was fine, for a while. But then eventually it started to cause a bit of friction, and one or two of them started to pass comment – you know, "You're not supposed to be running these sorts of races ...". I suppose it was fair enough – if the weather was bad they wanted to know who was up there. But there was a little bit of "us and them" about it. I thought, I don't want this. I was running for pleasure at the time. So I stopped.'

Fred Reeves, who has since emigrated and now lives in contented retirement on the flat shores of Lake Michigan, had similar experiences. 'I got tired of the looks people used to give you.' So he stopped too.

That didn't stop some of the amateur administrators from disapproving, or from expressing their disapproval in all sorts of other, pettier ways.

Several catalysts combined to ignite the feud. The formation of the FRA gave the amateur establishment an interest in a sport that had hitherto passed it by. The same year, 1970, saw the formation of the Northern Sports Promoters Association (NSPA), a fairly loose organisation designed to safeguard the interests of the few remaining professional fell-runners. No slight or challenge to the FRA was intended: the NSPA was concerned merely with saving the old guides races and shepherds' meets from extinction. No one seemed to mind – or even notice – when three runners who had competed professionally took part in the 1971 Burnsall race.

But the NSPA was more successful than anticipated. By the mid-1970s, the exploits of Reeves and Sedgwick were being reported in the *Westmorland Gazette* (though at considerably less length than the exploits of the amateurs) and were inspiring a minor renaissance in professional fell-racing. That, perhaps, was part of the problem; the other part was that the Northern Counties AAA had by then set up its own Cumbrian branch, based in Barrow-in-Furness. Three decades later, there's some dispute about the exact sequence of events. What everyone agrees on is that the brunt of the feud was initially borne by children.

Hostilities commenced in April 1976, when an AAA ruling came into force stating that any boy or girl over eleven who took part in an athletics meeting that was not registered with the AAA, where money was offered as a prize or where betting took place, would automatically be deemed a professional. This description covered every meeting in the NSPA calendar. To make matters worse, anyone who competed against a professional might be deemed a professional.

Given that there were around 800 boys and girls in the relevant age group who regularly competed at professional meetings – either in junior guides races or on the track – and that there were many thousands more who took part in school sports alongside one or more of those competitors, this was a fairly ambitious assault on the traditional practices of the region. But the general presumption against professionalism was such that the educational establishment went along with it. Peter Boulter, Cumbria County Council's Director of Education, announced that he had no alternative but to advise headmasters to stop 'professional' children from taking part in sport in schools. 'With the laws as they are, it is in the best interests of the children to abide by them,' he said.

'Children should beware of unwittingly entering professional races at local sports meetings this summer,' warned Mrs M. F. Bell of the South Lakeland Schools Athletics Association. 'My personal hope is that local sports associations will register their athletic meetings with the AAA ... There will then be less chance of youngsters jeopardising their chances of ever representing county and country.'

The effects were mixed but generally miserable. Attendance at Ambleside Sports plummeted, with entries in junior races down by 50 per cent. More devastating, perhaps, was the anonymous 'informer' culture that began to grow up around school sport in Cumbria, as the envious and the spiteful exploited the ruling to further their own malicious ends.

Roger Ingham, the colourful ex-guides-racer from Skipton who created the NSPA, remembers numerous instances of young runners 'being told they couldn't compete in their school cross-country team, or even their school netball team, because they'd run at meetings with cash prizes. It was mainly in the Lake District, but it started to spread to certain parts of Yorkshire too. You could never be certain who was behind it: they were all faceless, they'd do it behind your back.'

Scores of traditional fell-racing events found themselves in an impossible position. Most professional guides races formed part of little village shows that had been going on for as long as anyone could remember. Countless youngsters had had their first taste of fell-running by trying their luck at their local show. 'Most of them,' says Ingham, 'had never heard of the AAA.' A few of these junior races offered prizes of a shilling or two; most didn't. Nonetheless, all the shows featured professional runners. For the AAA to be appeased, either the senior races or the junior races would have to be discontinued, or both would have to submit to AAA rules.

What made the campaign against 'junior' professionalism particularly infuriating was the fact that organising events for younger age groups was one of the things that the NSPA – and its successor, the British Open Fell Runners' Association (BOFRA) – did best. By contrast, amateur fell-running, by the nature of its origins, made no provision for youngsters and, indeed, by the nature of its long-distance activities, was largely unsuitable for them. But it wasn't the amateur fell-runners who were behind the conflict. It was the administrators, who knew more about track and cross-country than about the fells, but who had assumed jurisdiction over fell-running through the FRA's affiliation to the AAA. Neither side particularly wanted a war; but neither would – or could – back down.

Trevor Batchelor, another ex-pro from Skipton, who helped turn the NSPA into BOFRA in 1982 and was BOFRA's secretary until 1994, remembers taking his son to run at Burnsall Feast Sports, one of the few amateur events that had a junior race. 'He was a really good junior, and he was on song. He'd won a prize two or three days earlier at Grasmere Sports. I took him along to Burnsall, and there were two or three other lads that had run at Grasmere with him. They were allowed to run, but not my son. They said: "You know we can't let him, because he's won money in a race that's not under rules." I said: "How come they're allowed to run?" They said, "Oh, no one's told us about them." And they wouldn't let him run.' Twenty years later, the memory still angers him. Burnsall was his local show – a celebration of fell-running, in which a local youngster with a gift for fell-running was not allowed to take part. But, he says, 'That's just the way some people are.' When I asked one of the administrators concerned for his views on such cases, he told me: 'Rules have got to stay rules, or things fall apart.'

Roger Ingham is unimpressed. 'Any kid in these parts, that was how you started. If your local show was on, naturally you'd go to it, and maybe you'd take part in the fancy dress or whatever, or the cakes and jam, and if there were a little fell race you'd have a go at that, too. And now they were being told that if they did that they were banned. Kids were being professionalised before they even knew there was a difference. Some of them may have won a few shillings, but that's literally all it was. And even if there wasn't any prize money at all, if it wasn't under AAA rules, you were classed as a pro.

'It was a shame,' he adds, 'that a few bigots who wouldn't stand up and be counted were trying to wreck what had been a part of our traditional heritage for years.'

Ingham feels strongly about this, not just because he has his own bitter memory of being barred from an amateur race himself ('They said, you can't run this, you've run at Kilnsey show; I said, but I've just paid ten shillings to enter – can't I just run along and not win? They said, no, you're a professional') but because he has devoted much of his life to helping young people realise their potential through sport. A former amateur boxer and rugby player as well as a runner – with the kind of gap-toothed, thick-eared appearance that such a combination of activities implies – he earns his living through a variety of odd jobs while devoting most of his time and energy to encouraging local youths to develop self-discipline and moral backbone by channelling their energies into various sports. Now almost sixty, he is rightly lionised in Skipton as a plain man whose goodwill and good sense have brought hope to hundreds of troubled young lives. He has also raised many tens of thousands of pounds for charity. But his proudest achievement was the creation of the NSPA and BOFRA, which simultaneously saved the tradition of fell-racing at local shows and created a framework that has introduced thousands of young people to running and to the fells.

'We got all the age groups sorted out,' remembers Trevor Batchelor, 'and had a championship in every age group. I don't know how many shows we saved, but we ended up looking after nearly a hundred events from around the country – all the old shepherds' meets and so forth. And kids started turning out. Everyone was really keen and offered the youngsters encouragement. And they still do.' Soon enough, young successors to Reeves and Sedgwick were emerging, several of whom – such as Kenny Stuart and Mick Hawkins – were demonstrably talented enough to run for their country. It was difficult for anyone in athletics to make a serious case for this being a bad thing. Nonetheless, some people tried to.

'It got almost as nasty as what's going on in the Middle East,' says Roger Ingham. 'There were kids in our local school, for example, who suddenly got banned from running in county sports championships, because they were classed as professional. But for anyone starting out, the professional circuit were basically the only one you could get into, because that were the only one that catered for juniors.'

In fact, after 1976, the AAA's official, head-on attack on events such as Grasmere rather petered out. The various professional organisations had been vigorously supporting their young athletes, and the Cumbria Boys' and Girls' Foot Racing Association (CBGFRA), under whose auspices most of the professional track races in question were run, eventually won a significant victory. At a stormy special hearing in which he had to insist on 'no interruptions from the Barrow contingent', Jack Payne, chairman of the CBGFRA and official timekeeper at Grasmere, managed to persuade the Northern Counties AAA that to separate the young foot-racers from the senior guides-racers would cause 'great hardship to all competitors and committees of all sports meetings in Cumbria'.

But the ban on competing at unsanctioned meetings remained in force for the over-sixteens, and the fact remained that, strictly speaking, the AAA's rules already entitled it to ban pretty much anyone it chose – especially those who ran for money; those who ran *with* those who ran for money; and those who ran with those who *had* competed for money. So although the amateur administrators subsequently backed off a bit, the conflict was there to be reignited whenever someone felt sufficiently officious to enforce the letter of the law. Individual cases of discrimination against young professionals – or, as the discriminators would have it, enforcement of AAA rules – continued: there were reports of juniors (that is, under-seventeens) running at Grasmere under false names as late as 1985. Meanwhile, the war spread to other age groups.

In 1984, a thirty-nine-year-old sports journalist called Jeff Connor moved house from Manchester to Eskdale Green in Cumbria. He was already a keen fell-runner, and joined the local club, Cumberland Fell Runners, when he moved. That October, he went to the Eskdale Show, and it seemed natural to enter the fell race that was held there, especially when 'my neighbours egged me on to have a go'. A few days later, he ran in a similar race at the Wasdale Show, a few miles up the road. In both cases, he came sixth.

But there was a problem. Cash prizes were awarded: £5 for the winner and, in each race, £1 for sixth place. Shortly afterwards, Connor's club secretary received an anonymous letter reporting that he had run professionally and should therefore be banned from running in amateur fell races. Connor sought clarification from the AAA, which confirmed that he had forfeited his amateur status, although there was nothing to stop him applying for reinstatement. Connor told them what they could do with their reinstatement. Instead, he resigned from Cumberland Fell Runners and from then on ran only in BOFRA events. 'Basically, I said: "Bollocks!" ' he recalls today.

Connor now lives and works in Edinburgh and insists that he feels no bitterness about the episode. 'I thoroughly enjoyed my time with BOFRA and made hundreds of friends all over the country.' Nonetheless, his case became a cause célèbre. Just a few weeks before the offending races, a British amateur runner, Steve Jones, had been paid $100,000 (into a trust fund from which he could draw expenses) for winning the Chicago marathon. Now amateur fell-runners were being asked to ostracise one of their own because he had won £2. At least some of them had no intention of doing so. Angry letters and articles appeared in the *Fellrunner* and in *Athletics Weekly*. An extraordinary general meeting of the FRA was called, resulting in a unanimously passed motion to the effect that: 'The FRA recognises that in principle there is no difference between amateur and professional in our sport. The Committee is requested by this meeting to seek an end to this distinction by means of negotiation with the AAA . . .'. But the AAA showed no interest in negotiating.

Connor and others launched an entertaining counter-attack, complaining about the 'commercialisation' of their sport through creeping amateurism. This became focused on a controversy over Ambleside Sports, whose organisers had recently introduced a 9-mile amateur race, the Rydal Round, to be run in addition to the short, professional guides race. This, claimed the anti-amateurs, not only had the effect of marginalising the professionals but also exposed a traditional Lakeland event to the malign forces of commerce. The Rydal Round was sponsored by a bathroom manufacturer based in Croydon and was supposed to be called the Metlex Rydal Round. Its first prize was valued at £75, compared with £40 cash for the Ambleside guides race.

One of Connor's most articulate supporters, the (amateur) Ambleside runner Selwyn Wright, wrote an article in *Athletics Weekly* warning that the egalitarian spirit of fell-running (in which 'everybody, whether champion or duffer, is in the same race and the same pub afterwards') was in jeopardy from commercial pressures that originated with the AAA. Wright foresaw a future in which members' subscriptions would be diverted to fund grandiose international championships, with a national squad too elite to compete in domestic races, and sponsored stars who would be seen 'sipping Bovril on TV every night'. Around the same time, a Keswick runner was banned from the Three Peaks race in Yorkshire after being caught cutting out the sponsor's name that was printed on his race number.

It was hard to know whether to laugh or wince. Selwyn Wright expressed the problem best: 'Fell-running,' he wrote, 'is in grave danger of becoming far too serious a business. To run up a fell is the simplest thing. Let's not make it complicated.'

Hundreds of fell-runners, both amateur and professional, heeded his advice and carried on trying to enjoy their sport, for the most part as if nothing much was happening. The quarrel had never been between the runners, many of whom conspired to frustrate the segregation by running under false names or turning a blind eye to those who ran under both codes. Rather it was an unintended consequence of administrative decisions made at a national level – and of the fact that fell-running was too insignificant a part of athletics as a whole to justify any change in the AAA's national policy on professionalism.

Yet the complications proved absurdly hard to unravel. In 1986, presumably following another anonymous complaint, the AAA Area 3 Committee instructed Ambleside Athletic Club not to accept the subscription of a member, Guy Russell, who had run in two races in which professionals were competing. (There were no prizes to be won at the races in question, but the runner was nonetheless considered tainted.) 'The club didn't have a lot of choice,' recalls Selwyn Wright, 'because the AAA rules were perfectly clear.' At the same time, Russell's clubmates had no desire to eject him. Wright counter-attacked by organising a petition in which more than a hundred runners from Ambleside and elsewhere 'confessed' to sins of professionalism and invited the AAA to ban them; Wright even ran in a professional race himself, so that he too could be implicated; he was subsequently banned – and, later, reinstated.

Since Wright had now been made secretary of the FRA, this was quite a dramatic state of affairs. It led to some top-level negotiations in London during which the AAA agreed to allow amateur fell-runners to take part in BOFRA races, on the grounds that the prize money was (by amateur standards) negligible. All they asked in return was that BOFRA should list its fixtures in the FRA calendar, so that the races would technically be sanctioned by the FRA.

But it wasn't obvious to Roger Ingham and Trevor Batchelor

why, after years in the wilderness, they should *want* to be sanctioned by the FRA. Their self-contained sporting world was now functioning very happily, and the prospect of hundreds of amateurs rushing in to compete in their little races was not an attractive one. So now a new set of negotiations had to begin, between the FRA and BOFRA.

Ultimately, the whole argument became too absurd to sustain (as it did in Scotland, where a whole parallel version of this story, involving the Scottish AAA and the Scottish Hill Runners Association, had been unfolding around the same time). By 1992, hundreds of athletes were earning a living from running. They were all amateurs. More or less the only top-class runners who still tried to fit their training around day jobs were the alleged professionals. Like the Berlin Wall, the artificial separation of professional and amateur fell-runners collapsed, belatedly, under the weight of its own grotesqueness. That year, by the agreement of all concerned parties, fell-running was declared 'open'.

Selwyn Wright, who was by then FRA chairman, considered this declaration 'my greatest achievement – and yet by the time it happened, hardly anyone noticed'. Its effect was to give runners official permission to do what most of them had been doing anyway: that is, to run and race on the fells in a spirit of camaraderie with whomever they chose, wherever and whenever they chose. And so they have been doing ever since, mostly under the auspices of the FRA, although BOFRA still administers a number of local events and its own championship, in which races for juniors feature prominently. Rivalry between the two traditions has evaporated, as experience has shown that the best runners in each code are of much the same standard. Most of the very best now try to combine the long-distance skills associated with amateurism with the more explosive qualities associated with the professionals; in order to win the British or English championship you need to excel at both extremes. The feared 'commercialisation' of fell-running has not, on the whole, materialised, partly because the FRA has – at its members' behest – deliberately maintained a 'low-profile' policy for its sport, as has BOFRA.

But the long years of hostility have left one sad legacy, which is that the sporting achievements that took place in the shadow of the feud remain, retrospectively, overshadowed by it. Who now – even among the contenders for today's fell-running championships – has heard of Sedgwick and Reeves, or of their predecessors, Broadhurst and Harrison; or, from the professional track, of George McNeill or Albert Spence or Michael Glenn? We have shed the prejudices of earlier decades, but our mental picture of the past is still coloured by those prejudices.

And, as a result, a whole slice of our past is almost invisible to us. Events of great sporting and social drama that took place in our country in the 1950s and 1960s are as distant and indistinct as events from the 1850s. No wonder so many of us are ill at ease with ourselves.

10

Scenes from a fell-running year: April

There's a fierce breeze slicing through Cumbria's
Newlands valley as more than 400 runners make
their way up a narrow lane behind Stair village hall,
towards the start of the Anniversary Waltz. It's only
the sixth running of the race, yet it has a special place in
many hearts, not least those of its organisers, Steve and
Wynn Cliff. Steve and Wynn are southerners: a
Leicestershire-based couple who fell in love with each other
and the Lake District at roughly the same time. When they
married, they did so in their favourite valley, in Newlands
Church, a low, white building hidden beneath gnarled trees at the
side of one of Cumbria's narrowest lanes, about 5 miles south of
Keswick. Wanting – as many fell-runners do – to 'put something back'
in return for all the happiness they had found in the mountains, they
inaugurated an annual race to mark their anniversary, with any
proceeds going towards the upkeep of the village hall. The Waltz is a
brilliantly simple horseshoe of around 12 miles that takes in
Robinson, Hindscarth, Dale Head, High Spy and Catbells. It's steep
but mostly runnable, with a nice balance between turf and rock and –
if you can snatch a moment to gaze around – views that can stay with
you for a lifetime. And, this year, it's one of the six races that count
towards the English championship.

At least half of those running are only here for the championship
points. But that still leaves one or two hundred of us who are here for
the joy of the race; and, with every local hand apparently on deck to
help with registration, traffic control, marshalling and catering,
there's an exciting buzz in the air of a community enjoying a big day.

The local clubs – Keswick, Borrowdale, Cumberland Fellrunners – are out in force, and the starting line is loud with companionable babble.

The race begins with a mile or more of awkward jostling, as the narrow lane and the narrow path that follows struggle to channel the heavy traffic. But we reach the steep sides of Robinson soon enough, and, from there on, it's every man at his own pace. Quite what this pace should be is hard to judge. Gut feeling suggests that one should plough most of one's resources into doing this one big ascent as quickly as possible, since the rest of the course is effectively just an undulating ridge. Experience suggests that undulating ridges can be deceptively demanding. I reach the top feeling vaguely guilty at not having pushed myself hard enough – and reach Catbells an hour later wishing I had kept more in reserve. In between, there's a fabulous, flying descent from Robinson to Hindscarth, on soft, curved turf that couldn't be more conducive to downhill running if it had been purpose-made; followed by a succession of rocky ups and downs over the next three peaks which all seem irritatingly larger than they appeared on the map; followed by another long, forgiving descent, over Maiden Moor to Catbells; after which a steep drop through thick bracken brings us back down to Stair. Gavin Bland, the Borrowdale shepherd, once did this final descent, peak to finish, in under five minutes. Ian Holmes doesn't take much longer today, reaching Catbells 100 metres behind John Brown – who has led from the start – and reaching the bottom 100 metres ahead of him. 'I'm just pleased I got down without breaking my leg,' says Brown afterwards. My attempt at a flat-out sprint down the hillside takes nearer ten minutes than five, giving me an overall time more than forty minutes slower than Holmes's new record of 1 hour 28 minutes 27 seconds. Lou Sharp wins the ladies' race in 1 hour 51 minutes 10 seconds.

It's a welcome change of fortune for Lou, who two weeks ago could only manage second, behind Angela Mudge, in the first 'counter' in this year's British championship: the Slieve Bernagh in the Mourne Mountains. (Rob Jebb won the men's race.) Perhaps there's a link between Lou's confident running today and her recent decision to take voluntary redundancy. She's hoping to spend a few months travelling and running with her husband in Europe and New Zealand. But it would be nice to sew up another championship first.

At Rivington Pike, Britain's second oldest amateur fell race, on the outskirts of Horwich, near Manchester, Billy Burns of Salford Harriers wins impressively in 17 minutes 12 seconds. Burns is a Commonwealth Games marathon-runner and a star of the relatively lucrative international mountain-running circuit, but isn't seen that often at domestic fell races. There is, however, plenty of local tradition at the back of the field, where Ron Hill, triple Olympian, four-time world-record-breaker and inventor of the famous Trackster leggings, comes 173rd. He's a few months short of his sixty-fifth birthday and hasn't gone a day without running since 1964. This is his thirtieth running of the 3¼-mile race, which involves 700 feet of ascent and descent, and he feels dreadful. 'My mind was telling me, "Never again, this is the last time!"' he reports afterwards. Nonetheless, he's eight minutes quicker than the last man home: seventy-five-year-old Harold Minshull. On two previous occasions, in 1957 and 1960, Minshull was the winner.

There's room to list only an arbitrary selection of the month's other highlights: Knockfarrell, Ross-shire, in the Scottish Championships; the Lara Shining Cliffs and the Kinder Downfall in the Peak District; the Wardle Skyline and the Pendle Fell Race in Lancashire; the Guisborough Moors in North Yorkshire; the Knockdhu Classic in County Antrim; the Wrekin in Shropshire. Tim Austin misses them all: for the second month running, he's down with a mystery virus. But the races are now coming so thick and fast that it's becoming hard to tell who's just running somewhere else, and who's missing altogether.

At the Manx Mountain Marathon, Ian Gale becomes the first Manxman to win the race in its thirty-three-year history – and is still nearly fifteen minutes outside Colin Donnelly's 2002 record. The MMM is not a mountain marathon in the technical sense of a two-day orienteering event; it's just a long race through the mountains. It's also a huge, wild beast of a challenge, staggeringly beautiful (especially on the final coastal section from Bradda Cairn to Port Erin), but so unrelentingly draining that the great Joss Naylor used to boast that he could win it and be back in Cumbria before all the stragglers had finished. Donnelly, a remarkable athlete who was British Fellrunning Champion in 1987, 1988 and 1989 and Over-40s Champion in 2000 and 2002, completed the 31½ miles and 8,000 feet of ascent in 4 hours 39 minutes 27 seconds.

In North Yorkshire, meanwhile, there's a disappointing turnout for the Three Peaks. This famous 24-mile circuit of Pen-y-Ghent, Whernside and Ingleborough, which celebrates its fiftieth anniversary in 2004, has traditionally been one of the high points of the fell-running year; some would say *the* high point. It's a satisfying route, also much prized as a challenge for walkers, who aim to complete it in a single day rather than within three hours, and it demands the full range of fell-running virtues: mountaincraft, navigation, stamina; sure-footedness and courage for the steep descents from Ingleborough and Whernside; and, for the long runs between the peaks, straightforward speed. Its early history is littered with the names of amateur fell-running's legendary hard men: Fred Bagley, Stanley Bradshaw and Alf Case (the only finishers of the first race); Joe Hand, Alan Heaton, George Brass, Eric Beard; and, more recently, Jeff Norman and Sarah Rowell, both multiple winners and Olympic marathon-runners. By the 1980s, the race regularly attracted 1,000 entries a year, of whom a maximum of 600 would be permitted to run. Such numbers allowed road- and cross-country-runners with little mountain experience to test their athleticism on the course, confident (not always justifiably) that they could find the route simply by following the crowd. In recent years, however, numbers and standards have fallen. Some say that this is because today's young runners are soft; others that too much pressure is placed on the best of them to focus their training on shorter, faster events. Either way, this year, despite perfect conditions, there are a mere 235 starters, most of them over forty. Wendy Dodds is among them, fifty-fourth in a slow-moving field. The foot gives her 'a bit of grief – nothing serious'; and at least she's on course for that twenty-first successive running next year. 'It was hard,' she says, 'on the background of so little training. I'm pleased just to get round.' The winning time, 3 hours 6 minutes 27 seconds, is more than twenty minutes outside the record. But there's widespread delight at the winner's identity: Dave Walker, of Clayton-le-Moors Harriers, is son of the famous Harry Walker, who won the race in 1978, 1979 and 1981. And you have only to see the two men choking back the tears at the finish to realise that, for some people, the Three Peaks still matters very much.

11

Bill gone home yet?

THE VILLAGE OF CALDBECK is in one of the less
fashionable corners of the Lake District. To reach it from Keswick,
the nearest town, you must follow a series of twisting lanes that
tangle obscurely northwards for a dozen miles across the great
shagginess of Mungrisdale Common. 'Back o' Skiddaw', they call
it. There are no lakes to look at, nor much in the way of mountains,
although the long, heathery backs of Blencathra and Bowscale Fell
stretch up behind you to the south and west. Instead, you are
drawn ever deeper into a strange semi-wilderness: more fen than
fell at first, with lank grass dotted with gorse and squat, wind-
dwarfed trees, giving way eventually to an old-fashioned working
landscape of small fields, thin lanes and high banks. There are
frequent signs of agriculture, and a few of human habitation; but
they seem to have had limited impact on the ragged vegetation.
The verges (and sometimes the centres) of the lanes are bright with
weeds, wildflowers, butterflies; the tractors and farm buildings you
pass are usually rickety and may even be abandoned. Nature and
time are in the ascendant.

Caldbeck itself is the birthplace and resting place of John Peel,
patron saint of hunting. As such, it is a minor tourist attraction.
The centre of the village has been prettified, with a manicured
green and a tea-room and bookshop near the churchyard (where
Mary Robinson, the Maid of Buttermere, is also buried). But the
fringes are as untamed as the surrounding hinterland.

Bushby House is on the fringes. It is a low, white house, set
back from the lane behind a dank, neglected garden. The gate falls
open to the touch; if you pushed too vigorously, I suspect it would

fall over. A damp path leads to a peeling front door that matches the peeling whitewash on the walls. I am sure I am not the first visitor to have wondered if anyone really lives here. The mouldering air of the place is not unpleasant; but you get the distinct impression that here, too, nature, not man, is in charge.

My initial doubts are compounded by the fact that, when I knock, there is no answer. One minute; two; silence. The kind of profound, immovable silence in which country afternoons were once saturated; in which flies buzz and birds sing and someone, somewhere, is using shears. I knock again: not too hard, for fear of damaging the door. There is, of course, no doorbell. Nor, I happen to know, is there a telephone. Perhaps that's the trouble: perhaps he has changed his plans – or his mind – since I last wrote.

More minutes pass. I am turning away, preparing to peer through some cobwebbed windows, when the door creaks open.

The figure inside is strikingly short but otherwise hard to make out in the darkness within. When my eyes have adjusted, I see what looks like a hobbit: bushy eyebrows; big, tufty ears; a flop of white hair hanging out from under a flat tweed cap; a twinkling eye; and a neat little bulge of a tummy under a buttoned cardigan. This is, I realise, Bill Teasdale: one of Britain's greatest-ever athletes; older, wheezier, more stooped, but still recognisable from all those old photographs, when he reigned unchallenged as King of the Fells for the best part of two decades.

I step down to follow him – for the floor inside seems to be lower than the damp earth without – and am led to the main room. It is dark here, too, for the window is small. And there's that same indefinable sense of decay, a faint smell of wet soil. Yet the room itself is clean and tidy: two worn armchairs, a Formica table, a dark wooden cabinet and an empty fireplace. An elderly grandfather clock ticks loudly in a corner. Fifty years ago, you might have called this a typical countryman's cottage. You wouldn't today. And you certainly wouldn't call it a typical dwelling for a sporting superstar.

Yet that is what Teasdale is. Look more closely at the wooden cabinet and you'll see that it is packed with trophies: more than fifty of them by my count, though they are hard to make out in the shadows. Wait for him to settle in his seat and get his breath back, and he's happy to tell you how he won them.

He was born in 1924, in Greenhead, a mile down the road, and grew up in Caldbeck with three brothers and four sisters, at Todcrofts, the farm his father managed a few hundred yards from Bushby House. Most of his uncles farmed too, and Bill was out on the fells from an early age, working for one or other of them as a shepherd and errand boy. When he wasn't, he was down milking cows in the morning, or helping his mother to churn the milk into butter. For a while he was hired out as a farm lad in nearby Ireby, but as his brothers married and moved out, his services were increasingly in demand at home. To help make ends meet, he found work as a gamekeeper as well, looking after the grouse on the Skiddaw Estate. All these jobs required constant physical activity, including much fast walking on the fells. Occasionally – as when his grandfather accompanied him on horseback – he was urged to walk faster. Inevitably, he grew fit.

'There were no sports when I was a boy,' he explains, in sing-song cadences that a Southerner might mistake for Scottish. 'There was a war. I couldn't run.' He admits, though, that 'I was always a bit inclined to run about' – for the sheer joy of it. Perhaps that is why, when he was twenty-two, a friend asked him to make up team numbers in a half-mile track race at Skelton Sports. He came third, in his stockinged feet, and was struck by how effortless it seemed. He tried again, over quarter of a mile, at Hesket Newmarket. He wore running shoes this time, borrowed from a family friend, and won. Soon he was racing and winning all over the North-West, and in the Scottish Borders.

'I used to run on track, like. I ran miles, half-mile, two mile.' How fast, I wonder? 'Well, like, we ran on some queer fields ... Four minutes fifteen would win most miles. But some of them were doing round four minutes in them days, running on grass. I won my share of miles, but if you won you got pulled back, because they were handicaps, like. You got to where you could give them quarter-mile in mile. That put me out of miling.'

He laughs: a high-pitched, musical giggle which comes to him often and which seems to denote thoughtfulness as much as hilarity. He stares into the gloom of the empty fireplace. Then he resumes.

'So I drifted into fell-racing. There's no handicaps in fell-racing.' His first win was in 1947, at Burton-in Holme – 'and that was more cross-country than fell'. His first major win was two years after that, at Ambleside Sports. Even then, the twenty-four-year-old Teasdale was so far from being an established figure that the race commentator couldn't identify him. 'It was a bit of a laugh. I were coming down, and I was a street of houses in front, and the commentator, he called me everybody: Colin Brown, Dave Temple . . . He had to give in at finish. A mate of mine was standing next to him – he says he turned to him and said: "Who the hell *is* it?" I was a bolt from the blue.'

Before long, though, he had made his name the best-known in fell-racing. In 1950 he won Grasmere, the biggest prize in guides-racing, for the first time. He went on to win it ten times more. He also won the controversially named British Hill Running Championship – held at Alva, in Scotland – eight times. And he won pretty much everything else in between. He set records that stood for years, and others that were broken repeatedly, but only by him. He once won two big races, at Bampton and at Tebay, on the same day. In so far as such a thing was possible in his prime, he became a celebrity. Journalists – from the *Westmorland Gazette*, or from *Cumbria* magazine, and later on from local radio and television – came to interview him. Bookmakers offered prohibitive odds against him, or took bets only on the margin of his win rather than the win itself. Fellow runners despaired of beating him. 'Has Bill gone home yet?' gasped Derek Ormondy of Rusland, after breaking the record at Ingleborough but still finishing three minutes behind Teasdale. The question became a finishing-line catchphrase among the defeated, as soon as they had regained enough breath to speak.

But his fame could only spread so far. Thousands of Cumbrians watched him at Grasmere and Ambleside, but most British sports fans knew nothing of professional racing in the 1950s, let alone of professional fell-racing. And even in the fell-racing counties there were places too far afield for a poor farmer's son to reach. 'I couldn't afford to be away for days on end. There was the farm to look after. The cows couldn't go days without milking. There was many went further to race than me.'

He did, however, begin to win regular money. 'Prizes were anywhere from three quid to fifteen. No one could really make a living from it, but if you could get a couple of races in the week, you made good pocket money.'

Whether or not that was enough to justify the tag 'professional' is debatable. This was a time when, as Teasdale points out, 'wages weren't much either – if you got seven or eight pound a week you were doing well'. But simply getting to races represented a significant expense, in money or in lost cash. 'It could take you two days to get to a fell race if you didn't have a motor car. You could get a train if you got to station, but trains never went to Grasmere – they used to go to Windermere. We used to do a lot of walking.'

Traditionally, the winner of a big guides race could expect a lift home from a wealthy fan, while the rest of the field – also classed as professionals – trudged home on foot. For the smaller races, even that incentive was lacking. Teasdale recalls an event in Dent, in the Yorkshire Dales, when he was still relatively unknown. 'I had to cycle to Carlisle [about 14 miles] to catch a train, because it was the only train that stopped in Dent. I got out at what I thought was Dent – at least it said Dent station – but it turned out Dent was way over mountain. I had to walk 6 miles to get there. Anyway, I won mile, and then I turned out and was third in fell race, so I won about ten quid. But I had to hire a taxi back to station, and that cost me five bob, because if I'd have missed that train, I wouldn't have been back at farm till next day.'

Later on, Teasdale bought a motorbike, a form of transport popular with fell-runners. (There was a famous occasion in the 1920s when the Metcalfe brothers crashed their motorbike on the way to the Burnsall race but still managed to compete, once the stewards had been persuaded that they were not, in fact, dead.) Several of his biggest victories, including his first Grasmere victory, were achieved after motorbike journeys in heavy rain; just as they were invariably achieved after early mornings of frantic farm work. 'That first time I won Ambleside, we were haytiming, in that field across road. We were mowing a field of corn with scythes, and after I'd won I had to come back and mow some more.'

This was what professionalism meant: fitting in your running around the demands of work. And for nine runners out of ten, there weren't even any prizes to compensate. 'There was one lad, he were a true amateur. He come from Barrow. He ran professional – it didn't matter where there was a race, he always turned up. But I never saw him win money once in his life.' Conversely, he remembers one amateur, a Yorkshireman, telling him mockingly: 'If I win a prize, I can sell it for more than you win.'

Nonetheless, the amateur establishment treated the professionals, Teasdale included, with confident distaste. In 1954, keen to test himself over a longer distance, Teasdale paid ten shillings to join the Youth Hostel Association, so that he could enter the Lake District Mountain Trial. The authorities were outraged: 'Are you Teasdale the fell-racer?' But eventually it was agreed that he could run unofficially, as long as he stood back at the start and waited until all the 'real' competitors were gone before he started. He did so, and won effortlessly, knocking half an hour off the course record (the Trial was run over a fixed course in those days). Or rather, he finished first, and was washed, changed, fed and back at the finish in dry clothes before the first official runner came in, thirty-eight minutes behind. The official runner – Joe Hands – was declared the winner, and all Teasdale got for his pains was a certificate saying that he had taken part. 'I was a real amateur that day,' he laughs. 'I didn't get owt.'

He doesn't seem to bear any grudges about this. 'As far as we were concerned, it was just the committees kept you apart.' But it's hard not to wonder what he could have achieved if he'd been allowed to contest some of the longer, amateur events. 'I would have liked to try something further,' he admits. 'The furthest we did was about 8 miles, I think, at Ingleborough, and most was much less. I would have liked to have run Ben Nevis – but they wouldn't have you. If you'd tooken five bob, that was it.' He once bet on himself to lower the Ingleborough record by between five and six minutes – an unlikely feat against which the bookies offered generous odds. Rather to his disappointment, he lowered it by six-and-a-half.

On other occasions, his betting proved more successful. 'The first time I ran Ambleside, I took off and left my brother at home. But when I came back, I'd taken a lot of cheap money off the bookies. I had twenty pound on myself – that's a lot of money – at ten to one.' For a professional pariah winning meagre prize money, such rewards offered considerable consolation, and helped reconcile his family and friends to his increasingly frequent absences. They also made the whole business of running significantly more intense, with every race conducted under pressure to deliver the result his supporters wanted.

'There was a hell of a lot more gambling going on than there is now. Ordinary people didn't have much money, but they still might put a pound on. And other folk would be big money – you know, double figures of thousands, like. I know when Albert Spence won Powderhall [the Powderhall Sprint in Edinburgh, the most prestigious event on the professional track circuit] he got £20,000 from the man that backed him.'

After 1949, Teasdale's odds were never twenty to one again. 'I was more odds-on than odds-against – I was never a big price, and it got to the point where you couldn't get a bet on yourself. If you put your hand in your pocket to get wallet out they used to wipe board.' But gambling remained an important part of what he did. 'We ran for the bookies. The bookies and the crowds.' This made for a febrile atmosphere. 'You couldn't run out [train] at Grasmere without someone watching you with a stopwatch on,' says Teasdale. And he recalls one race when he was heading for a rare defeat until a spectator bellowed in his ear: 'I've got my money on you, Teasdale!'

The guardians of amateur purity saw gambling as one of the chief reasons for considering professional athletics inherently corrupt. They had a point. All sports on which people bet attract would-be cheats; how much more so when the participants are human, and can be induced by fear or greed to bring about a desired result. Attempts to defraud bookmakers were being recorded from the earliest days of guides racing – a competitor was banned from Grasmere for cheating in 1890 – and most fell-running enthusiasts who were around in Teasdale's heyday will tell you that races were still, from time to time, being thrown. There was a scandal at Outgate Sports, near Hawkshead, in the late 1940s, when a Scottish runner rested behind a wall until he was overtaken; he was warned never to come south of the border again. And there was another in the Eden Valley in the 1950s, described in his memoirs by John Hurst, former editor of the *Cumberland & Westmorland Herald*, at which a rigged race turned into 'a ludicrous spectacle' because the chosen winner, a rank outsider, was manifestly incapable of beating his rivals even when they weren't trying. 'The set-up became obvious. Some of the other competitors tripped over non-existent obstacles and faltered at walls which they would normally have scaled with ease; one much fancied runner disappeared from sight altogether until the unlikely victor finally stumbled over the finishing line.'

The late Stan Edmondson, the Borrowdale farmer who was Teasdale's main rival in the late 1940s and 1950s, told the author Sheila Richardson that, when he was starting out, he was told 'by some fellas' to come fourth in a big race, and did so; but, he said: 'I think that would be the only time I did what I was told. I never did it again.' Fred Reeves, likewise, remembers being taken aside by a bookmaker before one of his first senior races, in the 1960s: 'He said, "We could make a fortune if you throw this race." I wouldn't like to repeat to you what I said, but I told him in no uncertain terms where to go. I didn't train fourteen times a week just to throw races. And I think after that word got around that I wasn't interested.' Another leading runner of the 1950s and 1960s told me: 'There was a lot of fiddling with the bookmakers. There were a couple of characters, they'd throw a race anywhere for a shilling. They'd work a race between them – they'd say, "Well, who's going to win today?" You knew about it, because of the language that was flying about, and fisticuffs now and again. They'd try to get me in, but I'd say no – my dad was very strict about that sort of thing – so the great problem was me splitting them up. I was disliked for that.'

Was Teasdale ever involved in such practices? He stoutly denies it, but implies that others were. One rival, he suggests, used to 'run about', probably because he had lost money gambling himself and 'the bookies were looking for him'. One obvious defence against gossips who doubt Teasdale's integrity is that there is no evidence of his ever having been rich (in contrast to the recently deceased Northern millionaire who is alleged to have built an entire furniture business on the proceeds of a fell-racing betting coup). Another is that, as his reputation grew, he became too public a figure to participate in dubious activities that flourished best in the shadows. The third, and most conclusive, is that he kept winning.

Actually, to say that he kept winning is an understatement. He kept on and on winning. And the strange thing was that, whereas most previous champions had begun to fade by their late twenties, Teasdale improved with age. In 1962, after a rare defeat at Grasmere, he announced his retirement. It seemed the thing to do, at thirty-seven. But he was back the following year, after getting into an argument with a local young hopeful and, to settle it, trouncing him in a practice race. The year after that, following two successive Grasmere failures, he retired again. He was still working on the fells, but had also found additional employment as a rigger for the BBC, which required frequent travel. Nonetheless, in 1965 – aged forty by now – he returned properly, not only winning Grasmere but reducing the record by a further nine seconds. He had, as usual, been up since dawn, tending sheep. His main rivals, Reg Harrison and George Broadhurst, were astounded. 'Sorry old man,' Broadhurst had told him beforehand, 'there can be only one winner today.' 'That's right,' said Teasdale coolly. 'And it isn't going to be you.'

His last serious Grasmere was in 1969, aged forty-five, when he came seventh – his worst position in twenty-three years. At the end of that year, he was awarded the MBE, which he thought was 'a good hint that it's time to give up'. But he didn't finally do so until he was forty-seven, shortly after coming third in the British Hill Running Championships at Alva.

Even then, his natural fitness didn't entirely desert him. When he was sixty-two, some television documentary makers persuaded him to run Grasmere one last time. He didn't win, but nor was he anything like last, and he still leapt up the hill with alarming ease. A younger runner, Trevor Batchelor, was asked to run alongside him to check that he was OK. 'By halfway up,' recalls Batchelor, 'I was knackered. I was ready to take it easy for a bit, but the bugger wouldn't slow down. I think he trotted in in about eighteen minutes in the end. I forget how old he was, but he had the heart and lungs of an eighteen-year-old.'

'I just seemed to carry on,' muses Teasdale, almost as if he were talking about someone else. 'I don't know why. I just seemed to carry on winning.'

Sports physiologists agreed that he was a superb human specimen, with a resting pulse rate of forty-one beats a minute and a superb power-to-weight ratio (he weighed just 8 stone 7 pounds at his peak). His oxygen uptake, measured for the first time for the same documentary when he was sixty-two, was, according to former British Olympic coach Tom McNab, 'comparable to an exceptionally fit twenty-year-old – his VO^2 max was pushing seventy.' We can only guess what such tests would have recorded in his prime.

Sports statisticians, meanwhile, agreed that, objectively, he compared favourably with any athlete alive. His Mountain Trial performance alone implied strongly that he was in a class above such Olympians as Christopher Brasher and Bruce Tulloh. And the form book also argued for his superiority in shorter events. In 1953, special arrangements were made for Teasdale to run a version of the Burnsall race (usually an amateur event) to see if he could beat Dalzell's record. He didn't, for various reasons (principally his choice of route), but he still returned a time of 14 minutes 47 seconds, the best since Dalzell. The same year, the 'real' (i.e. amateur) Burnsall race was won by Derek Ibbotson, the former world mile record-holder (and, incidentally, the first man to run a mile in exactly four minutes). Ibbotson's time was more than two minutes slower. Ibbotson subsequently turned professional, as did his fellow track superstar and mountain enthusiast Gordon Pirie; neither did much for his reputation by doing so. In 1962, Pirie was beaten by Teasdale's great rival, Reg Harrison, in a 2-mile track event in Jedburgh.

Yet Teasdale hardly seems to have trained, at least not in the conventional sense. He briefly had a trainer, Bob Thirlwall of Keswick, but he denies having done any serious training. 'I was lucky. I just turned out and ran, and that was it. I didn't have to train like a lot of these lads – they used to tell me how far they'd run.' Thirlwall had a reputation for feeding his runners a concoction of sherry and eggs shortly before a race, but Teasdale says that his main function in his case was 'to look after my clothes and my money and my false teeth while I ran'. (This gave rise to an interesting rumour: 'One bloke said, "Teasdale must be on something. There's always this bloke gives him something in a tin after a race, and he puts it in his mouth." ') But, with or without a trainer, he never seems to have got into the habit of regular training runs. 'Well, I maybe went up glen and ran mile in New Year. Then I turned out in spring and just ran in fell races once or twice a week. But I worked on farm and worked up on fell, so I used to walk a long way.

'But I think a lot of it is up in here –' he points to his head. 'I've seen boys with confidence used to fly, like, while really good runners would get beat. And of course, I never ailed out. I was never injured.' Which is true if you discount at least two instances when he was struck on the head by boulders dislodged by pursuing descenders above.

Even today, approaching eighty, he is fit and active, taking his spaniel for two long walks a day, on the same fellside he roamed as a gamekeeper. His doctor says he has high blood pressure, but he doesn't take that too seriously. 'I've always had high blood pressure. Anyway, I feel fine.'

If he does show signs of age, it's more in a sense of alienation from modern life. 'It used to be that you knew everybody and everybody knew you. Now there's a lot of folk in village I don't know owt about. A lot of the lesser farms have been sold off. I know my own folk like, but there's a lot of others have moved in, and I don't know what the half of them do for work.'

He worries about the traffic, too – one of his great-nephews was killed on the A66 – and about people disapproving of his enthusiasm for shooting. ('But there's a lot worse things I can think of, like keeping big dogs in the middle of towns.') There's no bitterness in his words, just a certain weariness. 'People talk about the march of progress, but I don't think it's made things any better.'

He still goes occasionally to fell races, notably Ambleside, where until recently he helped lay the hound trail. But, he says: 'It's all changed. You get more runners now, but there's more that hasn't a chance. And there's so much else for folk to watch [at the sports]. It doesn't mean the same. People used to do it and watch it because there was nowt else for them. Every village had its sports, and you used to get 18,000 folk at Grasmere or Keswick. Then TV came. Now most of the young lads aren't interested.' With so many more lucrative forms of sporting superstardom now theoretically open to them, and so many less demanding forms of diversion, it's not surprising.

Teasdale's name no longer appears in any record books, but his times were beaten only by modern champions in lightweight modern shoes. Teasdale ran in heavy kangaroo-skin boots ('heavier than these,' he says, pointing to the hefty walking boots which are his usual daily footwear) with metal studs and a metal plate to prevent the studs from being driven back into the foot. He 'used to send off for them from Foster's of Bolton' – where they were made by a young Norman Walsh, who decades later would create his own celebrated brand of fell-running shoe. 'You had to draw the outline of your feet on a piece of paper. But they were still hard on your feet – sometimes you could see the studmarks on the bottom of your feet.' The courses, too, were rougher: there's many a stone wall that the 5-foot-4-inch Teasdale used to scale that now has a permanent gap in it; and many a brackened slope into which a permanent path has since been worn.

Talking to Teasdale today, however, as the chill of evening creeps through his living room, it's hard not to be struck by thoughts of impermanence. Apart from the trophies in his cabinet, he doesn't have much to show for his triumphs, although money put aside from winnings did help him buy Bushby House four decades ago, after he was turfed out of Todcrofts on his father's death. For a man who took the art of distance running to previously unimaginable heights, he has left little trace on the national psyche. As for fortune, the brown envelopes on the mantelpiece, over an empty grate, look suspiciously like unopened bills.

Yet, unlike many sporting millionaires, he seems at peace with himself. He won his glory in a world that has vanished – a world of professional cycling and pony-trotting, of hound trails and Cumberland wrestling, of five-lap miles and dodgy sprint tracks and quick-fisted bookies – but he knows that, in that world, the honour he won was real. That was a world with boundaries, in which a journey beyond your own valley, let alone your own county, was not something to be undertaken lightly; and in which a hero measured his worth not by his nationwide celebrity but by the respect of his neighbours.

In fact, he does have one other treasured possession, kept under an old cloth in a tiny, seatless dining-room-cum-junk-room. It is a silver plate, given to him by his fellow competitors on his final retirement, inscribed with a picture of Teasdale running and, beneath, the words 'To a great sportsman'. 'Needs a clean,' he says, putting it back. But somehow I'm not convinced that it will get one.

He never married, and has lived alone since his mother died. It's tempting to wonder why – and whether any secrets or sadnesses underlie those stark statements; but something about this little old man commands too much respect to allow prying. It's tempting, too, to ask if Bushby House has electricity, for after a couple of hours of talk the half-light has deteriorated into almost total darkness – but it seems less rude just to sit back and listen to the patient ticking of the old clock.

'Aye,' he says, emerging from a long reverie, 'I did well, didn't I?'

He laughs, then adds: 'And I enjoyed it. You met a lot of folk you wouldn't have met, and you got friendly with a lot of blokes, like. I got to places I would never had gone to.' Which is true enough, but in an infinitely more local sense than most people would imagine. When he visited London to collect his MBE, it was the furthest he had ever been from Caldbeck.

12

Scenes from a fell-running year: May

Thin mist rests lightly on the wet hilltops of Jura: nothing serious, but enough to dampen the spirits of at least a few of the 165 runners who wait on the cold seafront at Craighouse while the Islay Pipe Band serenades them with bagpipes. In a few minutes' time, a blast from a shotgun will send them off for the twentieth running of the island's famous race, the Bens of Jura. Even a suggestion of worsening weather can be demoralising at such moments.

But at least one man present is conscious only of the scene's heart-breaking beauty. Mike Rose, recently retired secretary of the Fellrunners' Association, won't be running in the race. He's in the advanced stages of lung cancer, and is unlikely to leave his wheelchair. But his life has revolved around fell-running for thirty years, for most of which he's been coming up to Jura in his camper van every May; so now three similarly inclined friends, Jon Broxap, Arthur Clarke and Selwyn Wright, have brought him up here in that same camper van for one last chance to savour the race's romantic atmosphere.

You might wonder why he holds this particular event so dear. It's not particularly long, as long races go. But its 16 miles are notoriously wild and tough, with 7,500 feet of ascent over rugged, trackless terrain and a microclimate that can turn both Arctic and impenetrably claggy in an instant. In a bad year, of which there have been many, competitors can find their powers of navigation and resilience tested to the limit – it's been known for more than a third of the field to retire in distress before the finish. A handful of those who finish today will do so in less than three-and-a-half hours; many will take nearer seven.

But true fellsmen relish such challenges. And Mike Rose is a true fellsman. A Cheshire-born engineer, he stumbled into fell-running via walking when he was in his mid-thirties. Ever since, he has lived for the sport. Not that he's ever won anything – his best-ever position in a race was fifth, and that, he used to boast, was in a field of six. But in some senses he's closer to the heart of the sport than many champions. He understands absolutely what it is all about – the adventure, the integrity, the camaraderie, the joyous engagement with wild places, the epic battles with impossibly hostile weather, the cheerful discomfort in the campsite before and afterwards. His distinctive figure – simultaneously bald and tousle-haired, with a cigar usually in hand and his long legs rarely protected by anything more than the shortest shorts – has been part of the scenery of British fell-racing for getting on for two decades. And, since he took advantage of early retirement in 1991 to become FRA secretary, his abrasive charm has been part of the sport's public character. 'He could,' according to one friend, 'be quite staggeringly rude. But there was terrific kindness underneath, and he's been a real force for good in the sport.'

One can only guess at the thoughts that go through his mind as the runners head for the hills and quiet returns to the cold seafront. But poignant memories will undoubtedly be among them, for this is a man to whom the social side of fell-running is as important as the athletic side. Since announcing his diagnosis in the February issue of the *Fellrunner*, he has been both overwhelmed and mystified by the support he has received from a community not much given to articulating its gentler feelings: 'Why is everyone bothering with a cantankerous old buffer like me?' The kindness of Broxap and Wright will have moved him particularly, for these are two of the hardest men ever to set studded foot on mountain. But, being the kind of man he is, he keeps most of his feelings to himself.

Out in the hills, the runners have a relatively pain-free time of it. The ground is heavy to the point of saturation – one woman briefly achieves total immersion in an unnoticed wet patch – but there's enough visibility to make it a contest of running rather than navigation. This is welcome news for those with Scottish championship points on their mind. Yet it's the English visitors – among the men, at least – who rise best to the challenge. Nick Sharp wins in an impressive 3 hours 20 minutes 14 seconds in his first attempt at the race. Rob Jebb is second, with his Bingley team-mates Andy Peace and Ian Holmes third and fifth respectively and Borrowdale's Phil Davies fourth. Ninth home, in 3 hours 45 minutes 31 seconds, is Angela Mudge – which would be a staggering achievement were that not the sort of level at which she habitually performs; the record she breaks – by four minutes – is her own. Afterwards, there is, as ever, plenty of party spirit at the prize-giving, with a ceilidh and whisky galore courtesy of the local distillery; and, when the ferry pulls out of Craighouse on a perfect spring morning for the long return journey, most of the weary passengers are already thinking about repeating the experience next year. Except, of course, for Mike Rose.

Back on the mainland, there's less joy than you might imagine in the Sharp household. Nick and Lou have made the painful decision to split up. This leaves Lou looking for a new home and, since the couple's plans to go travelling are now in ruins, for a new job. But the strain doesn't seem to harm her running: she wins her first major victory of the season in vile weather in the Moel Eilio, a British and Welsh championship counter at Llanberis; Mercia's Tim Davies takes the men's prize.

Earlier in the month, there's a big turnout at Stuc a Croin, in the British and Scottish championship. Heavy going, following a week of torrential rain, makes the 13-mile course even more demanding than usual. Ian Holmes, Rob Jebb and Andy Peace are among those who cope best with the conditions, taking the first three places respectively for Bingley. But Angela Mudge's performance is arguably more memorable. She's twentieth overall – and first woman home by nearly twenty minutes. For Mudge, the race is a good warm-up for the Scottish Islands Peaks race later in the month, a four-leg marathon for teams comprising two runners, three sailors and a yacht; Mudge's team wins this too, with two-and-a-half hours to spare.

Mark Croasdale returns safely from Iraq, where his duties, just south of Basra, have consisted largely of routine patrols. ('Not like when I went to the Falklands twenty years ago – that was the real thing.') He's fitter than he'd feared – at one point he even ran in a half-marathon, round and round the perimeter of his camp – and now he tries to shake off the rest of the athletic rust with three races in two weeks: the Belmont Village Winter Hill and the Clougha Pike (both in Lancashire) and the Hutton Roof Crags (in Cumbria). He comes second, first and first respectively, and the odds against mankind finally out-running horsekind shorten slightly.

Elsewhere, the calendar bristles with famous and arduous events: Cader Idris in Gwynedd; the Llanghorse Loop in Monmouthshire; the Donard-Commedagh in the Mourne Mountains; Alwinton in Northumberland; Shining Tor and Burbage in Derbyshire; Pinhaw Moor in Lancashire; Totley Moor in South Yorkshire; and the Coniston, the Old County Tops and the Fairfield Horseshoe in Cumbria. Everyone has their own favourite, and the best-loved races are not necessarily those that feature in the championship-chasers' scheme of things.

At the Duddon Valley, for example, it's the atmosphere that counts. It's the twenty-fifth running of the event, a 20-mile classic in the heart of Borrowdale, whose creator, Ken Ledward, used to run it in defiance of AAA regulations as an unregistered race, open to both amateurs and professionals. There aren't that many runners this time – long, rough races are out of fashion – but there are some distinguished names among them, including Mark Hartell and Wendy Dodds, while two old champions, Billy Bland and Joss Naylor (respectively winner and runner-up in the first running) turn up to pay their respects at the start. Naylor even competes, aged sixty-seven, to widespread delight – and doesn't come last. Hartell comes fifth, nearly an hour ahead of Dodds but twelve minutes behind the winner, Andrew Schofield of Borrowdale – who in turn is thirty minutes behind Billy Bland's 1981 record.

And then there's the Fellsman Hike, a 61-mile yomp through the Yorkshire Dales, organised by the Keighley Scout Service Team. Winding from Ingleton to Threshfield (via Ingleborough, Whernside,

Gragareth, Great Courn, Blea Moor, Great Knotberry, Dodd Fell, Middle Tonge, Cray, Buckden Pike and much else), it's arguably a walkers' challenge as much as a runners' one. But it makes demands – for toughness, resourcefulness, stamina and mountaincraft – that go to the heart of the sport's character. It was here that this year's winner, Warwickshire-born Mark Hartell, had his first encounter with the mountains, nearly twenty-five years ago. His knee locked up and he had to withdraw, but the failure left a residue of dissatisfaction that he subsequently purged with spectacular effect. He's now won the Fellsman Axe – as the trophy is called – six times, and has his eye on Alan Heaton's record of nine. He has also won more mountain marathons than he can remember, has completed all three great British twenty-four-hour rounds (doing the Paddy Buckley in the fastest time ever and the Bob Graham in the second-fastest time ever), and since 1997 has held the record – seventy-seven – for the number of Lake District Peaks climbed in twenty-four hours.

You might not take Hartell for a mountain man if you saw him at work – serious, ambitious, well-spoken, neatly dressed, spending much of his time in anonymous hotels or driving too fast in his company car (he has, he says, a tendency to road rage). But beneath the focused surface is an extravagant dreamer who always tries 'to reach a little further than I can grasp' and who realised long ago that 'each time I made one of these dreams come true, I would simply find new, harder ones to fill the gap'. He's having a quiet year this year: he too is in the throes of a painful marital separation, and is also unsettled in his job; he isn't yet ready to push himself too hard, believing that 'for distance running you need stability and a strong base'. In 2002, however, he took a year off work to concentrate on running the 'hottest, coldest, highest and hardest' ultra-distance races in the world – respectively, the Marathon des Sables in the Sahara, the 350-mile Iditarod in Alaska, the Everest Marathon and the Hardrock 100 Endurance Run in south-western Colorado's San Juan Mountains. The scheme foundered when the Hardrock 100 was cancelled; hence his plans for a visit to Colorado this July.

'I hate unfinished business,' he explains grimly.

13

The club

CUMBRIA, MAY 2003. A MUGGY THURSDAY
EVENING IN KESWICK. A dozen fidgeting figures have
assembled by the war memorial. Most wear Ron Hill tracksters and
Walsh fell shoes; Lycra and trainers are also in evidence. No one
gives any noticeable thought to the twenty-second name down in
the 1914–18 section of the monument; in fact, I'm not sure that any
one present has even heard of E. H. Dalzell, who was killed at
Monchy in 1917 (causing the *Westmorland Gazette* to mourn a
'fearless human antelope ... who gave his life for his country
running an even greater race than lovely Grasmere can provide'). I
don't like to ask, because, to be honest, I feel like a bit of an
intruder, and I don't want to come across as a clever Southern git.

Instead, I smile politely at those who notice me and tuck in near
the back as Mark Denham-Smith, club fell-running champion,
leads us off at a jog towards what *Pacemaker*, the Keswick Athletic
Club newsletter, has intriguingly billed as 'fell drills'. Perhaps this
could be my chance to discover the secret techniques of the fell-
running masters. Or perhaps it's just a fancy Cumbrian term for
'training run'.

No one could accuse Mark of not looking the part of the drill
sergeant: lithe, athletic, hairless, he emanates toughness and
intensity in equal measure and runs with the effortless bounce of a
man unacquainted with excess fat. But it is Duncan Overton – a
tanned, Lycra-clad fortysomething bulging with toned muscles –
who is leading tonight's session. I suspect this is bad news, because
Duncan – crow's-feet clustering around a firm, clear-eyed gaze –
appears to be an even harder case than Mark.

But neither looks anything like as tough as Skiddaw, the 931-metre peak that towers over Keswick as Table Mountain towers over Cape Town, curved, majestic and palpably enormous. Its sphinx-like immensity makes a toy town of our surroundings; in the wrong frame of mind you could look at it and feel your limbs go limp at the thought of its sheer mass. But no one else here seems the kind to succumb to such fancies, and I fear that it is only me whose heart is in his fell shoes as we jog off to torture ourselves on its slopes.

There are half a dozen of us, from a club membership of getting on for 200 (of which I am the newest). A second group, of half-a-dozen women, has opted for a lakeside track run instead. This is a fairly typical Thursday night turnout. Not all members are runners; not all runners are fell-runners; not all fell-runners feel like club training on any given night. Anyway, an audience of half a dozen is more than enough people in front of whom to humiliate myself in my first midweek training session.

We head easily up Station Road, past the Leisure Pool and along the tree-lined back lane; people chat about injuries and fellow members. A right turn, and the town gives way abruptly to sloping track; shortly afterwards, the sloping track gives way to steeply sloping track. Conversation peters out.

We stop. 'All right,' begins Duncan, sounding like an NCO who may or may not be a sadist. 'This is very simple. Hard up for ninety seconds, then ninety seconds' rest. Twelve repetitions. I'll shout when the ninety seconds is up. Rest means walk, or an easy jog. Hard means hard. But don't go off like a bat out of hell. It's a lot tougher than you'd think.' I believe him. I'm right to do so.

I set myself the modest target of not being last. Or, rather, not last every time. After three repetitions, I'm setting myself the target of simply completing the twelve repetitions. By the sixth – by which time we have left the original track for the steep, loose scree of the open mountain – I've revised that to not being sick. After eight, to not being left to die on the fellside.

There's nothing particularly technical about the drills; it's just old-fashioned interval training. But we're doing it up a 45-degree slope – every step we've taken to date has been upwards. And, as each successive repetition takes us further on to the steep section known as Jenkin Hill, so the task of running hard in a forward direction for a minute-and-a-half grows in its severity. It is, I suppose, a powerful incentive to develop an economical uphill gait.

After nine repetitions I can hardly see, so freely is the sweat streaming down my face. I'm not sure if I feel winded or sick, but there is a discomfort in my torso that I know can be relieved only by lying down. Blind vanity keeps me upright.

After ten, I find that my gentle jog-cum-walk during the recovery periods is occasionally taking me backwards down the hill. There is not enough air in Cumbria to satisfy my heaving gasps for oxygen.

After eleven, Duncan says: 'Two to go.'

Mark says: 'It's the second twelve that really hurt.'

I try to swear but the words won't come: not just the breath – I can't even call to mind any swear words. At some point, presumably, my lungs or my brain will explode. I wonder if anyone will clear up the mess.

And then – the recurrent miracle at the heart of every runner's faith – it is over. We're done; we're still alive; we're starting to feel better already. All that remains is to jog down, chatting and marvelling at the view. The sun has sunk somewhere behind us, on the far side of the mountain, and the slopes are flooded with deep, prehistoric shadow. A white moon glows icily out of the deepening blue ahead; and, though the necessities of downhill running mean that one cannot glance at it for more than a second at a time, the sea of ancient Cumbrian twilight that stretches for miles ahead must look much as it did to Ernest Dalzell when he ran (and worked) here; or, for that matter, to that other famous gamekeeper of these parts, Bill Teasdale.

But the great orange glow of Keswick itself, down to our right, would have struck Dalzell as bizarre – and so, of course, would we. Our purpose-made kit would have mystified him. So would the idea of a Keswick-based running club with a membership running into three figures. (Keswick Athletic Club was founded in 1973 and is one of Britain's oldest fell-running clubs.) As for what we have been doing, neither Dalzell and his trainer, Jack Cowperthwaite, nor Teasdale and his, Bob Thirlwall, would have had any conception of interval training. (Dalzell's preparations would probably have revolved around long walks and extra food; Teasdale occasionally ran fast around the grass track in Keswick's Fitz Park.)

But the thing that would really have baffled Dalzell – and, to a lesser extent, Teasdale – would have been us: our backgrounds, our world-views, our life stories. In his world, there were people like him, who lived and worked and in some cases ran in the fells; and there was another variant of the species that came in cars and carriages to marvel at the views and mountains and the curious creatures who ran on them. You'd expect the fell-runners of Keswick to have more in common with the first group. But do they?

Here's Mark Denham-Smith, thirty-five years old and altogether less intimidating once you've been in his company for five minutes. A short, effervescent man with a grin that verges on a beam, he earns his living from quantity surveying and only moved to Cumbria – from Cambridgeshire – three years ago, whereupon he took to the fells with a degree of nervous caution. Today, he's not only the club's most successful fell-runner but has also 'taken on the mantle of hustling the boys down for championship races, organising transport, maps, recces, etcetera'; many see him as a future club captain. Here's Duncan Overton (who, I discover to my shame, is actually a tanned, Lycra-clad *fiftysomething*, recently recovered from a heart operation): a retired RAF training officer who now runs his own e-learning business, he's originally from Lancashire, and although he's spent much of his life in Cumbria, he's only recently returned from a stint in Swindon. Here, a bit further back in our group, is Stephen Fletcher, three years out of London after taking a career break, painstakingly building a new life as a project manager based in the neighbouring village of Threlkeld. Here, just behind him, is Stephen Kemp, a chartered surveyor who moved here from Nottinghamshire seven years ago . . .

I'm beginning to realise that, apart from our geographical differences, many of our stories are essentially much the same. This is new Britain, and while nobody present would feel any disrespect for the venerable tradition of guides, gamekeepers and farmworkers in whose footsteps we run, the fact is that we're all, to some exent, new Britons. We earn our livings as we can, from jobs that change, move, vanish, reinvent themselves. Whether we're manual, managerial, entrepreneurial, professional or something else, we're all more likely than not to be mobile, wired-up footsoldiers in the service industries – flexiworkers, downshifters, self-employed, even commuters. We've nothing against the more rooted lives of our forerunners – the idea of one life, one job, one home seems positively enviable. It's just that those options hardly exist any more.

As time goes on, I meet other Keswick members; and, the more I meet, the more I am struck by this sense of social transformation. There's Dave Spedding, for example, club captain and former British Over-50s Fellrunning Champion, until recently proprietor of the gift shop over which he lives, but now retired on the proceeds. There's Patric Gilchrist, another relative newcomer, who manages the Theatre by the Lake. There's Nimrod Lockwood, probably the club's best young hope, who helps run his family's guesthouse in nearby Thornthwaite, where they've lived since moving from Yorkshire twenty years ago. There's Chris Knox, conservationist and lecturer, a respected figure in fell-running for more than twenty years but no more Keswick-born than I am – he migrated from Tyneside in 1980. There's Lyn Thompson, former club chairman, who runs her own firm of surveyors in the town. And of course there's Lou Sharp, ladies' captain, until recently commuting from Kendal, half an hour to the south – and now looking to rebuild her life from scratch.

And here's Pete Richards, club secretary, semi-retired photographer and co-proprietor of Dunsford guesthouse in Stanger Street. A slim, cheerful man with a foxy beard and an accent that owes more to his native Yorkshire than to his adopted Cumbria, Pete has spent most of his sporting life running on roads around Scarborough, and only took to the mountains when he came to Keswick because it seemed perverse not to do so. He knew next to nothing about fell-running – but he did know about running running clubs; and so, with the inexorable dynamic that governs amateur organisations everywhere, he soon found himself running this one. His wife, Pat, a strikingly bright-eyed woman in her early fifties, is another of the club's leading organisational lights; she's taking the women's session tonight. 'I felt like a bit of an imposter at first,' Pete told me the first time we met. 'But it's remarkable how quickly people expect you to know everything about everything.'

You get the picture. Keswick AC drips with fell-running pedigree and tradition – it famously won five British championships in six years between 1983 and 1988 – but these are not, by any stretch of the imagination, the kind of fell-runners that Dalzell and Teasdale knew. Indeed, jogging down from our fell drills, I am unnerved by the ease with which I feel myself fitting in. I know people are going out of their way to make me feel welcome, but it strikes me that, for all my form as a privileged Southern graduate and semi-urban media type, I'm not really that much of an outsider at all. 'This is so much better than running in London,' says Stephen Fletcher, as we jog down the wide stone path. My own thoughts exactly – I just hadn't expected to hear them echoed here. Stephen, it turns out, is a hands-on young father who recently persuaded the club to start a junior section, of which he is now in charge. It's proving highly successful, he tells me, with ten to twenty children at a time turning out on Saturday mornings – which doesn't sound that different from how nice families spend their Saturday mornings down in my part of Northamptonshire, ferrying their children to music school and football practice.

It's the pedigree, though, that has persuaded the FRA to mount a bid for Keswick to host the 2005 World Mountain Running Trophy – an event that could provide a significant boost to a local economy still finding its feet after the foot-and-mouth catastrophe of 2001. Keswick has hosted the annual event before, in 1988, the fourth year of its existence. But it's a much bigger business these days – twenty-seven countries will compete for the trophy in Alaska this October. And the bidding process is more competitive too, with most rival bidders getting considerably more official support than Keswick can expect. Wellington, New Zealand, has a £200,000 budget already in place – nearly twice what the FRA would hope to raise for Keswick. Sport England, by contrast, has repeatedly turned down applications from the FRA for National Lottery funding to make bids for major events. An attempted bid to hold the 2003 championships in Sedbergh ran aground when UK Sport (Sport England's parent body) initially lost the FRA's grant application (for a £31,500 contribution towards a £90,000 budget) and Sport England then scorned the duplicate on the grounds that fell-running is not an Olympic or Commonwealth sport and does not have a Lottery-funded 'world-class performance programme'. The current bid is relying on support from the local council and a local quango, Rural Regeneration Cumbria; and on the enthusiasm and commitment of FRA officials and individual club members.

Many of Keswick's hopes are focused on the famous Skiddaw race, which takes place in July. It's a 'counter' in both the English and the British championships this year, and up to 500 of the country's best fell-runners are expected to take part. It's also a big chance to demonstrate that Keswick has what it takes to host a big fell-running event.

Not everyone in the club is enthusiastic about the World Trophy bid. Some traditionalists despise the whole idea of international mountain-running, because most of the other nations that participate refuse to run on the rough, steep, rocky descents that characterise the classic British races. Some favour uphill-only racing; others insist on terrain that is either tracked, tarmaced or, at worst, grassy and smooth. That doesn't make it easy; it does make it different, and the Britons who excel on the international circuit tend to be top marathon- and cross-country-runners rather than familiar faces from the domestic fell-running circuit. ('And in any case,' says one dissenting voice, 'the town's already full at that time of year.')

Nonetheless, the bid organisers intend to make this year's high-profile Skiddaw race a central item of evidence in their presentation to the World Mountain Running Association, and everyone at Keswick seems to agree on the need to 'showcase our club in the best possible light' – as Pete Richards puts it in one of many e-mailed appeals for help. Allan Buckley, a retired health manager from nearby Greystoke, is in overall charge of the race plans, but dozens of people have already volunteered to help with marshalling or registration or catering. And the committee has spent many long hours agonising about the precise format of the race – which must, at all costs, run smoothly.

One headache concerns erosion. Should runners be forced to stick to the stony path that goes much of the way up Jenkin Hill? Or should they, as is traditional in fell races, be allowed to choose whatever route they please? Going up, the path – which was recently restored – is a help to runners; on the way down, however, you could lose a lot of time if you stuck to every zig and zag rather than just plummeting cross-country. But if 500 runners all take the same short cuts it won't do much for the well-being of a hillside that has already been badly worn away by walkers.

Another headache is the start. 'That's what everyone gets worked up about,' says Pete Richards. 'There's a bit of a bottleneck very soon after the start, while you get from the park to Briar Rigg. No one likes that, and when you've got this many runners it's a definite problem. So we've talked about all sorts of alternatives, like getting people to do a lap of the park first, to spread them out. But then people complain that the distance won't be the same, so there's no chance of challenging the record. We even worked out a way of getting round that, but some people still weren't happy. There's always someone,' he adds, 'who isn't happy.'

He's right; but he's quick to point out that, most of the time, harmony reigns in the club. Trawl through its archives – or, more accurately, Dave Spedding's complete set of quarterly newsletters – and you get a sense of a big, cheerful, chaotic family, evolving over three decades in much the same way as Britain has evolved. The early issues of *Pacemaker* are roneographed and consist largely of results of local fell races. By the 1980s, hints of graphic-design awareness are creeping in; for a few issues there is even a staple.

The editorial carries echoes of the road-running boom in the world beyond Cumbria, and occasionally airs anxieties about the growing commercialisation of athletics. In the 1990s, the newsletter is photocopied, and, as a result, more discursive. The warm, faintly anarchic character of the club becomes unmistakable. There are hints of excess at the annual dinner, moans about the length of committee meetings, apologies for inaccurate race details and appeals for information about the whereabouts of missing trophies. There are also accounts of members' racing experiences in Scotland, Wales, Ireland, the Isle of Man, even mainland Europe. By 2000, the list of members' addresses on the back page includes some e-mail addresses. By 2003, only a handful don't have them, and, for the first time, the newsletter is distributed electronically. As for the content: ordinary week-to-week news (race details, appeals for help and so on) now reaches most members as it happens, e-mailed by Pete Richards, and so *Pacemaker* is once again filled mainly with results and league tables, leavened by occasional accounts of members' more exotic running adventures.

Some people feel that Keswick isn't the club it used to be: that its subtle modernisation has robbed it of the rock-hard core that made it invincible in the 1980s. Some claim that Borrowdale, further down the valley where the shepherds and farmers live, is a more authentic club and (with three individual Fellrunner of the Year title-winners and seven team titles since 1993) a better one. Others look to Cumberland Fellrunners and Clayton-le-Moors, to the west and the south; or, beyond the Lakes, to such great fell-running clubs as Bingley, in whose colours Ian Holmes, Rob Jebb and Andy Peace have won so many trophies; Macclesfield Harriers, home of such ultra-distance greats as Mark Hartell, Mark McDermott and Anne Stentiford; Dark Peak, famous for its prowess in guiding members round the BG; or, beyond England, Carnethy and Eryri. Such claims may well be true; they are also, I think, rather patronising, implying on the one hand that there is something inauthentic about anyone running on the fells who wasn't born and bred among them; and, on the other, that those who were born and bred among the fells are somehow incapable of engaging properly with the modern world.

In fact, all the above-mentioned clubs have their websites and their teleworking 'off-comers' (i.e. newcomers) too. Nor is Keswick only the sum of its novices: I don't think Harry Blenkinsop, club president, would take kindly to that suggestion: he's been running Mountain Trials in these parts for forty years, was British Over-40 Fellrunning Champion in 1979, and is member No. 11 of the Bob Graham 24 Hour Club; nor would Colin Valentine, the veteran Penrith forestry worker famous for his spectacular descents, who in the 1980s used to toughen himself up by running fell races barefoot; or, for that matter, Duncan Overton, who ran his first Lake District fell race thirty years ago, and is strongly fancied to win his second British Over-50 title this year.

The truth is, no modern fell-running club can conform to the clichéd stereotype of a tight-knit band of shepherds and gamekeepers deeply rooted in their unchanging rural community. Such communities no longer exist: we are all new Britons now. And Keswick, where runners chat by e-mail and mobile phone almost as often as they bump into one another in the street, is as close-knit a modern community as any. In any case, whatever its faults as a club for fell-runners, Keswick does have one unquestionable advantage over its rivals: the miraculous ring of mountains that encircles it. Steep, rough, green and large, these are generally acknowledged as classic fell-running hills. And the most spectacular of them all, with the biggest bottom-to-top ascent, is Skiddaw.

For running on, and particularly for running downhill on, slopes don't get much better than Skiddaw's, especially the wide, even descent of Jenkin Hill. I don't doubt for a moment that people have run down it for pleasure since mankind first lived and worked here. There is something about it that cries out to be run down: the relatively gentle slope that brings you to it from the summit, so that by the time you reach the top of Jenkin Hill you are already flying, without really having decided to do so; the abrupt falling-away that follows, after which your only options are to fall flat on your face or to accelerate; the relatively stable surface, firm underneath but with turf on top; and the final uphill curve at the end, guaranteed, like the end of a racing piste, to bring even the most lunatic descent gently back under control.

We gallop down it now: slowly at first, for this is meant to be a jog, but gradually accelerating as the laws of physics kick in and we're reminded how much harder slow is than fast. By the bottom I, at any rate, am close to racing speed, hanging in the air in the midst of each leap-sized stride, scarcely remembering to breathe, and oddly conscious of the fact that, with each impact, great drops of sweat are flying from my face in the chill evening breeze.

'Is it true,' asks someone, as the counterslope finally brings us back to an exhilarated jog, 'that Kenny Stuart once ran the fastest mile ever run by a human being coming down that slope?'

It seems a reasonable question, but no one knows the answer. The simplest solution, I decide, is to go and ask him.

14

The flying gardener

KENNY STUART LIVES IN A FORMER COUNCIL HOUSE in a modest terrace on the edge of Threlkeld, the little village squeezed between the southern foot of Blencathra and the lethally busy A66. If you don't count the view, it's an unremarkable place: just an ordinary home with a neat little garden outside and, inside, clutter and pets and children moaning about homework.

You could stand outside it many times, as I have (for this is a corner where Bob Graham rounders traditionally meet their supporters at about 4.50 a.m.), without imagining who lived there. And, to be honest, you could visit the Stuart household many times without suspecting that you were in the presence of one of the very greatest of British athletes. There are none of his trophies in sight, no photographs; and he, though there's still an unmistakably athletic spring in his step, is not the sort of person to brag.

Yet here he is, still implausibly small and delicate, still with a curiously confident glitter in his brown eyes: Kenny Stuart – or, as he's universally known round here: Kenny.

Athletics fans of a certain age may vaguely remember him. His name floated into the national consciousness in 1986, when the combined attractions of sponsorship and fresh challenges lured him from the obscurity of fell-running into the lucrative new sport of international marathon-running. At his very first attempt at the distance, he beat 8,200 other runners to win the Glasgow Marathon in 2 hours 14 minutes 3 seconds – a record for the course and within seven minutes of the then world record. Three years later, in the Houston Marathon, he ran 2 hours 11 minutes 20 seconds – one of the half-dozen fastest times ever recorded by a

Briton until then. He was still only thirty-one, well short of a distance-runner's peak, and although Britain had a plentiful supply of world-class marathon-runners in those days, admirers began to think of him as an Olympic champion in the making. Then, inexplicably, he vanished.

This is what happened.

Kenny was born in 1957, the eldest of four brothers. His family, on both his mother's and his father's side, had lived in Threlkeld for generations. They weren't rich: his father worked in the local quarry, as had his father before him. But they were respected members of the little community, and the boys grew up in a stable, old-fashioned village environment. Threlkeld is small – about 500 souls – and somewhat isolated. Few villagers had cars – 'just four families out of fourteen houses on our estate' – and few children saw much of the wider world. Instead, they went to school in the village, and played in the village, with visits to local shows among the social highlights of their year.

He was a small, rather sickly child, without noticeable athletic potential. Nor were there any runners in his immediate family. Yet fell-running of a sort was hard to avoid. 'If you were interested in the fells, it was natural to want to run on them,' remembers Kenny, who lives within 100 yards of the house he grew up in. 'And it was natural for us to be interested in the fells. If we wanted entertainment, we had to go outside. There was nowt in the house.' Given Threlkeld's position, 'outside' tended to mean the lower slopes of Blencathra. 'So we got quite fit,' he continues, in his quiet, conspiratorial voice. 'We used to walk for miles to find apples or plums. Or, you know, we'd chase each other, or maybe it would just be: "I'll race you from here to there." ' There was also football and, in the winter, 'many hours spent tramping the hills following the local foxhounds and beagles'.

Occasionally, Kenny and his friends would try their luck in the junior guides races at the summer shows. His father would ferry them to the more distant ones on the back of his motorbike, one at a time. Duncan, the next eldest brother, showed some promise as a runner; Kenny showed less, but did win one junior race in his local show, which was enough to sow a seed of ambition. Later, when he was thirteen, he came fourth in a junior race at Ambleside, which was then one of the most important meetings in the guides-racing calendar.

That was better than he could manage academically. 'I did badly in my exams. I would have left school at fifteen, except that the work situation was bad round here. So I stayed on, and got in the school cross-country team. It turned out I was quite good. In fact, it was about the only thing I was good at. I remember doing the county championship just before my sixteenth birthday.' Then, the day he turned sixteen, a letter arrived from the Northern Counties AAA, telling him that if he wanted to continue competing at county level after he left school he would have to stop running in professional fell races. Forced to choose, he chose the tradition he knew best – the professional one – and resolved to do better in it.

Improvement was slow. That year, he came sixth in the junior guides race at Grasmere; his prospects of ever earning anything from running, let alone a living, seemed slim. But somewhere inside this quiet, almost feckless youth was a merciless determination. 'I always thought,' he says, 'that it was in my hands to improve a lot.' Time would tell.

He was working now, though still living at home, and wasn't finding work – as a gardener – very interesting. Running, by contrast, seemed full of exotic potential. The running boom had just begun, and its echoes could be heard even in Threlkeld. Heroes like David Bedford and Kip Keino could be seen on television, while popular magazines – *Athletics Weekly*, or Ron Hill's *Running Review* – were for the first time giving ordinary readers a flavour of the adventure of elite running.

Kenny sent off for some training manuals, and immersed himself in the ground-breaking theories of Percy Cerutty and Arthur Lydiard. He began to train every day: not just endurance runs, but intervals, repetitions, 'fartlek' (that is, mixing fast running with slow). He also watched what he ate and drank, which his mates in the village thought strange. 'I'd go for weeks without a drink – just tagging along with the pool or darts team drinking orange juice.' Slowly the improvements came.

In 1975, aged eighteen, he came seventh in the Senior Guides Race at Grasmere; in 1976, he came fourth; in 1977, third; in 1978, fourth; in 1979, second. (All these races were won by either Fred Reeves or Tommy Sedgwick, with the other usually in second place.) It was a slow journey, not least because Kenny had yet to reach full physical maturity. But by 1980 he had got there.

That year, the lights came on. After spraining an ankle at Alva in July, he won Ambleside in August, ending Fred Reeves's ten-year winning streak. (Fred's young son, Phillip, cried, asking his dad why he had let himself be beaten; 'I didn't have much choice in the matter,' said Fred.) Later that month, Kenny won Grasmere, in what was then the second-fastest time ever (12 minutes 37 seconds). He also won Kilnsey Crag, Malham, the new professional version of the Burnsall race, and thirteen other races.

But it wasn't just what he won that excited people: it was how he won. Even today, Kenny is a frail-looking man; in his racing prime, he was almost impossibly slight, with the power and delicacy of a pedigree whippet. His 5-foot-5-inch frame was almost perfectly balanced (despite a slight lopsidedness in his arm movements); the 8 stone he weighed was almost entirely accounted for by perfectly conditioned muscle. When he ran, it looked effortless; he seemed to glide. You could be entranced by the economy and symmetry of his stride without even considering the broader context of the race or the racing environment.

Running enthusiasts observed a similar beauty in the gait of Sebastian Coe. But Coe ran on smooth track. Kenny was running on some of the roughest terrain it is possible to run on. 'He ran on scree as if it was Axminster,' said one observer. 'He just seemed to float,' said another. 'He could run over scree and the stones didn't even move,' says Trevor Batchelor, who ran against him. 'He sort of glided over it, he was so light-footed.'

Dave Spedding, who also raced against him, remembers his twelve-year-old daughter's crushing question after he had been trounced by Kenny at Grasmere. 'Why,' she asked, 'was Kenny

Stuart the only one who was *running*?' Spedding adds that Kenny was 'a real thoroughbred' – a description repeated again and again by those who saw and raced against him.

In 1981 – the annus mirabilis that confirmed Coe on the path to being an 'amateur' millionaire – Kenny was champion guides-racer for the second year in succession. He had thirty wins from thirty-two starts, setting records at, among others, Braemar, Kilnsey Crag and Sedburgh Hills. Altogether, he won £687 in prize money. 'A lot of that went on entrance fees and petrol,' he says. 'But it was useful pocket money. You got £75 for winning Grasmere, which was about what I was getting in my weekly wage packet.'

He could have carried on like this for years. Reeves and Sedgwick were now definitely in decline, and no one else could get close to him. But Kenny had his eyes on a bigger prize: greatness. 'I knew that I was good. But I wanted to measure myself against my heroes, and they were all amateurs.'

In the spring of 1982, he applied to be reinstated as an amateur. This was an unusual step, and 'many people in both codes were very negative about it'. But Christopher Brasher, one of Kenny's many admirers on the amateur scene, advised and encouraged him. 'It took nearly eight months,' says Kenny. 'I missed almost a full season while they considered my case – because I wasn't allowed to run in professional races any more, but I couldn't run in AAA races either.' Quite why it needed to take so long was never explained. 'They weren't friendly or encouraging. I was never contacted by them, or asked to give my opinion or state my case. But they were known for being very officious.' Presumably he was thought to be going through some kind of decontamination process.

In fact, he was persuaded to take part in one amateur race in May: the Duddon Fell Race, whose organiser, Ken Ledward, loathed mountain bureaucracy and had always refused to run his race under anyone's rules but his own. (Ledward's teenage son was banned from running for his county after winning the Ambleside junior guides race in 1977.) Several leading amateurs – including Joss Naylor, Billy Bland and Chris Brasher – dared the AAA to ban them by competing in an event in which an unsanctioned athlete was taking part; Kenny rewarded them by spending the entire race on Billy Bland's shoulder before outsprinting him at the finish.

Finally, in August 1982, he was allowed to run officially as an amateur. His first race was at Burnsall – a short event in the Yorkshire Dales that had once been professional. Up against him was one of the best athletes amateur fell-running had yet seen: John Wild, British champion for 1981 and a former national cross-country champion and Commonwealth Games steeplechase finalist. An electronics instructor with the RAF, Wild was educated, well travelled, well spoken and an extrovert. Many people remarked on the contrast between Wild and Kenny; some made much of the contrast. To them, the contest between the dashing RAF officer who ran for running's sake and the grasping professional who ran for money was an ideological struggle as well as an athletic one.

Roger Ingham saw the race. 'Kenny and John came up the fell neck and neck, and the abuse that Kenny Stuart got was horrible. I told them: you should be running, not slagging folk off like that.' He particularly remembers one 'horrible V-sign – like *that* . . .'

Wild won – not surprisingly, given Kenny's long lay-off – and told journalists: 'I have heard nothing but Reeves and Stuart since I got here. Yes, the win gave me a great deal of satisfaction.' 'Should have been banned for life,' shouted a heckler when Kenny collected his second prize. (That prize, incidentally, was a silver tray – worth more than most of the prizes he had won as a professional.)

But Kenny, despite appearances, was not fragile. Wild notwithstanding, he fought on and began to win races: Ben Nevis, Langdale, Butter Crags, the Blisco Dash. He was doing about 70 miles' training a week by now – 'mostly on the road, in the dark' – and the investment was paying dividends. He still had difficulties in the very longest events, coming eleventh in the Vaux Mountain Trial, forty minutes behind the winner. But he was adapting fast.

His first full season, 1983, was marked by ferocious rivalry with Wild, who had won the 1982 championship. The two men had become friends by then (as, indeed, the amateur community at large had made friends with Kenny), but they raced one another as if defeat meant death. Week after week, up and down the country, each pushed the other beyond his assumed limits, and record after record fell to one or other of them. Their rivalry began to be noted in mainstream athletics magazines. 'Mentally, he was as strong as I was,' says Kenny, 'and he was incredibly well trained. So we used to race each other to our hands and knees.' Afterwards, they played hard too, for Wild was known for his extravagant post-race celebrations (think champagne, streaking, fire extinguishers). 'It was the forces mentality,' says Kenny. 'Stability during the day, but let the hair down when they're off duty.' For a quarryman's son from Threlkeld, it was a mind-broadening period.

The 1983 British championship stayed in the balance until the very last race of the season. 'It was Thieveley Pike,' says Kenny. 'John really fancied his chances. It's not too steep, the kind of course that really suited him. So his wife had brought along a bottle of champagne to celebrate when he won. But I beat him [breaking the course record]. And after that he didn't really race so much.'

Kenny's life was by now not noticeably different from that of an Olympic athlete – except, of course, that he still lived with his parents and was fitting his training in around a 40-hour working week. The job – as a gardener at Hope Park, on the Keswick shore of Derwentwater – was not stressful, but it could be physically tiring. Somehow he had to fit a quality 5-mile run into his lunch hour – leaving time to warm down and change but not to shower – and then summon up the energy for a proper evening session after work. It's curious to imagine this while strolling in Hope Park today: such a quiet place, a few yards from Bob Graham's old house in Lake Road, sheltered from the tourist hubbub, with the waters of the lake just visible through the leaves. What self-belief it must have taken, and what hunger, to drive himself so relentlessly amid such calm.

There was less cash in his pocket than there had been in his professional days, and more travel expenses to pay. Then again, there was more useless glassware, and so much training that there wasn't much time for spending money. His training diary – meticulously recorded for more than a decade in neat pencil – records a relentless schedule, twice a day, 365 days a year; the distance (rarely more than 90 miles a week) was quite low by modern standards, but not the quality. 'I used to do the most incredible interval sessions. All my competitiveness went into my training as much as my racing.' It also shows his weight hovering 2 or 3 pounds above his preferred racing weight of 8 stone. 'I watched every single thing I ate. I was always hungry. It was like being a human hound.' But the dedication paid off. 'Even I was surprised at how big the improvement was.'

In 1984, he won pretty much everything he entered: Fairfield, Ennerdale, Snowdon, the Northern Counties. He set records – some of which stand today – for Black Combe, the Blisco Dash, Coniston, Eildon, Butter Crags, Skiddaw. What such lists don't convey is the grace and majesty of his performances. Some of the best-ever fell-runners were in their prime that year – Billy Bland, Hugh Symonds, Colin Donnelly, Jack Maitland, Jon Broxap. Yet Kenny brushed them aside with scarcely a second thought. 'The thing about Kenny,' says Dave Spedding, 'is that he wasn't even trying when he set those records. If he'd had someone to push him, he could have gone a lot faster.'

That year's Skiddaw race is a case in point. This was the day when he is alleged to have run the fastest mile ever, down the long steep side of Jenkin Hill. (If he did, no one ever told him about it. The fastest recorded mile that either I or he has heard of is 3 minutes 24 seconds, set in 1993 by Craig Wheeler – breaking a record set by the fell-runner Mick Hawkins – in the Meltham Maniac Mile, a downhill road race in Yorkshire. 'I'd be surprised if I'd gone faster than someone running on road,' says Kenny. 'Then again,' he adds, 'Jenkin Hill is very steep – I would have been going pretty fast.') But after that descent he was easing off: his nearest challenger was a minute behind. And although few subsequent winners have got anywhere near his time of 62 minutes 18 seconds (despite the recently added assistance of that improved stone path), the *Fellrunner*'s report remarked on the 'casual' manner of his victory and suggested that, if pushed, Kenny could have broken one hour. 'It was in my training that I really used to dig deep,' is all Kenny will say. 'The races were more like a bonus – the reward, if you like.'

Perhaps that explains why a man so gentle – shy, even – could demolish his opponents so ruthlessly. One 1984 race report talks of him 'warming up with a grim determination, a glint in his eye, and a quiet confidence that spelled danger for those who could read the signs . . .'. This was not racing as personal confrontation: this was racing from deep within the self – victories carved out in the kind of brutal lone training sessions to which only the most fearlessly honest runners will subject themselves.

Naturally, he won that year's British championship. Most memorably of all, on a wet, slippery September day, he set a record for the Ben Nevis race – 1 hour 25 minutes 34 seconds – that no one has come close to equalling since. To appreciate the enormity of this achievement, you really have to try the race for yourself (see Chapter 26). But you can get some measure of it from the fact that, two decades later, the organisers are offering a £1,000 prize to anyone who can break it, and have publicly stated: 'We think our money's fairly safe.'

Finally, for good measure, Kenny went to Italy, the world capital of mountain-running, for an international event that was a world cup in all but name. The Italians were hot favourites and duly humbled the British contestants, taking six of the first seven places; the exception was first place, taken by Kenny, who won with more than thirty seconds to spare. If anyone had doubted that this was an athlete of extraordinary gifts, there could be no doubting it now.

One person who had never doubted it was Kenny's Threlkeld neighbour, Pauline Haworth. Six months older than Kenny, Pauline was born in Northampton and spent her early adult life as a nurse in Liverpool and Southport. She drifted into fell-running via rambling and, later, her husband, Pete Haworth. After a spell working at the Llanbedr Youth Hostel, the couple had moved to Threlkeld in 1980, where they worked for the National Parks Commission at the Blencathra Centre at the back of the village. Pauline had tried her hand at fell-running in 1977, in a race round the Fairfield Horseshoe organised by the YHA, and had found that, without training particularly hard, she could beat most female fell-runners – still a rare breed – with ease. In 1980 she was Lady Fellrunner of the Year (as the title was then styled). Naturally, she became an active member of the local running club, Keswick AC, of which Kenny was also a member. By 1984, she was running *Pacemaker*, the club newsletter, whose function at the time was largely to record Kenny's triumphs and records.

She was also in the process of splitting up with her husband. And, by way of diversion, she was pushing back the frontiers of female fell-running. In 1984 she won the British championship for a second time, setting numerous new records, notably a time of 1 hour 43 minutes 25 seconds at Ben Nevis. Yes, the competition was limited: the number of serious female competitors barely reached double figures in some of these races. But there's £1,000 on offer today for anyone who can beat Pauline's Ben Nevis record too.

You can guess what happened next. If you can't, you have only to look at the photograph of the two of them at the Ben Nevis finish: both suffused with joy and sweat, Pauline's arm round Kenny's shoulder, simultaneously congratulatory and protective. Such scenes were repeated at every major fell race of the season. By the end of that summer, Kenny and Pauline were an item.

Love helped Kenny to deal with the blow of his mother's death in May 1985, from cancer, aged forty-eight. It also seemed to lift both him and Pauline to new athletic heights. Each won the British championship again that year. Kenny set more spectacular records – notably his still unbroken 62 minutes 29 seconds for Snowdon, and, in July, an unbelievable 12 minutes 1 second on the Grasmere Guides Race course – twenty seconds faster than Reeves's celebrated record. This was a special race, the Grasmere Dash, held as part of the inaugural Reebok International Mountain

Challenge, a kind of proto-world cup held around Grasmere. Kenny won every event in the tournament, as did Pauline, and the couple were duly crowned King and Queen of the Mountains. The titles almost seemed to make the relationship official.

In the September 1985 edition of *Pacemaker* – edited, by this stage, not by Pauline but by Pete Haworth – Kenny writes an account of his trip to Switzerland for the International Danisberglauf Race, in which Pauline was also competing. Typically, he's more concerned to thank the organisers ('A superb guesthouse/hotel with private bathrooms and even a "mini-bar" fridge in the rooms') than to enthuse about his own achievements, but there's an interesting aside about how, after the post-race meal, 'Pauline and I left [the others] to walk back down the mountain and followed a path that twisted through woods and fields. Wild flowers grew among these hay meadows in abundance, and this at 5,000 feet . . .'. At around the same time, rather behind the times, 'Wife runs off with fell-runner' headlines began to appear in the local papers.

Almost as an afterthought, Kenny and Pauline competed in Italy that same month, in the first proper mountain-running World Cup. Pauline ran disappointingly; she later discovered that she was pregnant. But Kenny won the short race, making him an official world champion, and came fifth in the long one.

The December 1985 edition of *Pacemaker* begins as follows: 'Congratulations to Pauline and Kenny Stuart on their marriage on Saturday 6 December.' The paragraph continues: 'Congratulations to Kenny Stuart for recording his third successive club championship and to Pauline Stuart for winning the ladies championship, also for the third time.' The sign-off: 'Peter Haworth'.

For their first winter, Kenny and Pauline looked after a borrowed house in Brocklecrag, a remote spot at the back of Skiddaw, up Bill Teasdale's way. It was the first time Kenny had lived out of sight of Blencathra. Work, in Keswick, was a 7-mile walk away, straight over the top of Skiddaw. The twice-daily journey left him with plenty of time to consider what further mountains remained for him to climb.

Enter Dave Cannon, a Kendal runner and minor athletics celebrity. A five-times winner of the Ben Nevis race with a reputation for implausibly fast descending, Cannon had switched in 1976 from the fells to the road, where he had become a leading international marathon-runner. By 1986, however, he was in the process of succumbing to the illness that would end his career: ME, the debilitating condition associated (but not necessarily synonymous) with post-viral fatigue. He was also becoming increasingly involved in coaching.

'I'd noticed Kenny,' he remembers. 'His name kept cropping up, winning the races I used to win, and beating my records. Then I saw him running in a road-race [possibly the Derwentwater 10, in which Kenny ran 10 miles in well under 50 minutes], and I think I mentioned to someone, maybe in an interview, that I could help him become a good marathon-runner.' Shortly afterwards, Kenny rang him up. The two men agreed to collaborate, and the King of the Mountains set out to conquer the roads.

'He'd left it quite late to switch,' says Cannon, 'but he had great natural talent. He also had great hardness and determination, and a lot of sense. He knew exactly what he wanted to do, and he thought about how to do it.'

Nonetheless, no one who understood running expected it to be easy. It wasn't. Even the fastest fell-racers lack pace on the road in comparison with flat-racers, even marathon-runners; and, as Cannon points out, 'you use a completely different lot of muscles on the flat'. Kenny faced a long, patient struggle to convert his powers of endurance into greater basic speed.

No one who understood running expected him to make much impact in his first attempt at the marathon distance. But he did. The 2 hours 14 minutes 3 seconds he recorded in Glasgow that September was one of the most sensational debuts in marathon history. There is a much-reproduced photograph of Kenny crossing the finishing line, arms aloft, beaming from ear to ear. This is joy of a rare and precious kind: the joy of a man who has realised that nothing is beyond his reach.

It is at moments like these that the gods like to put a spanner in the works of human affairs, and so, in their own good time, they did.

Kenny was still working at Hope Park, while once again living (with Pauline and new-born Matthew) in Threlkeld, in council accommodation. His Glasgow triumph had opened up the prospect of a share of the riches of amateurism – from four- and five-figure slices of prize money and appearance money – but that was still in the future. There were no Lottery grants available then for champions in the making. And so his relentless schedule continued: work, train, work, train, help with baby, train, sleep. He had always been troubled by allergies, and now, imperceptibly, they began to trouble him more.

In April 1987, he had breathing problems in the London Marathon – where the air is considerably less pure than on the fells – and ran a disappointing race. He blamed a virus. The same thing happened the following year, although he still managed to come fourteenth, in 2 hours 13 minutes 36 seconds. He blamed pollen: 'I've always been prone to allergies.' It didn't seem much to worry about. Later that year he came second in the Berlin Marathon and then, in January 1989, second in the Houston Marathon, in his most impressive time yet: 2 hours 11 minutes 36 seconds. Again, the place names and times may not convey the essential truth: that here was a virtual novice who was already doing what scarcely twenty specialist marathon-runners in the world could do: run three marathons a year at the super-elite sub-2-hours-15-minutes level. (There are plenty of full-time marathon-runners today who can't reach that level at all; at the time of writing, I am aware of only three British runners who can do so, none regularly.)

Consistent success meant that, for the first time in his life, Kenny's talent earned him significant sums of money: $15,000 prize money for Houston, with a further £4,000 just for appearing in that year's London Marathon (where he came fifteenth in 2 hours 12 minutes 53 seconds), and a couple of thousand more for a race in Birmingham. There was sponsorship money, too: initially a small shoe contract with Nike, then a bigger one with the company now known as Asics. The Stuarts bought their council house, and a car, and a bit of furniture.

But the allergy and virus problems kept recurring. His training diary for the early 1980s is full of comments such as 'Felt strong' or 'Good session'. By the late 1980s, as he steps up the mileage to around 100 miles a week in pursuit of that final 3 or 4 per cent improvement, there's a negative tone creeping in: 'Stale', 'Felt flat' and so on. 'Nearly every year, something happened where at some point I just couldn't race,' he admits. 'But I always managed to run through it.'

At the end of that year, he gave up his job. It was a sensible decision, but it came at the worst possible time.

His training diary for 1990 makes bleak reading: 'Fed up of training', 'No energy', 'Knackered'. The mileage drops, and then there is week after week of complete blanks. He dropped out of that spring's London Marathon – 'Not going well' – and from then on more or less stopped running. 'It went on all summer. I couldn't run through it – it just got worse, month after month.'

Was it all in the mind? He couldn't help asking himself – yet his approach to his health had always been robust in the extreme. 'I'd always be thinking, I'll get another run in before this cold really starts, or I'll do one now to shake it off. I never listened to my body. If you listened to your body that much you'd never train at all.'

Now, though, his body demanded to be heard. 'In the end I could hardly drive a car. I was tired all the time. Not sleepy [although he spent most afternoons asleep] but really, really stale. I was so blooming ill by the end I was really worried.'

And where was the end? 'I never quite decided to stop. I just didn't get better. I'd stop for six months, then start again, and then I'd get ill.' What he did do was refuse to take his retainer from Asics that year – 'I hadn't done owt, and I didn't deserve it'. And then, luckily, he found another job, in the gardens of Newton Rigg College in Penrith, which at least provided a framework for something he had never imagined: a future without running.

The medical tests went on for years, without ever really solving anything. ME was the obvious answer, except that experts could not (and still cannot) agree on precisely what that might mean. One way or another, though, it was clear that the problem was serious. 'I remember making these trips to Northwick Park [the hospital in London where the British Olympic Medical Centre is based] and hearing about people who had this who ended up spending years in wheelchairs. That really frightened me.'

Because world-class marathon-runners race so rarely, his enforced retirement was not immediately obvious; and, of course, he had already ceased to be a regular feature on the local fell-running scene. But as season followed season, his absence continued, and became more noticeable. Gradually, word of his mystery illness spread, and the story grew more extravagant with each retelling. Even today, there are many people who believe that Kenny Stuart has been confined to a wheelchair for years and never leaves the house.

In fact, he now leads what most people would consider an active life. He works a forty-hour week, most of it on his feet. He takes his two dogs for two long walks a day – in the meadows or on the low fell. He works in his garden when he has the time. And at weekends he follows the local hunt, when they are (or were) out, which usually involves several hours' fast fell-walking. He is fervently opposed to a hunting ban, and sits on the local hunt committee.

He also receives endless invitations to give prizes and make speeches at various fell-running occasions, and when he turns out to watch races there are generally queues of admirers wanting to say hello. ('The trouble is, though, it was all a long time ago, and I don't always recognise who people are.') He also accompanies his children around the junior fell-racing circuit. All three have showed great promise, although Matthew, the eldest, no longer races. Emma (born 1988) and Rosie (born 1991) have both been junior champions.

But Kenny himself doesn't, and won't, run. He tried a mini-comeback in 1991, when he entered six short fell races, winning one and coming second in another. He tried again in 1994, when he did a few weeks' light training before entering (and winning) the

Gatesgill race, which starts and finishes in Threlkeld. He even entered another short race five years after that – at the Rusland Show, on the spur of the moment, without having trained for years, wearing Emma's shorts and Matthew's shoes – and came sixth. But, each time, there was a price. 'I was so ill afterwards, I had to spend all the next day in bed: high fever, everything.'

And so he remains earthbound. The man who once defied the laws of gravity, humbled by the immutable laws of human decay. Yet his spirit is not broken. On the contrary, talk to Kenny today, and you meet a man who has more or less shrugged off the twin impositions of triumph and disaster.

'I was pretty lucky in most ways. In fact, the doctor said I was lucky to get in as much running as I did. I was certainly lucky on the injury side: never really did anything apart from the odd sprain. But that's probably why I ended up getting ill. Something's got to give, and often other people get a forced rest when they're injured.'

If he thinks about his misfortune, it's with a detached curiosity, for he has always been interested in the science of running. 'It was all linked to the immune system. I was born atopic, which means you're prone to allergies, so even as a kid I had lots of colds and was bothered a lot by pollen. But all that marathon training didn't help. It's like flogging a car on the motorway, churning out all those fast miles, and the racing is really unforgiving. And pounding on the roads, at that level, destroys red blood cells.'

Pauline sees it differently. 'Remember, you were working full-time as a gardener,' she says, as the three of us mull over old times one winter evening. 'You were running 100 miles a week, running three marathons a year . . . You think of all these marathon-runners now who can't even run 2:15, and they're full-time athletes. You weren't a full-time athlete. If you want to know what your problem was, it was called overdoing it.'

To which Kenny responds with the enigmatic grin of a man who decided long ago that he was the best judge of what he could and couldn't do, and who has never really been deflected from that belief.

'Those were hard days,' he says after a while. 'Looking back, you wonder how you could have become so fit.' Which, of course, you do. But what you also wonder is how such a frail, gentle man could have achieved such greatness in such a tough environment; and, though one hardly dares say it, whether the switch to the roads was his undoing.

'It was terrain that suited me,' he says, as if reading my thoughts. 'I don't regret moving to the roads, because I wanted to try it. But I always missed running on the fells. My one regret is that when the world championship came to Keswick in 1988, I had to stand on Latrigg and watch them. I was training for the Berlin Marathon. My one regret, really, is that I didn't say: let's leave the road for six months and go back to the fells for that.'

He takes another sip from his whisky, with a distant look in his eye. 'But what I really regret is that my career came to an end two years earlier than it should have done. Sometimes,' he adds, 'I wonder where all the time has gone.'

It is dark outside, and, as I leave, I am conscious of the overwhelming blackness of Blencathra behind the house, its hugeness undiminished by the fact that much of it is hidden in cloud. I've often looked up at that same giant shadow before a nocturnal run and felt my blood chill. But tonight I look up and see it through Kenny Stuart's eyes: as a reassuring presence, sheltering us like the protective wing of some giant mother bird.

And I think, too, of the times when, wandering on its summit in cloud and feeling the sinister silence of the abyss beyond, I have had my bearings restored or confirmed by the sight of the two pale crosses laid out in stones on the ground, 100 metres or so north of the true peak. Countless walkers and runners must have had similar experiences, yet the story of how they come to be there is seldom told.

The smaller, scrappier cross is a recent imitation, made by assorted passers-by with stones cannibalised from its larger neighbour. The original, however, was painstakingly created by one man: Harold Robinson, a Threlkeld fell-runner, in the years immediately following the Second World War. For a decade or more, Robinson climbed Blencathra every day, silently and alone, bearing prize pieces of quartzite-veined slate gathered from the scree-slopes below. The eventual result was a memorial to his close friend, a Mr Straughan, the gamekeeper at Skiddaw House, who was killed in action in 1942.

Perhaps you need to have climbed Blencathra alone to imagine the broodings that must have sustained Robinson. But once you start imagining, it is hard to stop. What sort of friendship was it? What sort of life was Robinson's? How did the world seem, from where he walked? Could he have imagined the modern mindset, to which such a patient private act of remembrance must seem futile to the point of lunacy? Or did he perhaps see it coming?

Such questions have little to do with fell-running; and, in any case, it is too late to ask them, for Robinson died in 1988. But today his great-nephew – Kenny Stuart – walks the same fellside, alone apart from his dogs, thinking equally private thoughts. Is he brooding about the way the world is going and the lost joys of his prime? Does he dream of the days when he could fly across the fells as no man has done before or since? Or is he absorbed in the texture of the landscape and the creatures that live on it?

Who knows? But it would be surprising if the man who resolved as a slow-growing teenager to throw off his limitations and become a champion did not sometimes nurture an equally audacious ambition for his later years. Or perhaps it is only me who from time to time daydreams that, one of these days, the once and future king of the fells will repudiate the limitations of his body and stride again over the slopes he once ruled.

15

Scenes from a fell-running year: June

Only the cars parked along the edge of the lane give any clue that a sporting event is in progress – that and a couple of scraps of tape on the grassy slope. There are more participants than spectators, more children than adults. In one of the cars, a teenage runner is in charge of registration. The atmosphere is closer to a school sports day than to a top-level athletic event. In fact, this is the modern face of professional fell-running.

The scene is a green hill just outside Kendal, and the occasion is the annual Helm Hill race, organised by BOFRA. Some of the most famous names of fell-running are in evidence: Kenny and Pauline Stuart, here to watch their children; Helen Sedgwick, Tommy's daughter, running for Ilkley Harriers; and Bill Smith, still competing at sixty-seven. (Smith, in addition to writing *Stud Marks on the Summits*, was a runner of considerable talent who in 1976 ran a Bob Graham-plus of sixty-three peaks. This will be his fifth race in seven weeks.) None of them attracts any particular notice: people are too wrapped up in their families to spot celebrities.

The weather is mild, and the hill is neither very steep nor very rough; which, since most of the races involve children, is just as well. But it's demanding enough to tax most of the runners to their limits. Even the Under-9s, whose race is over in less than three minutes, slump to the ground in exhaustion at the finish.

The distance increases with each age bracket, and some competitors are confused by the circuit of grassy tracks on the flat hilltop. 'Lost? How could you get lost?' says Pauline Stuart to a friend of her daughter's after the Under-12s. 'You need a homing device.'

But everyone gets back safely in the end, and the frontrunners – and their supporters – are fiercely competitive. 'Go on, one last push!' shouts an adult as the two leading Under-12s approach the finish neck and neck. Both subsequently fall flat on the grass. 'Keep trying, you'll get him next time,' says the attentive parent of the runner-up. 'Where's my drink?' he replies. 'I'm knackered.'

There are no losers' tantrums, though, and everyone seems to be enjoying themselves – even Andrew Biddle, the organiser, as he rushes around with his megaphone while finding time to congratulate his two daughters on being first girl home in the Under-9s and third girl home in the Under 14s. The Stuart girls, Rosie and Emma, are, as usual, first girls home in their respective events (Under-12s and Under 17s). Both seem relatively fresh at the finish, although Emma complains of 'tight hams'.

When it's time for the senior event, Biddle puts down his megaphone and joins in. Once all thirty-five runners have disappeared over the brow of the hill, there is scarcely an adult to be seen down at the roadside. But the first runners are back in just over twenty minutes, and although Biddle takes slightly longer – he comes thirty-first – he's clearly glad to have had a run. Bill Smith trots in three-and-a-half minutes later but avoids last place. A brief prize-giving follows in the pub on the corner. Then it's 'See you next week' and back to the cars.

In athletic terms, it's not a memorable event. But as an example of how, with a bit of collective effort and goodwill, families can still enjoy an inexpensive, friendly, well-behaved, challenging and healthy day out, it's exhilarating. This, remember, is the strand of fell-running once shunned for its violation of decent amateur values.

But there are other strands, too, several of which are in evidence this month, and some of which are thriving more than others. There's a good turnout for Allan Greenwood's Calder Valley Midsummer Madness three-day series. Ian Holmes, who lives about 10 miles away, arrives for the first event, the Wicken Hill Whizz, by bicycle, prompting Greenwood to offer him £5,000 and a new bike if he breaks the course record. Holmes sportingly lets him off after breaking it by ten seconds. A few days earlier, there is a disappointing turnout – scarcely two dozen – for the Hallam Chase near Sheffield. As Britain's oldest amateur fell race, this used to be regarded as a blue-riband event. But its unconventional handicap format – the slowest start first, with a view to everyone finishing together – may have contributed to its marginalisation.

Then there is, or should be, the Ennerdale Horseshoe. For many people, this is the defining June event: one of the most notoriously brutal tests of fell-running manhood, first run in 1968, with a steep, rocky, 23-mile course that takes in Great Bourne, Red Pike, Scarth Gap, Green Gable, Kirk Fell, Pillar, Haycock and Crag Fell – and a minimum age limit of twenty-one. Few races are so steeped in fell-running's great traditions: past winners include such all-time greats as Joss Naylor, Mike Short, Andy Styan, Hugh Symonds, Billy Bland and Kenny Stuart – whose 1985 record of 3 hours 20 minutes 57 seconds still stands. Yet this year's race, unprecedentedly, is cancelled, after entries fail to reach double figures.

The immediate explanation is competition from the British and English championships, which draw more than 500 leading fell-runners to Yorkshire for the 5.5-mile Pen-y-Ghent race on the same day. But many people feel that the calendar clash is only part of the problem. Long, brutal challenges have less appeal than they used to, especially for the young generation who see fell-running as a branch of athletics rather than a branch of mountaineering, and who need to focus on short-distance speed if they are to have any hope of competing internationally. Another long-distance classic, the Dockray Helvellyn, is cancelled a few weeks later. And while the disappointing turnout for the 22-mile Welsh 1,000 Metre Peaks (just eighteen finishers) can be partially explained by that same clash with Pen-y-Ghent, those who remember the heyday of this once-prestigious event can't help wondering what their sport is coming to.

But the elite are too busy travelling and training and accumulating points to worry too much about that. At Pen-y-Ghent, Mark Roberts of Borrowdale narrowly beats Salford's John Brown, with Nick Sharp, Ian Holmes and Rob Jebb third, fifth and ninth respectively; Holmes might have done better had it not been for what he calls 'poor route choice' towards the end. In a separate women's race, Tracey Brindley of Carnethy beats Lou Sharp by thirty seconds. Lou's disappointment is eased by the knowledge that she has at least found a new teaching job, near Penrith, for the autumn; all she needs now is somewhere to live. Elsewhere, Keswick's Angela Brand-Barker is first lady home in the Nant-y-Moch Skyline in the Welsh championship; Deon McNeilly seals his fifth Northern Ireland championship at Slieve Donard in the Mourne Mountains; and Borrowdale's Phil Davies wins the Durisdeer Hill Race in the Scottish Championship, with Keswick's Dave Spedding (ninth overall) the first over-50 veteran. There's another record for Angela Mudge in the Glas Tulaichean uphill-only race in Grampian – good practice for next month's uphill-only European mountain-running championships (for which Lou Sharp qualifies in the trials at Llanberis). The Waugh's Well fell race in Lancashire sees a welcome victory for Bashir Hussain, a leading runner of the 1990s who has recently been living abroad; scarcely less welcome is a sensational seventh place (in a field of 112) by the teenage Wajib Ali, a junior runner who has been tipped as fell-running's next big thing. And there are plenty of top contenders at Buckden Pike, West Yorkshire, where Ian Holmes is comfortable winner on a scorching day. There's a minute's silence at the start of the race to mark the death of Mike Rose the week before.

Rose was sixty-five. Although he was an FRA official, his death is a reminder that fell-running isn't all about championships; rather, it is about people, who run in the mountains for the joy of it. For many, it is also about more private challenges. There are, for example, twenty-seven people who achieve membership of the Bob Graham 24 Hour Club this year, and many more who attempt it; most do so in June. One of them, Jonathan Steele, an ex-Marine turned fitness instructor from Hull, grinds to a miserable halt after just two sections: 'I should have prepared better,' he grimaces, white-faced and staggering at Dunmail Raise. 'I was so stressed out by it all, I was knackered before I started. But I'll be back.' Another, Borrowdale's Andrew Schofield, attempts a super-fast round, following in hallowed footsteps about which we'll be hearing more shortly. His first 60 miles are blisteringly fast, but by Honister he has nothing left and is reduced to something approaching normal speed. His eventual time,

17 hours 1 minute, is nonetheless pretty sensational; only three men have ever got round faster.

One of those three, Mark Hartell, is narrowly beaten – in partnership with Mark Seddon – in the Lowe Alpine Mountain Marathon (another topic to which we'll soon be returning). John Hunt and Ifor Powell win the Elite class in this two-day test of stamina and self-reliance in the Scottish Highlands. Wendy Dodds and Nicky Lavery come fifteenth in the A class.

And then, of course, there is the Man vs Horse Marathon. Mark Croasdale is once again first human finisher – the 22 miles of Welsh hills take him 2 hours 11 minutes 16 seconds. But his tour of active service has taken too much out of his legs, and he can only get within 17 minutes of the winning horse. 'It took its toll,' he admits. There's always next year, though: the twenty-fifth running of the event, for which the sponsors, William Hill, are offering a £25,000 prize as an incentive for an unprecedented human victory. After that, Croasdale suspects he'll probably be too busy ferrying his three eldest children to rugby, football and hockey to be able to carry on competing at that level much longer. 'I've had my turn,' he says philosophically. 'It's their turn now.'

16

The Londoner

SOUTH LONDON, THE MID-1990s. The scene: a standard-issue yuppie flat near the Oval, unimaginatively furnished, worn at the edges, with a semi-abandoned air that makes you wonder if anyone currently lives in it.

Someone does: one yuppie, too busy and focused to chat to his neighbours and, to be honest, too rarely there to know who most of them are.

On weekday mornings he can be seen out at dawn: a sleepy walk to the corner, then off with a bound on his pre-breakfast run, northwards via Kennington Road to Westminster Bridge, over the river to the stately parks of SW1, around them all, then back for a final sprint – more than an hour later – across the cracked pavements of Lambeth. He seems to run quite hard. On his return his clothes are so drenched he might have been swimming in them.

Shortly afterwards, he disappears on his motorbike to work. Thirteen or fourteen hours later, he returns. He looks exhausted. As often as not, he is carrying another set of drenched sports clothes with him – the result of an hour or so in the office gym. The puddles of sweat he leaves behind him at the exercise bikes and step machines have been known to provoke complaints from other gym users.

Before long, he will collapse into bed. First, he has other tasks to perform. Over a giant bowl of muesli, he studies a volume of Alfred Wainwright's *Pictorial Guide to the Lakeland Fells*, memorising the identifying features of various peaks, including the layout of their summits and the shape of the cairns thereon, before testing himself and, if necessary, going over it all again.

Then come the pre-bed routines. Five minutes of standing on one ankle with his eyes closed – to strengthen damaged ankle ligaments. Five minutes with his bare feet in a bowl of surgical spirit – to harden the skin. Ten minutes or more of inner and outer thigh exercises, using an enormous rubber band attached to a table leg – to strengthen various muscles in the pelvis and upper thigh, with a view to protecting a chronic injury in the sacro-iliac joint. The next five minutes, spent standing in an upright but foolish-looking posture loosely based on the Alexander Technique – have a similar purpose.

Then comes a ten-minute routine on the sofa – based on a borrowed, ten-year-old self-hypnosis tape narrated by an obscure Swedish sports academic – during which our yuppie visualises his way down from the frenetic alertness of daily London life to a state of deep, secure relaxation. Clench the left fist tightly, then relax, breathing out smoothly from the stomach, letting go a little more with each breath and each preprepared mental image. This not only trains his mind to master his body, but develops the little-known skill of deliberately lowering the pulse rate. By the time he has finished, his heart is beating scarcely forty times a minute. He knows because he times it.

Next, the bathroom, where he cleans his teeth in front of a huge Ordnance Survey map – four Pathfinders chopped up and stuck together – on the wall. A large circular route is drawn on it in orange highlighter pen, and forty-two key points – all mountain peaks – are marked with bright red stickers. Every half inch or so – every time the orange line changes direction – a compass bearing is written nearby; while a typewritten sheet stuck to the top left-hand corner lists the names of the 42 peaks in question, with scheduled arrival times for each and estimated distances between them.

He brushes for three, four, five minutes – his dentist would be delighted – all the while peering at the contour lines, trying to recreate in his mind the reality they depict. Due south from Helvellyn, 500 gently downhill metres, that's about two minutes, a wide, rock-strewn path, watch out for the remains of the little cairn – on the left? – then fork left with the path, keep left until the path drifts right and then keep straight on. A hundred and fifty, 200 metres – a minute or so, gently uphill? – and that's the summit of Nethermost Pike there, just on the edge of that big drop to the east. Easy enough on a clear day but damnably confusing in mist. Distinguishing features? None. The top's just a flat, turfy field scattered with boulders. So how do you tell if you've gone too far one way or another? Think. Too far left, you go over the edge; so you must see the downhill slope coming. Too far right ... Well, you keep drifting on without finding anything. What does Wainwright say? Something about a 'small ruined circular wall 100 yards south-west'... Where's that, then? Must be those little dashes – or is it under the 'e' of 'Nethermost Pike'? Whatever. If you hit that, you've gone too far. Best to keep left, and you can hardly miss it. But what *is* it? What sort of summit cairn is there? (He screws up his eyes at this point, trying to remember.) Nethermost Pike ... Is that the big, domey one, with a pointy cairn that makes it look like a German officer's helmet from the First World War? No, that's Dollywaggon Pike. 'D' for 'Dollywaggon', 'D' for *'Deutsch'*. *Deutsch*-wagon. Volkswagen. All right, so what about Nethermost? That's the scrappy little one: just a half-hearted cube of rocks that you'd never notice if you weren't looking for it. 'N' for 'never'. Just as, if we look, the Nethermost cairn is at the near edge of the summit area (going south), whereas Dollywaggon Pike (the next one), is at the furthest, southern edge. 'Never notice' – 'Nethermost' – at the 'near' edge of the spur. 'Dollywaggon' – *'Deutsch'* – 'distant'. That's that fixed. And as for getting from one to the other: precisely south-west from the summit should take you first to that ruined circular wall and then by the best possible line to the path you left on the way from Helvellyn, after which . . . but perhaps that's enough for one night.

He rinses the remains of his toothbrush and goes to bed, where he tries to read but is usually asleep within seconds. And what seems like a few seconds after that it's morning, and he – or rather, I – am dragging myself blearily out of bed to start again.

Mike Cudahy, the first man ever to run the entire Pennine Way in under three days, was once asked to give a talk about his exploits to Horwich Athletic Club. 'What sort of thing shall I talk about?' he asked. 'Oh,' said his host, Denis Weir, 'just talk about all the amusing things that must have happened to you in the course of your eight attempts on the Pennine Way record.' Cudahy thought carefully. 'Denis,' he said, 'there weren't any amusing events.'

So it was, at the height of my Bob Graham obsession, with me. Ask me to cast my mind back to that period and the first thing that comes back is the mental focus: driving myself forward on the streets or the exercise bike with the same unvarying mantra pounding bizarrely in my brain: '(Keswick: 01:00); Skiddaw (02:22), Great Calva (03:16), Blencathra (04:26); (Threlkeld: 04:50–04:55); Clough Head (05:54), Great Dodd (06:25), Watson's Dodd (06:32), Stybarrow Dodd (06:41), Raise (06:59), Whiteside (07:06), Helvellyn Low Man (07:19), Helvellyn (07:25), Nethermost Pike (07:48), Dollywaggon Pike (07:57), Fairfield (08:35), Seat Sandal (08:59); (Dunmail Raise: 09:19–09:39); Steel Fell (10:06), Calf Crag (10:27), High Raise (11:05), Sergeant Man (11:10), Thunacar Knott (11:25), Harrison Stickle (11:33), Pike o' Stickle (11:44), Rossett Pike (12:24), Bowfell (12:59), Esk Pike (13:19), Great End (13:41), Ill Crag (13:57), Broad Crag (14:08), Scafell Pike (14:20), Scafell (14:51); (Wasdale Head: 15:17–15:47); Yewbarrow (16:17), Red Pike (17:04), Steeple (17:30), Pillar (17:55), Kirk Fell (18:56), Great Gable (19:35), Green Gable (19:51), Brandreth (20:06), Grey Knotts (20:15); (Honister Pass: 20:28–20:53); Dale Head (21:33), Hindscarth (21:58), Robinson (22:28); (Keswick: 24:00).' I can type it now, years later, without a moment's hesitation or reflection. It's the schedule worked out by Fred Rogerson, based on averages of times taken in all successful BG attempts to date. (The places in brackets are the road crossings, where it's traditional to take some rest; the schedule is a twenty-three-hour one, giving you an hour in hand for mishaps, diversions and delays.) There was nothing to be gained from knowing it off by heart – but much to be lost from attempting the BG without having the stark facts of its enormity continually in one's thoughts.

Did I ever go out at that time? Presumably; yet it's hard, looking back, to remember when. I was so focused on that single theme that nothing else seems to have made a lasting impression on my mind. Just as an addicted gambler loses the capacity to see money as anything but the wherewithal for further gambling, so the obsessive runner measures all things in terms of their effect on his running. A night out with an old friend? Yes, I suppose so, as long as it doesn't start so early that it interferes with evening training, or finish so late that I'll be too tired to run in the morning. A nice meal? Perhaps, as long as it's not too heavy. A party? Well, up to a point; but not if it's going to be smoky, or drunken, or late finishing – and just think how much extra fitness I could squeeze in if I spent the hours in question training instead.

In fact, if I reconstruct my past logically, I realise that there can't have been more than a few dozen weeks – in various discrete clusters spread over several years – during which I pursued my obsession uninterruptedly. Between my first BG attempt and my fourth, I had two children, changed jobs twice, and evolved from a rather wild thirty-two-year-old into a somewhat wiser, less selfish thirty-six-year-old family man.

I also moved out of London, to a small village in Northamptonshire. The routine described above relates to a period shortly after we moved, when I found myself working in London again and was forced to spend most of each week away from home. But it wasn't hard to transfer my obsession to Northamptonshire, with endless undulating ploughed fields and rutted tracks on which to simulate the challenges of the fells. My favourite route lasted about 15 miles and had the additional attraction, in summer, of several fields thick with vicious thistles. The practice they provided in shrugging off incidental pain was invaluable, and I imagine that in the long run the scarring toughened my skin.

What I didn't realise until later was quite how *normal* such behaviour is among long-distance fell-runners. Disregard the elite three or four each year to whom the BG comes relatively easily, and you have perhaps ten or twenty people a year whose only hope of success lies in total dedication to the challenge. Each will go through some form or other of the same derangement; as, indeed, will the greater runners on their greater challenges. The circumstantial details will vary, but the spirit of the thing is the same: unless you immerse yourself in it, utterly, you will never succeed.

I know of at least three members of the Bob Graham 24 Hour Club (four if you count Bill Smith) who have succumbed to the urge to write books about the BG; Peter Travis's, *The Round*, is a novel. Another club member, Howard Pattinson, has created a series of artworks on the theme. My favourite, called *The Night Section*, depicts the twelve peaks on the Thelkeld-to-Dunmail section in typographical form: just the twelve names, reversed out of a dark, nocturnal background, rather like place names on a surreal motorway sign, arranged in the same zigzag relationship to one another that they have in real life. I'm not sure what anyone without first-hand experience of the BG would make of it, but for me it captures perfectly the way one's visualisations echo in the mind. (Different people, I should explain, choose different times of day to start the round, and thus do different bits in darkness.)

I also know of any number of members and would-be members whose love affair with the Bob Graham is conducted from afar: from London, from the Home Counties, from the flat east coast. If anything, distance makes our involvement all the more intense. For us, the lure of the challenge lies not just in the chance to prove our physical and mental resilience but also in the whole process of refreshing our office-worn spirits by flinging ourselves deep into a mountain landscape. Yes, there are fields and hills in the South; there's even the odd fell race, such as the Box Hill race or the Isle of Wight series. But occasional hills are not the same as fells in which you can get lost, cold, frightened, overawed; to escape, you need the poetry of a mountain range.

In fact, by the time of my second BG attempt, I was escaping to the Lakes relatively infrequently. I knew the route quite well, and time spent on long motorway journeys seemed like time that could have been better spent on training (or on more inclusive family activities). But my determination to get round the bloody thing was, if anything, even greater. Gawain had made another attempt by then, and succeeded. Charlie, by contrast, had resigned himself to never getting round, arguing that it wasn't fair on his family to keep on trying. I could see the pain this decision caused him, and I feared that the failure of my first attempt would rankle indefinitely if I did not do something to erase it.

My interest was further sustained by the appearance of another challenger in our group of Southern enthusiasts: Charles, an ex-army officer who now worked with Gawain in the City. Charles was much younger and fitter than me, with considerable experience of mountains and orienteering, and was reasonably confident of succeeding first time. Nonetheless, he welcomed the advice of more experienced peak-baggers, and he and his friends gave us a new excuse for reconnoitring sessions – which, as any outsider will confirm, can be enjoyed as much for the general buzz of the expedition as for the fell-running itself.

Oddly enough, much of our time in the Lakes was spent among local people who had never heard of fell-running, and who – if they ran the bed-and-breakfast where we happened to be staying – were as likely as not to be horrified by people coming back steaming and dripping with sweat and mud, or tiptoeing out in the small hours to practise or support a night section. Then I discovered Gary and Donna McRae, who had just renovated and reopened the derelict Langstrath Hotel in Stonethwaite, Borrowdale. Not only were they keen supporters of fell-running, they actually sponsored the local Langstrath race. Donna even ran herself, for Keswick. Far from considering us eccentric, they actively encouraged us in our endeavours, finding us rooms with friends and relations when there were none left in the hotel and introducing us to local runners who could help support our attempts. On one attempt, Donna acted as pacer for a section, while Gary came to Keswick with us more than once to see off a challenger at 1 a.m. If we had ever worried that outsiders were not welcome to run on the Lakeland fells, Gary and Donna dispelled our concerns.

And so it was that, two years to the day after my first attempt, I found myself being shaken awake at midnight from a comfortable Langstrath bed and told that breakfast was ready downstairs.

Never has a reluctant office-worker dragged himself more miserably into wakefulness on a dark Monday morning. Wind and rain were rattling the windows so loudly that you would have sworn there was a stormy sea outside; my sleep, which had begun scarcely an hour earlier, was warm and still; nothing could be more horrifying than the thought of exposing my snug body to the vicious mountain elements.

But it had to be done. Charles was up already, while Jim and Mick, two middle-aged Keswick runners who had kindly agreed to pace the first section of our joint attempt, would already be on their way to the Moot Hall.

And so it was done. As usually happens, the reality was more tolerable than the apprehension had suggested – at first, anyway. The night was cold and damp, but not so bad that we really noticed it once we had got going. Clouds were hanging ominously low, but we didn't get lost. In fact, the only real surprise of that first section came when, crossing Wiley Gill on the way from Great Calva to Blencathra, Mick sunk up to his chest in a small bog, in which a sheep appeared to have drowned some weeks previously. This meant that he actually fell *through* the decomposing sheep – an experience that I would not wish on anyone. It was probably no comfort to him that our amusement kept our morale up for the best part of an hour afterwards.

From then on, it got worse. The clouds sank lower and lower, thick as mould. We struggled through the second section with only a few minor navigational errors, but by Dunmail Raise we were already slipping behind schedule. Charles, especially, was still moving well, and we did the third section with separate pacers so that I wouldn't hold him back. The clouds were less easily dealt with. We got badly lost around Rossett Pike, where Charles's brother was supposed to be joining us. Time rushed by; tension rose; morale fell. Meanwhile, the wind was getting up. By the top of Bowfell, at the south-east end of the high plateau that curves round to Scafell Pike, I was starting to think of warm baths and beds. By Scafell Pike, I was an hour-and-a-half behind schedule, with Charles perhaps ten minutes quicker. Theoretically, it could still be done: but only by putting myself through extremes of exhaustion and pain in conditions that were becoming hazardous. Would I do so? I preferred not to think about it.

At Wasdale Head, with twelve peaks to go, I was two hours down but stubbornly went through the motions of starting up Yewbarrow with Gawain. By the top, we both knew with depressing certainty that I wasn't going to do it, and we decided to turn back. It felt like being relieved of a great burden. We returned to the bottom and, half an hour later, were joined by Charles and his brother, who had only got a mile or so further before reaching a similar conclusion.

Looking back, it's hard to explain how we can have been so feeble – except to say that, in reality, it isn't like that. Going up and down mountains isn't easy. After sixteen hours or so, and more than thirty ascents and descents, it hurts. Your joints hurt. Being exhausted hurts. Being cold and wet hurts. And when you're cold and wet and exhausted and sore-jointed and faced with an unimaginably long gauntlet of sharp, slippery mountains to cross, morale and warmth leak from your body like air from a punctured tyre.

Twenty-four hours later, warm, dry and rested, we once again contemplated our maps. How tame the mountains seemed, reduced once again to curving contour lines. Did we really want to admit defeat? Or should we try again and hope for better weather?

After a modicum of soul-searching, we agreed to try again as soon as possible.

First, though, we would seek some advice.

17

King Billy

'IT'S JUST A WALK,' SAYS BILLY BLAND, stretching out two chunky legs from his small armchair. There's an amused gleam in his bushy-browed eyes that makes you wonder if he's joking. He isn't. A decade or so ago – 1988, to be precise – Billy did the Bob Graham round entirely at a walk, just to show how easy it was. It took him a little under twenty-one hours. 'It was,' he adds, 'just about the only time I ever got injured – torn knee ligaments, from all the holding back downhill.'

Twenty-one hours strikes me as unimaginably fast for such a challenge; for Billy, it was absurdly slow. Six years earlier, in June 1982, he completed the round more or less entirely at a run. It took him 13 hours 53 minutes, which stands today not just as the record for the round but as arguably the most extraordinary record in this or any other sport. Only the very finest fell-runners can do even a single section of the BG at that pace.

Nor is this his only claim to fell-running fame. He won the Mountain Trial nine times, the Borrowdale ten times, the Wasdale nine times, the Ennerdale five times, and most other major races at least once. His records for the Duddon, the Borrowdale and the Wasdale still stand more than twenty years later, as does his record for the four Lakeland 3,000-foot peaks. He had speed, stamina, a genius for rough descents and great natural mountaincraft – and he stayed at the top for the best part of a decade. Some consider him the greatest fell-runner ever; few would deny him a place among the all-time top four or five.

Charles and I are paying Billy a visit on Donna's advice, to see if he can offer us any tips. We are well aware of his reputation and achievements, and it is with some apprehension that we have walked up the hill to his Borrowdale cottage on a rock-grey Sunday morning. Bland himself is physically an unimposing figure – about 5 foot 10 inches, lightly built, with unruly ginger hair and a pair of black Ron Hill dungarees so faded that I wonder if he ever takes them off. (He does.) But there's a relaxed confidence about him that does little to dispel our awestruck sense of inferiority in his presence.

When people try to capture the essence of Kenny Stuart's running, they often compare him to a gazelle. With Billy Bland, they tend to invoke the mountain goat. I can't vouch for the precise zoological accuracy of either comparison, but in Billy's case I suspect that the imagery may have as much to do with his character as with his gait. He is celebrated not just for his athleticism but for his equally phenomenal hardiness; and for his stubborn, ungovernable independence. In the flesh, there's a suggestion of wildness about him; something – his eyebrows? his hair? – that makes you think: headbanger. It's a word that's often used about him (not least by him). 'Ah, Billy,' more than one person has told me, smiling knowingly. 'He calls a spade a spade, does Billy.'

Yet the man who invites Charles and me into his front room – and who on a later occasion spends several hours sharing his thoughts and memories with me in his kitchen – is irreproachably kind and polite. We assume that he finds us ridiculous: two southern toffs who for some reason can't even get round the BG in twenty-four hours. He himself has done it three times: in 1976, when he became the fifty-second member of the BG club; in 1982, when he set his record; and in 1988 (by which time he was semi-retired from fell-running), when he did his walk. The first time, he did it in conjunction with his brother, David, and his cousins, Anthony and Chris. There are, you should understand, a lot of Blands in Borrowdale. 'I wanted to go faster,' Billy tells us, 'but I kept having to wait for my fat cousin.' Eventually he left the others behind, only to find that the pacers had not arrived when he reached Wasdale. His eventual time of 18 hours 50 minutes was a new record, but he felt 'a bit embarrassed by it'. (David and

Anthony, 'fat' or otherwise, took 20 hours 4 minutes; Chris failed to finish, but did succeed the following year, in 22 hours 50 minutes.)

Patiently, Billy searches his mind for insights that might be of use to the likes of Charles and me, and offers those he finds: 'You mustn't be too cautious descending'; 'If you've a bad patch, just hang on and it'll pass'; 'Don't get caught up in someone else's attempt – go at your own pace'; and 'Don't take long breaks – you'll stiffen up. You can eat and drink on the move.' Above all, he urges us: 'Don't get too bothered by it. It's just a walk.' Which causes us to speculate afterwards as to what exactly he would get bothered by. 'Do you think,' asks Charles, 'that he belongs to the same species as us?'

In a sense, he doesn't. He has lived all his life in the Borrowdale valley, and has been running in the hills since he was a small child. The son of a guides racer, he was born in 1947, in Nook Farm, Rosthwaite. He went to school in the valley, and has always earned his living in and around it; for the past few decades he has lived just a mile or so south of his birthplace, in a small grey cottage near Seatoller, in the shadow of Dale Head. He ran his first professional fell race at seventeen, and continued on the guides-race circuit into his mid-twenties before being reinstated as an amateur in 1974. If ever a sport was in a man's blood, fell-running was in Billy Bland's.

Yet it would be a mistake to assume that it all came easily to him. In that first race, at the Keswick Show, he came last, despite desperate efforts to avoid that indignity. (Unfortunately, the one runner he managed to overtake promptly retired from the race.) Thereafter, he lost more than he won, despite an obvious talent for fast descents on steep, rough ground. Bill Teasdale, who raced against him a few times, reckons that 'he never won the races he should have done when he ran with us. He was a good lad, but I think it was in his mind.' Billy admits that he suffered badly from pre-race nerves, sometimes to the extent of opting out of races altogether: 'I enjoyed the training, but hated racing.' Teasdale suspects that local supporters' hunger for gambling coups may have added to the pressure. (Sometimes, though, this hunger was satisfied, as when Billy beat Teasdale at Patterdale in 1967. He had told his friends to bet on him if he was well placed at the top. He was; they did; the bookies paid out at five to one.)

Because of these difficulties, Billy drifted away from running and towards football, in which he represented Westmorland at county level. He was running only sporadically when, in 1974, a new fell race appeared on his doorstep. The Borrowdale race was the brainchild of Billy's cousin, Chris Bland, and of the jovial new proprietor of the local Scafell hotel, Miles Jessop, who sponsored it. Chris had only recently taken up running, after becoming alarmed at his weight and lack of fitness in his mid-thirties. But he knew and loved the mountains, and he knew exactly what it took to devise a great race. The Borrowdale, a 17-mile epic that takes in Bessyboot, Scafell Pike, Great Gable and Dale Head, was immediately recognised as a classic course – and interest in the valley was considerable, not least among the twenty-two different members of the Bland clan then living there. (For our purposes, the key Blands to remember are: Stuart and David, respectively Billy's older and younger brother; Anthony and Chris, his cousins; his nephews, Jonathan and Gavin, who are sons of, respectively, Stuart and David; and Ann, Billy's wife. All these are, or were, distinguished fell-runners; as were Pete, Anne and Denis Bland, who live in Kendal and are not related to the Borrowdale clan.) But one person in the valley who wasn't allowed to enter the race was Billy – because he was a professional and it was amateur. So he 'ran along' instead, decided that he quite liked it, applied for reinstatement (with the encouragement of, to confuse you further, Pete Bland) – and by 1975 was running as an amateur.

At first he trained modestly – perhaps 40 or 50 miles a week – and, though he entered most of the amateur events in the area, rarely achieved a placing in single figures. He enjoyed it, especially the 'relaxed, friendly' atmosphere at the starts; but you wouldn't have marked him out as special. He couldn't even finish the 1975 Borrowdale race. Some people thought that the Bland to watch was David.

But Billy is not a man who takes kindly to being eclipsed by anyone, let alone a member of his own family, and least of all his younger brother. He began to train 'properly'. Gradually, but relentlessly, he increased his mileage, until he was running more than 70 and, ultimately, up to 100 miles a week.

This was where the talk of headbanging and goats began. No one ran such distances on the fells in those days; nor, for that matter, has anyone since. A handful of ultra-obsessive Olympians (David Bedford, Ron Hill) were doing 100 miles a week on road or track in the mid-1970s; but Billy's miles were all carved out on the high fells, where, as a rough rule of thumb (based on race times), each mile takes as much out of you as 2 miles on flat road.

And Billy didn't just run: he ran with a kind of madness, rarely setting himself any specific target beyond running until he was ready to drop. Anyone with a smattering of sports science knows that just banging out miles without rhyme or reason is a recipe only for injury and exhaustion. Real gains in performance come from quality, not quantity; long slow distance sessions need to be interspersed with speed work, interval training, recovery runs.

Billy scorned such wisdom. He just hurried back from work – at the Honister slate quarry up the road – put on his running things and headed up the hillside. 'If my wife said, "Where are you going tonight?" I couldn't say, because I didn't know myself. Or if I did know, nine times out of ten I'd change my mind. I just did what I felt like. Sometimes it would be 8 miles, sometimes 17. There was no real structure. I just made it up as I went along.'

Stuart and David occasionally tried accompanying him. It didn't work. Billy would just burn them off. That didn't prevent them from giving him a run for his money in races, for familial rivalry is a Bland trait. 'It gives me a boost in a race,' David once admitted, 'to know either my brothers or cousins are going badly a mile behind.' But no other Bland could bring himself to make the huge investment in training that Billy did; and, with each passing year, that investment paid greater dividends.

In 1976 – the year of his first BG – Billy won the Borrowdale, but otherwise was coming third or fourth in races rather than winning them. Likewise in 1977. But each year he was getting better – 'and the better I got, the more I could train'. In addition to making him fitter, this honed to perfection his already exceptional gift for running on rough and steep ground. Kenny Stuart may have been more obviously light-footed (Billy weighed 10 stone 7 pounds, compared with Kenny's 8 stone); but Billy was faster on the really difficult descents.

By 1978, Billy had overtaken most of his rivals, winning both the Ben Nevis and the Mountain Trial, among much else, and coming third in the British Fellrunning Championship. His Ben Nevis time – 1 hour 26 minutes 56 seconds – was within a second of the then record; he would, he said, have gone faster if he'd known. By 1980, when he started using a high-carbohydrate diet devised by Ron Hill (a fellow member of Keswick AC), he was almost unbeatable. Ten wins and six seconds made him undisputed British fell-running champion. He never totally imposed himself on the very shortest races (although he was second at Burnsall that year), but in the longer events – the Ennerdale, the Wasdale, the Borrowdale, the Mountain Trial – there was no one to touch him.

Nor was there for most of the next decade. Kenny Stuart caused him difficulties in his glory years, but even then Billy generally came off best in the Borrowdale and the Mountain Trial. Billy's big gripe was that Kenny (and others) tended to tuck in behind him, letting him find the way before sprinting off at the finish. Billy, who knew the Lake District mountains better than anyone, sometimes retaliated by deliberately leading his followers on to harder-than-necessary routes, knowing that they would suffer more than he did on the roughest ground. On one occasion – the 1986 Ennerdale – he waited at the start until five minutes after everyone else had begun, so that no one could follow him. He then ran through the field, beating everyone except Hugh Symonds (no mean performer himself) to come a narrow second.

It was his 1982 Bob Graham record that really established Billy as an all-time great, although there was little fanfare about it at the time. Only the absolute cream of the fell-running community were quick enough to act as his pacers: Kenny Stuart, Joss Naylor, Jon Broxap, Pete Barron, Tony Cresswell. Yet Billy seemed scarcely uncomfortable for most of the 66 miles, which passed almost too quickly to merit the adjective 'epic'; only twenty-one minutes of his time, on a still, misty day, was spent resting. The current record for a relay Bob Graham – in which a different runner runs each of the five legs – is 13 hours 21 minutes, held by Cumberland Fellrunners. There is, of course, no need for any resting time in a relay – which makes Billy's 13 hours 53 minutes seem all the more astounding. Billy's times for the first three legs were faster than those in the relay record.

In fact, it had been Stuart Bland's idea to try a flat-out round; when Billy heard about it, he decided to get his own attempt in first. Stuart ran a scarcely less creditable round, 14 hours 56 minutes, a few weeks after Billy's. As one of his pacers, Neil Shuttleworth, succinctly puts it: 'That sunny day Stuart went round in the hours of daylight and had many to spare.' Only in years to come did the enormity of both these achievements really sink in, as champion after champion tried and failed to get anywhere close to them. Mark Hartell finally knocked two minutes off Stuart's time in 1999, but no one else has even approached Billy's. It's possible that they never will.

But the legend of Billy derives not so much from his results and times as from the single-mindedness in which they were grounded. 'There was no bugger trained harder than Billy,' says Joss Naylor, a fell-running demi-god in his own right, whom we shall meet in a later chapter. 'He put the miles in, and he put them in hard. He was so self-centred, so self-destructive – he put himself through a hell of a regime. But I'll tell you what: he had a lot of bloody guts and determination in his training. He really got stuck in.'

Many people tried to urge him to adopt a more scientific approach to training. Billy wasn't interested. Coaching? 'If I had a coach telling me where to go, I wouldn't want to do it – I just won't do as I'm told. That's how I am.' Track sessions? 'I just cannot get it into me head to do two laps of anything.' Repetitions? 'I tried reps the very odd time, but I didn't like it.' Rest and recovery? 'I haven't heard such bloody rubbish in all my life. There was one five-week period when I set the Bob Graham record, the

Ennerdale record, the Wasdale record – and the Ennerdale and the Wasdale is two of the hardest races there is. I was never in better form in my life. Another time I won the Ben Nevis, the Mountain Trial and the Langdale on consecutive weekends.

'It really does annoy me,' he says, when I mention the fashionable term 'over-racing'. 'Honestly, it just makes the hairs on my neck stand on end – the FRA and their so-called bloody coaches. If you're interested in being picked for the England team these days, you haven't to run in long races at all.'

He used to argue about training with Kenny Stuart, too. Kenny's approach to running was pretty much state-of-the-science in the 1980s; but Billy felt that he didn't put in enough miles. 'Kenny was class, absolute class,' says Billy today. 'I freely admit he was a lot better runner than me. But he just couldn't apply himself. He used to say: "My body won't stand it." But I reckon it was up here.' He points to his head. (Kenny, asked about this, laughs. 'Billy,' he says, 'was a beast when it came to training. But there's no way I could have coped with what he was doing – two or three hours on the high fells every night.')

'They think I'm just a headbanger,' says Billy, whose attempt some years ago to offer his services as a coach to the FRA ended in acrimony. 'But I'll let my record speak for that.' He certainly seems to have done something right.

His success did little to soften his native stubbornness, or to calm a quick temper. ('He can,' says one admirer, 'be a miserable old git.') Towards the end of his career (there weren't really any international events to speak of before the mid-1980s), he ran a few races for England, only to fall out with the selectors. 'I'd been out with summat, sick, just for a week or two, and they thought I wasn't fit. But the week before the selection I won a race, which should have told them I was fit, and then I went to the Welsh 1,000 Metre Peaks and won that, and that morning I got a letter saying I'd been picked as a reserve for whatever it was. Well, I told them, you can stuff that up your arse. It was an insult, that's how I saw it, and I maintain it was an insult. The lads who got in the team I beat every week. So I wasn't having that, and so I put a few backs up.

And then that set us up for other arguments . . .' That was one reason why he never made much impact internationally. The other was that he was contemptuous of the Continentals' 'soft' approach to fell-running, which tends to involve races on marked tracks and to exclude rough descents altogether. Asked once why he didn't take part in more international hill races, Billy replied: 'Because I'm a fell-runner, not a bloody road-runner.'

Meanwhile, there was plenty else to quarrel about, and people to quarrel with, not least in his own family. Chris Knox, the Keswick runner, remembers sharing a car with Billy and Stuart on the way back from a race in the 1980s. 'We were driving back, and Stuart had done badly, in fact he'd dropped out, and you should have heard the effing and blinding in the back of the car. I thought I'd done badly, but Billy said, "At least he finished. You just gave up." Stuart said: "But I was feeling terrible." But Billy just kept on at him. I thought there was going to be a fight. Eventually, Billy told Stuart: "Right, now you can get out and buy everyone ice-creams." ' Tony Cresswell (owner of one of only four dogs to have completed the BG) witnessed a similar flare-up during Stuart's 1982 BG record attempt. Stuart went through a bad patch going up Yewbarrow, but Billy was by his side, 'giving, shall we say, words of encouragement,' Cresswell reported in *The Fellrunner*. 'I had feared it might all end up in a punch-up.' It didn't; and nor, as far as I am aware, did any other such incidents, which seem to have been common but which – being fuelled by love rather than hate – seem to have caused no lasting rifts: Billy's anger passes as quickly as it comes, and his nearest and dearest make allowances for it.

In 1991, however, he performed one of his more controversial acts of independence when he led a breakaway from Keswick Athletic Club, to which he had belonged since 1974. 'A lot of people wouldn't agree with me,' he says today, evidently trying to be conciliatory, 'but I thought . . . well, there was a lot of good runners, but they weren't all turning out to run, and it wasn't really working as a team. You know how when you have a club of a hundred, everybody don't always like everybody else . . . And I thought it could have been better than that, and broke away from it.'

Bob Graham (*centre*) pauses at Dunmail Raise with two pacers, Phil Davidson (*left*) and Martyn Rylands, during his epoch-making 1932 round. (G. Abraham)

Fred Rogerson (*right*) planning a record attempt with (*from left*) Ken and Alan Heaton in 1961. (Courtesy of Fred Rogerson)

Members of the Youth Hostels Association line up outside the Old Dungeon Ghyll hotel in Great Langdale for the start of the first Lake District Mountain Trial in 1952. (Maurice Dean)

George Brass, broken shoe in hand, limps into Glenridding to be the only finisher in the 1962 Mountain Trial.

Happy runners leaving Rosthwaite at the start of the 17-mile Borrowdale race. (Pete Hartley)

Marginally less happy runners struggling up the long, rocky main ascent in the Ben Nevis race. (Pete Hartley)

The view from the top in the Burnsall race, with the village (and finish) visible far below. This is the descent that took Ernest Dalzell 2 minutes 42 seconds in 1910. (Pete Hartley)

Ernest Dalzell (*centre*) with Lord Lonsdale after one of his seven victories in the Grasmere Guides Race between 1905 and 1913; his trainer, Jack Cowperthwaite, is on the left. (Courtesy of Lord Lonsdale)

Bill Teasdale (*centre*) is congratulated by the second- and third-placed runners after winning the Grasmere Guides Race by more than 150 yards in 1954 – the fourth of his eleven victories in the event. (*Westmorland Gazette*)

Eddie Campbell, aged fifty-eight, towards
the end of the fortieth of his forty-four
Ben Nevis races (in 1991); he is thought
to have run up and down the mountain
800 times in his life. (Pete Hartley)

'It was like being in a dream – I had no pain.'
Pete Bland finally wins Ambleside in 1968.
(Courtesy of Pete Bland)

Mark Hartell, holder of the Lake District twenty-four-hour record, runs the Everest Marathon during his 2002 attempt to complete the world's 'highest, hardest, hottest and coldest' races in a single year. (Courtesy of Mark Hartell)

Ian Holmes leaving the summit of Corra Bheinn, the final peak, on his way to victory in the Bens of Jura, 1993. (Pete Hartley)

Helene Diamantides (*right*) with Angela Mudge at a checkpoint in the 1999 Karrimor International Mountain Marathon, on the Cowal Peninsula, Argyll. (Pete Hartley)

The author on his way down from the summit in the 2003 Ben Nevis race. (Darian Bridge/Borrowdale Fellrunners)

Twenty-eight peaks down, thirty-two to go: Joss Naylor (*right* with dog, Fly) passing through Buttermere during his 1996 '60 at 60' round. (Courtesy of Monica Shone)

Fred Reeves (*left*) and Tommy Sedgwick (*right*) after Reeves's 1978 Grasmere victory and record. (*Westmorland Gazette*)

Billy Bland in the 1990 Borrowdale race; after coming down Scafell Pike by the Corridor Route (visible in the background), he is beginning the ascent of Great Gable. (Pete Hartley)

Kenny Stuart on the steepest section of the Blisco Dash, on his way to yet another victory in 1985. (Pete Hartley)

He was, by now, working as a self-employed stonemason, and running rather less than he had done in the 1980s. But even in semi-retired mode he trained more than most – working, for example, on Miles Jessop's house in Grasmere, and getting there and back by running for an hour and ten minutes (each way) across the fells. (If you're not impressed, look at the terrain on a map.) And he still believed passionately in the runner's duty to make the most of whatever talent he had. Neither the club, he felt, nor some of its most gifted members (such as his nephew, Gavin) were developing to their full potential.

'Within two or three days of leaving it, I thought, why not start one up here? So I had a word with a few of the lads, and my two nephews who were starting to run, Jonathan and Gavin, and a few more lads, and we kicked off with seven or eight members. We've never been above the mid-thirties, yet we've won the British championship I don't know how many times . . .'

There are still those in Keswick who see this as one of the great betrayals of modern sporting history, and who (as one member puts it) 'go a funny colour when you mention Billy Bland or Borrowdale Fellrunners'. More than a year after the split, *Pacemaker* was still pointing out how sad it was 'that in such a small area we have two clubs competing independently with moderate team success when combined we could be challenging for top honours'. It was certainly true that, after the best part of a decade as undisputed king of fell-running clubs, Keswick rejoined the also-rans after the split – whereas Borrowdale went on to win repeated British championships. But, in so far as Billy's analysis was accurate, the lackadaisical types who remained probably weren't too worried about that.

For the most part, the wounds have healed. Borrowdale remains a smaller, more local and perhaps more driven club – with a higher concentration of elite runners, and a higher proportion of born-and-bred Cumbrians. Keswick members are perhaps more likely to be middle-class outsiders and converted fun-runners, although their women's team have been British champions two years running. But since there's nothing to stop anyone joining whichever club they prefer, there's really not much left to fall out about.

Meanwhile, there are plenty of other erstwhile clubmates of Billy who will point out that, however headstrong his spirit, it is also generous. In the 1980s, for example, when he was winning the Borrowdale race more or less every year, he regularly forewent his prize – a weekend for two at the Scafell Hotel – and instead persuaded Miles Jessop to lay on a buffet for all his fellow Keswick club members, to be enjoyed at the end of a special event, Billy's Race, in March. It would be odd if many of them bore a grudge against him.

In fact, although everyone agrees that Billy has put plenty of backs up in his time, and isn't a great one for admitting that he's wrong ('and if he doesn't like any bugger,' one runner added, 'he'll tell them'), I've never actually met anyone who doesn't speak warmly of him. 'He's an idol round here,' says Miles Jessop. 'He's charming, he's generous, and no one could do more to encourage other fell-runners – his attitude is, if you put your mind to it, you can do it.' That attitude springs as much from modesty as from positive thinking. He seems genuinely to believe that there is nothing about his achievements on the fells that marks him out as special.

'I was never any good as a runner,' he told me – and has told many others before and since. 'Never what you'd call a champion. I had a talent to run rough ground and downhill, but that was it really. All the rest I had to work for. But I do believe that nobody ever trained harder than me. And I can honestly say that I became as good as I could be. There was a lot I beat that had more ability than me: they just didn't work hard enough at it.

'I don't even think I was really that strong mentally – not in races. I was beat quite easy. Well, I wouldn't give in until I was satisfied, but I wasn't a real fighter. I've seen people being sick, or lying on the ground after a race. Well, that didn't happen with me. The mental strength was getting yourself prepared properly. As someone said, it's not the will to win, it's the will to prepare to win.'

What he also had – to such an extent that perhaps he hardly

noticed it – was an affinity with the mountains. He was comfortable on them; at home on them. And, as a result, he could safely push himself to his uttermost physical limits on them. 'Anyone who says he's never been lost is a liar,' he says. 'But I've never been lost in training. I had a good memory, and I could read ground, especially in the Lake District. For long races I would write bearings on the back of my hand, but if I ever got the map out, it meant I was lost. Generally I'd find my way off memory.' For a nine-times winner of the Mountain Trial – one of the most demanding orienteering events anywhere – this is quite an admission.

'I've never really been injured, either,' he adds. 'I've been lucky really. I've run the equivalent of twice round the world on these fells out there, and I've done it on my own, and I've never needed to be rescued or anywhere near it. People used to say, when I was young, "Anyone who runs downhill like that is reckless – he's bloody mad." Well, I was always in control.'

Yet he was also – in answer to Charles's question – human, and, as such, subject to exactly the same trials and disasters as more ordinary fell-runners.

When I mention one of my less pleasant fell-running moments, in which my spent legs ceased to obey me many miles from home, he acknowledges this as a shared experience: 'Aye, you find something out about yourself, don't you, when you're nearly out of petrol. And that happens to the best.' He then recounts a painful Mountain Trial victory, where 'at the end I was sat on the skyline eating blaeberries, staggering about like a drunk in the bracken, run out of petrol. I'd had a twenty-minute lead two checkpoints earlier, and I nearly blew it. But,' he adds, 'I won it.'

The winning seems almost incidental, as it does in this account of one of his more glorious victories, in the Welsh 1,000 Metre Peaks in 1985. 'It was absolutely pouring down. Paths were just like streams. And it was in mist, and windy. I liked it wet, but windy I didn't like. It was a championship race, and it finished on the top of Snowdon. Kenny was there, and Bob Whitfield. We were trying to get over this ridge and it were reet misty, and Kenny was sitting on us. And I turned to Bob and said: "Right, let's get shot of Kenny." So we bombed down this stream and lost Kenny, and dropped out of the mist. Then we crossed to the top of Pen-y-Pass and set off up the PYG track, as they call it. And I started to die, but I had this Mars bar, and I knew that my only chance was to get this Mars bar inside me. So I let Bob go, had a drink of water from a stream, and ate the Mars bar, walking along, and gradually the Mars bar started to get through . . . And I just caught Bob just before the finger stone, on the zigzags. We were neither of us doing anything, but my Mars bar was starting to get through and gave me that little bit of energy he didn't have. So I just won. But God it was cold on the top. And then, after, we went down on the tourist railway. Our clothes had been sent up to the top and they asked me what colour my bag was, and I couldn't tell them. Because you do, don't you? You forget people's names if you're in that state. Anyway, eventually they found it. And then going down they were giving us cups of tea, but I was like that –' he waves his arms wildly '– and there was only about that much left in my plastic cup. My bloody ribcage was just shaking uncontrollably. It was just hypothermia, I suppose. God that was a bad day. If we'd had to go on a bit further I might have been in trouble.'

Was that his hardest race? He thinks for a moment. 'No. The hardest races, I always think, are when you come second. When you win, you've always got that little bit in hand, but, if you're second, even trying your hardest hasn't been able to get you to the front.' Which, for someone who tries as hard as Billy, must be quite demoralising.

Does it ever bother him, I wonder, that all that effort – all those thousands of hours of merciless self-punishment – has brought him so little material reward? This is, after all, an age in which Britain counts its sporting millionaires by the score. 'No,' he says firmly. 'Once you get big rewards, you get nastiness. This is a wonderful sport, with good sport in it. If someone fell in a race, you'd check they were all right, though you wouldn't stop unless you absolutely had to – just as, if I fell, I wouldn't want someone to lose their race because of me. But once there's money, there's trouble.'

'Anyway,' he continues, returning to the theme of millionaires, 'if I'd ever become that sort of figure – and I don't think I ever had the talent for that – then you become the property of agents and the like. But I couldn't have performed for anybody but myself. I would have been: "On your bike." No one's the boss of me.'

I believe him; and, on the whole, I envy him. His house is small and sparsely furnished. He works hard every day – and will presumably have to go on doing so until he drops. Yet few people in twenty-first-century Britain can lead lives so centred, with so many of their family and their friends and their passions so close to them. His skills as a stonemason and builder are much in demand – largely from local clients. And, although his years of sporting glory are behind him, he is at least still in his kingdom – among people who appreciate his experiences, and with whom he can share them.

He gets together regularly with other members of the Borrowdale club – 'It's nearly like a family' – and tries to persuade the more talented members to train harder. (Gavin Bland, he says, is 'far more talented than I was – but he's the laziest bugger you'll ever come across'.) He has a devoted wife, Ann, who supported him unquestioningly through his years of mad dedication and who proudly reminds him of past triumphs when she comes in to join our reminiscing session.

For Billy, these are things that matter: the respect of your family and neighbours. 'If you're nowt at home,' he has often said, 'you're nowt anywhere.' Which was why, when he was running, he 'would rather win the Borrowdale than any other race in the world'. He'll never win it again, of course – although at fifty-five and with virtually no training he wouldn't expect to come last either. But he's secure in the certainty that 'I know that what I did was as good as I was. If someone breaks one of my records, I'm the first to shake his hand, because he's obviously better than me. I know I became as good as I possibly could be with the talent I had. And you can't ask any more of yourself than that.'

Yet for all his equanimity, he is not entirely at peace. 'Borrowdale has changed for the worst in my lifetime,' he says. 'Too many people have been forced away by all these second homes. A lot of outsiders have come who can produce lots of money. Good luck to them, they're not breaking any rules – but there's too much greed. Even the farming community fall out over land now.

'There are so many off-comers. Our new next-door neighbours are nice people. But there are two sorts of human being in this country, and they have different outlooks on life. The way they think is completely different to how we think.'

You wouldn't guess this if you watched what looks like the whole of Rosthwaite turning out to support and help with the Borrowdale race, of which Ann is now the chief organiser; or Billy directing the traffic and the crowds before and after the event, beaming among friends. But Billy insists that 'the community spirit's gone' and that 'a lot less people volunteer to help these days.'

Ann confirms this, as does Miles Jessop, now approaching his thirtieth year of sponsoring the race: 'We have a lot of difficulty getting people to help. People like to enjoy it all, but they don't like to get involved in running it. The community here is not as strong as it used to be.'

It's easy to blame the outsiders and weekenders; yet without the money that they and their like bring in, it would be hard for the valley to sustain itself at all, especially after the calamity of foot-and-mouth in 2000–01. The truth is, the whole thrust of twenty-first-century progress and economy works against that kind of close-knit rural community.

As far as Billy is concerned, that may or may not be true. All he knows is what he sees. 'I just wish,' he says sadly, 'that things could go back to how they were. I wish Londoners could stop in London. I wish people who take a house out of this valley would only realise what they're doing.

'Those of us who've always lived here, we're like the Maoris or the Red Indians – gradually fading away. I'm not bitter about it. It's just a pity.'

18

Fell science

A FAT LOT OF GOOD BILLY BLAND'S ADVICE DID ME. A month or so later, I set out again from the same place, at the same time, with the same objective in mind. This time, the weather was perfect. Too perfect.

We set out up Skiddaw on a balmy summer night that felt like a scene from a dream. Bright moonlight made head-torches unnecessary, touching every clump of turf with silver. The stars shone so crisply that navigation was effortless, even across the sea of boggy heather between Skiddaw and Great Calva. And, every now and then, like a golden firework, a shooting star would float across the sky. I cannot describe our awe, the sense of privilege we felt at being in such a place at such a time. Naturally, we were not so superstitious as to read an omen into the spectacle; nonetheless, it did wonders for our morale.

Or, rather, my morale. Charles had returned for a fresh attempt a few weeks earlier, while I was otherwise engaged, and had sailed round comfortably in less than twenty-three hours. Now he was pacing me for the first two sections of my next attempt. It was clear that he had been converted to the Bland belief that there really wasn't a great deal to it.

For the first few hours, I was open to persuasion. There's nothing like an enchanted night to raise your spirits; nothing like effortless route-finding to keep them raised; and nothing like sustained high spirits to banish pain and weariness from the legs. As we trotted down from Blencathra, the first warmth of dawn was spreading across the valley below; a light grey mist of evaporating dew cocooned the sleeping cottages of Threlkeld and, beyond it, the ancient river meadow. Normally, after a few hours of running in the dark, one yearns for morning. This time, I wished the sun would hold back, so that the magical night could continue a little longer.

Yet the magic continued. After a brisk crossing of the damp valley and a surprisingly cold ascent of Clough Head, we found ourselves bounding through the most breathtaking mountain landscape I had ever seen. Ahead of us, the green undulating ridge wound its way through the Dodds towards Helvellyn, just as it had always done. Yet somehow it seemed to have been recreated: brighter, bigger, bolder. To our left, the sun burst out below in a flaming dawn; to our right, the entire Lake District shone in the fresh light, vast and spectacular as any Himalayas, every curve sharply defined, every rock so distinct you could imagine the feel of it – and all untouched by any trace of modern civilisation or industry. Somewhere far beyond, something glittered that must have been the sea. Somewhere behind us, birds sang.

Any doubts I had ever felt about the wisdom of putting myself through this ordeal were resolved in these moments. If you have never seen such spectacles – and not just seen them, but been *in* them, saturated by the shapes and the colours and the curves as if you were in a fresh oil painting – it's arguable that you haven't lived.

But enjoying a BG attempt is one thing; completing one is another. As the day progressed, the brilliance of the day became oppressive. Warmth gave way to heat, dawn to noon, dazzling views to unremitting glare. Route-finding was easy; moving quickly was not. First one then another pacer dropped out, complaining of headaches and dehydration. Others struggled to keep up. This wasn't a problem in itself: I had plenty of other pacers still going strong. But it didn't bode well.

Sure enough, after fifteen or sixteen hours, I began to wilt. Though I'd been drinking religiously – both water and isotonic drinks – my muscles seemed suddenly to tighten and shrink. Whereas previously I'd been pressing forward on a kind of autopilot, scarcely conscious of the effort involved, now every step sapped me to the depths of my being. My shoes seemed heavier than rock; my legs limp as rags.

I tried to gorge myself on banana-honey-and-Lucozade mix when I rested at Wasdale Head, but it was too late. My legs had gone – my whole body had gone. Climbing up from Wasdale Head to Yewbarrow, at the start of the fourth section, I almost fell asleep on my feet. On and on, up and up, heat blasting from the bracken as if from an open oven, the summit further away than ever . . .

I won't bore you with the details, most of which I have long since mentally shredded. I know that at some point I insisted on sitting down for a minute, and that that was the beginning of the end. An hour later I had to sit down again, then again half an hour after that. I hobbled most of the way from Pillar to Black Sail Pass – a long, easy descent that one can usually enjoy running flat out. For the ascent to Kirk Fell – not a particularly demanding climb – I was not so much walking as crawling.

I don't remember consciously deciding to give up, but at some point – somewhere between Kirk Fell and Great Gable – the attempt ground to a halt. We had realised that I was once again more than two hours behind schedule, and that with each passing peak, far from catching up, I was losing another five or ten minutes. My chances of finishing within twenty-four hours were zero. Someone finally summoned up the brutality to point this out. I accepted that there was no purpose in carrying on.

Except, that is, for the rather important purpose of getting off the mountain.

This proved spectacularly difficult. As my hopes evaporated, so did the last drops of life in my muscles. The pig-headed optimism that had been keeping me going vanished in an instant, to be replaced by limp, miserable hopelessness. I could barely put one foot in front of another, barely stand. The sense of failure was crushing.

Behind me and to my left, a sunset of miraculous brilliance flooded the valley. Even the dawn faded by comparison. The golden sky had an unfathomable depth to it, with hints of clouds of glory just below the horizon; the Buttermere mountains seemed to recede to infinity, every edge rock-sharp, every shadow soaked in mystery. No one could have seen it without thoughts of heaven rising unbidden in their minds. Yet there was no suggestion of all being right with the world. On the contrary, shame and despair had almost robbed me of the will to live.

BG-runners usually take just over one hour to get from the top of Great Gable to Honister Pass, via Green Gable, Brandreth and Grey Knotts. It took me nearly three, without any detours to no longer relevant summits. By the end, a black night had descended, and I was scarcely conscious. Even now, I feel humbled by the patience with which my pacers helped me along, eventually even providing shoulders to lean on when my legs stopped functioning altogether. And, even now, I am astonished by the totality of my collapse: the instantaneousness with which, at the moment I abandoned hope, every last drop of my strength deserted me.

Afterwards, I resolved, to general approval, that I would never make another attempt. If I couldn't do it in fine weather and I couldn't do it in foul, there wasn't much point in pretending that I could ever do it. No one could dispute that my three attempts had directly and indirectly brought us innumerable hours of pleasure, but to continue without hope would be silly. Now was the time for me, like Charlie, to accept my limitations like a man.

It ought to have been a heart-breaking moment. Actually, it was a relief. It wasn't that I was fed up with the pain – as usual, the memory of that soon faded. It was just that my obsession had suddenly begun to seem grotesque. What was it, after all, but an arbitrary attempt to run around in an enormous circle? Think of all that time and energy, expended to no avail – wasn't there something more constructive that I could have done with it? I resolved to lead a more rounded life in future.

Nonetheless, over the next couple of years, once the initial clouds of shame and depression had cleared, I found that my thoughts continued to dwell on the question of precisely why I had failed. I enjoy watching and reading about running as well as doing it, while from time to time I have written about sports science in a professional capacity. Questions about the mechanics of athletic achievement intrigue me. And I felt that my failures would be easier to accept if I could understand where I had gone wrong.

And so, in a spirit of curiosity rather than self-improvement, I applied myself to finding out more about the sport, and specifically about why this relatively straightforward challenge – of putting one foot in front of the other for twenty-four hours while crossing a few hills – was beyond me. My discoveries were less enlightening than I might have hoped.

In basic physiological terms, I had been suffering from no obvious handicap. True, I was large for a fell-runner, but I wouldn't have been the biggest person ever to have completed the BG, had I done so. I was also, I had assumed, old – I think I was thirty-four at the time of my third failure. Yet my subsequent research showed that, for ultra-distance running, your mid-to-late thirties are your peak. The average age for people completing the BG is thirty-six.

Perhaps I simply lacked natural athleticism; I'm certainly not over-endowed with speed or co-ordination, and have never shown much aptitude for sports that require too many attributes beyond general toughness and resilience. Yet look at Mark Hartell: he was hopeless at school sport ('When they couldn't kick the ball, they'd kick me'), came to the mountains as a hiker rather than a runner, and was struggling with a dodgy knee even as a teenager. When he first did the BG, he was a smoker, and he gave up only six years before extending the Lake District twenty-four-hour record to seventy-seven peaks. General toughness and resilience, rather than athletic perfection, would seem to be precisely the kind of attributes required.

A neutral observer, examining my body, might have concluded that I was simply crocked. Consider: ten toes, of which two (the second smallest on each foot) are permanently bent inwards and two (the big toes) have lost their toenails so many times that the current nails are both misshapen and thicker than some of my teeth; two arches in my feet, one now perceptibly lower than the other; two ankles, both several inches thicker than they used to be, with most of the ligaments so stretched and frayed that I have forgotten what it is like to run without fear of spraining; two knees, one of which functions normally while the other is prone to slipping out of line, resulting in pain, stiffness, muscular problems, tightening of the Achilles tendon and occasional build-ups of scar tissue that on one occasion had to be dispersed by (it's hard to write this without wincing) grinding it between the kneecap and the femur; two hips and a pelvis, which between them have, over the years, become so crooked that the sacro-iliac joint and lower left facet joint are more or less permanently inflamed; assorted scars, too numerous to list; and that's just below the waist . . .

There's more, but you get the picture. (If space permitted, I would tell you more about those toenails, and how they can swell and blacken after a long day in imperfectly fitting fell shoes, and how you can save them from dying and falling off if you lance them soon enough with a red-hot paper clip, and how this can result in spectacular fountains of pus. Sadly, it doesn't.) And yet somehow I knew that general wear and tear wasn't the problem. Lots of runners carry chronic injuries: a study by Wendy Dodds in 1979 found that fifty-two out of 165 competitors in the Karrimor International Mountain Marathon (the KIMM) suffered from recurrent ankle sprains. But we *know* when these injuries are holding us back. In my BG attempts, mine didn't (apart from the ankle the first time). And while my accumulated injuries do prevent me from banging out vast mileages on the roads, that's no bad thing for a fell-runner. In any case, go to any big fell race – or, better still, a road race – and you'll find countless cases worse than mine.

So what *was* the problem? As the memories of my attempts receded, my investigations took me far and wide. I began to learn of the various studies that have been made of top fell-runners over the years – measuring their VO^2 capacity, heart rate, recovery rates and so forth, as well as their diets and training regimes. I learned that a champion fell-racer typically weighs 10 stone 2 pounds, trains every day (usually more than once), runs more than 70 miles a week and gets eight hours' sleep a night. But I didn't discover anything useful that I didn't already know, or couldn't have guessed. The very best fell-runners are roughly comparable as physical specimens to the very best track and road athletes (although their forte tends to be endurance rather than speed). One can argue about specific comparisons, but there have been enough overlaps over the years – from Brasher, Pirie and Ibbotson to Kenny Stuart, Mick Hawkins, Dave Cannon and Jeff Norman – for it to be obvious that, broadly speaking, a champion fell-runner is the same sort of creature as an Olympic champion.

Clearly, there's a huge physiological gap between such creatures and me. Equally clearly, you can be on the wrong side of such a gap and still be a reasonably successful recreational runner. In most fell races, for example, if you run a time that's 50 per cent slower than the race record – which is what I usually seem to do – you will finish in the first half of the field (just). And if it's a good race, there will probably be several Bob Graham veterans behind you.

That was the crucial fact – and, from my point of view, the baffling one. I knew I could never compete at an Olympian level. I knew I could never compete with many – perhaps most – members of the BG club. But research proved beyond doubt that there were at least some members who were no more elite athletes than I was. Why had I failed where they succeeded? That was what I still couldn't understand.

As the years passed, I learnt more about successful fell-runners' training and dietary regimes – but, again, I knew most of it already. Apart from doing more work on the fells, and less (or none) on track and road, long-distance fell-running is essentially the same science as the rest of long-distance running. There's more emphasis on hills, obviously, but most of the basic principles – of building a foundation of stamina and lactic tolerance through long, slow distance sessions, of improving base speed by repetitions, of improving oxygen uptake with sessions of fast continuous running, of maintaining all-round flexibility and balance, of rehydration, of a high-carbohydrate, low-fat diet – are the same.

The only training principles specific to fell-running that I could find, in terms of physical conditioning, were the following:

(a) Keep your body-fat ratio below 10 per cent (i.e. very low indeed).

(b) Develop leg strength, both in the calves (for uphill) and in the quadriceps (for downhill) – not just with weights but also through plyometric jumps and bounds (for 'elastic' strength).

(c) Practise controlling your breathing patterns through use of the diaphragm.

(d) Develop ankle strength and proprioception (try standing on one foot with your eyes closed, or do resistance exercises against a large rubber band).

And, of those, (a) and (c) would probably be aspired to by road- and track-runners as well.

Apart from that, fell-running coaching is largely about developing racing technique – that is, of making more efficient use of the athlete's conditioned physique. Key skills include placing your feet correctly; varying your gait to spare your muscles; leaning correctly; and maximising stud contact with the ground – all of which undoubtedly help but none of which can be developed except by the time-honoured technique of going out on the fells and running on them. This was something that I had already been doing as often as my circumstances permitted – and, though I say it myself, my technique, especially downhill, had improved dramatically.

Theoretically, I could perhaps continue to improve – and thus become a better Bob Graham prospect – by spending more time practising in the mountains. This didn't really seem to constitute a major scientific discovery. Nor was it a helpful one. I already knew the most important training principle of all for recreational sport: that the only regimes that work are those you can accommodate in your life. And I was confident that, given the constraints of age and geography and my various commitments to work and family, I had been making the best possible use of the training time and energy available to me – especially as, over the years, I had shifted the emphasis of my gym and road sessions away from middle-distance power and speed and towards extreme stamina.

In the same way, it was clear that a large proportion of the best fell-runners did jobs that required them to be on their feet all day. But this was hardly a helpful insight. No doubt I too could benefit from switching to active rather than sedentary employment – especially if it involved chasing sheep on the fells. But that wasn't going to happen. Even I wasn't obsessed enough to change careers just for the sake of a fell-running challenge. (I might as well have had liposuction to get my weight down.)

And that, scientifically, was more or less that; until, years later, I remembered the single most striking physiological phenomenon I had observed in all my years of fell-running – the complete physical collapse that followed my decision to give up on my third attempt. It's obvious enough why such a collapse should occur; had I been asked I could probably have predicted it. But what took me by surprise – and what still fascinated me years later – was its magnitude. One minute I had been pressing desperately on, profoundly knackered but still essentially functional; the next, I had collapsed completely. Nothing had happened to change my physical condition, and yet my physical capabilities had been transformed. My engine had cut out.

Such abrupt deteriorations are not unknown in people who have run out of fuel. In this case, I'm certain that fuel wasn't the problem. That dramatic slump was clearly a direct result of a simple mental decision to give up; my energy had declined in exact proportion to my hopes.

So far, so obvious. But did it not follow that the ability to keep going that preceded the slump was sustained by the mental act of not giving up? Of course it did. All my experience of fell-running supported this view: in a positive frame of mind, you power over the mountains, subduing them, trampling them beneath your feet. You, and not the mountains, are in charge. And, as long as you believe that, your strength remains, and feeds off your morale.

There is no scientific proof that this happens, nor any demonstrable mechanism by which it does so – beyond the obvious fact that physical adversity encourages negative thoughts. Nonetheless, it self-evidently does happen; in which case the athlete with the mental strength to sustain morale in the face of physical adversity is significantly more 'fit' than the athlete without such strength.

And in that case, the explanation for my failures was staring me in the face: the weakness was in my mind – in my inability to sustain the belief that I could and would succeed.

'It's all in the mind' is among the tiredest of sporting clichés. It isn't all in the mind, obviously; otherwise no one would bother to train. Equally obviously, we all know that some of it *is* in the mind. But what we generally assume, and what I had always assumed, is that the mental component of any sporting achievement is relatively minor: somewhere in the region of 10 per cent, say, of the achievement as a whole – or perhaps as much as 20 per cent.

Now, suddenly, I was beginning to suspect that, at least where the Bob Graham was concerned, the mental component might be far, far higher, perhaps nearer 70 or 80 per cent.

Maybe that humiliating third failure hadn't been a physical failure at all. Maybe it was a spiritual failure.

If I hadn't foresworn any further attempts at the BG, I might have been tempted to put this theory to the test. As it was, I didn't have far to look to find someone who already had.

19

The Legend of Iron Joss

THERE IS ONLY ONE JOSS NAYLOR. Which is not to suggest that there is more than one Billy Bland or Kenny Stuart, but rather that, while one can accept theoretically that some future fell-runner might eventually emerge with athleticism, grace and courage to match that of Billy or Kenny, Joss Naylor is inimitable. No one else will ever achieve comparable sporting greatness in such an idiosyncratic way. He is, literally, a legend.

Literally? Well, the story of his life and heroics is true, but it has been overlaid through constant retelling with layers of myth, to such an extent that facts sometimes get lost in the mists of fantasy. People who have never met him feel that they know him; people who have never seen him run have a place for his exploits in their mental landscape. 'I know nothing at all about fell-running,' more than one sedentary Cumbrian has told me, 'although obviously I know about Joss Naylor.'

This is the man who, as a teenager, was told that he should never engage in strenuous physical activity again; whose back was so damaged that he spent five years in a special corset – and two decades in more or less constant pain; who, before he even started running, had two discs removed from his back and all the cartilage removed from one knee; who once went six weeks with two broken feet without noticing; who is accident-prone to an almost laughable degree. And yet, when he took to the fells in his late twenties, he transformed his fragility into indestructible resilience. Few people have ever conquered themselves so completely, or so utterly subdued the weaknesses of the flesh to the will of the spirit.

No one has ever absorbed the punishments of the mountains so imperturbably, so inspirationally, as Joss.

This is also, according to legend, a man who habitually interrupted his record-breaking runs to help lambs in distress (true-ish: he did so once, and another time while supporting someone else's BG); who once won a race the day after breaking his leg (untrue: 'Joss'll break a leg on Friday and win on Saturday' is just a local figure of speech, expressing Naylor's habit of suffering traumatic injuries shortly before big events and then winning them regardless); who thought nothing of running 18 miles across the fells to get to the stadium where he was doing a twenty-four-hour track record attempt (not strictly true: he did so for a training session, but not for the record attempt itself); who defied a warning that he would be wheelchair-bound for the rest of his life if he didn't give up running (in fact, the warning was against continuing in his farmwork, not his sport; and, what's more, he didn't entirely defy it).

But there is more than enough remarkable detail in his undisputed life story to make apocryphal embellishments superfluous. Joss Naylor is the only fell-runner apart from Bill Teasdale to have been made an MBE; the only one whose name features in a book title; one of the few to have had a long-distance challenge named after them; the only one to have had a racehorse named after him (the beaten favourite in the 2004 Grand National); the only one to have had a song written about him; and, I think, the only one to have won the Biggest Liar in the World competition (held annually at the Bridge Inn in Santon Bridge, Wasdale). He has had more television documentaries made about him (on both sides of the Atlantic) than all other fell-runners, living or dead, combined. He has probably raised more money for charity than any other fell-runner. And he has certainly had many, many more words written about him. In trying to condense his life into a single chapter, where does one start?

One obvious place is Wastwater, England's deepest lake, which shines at the foot of England's highest mountain on the western edge of the Lake District. This is where Joss was born, at

Wasdale Head, at the north-eastern end of the lake, and where he has lived all his life. Corners don't come much more out of the way than this: cut off by mountains from the crowded tourist zones of the central Lakes, the village can be reached by car only from Cumbria's grey west coast, along miles of single-track lane whose interminable twistings can drive impatient Southerners to despair. Wasdale Head is not so much a village as a place: the end of both the lake and the lane, where a few farmhouses and cottages are scattered (together with England's smallest church) along the valley. Most of the farmhouses have at one time or another been occupied by members of the Naylor family, whose connections with the valley go back to 1928 (longer on his mother's side).

Joss was born here in 1936, in Middle Row Farm. He was the youngest of three brothers; a younger sister followed. He went to school in Gosforth, 10 miles down the lane – but (disappointingly for mythologists) was able to get there and back by school minicab rather than by running. From the age of seven, however, he was out on the fells helping his father and brothers with the farming: fetching sheep, milking cows, or learning the basics of dry-stone-walling and fence-mending. There's an annual show at Wasdale, in October, with its own little fell race, but Joss was more interested in Cumberland & Westmorland wrestling, at which he showed some promise until the age of nine. He then got a slight knock in an impromptu grapple at school, which was exacerbated a few days later when he slipped and fell while climbing a fence and landed on the base of his spine. That was nearly sixty years ago. He's never been right since.

Another good place to begin this story would be at Manchester Royal Infirmary. Joss made his first visit there shortly after those twin knocks; he has lost count of the number of times he has returned. His initial treatment seems to have made things worse, and he wrestled rather less after that. But he continued to lead an active life, with much bending and lifting, as a young farmer-in-the-making. He left school at fifteen, to work full-time on the farm, but his back – and his musculo-skeletal system generally –

deteriorated. In 1955, aged nineteen, he had an operation to remove all the cartilage from his right knee, and was given a special corset to wear to support his back. Further wrestling was out of the question. The doctors also advised him to give up farmwork. He didn't; he couldn't.

Three years later, he had a major operation in which two discs were removed from his back. He spent six weeks encased in plaster. Afterwards, he continued to wear the corset, and the doctors continued to advise against overexertion.

One day, in 1960, he decided that he'd had enough. He was twenty-four now, and had spent more than half his life as a semi-invalid. The pain seemed just as bad whether he obeyed the doctors' orders or not. So he threw the corset away and took up running.

He didn't race at first. Circulation problems in his legs made him susceptible to spectacular attacks of cramp – which on several occasions caused him to pass out with pain. 'It was a wonderful feeling,' he observed once, 'when I came to life again and the pain was gone.' But several experienced fell-runners encouraged him, notably the great Eric Beard, and when that year's Mountain Trial started at Wasdale Head, Joss decided on the spur of the moment to have a go. He ran in his work boots and long trousers cut off at the knee, and led for about 8 miles until the cramp got him; eventually, after finding some picnickers to give him some salt, he finished fourteenth.

Undeterred, he came back the next year with a bit more training in his legs and once again started well, only to get lost after the third checkpoint. 'My sheep don't range that far,' he complained afterwards. But he'd seen enough to realise that he was a natural.

And the pain? Well, he was in pain anyway. Letting the mountains do their worst wasn't going to make a significant difference to his life. In fact, one of his weaknesses – the fact that his cartilage-free right knee would no longer straighten enough to lock – was arguably an advantage. Many runners, trying to run downhill fast, slip into a completely straight-legged gait that is unstable and potentially ruinous to their joints. Joss could relax more naturally into a controlled descending gait, with the knees slightly bent, forcing the muscles to do some cushioning.

That's not to say that he didn't experience physical problems. In his next Mountain Trial, in 1962, he tore a thigh muscle and had to be stretchered down from Grisedale Tarn. The same year, he joined Barrow AC (to which Fred Reeves also belonged) and was persuaded to take part in something he had never tried before: a 6-mile road race. For some reason this left him with broken bones in both feet. For six weeks afterwards he assumed that the pain was just bruising, and by the time the fractures were diagnosed they had set, wrongly, leaving him with two flat feet. More than forty years on, the left foot still gives him trouble.

No matter. He trained a bit harder; tried a bit harder; grew a bit older; and grew a bit harder inside. In 1966, he finally won a race: the Mountain Trial. Further victories followed over the next five years: the newly inaugurated Ennerdale (four times in a row from 1968); the Karrimor International Mountain Marathon, or KIMM (in 1970 and 1971); the Mountain Trial again (in 1969 and 1971). He had looked like winning the 1970 Mountain Trial as well, but faded to second after being kicked by a cow. He wasn't unbeatable, not least because he lacked a real turn of speed. But, given that long amateur races were still in their infancy then, and that relatively few runners competed in them, he was certainly becoming known as one of the best.

'He was the one – the Mr Big,' says Pete Walkington, Joss's partner in many KIMMs. 'He was a real stick insect, with this sort of gangly, leaning forward style. But he was good. I was quite a lot younger than him, and I could more or less keep up with him going up, but as soon as we reached really rough ground – you know, really serious boulder-hopping – he just maintained the same speed. It was unbelievable.'

Opinions differ as to how much training he did: Joss is the kind of runner who prefers not to admit to doing any at all. But his friend Ken Ledward – an Outward Bound instructor turned boot designer, mentioned earlier as organiser of the Duddon Valley race, who holds the record for running up and down Mount Kilimanjaro and who now runs his own business in the Newlands valley testing mountaineering equipment – remembers doing lengthy weekend sessions with Joss in the 1960s. 'Joss would run from Bowderdale through Eskdale and over into Duddon to collect me. We would then do some five or six hours in the Conistons or Langdales and back. Then I'd struggle down my valley and he would set off back to Bowderdale. Many of his sessions will have been nine hours.' Joss's wife, Mary – a Newcastle girl whom he met and married in 1963 – remembers several nights 'being worried sick when he was out on a training run and wasn't back by midnight – I'd be that close to ringing the mountain rescue, but I knew he'd go mad if I did.' A typical evening 'run-out' might be a 12-mile circuit from Wasdale over Haycock into Ennerdale and then back over the Pillar ridge to Yewbarrow; but the truth is, the line between training and work – roaming those same hills checking and tending his sheep – was often blurred. What's not in doubt is that whatever training – and working – he did do was done on the steepest and rockiest mountains in England; and that his idea of the meaning of 'hard' and 'long' was already diverging markedly from what normal people understand by the words.

In 1971, he became only the sixth person to complete the Bob Graham round. Two of those six were dead by then: Bob Graham himself, who died in 1966, and Eric Beard, who was killed in a car crash in 1969. Beard's 1963 round had, to general amazement, taken in fifty-six summits rather than the customary forty-two. Naylor now raised the record to sixty-one. The same year, he won the Ennerdale, the Mountain Trial and the KIMM, and set a record of 11 hours 54 minutes for the Three British Tops (Ben Nevis, Scafell Pike and Snowdon, including driving time). Clearly, this was no ordinary runner.

The following year, on midsummer's eve, he attempted to extend the twenty-four-hour record still further. The weather was against him; in fact, it was one of the foulest weekends in local memory. Yet Joss, uncowed, managed to take in sixty-three peaks within the allotted time. This, I think, was when his exploits first took on a legendary aura. There are some occasions in the mountains when the conditions become so hostile that the only sane thing to do is to retreat to civilisation as swiftly as possible. The 1962 Mountain Trial (see Chapter 22) was one such occasion. This was another. One of Joss's eleven pacers that day, Eric Roberts, has recalled wandering around in driving rain and black fog on Sergeant Man at about 2 a.m., trying to find the true summit; he and the two other pacers present decided that the cairn they had found would just have to do; Joss disagreed, and insisted on disappearing into the darkness and the gale until he had found the real summit. Much later, Christopher Brasher joined him at Langdale and paced him to Wasdale. Dawn had broken by then, but the weather had worsened. 'It did not seem possible,' Brasher wrote afterwards in his weekly column for the *Observer*, 'that anyone could be moving on the mountains on a night like that.' Perhaps you need to have tried the challenge, or something vaguely like it, to appreciate the sheer inner hardness that Naylor showed on that occasion. Or you could just try standing outside for ten minutes the next time there's a really vicious storm raging in the middle of the night. Generally speaking, extreme exhaustion and extreme exposure make cowards of us all – especially when exacerbated by darkness and bruised joints. Joss shut it all out. Years later, Brasher was still sharing the memory with *Observer* readers: 'I tried vainly to stay with him as the rain drummed on my hood so fiercely as to obliterate thought . . . . [It is] still a memory equal to any of the greatest Olympic races that I have ever seen.' And Brasher had witnessed more great Olympic races than most.

Later that year, Joss dropped a railway sleeper on his foot and was back in Manchester Royal Infirmary. Just over three weeks later, he was back running the KIMM, in which he and Allen Walker came second. Other achievements that year included victories in the Mountain Trial, the Manx Mountain Marathon and the Welsh 1,000 Metre Peaks.

Countless further achievements followed. I'll pass most of

them over. Stripped of its context – the interminable slogs and struggles and failures of several thousand also-rans – a chronicle of fell-running's all-time highlights can too easily dull rather than dazzle the mind: like a diet of endless spectacular goals without the drama of the football matches that gave them meaning. The last thing I want to suggest is that Joss's achievements, which account for many of those all-time highlights, were in any way normal or routine. On the contrary, the best of them were freakish; and he was doubly freakish for being associated with so many of them.

Let us merely note, therefore, that Joss's racing triumphs continued well into the 1980s (that is, his forties); and that, for most of the rest of the 1970s, he won most of the big long-distance events, most years; and that his trophy cabinet is one of the biggest and most densely packed you will ever see. I should mention, too, that he won the Mountain Trial every year from 1971 to 1977 (in all, he's run thirty-seven, and won ten); and that in 1974 he knocked more than twenty-four hours off the record for the Pennine Way, completing the entire route in 3 days, 4 hours and 36 minutes (despite severe problems with blistering). One of his secret weapons for this latter challenge – apart from the rock cakes and apple pies that were his main sustenance – was his ability, developed through all those decades of chronic pain, to survive on very little sleep. On ultra-distance challenges lasting several days or more, the man who can survive on two or three hours' sleep a night, rather than six or seven, is at an obvious advantage. So, for that matter, is the man who has spent so much of his life in pain that he has learnt to screen his conscious mind from awareness of it. I have already cited his remark, made around this time, that: 'If you ever want to do anything on the fells, then if you're suffering with some ailment, you've just got to shrug it off.' In my Bob Graham days, we used to recite that as a mantra.

It's also worth noting that, in 1975, Joss raised the Lake District twenty-four-hour record still further, to a scarcely comprehensible seventy-two peaks. Once again, the weather was against him: this time there was a heatwave. Once again, Joss shrugged off the discomfort, while his pacers struggled to do the same. 'I started off with him up Yewbarrow,' recalls one of them, Neil Shuttleworth (a former Keswick club champion with a marathon best of 2 hours 29 minutes), 'and was burnt off after just a few peaks.' 'He's inhuman,' complained another, Eric Roberts. 'We can't keep up with him.'

Later on, Roberts – member No. 12 of the Bob Graham 24 Hour Club – discussed with Brasher, who was again acting as pacer-cum-chronicler, how to equate what they were witnessing with any previous athletic achievement. Brasher reported Roberts's words thus: '"I thought of Ron Clarke when he first ran under thirteen minutes for 3 miles – great performance but not great enough. I thought of Emil Zatopek and his three gold medals in one Olympic Games – still not good enough. And then I decided that there was only one man in athletic history who was in this league – Wilson of *The Wizard*." And he laughed: "A man of fantasy for a fantastic performance."'

Another, more sober comparison is simply to point out, as Brasher did, that what Joss did that day was the equivalent of climbing Everest, and then climbing Ben Nevis, and then climbing Snowdon, and then climbing Kinder Scout, and coming down them all again – all in blistering heat, all within twenty-four hours. Or, to be precise: 23 hours and 11 minutes.

Brasher, who wasn't given to understatement, described it as 'the end of the second era of fell-running . . . a record which, like Bob Graham's, will last for over a quarter of a century'. Joss said little, and went back to his farm.

There were more landmarks to come, notably – in 1976, 1980 and 1983 respectively – records for Robin Hood Bay to St Bee's (just over 41 hours – at the end of which all ten toenails and the skin on the soles of his feet fell off), for Hadrian's Wall (10 hours 53 minutes) and for linking the Lake District's twenty-six 'lakes, meres and waters' (19 hours 15 minutes). And there was the small matter of being created MBE in 1976. But the landmark that perhaps deserves no less consideration is 1977 – which was the year that electricity finally reached Wasdale Head.

It's hard to imagine – or, at least, I find it so – that, scarcely twenty-five years ago, a part of England can have been so cut off from the comforts of modern life. Not that being without electricity necessarily implies hardship; but for those of us who have never known a world without electric lights and television and Hoovers and fridges, it's a useful reminder that life in late-twentieth-century Britain came in more than one form – and that the lives with the fewest mod cons were not necessarily the most impoverished.

Joss planned his epic runs by the light of paraffin lamps, assisted by a few close, local friends and encouraged by Mary, whose support for his endeavours has been devoted and unflinching. 'It is,' she says philosophically, 'no good trying to change someone.' Those who have been involved in Joss's record-breaking exploits invariably enthuse about the huge quantities of food and drink that Mary would prepare for all concerned. 'Their generosity knew no bounds,' says Ken Ledward.

After they married, Joss and Mary lived at Bowderdale Farm – a couple of miles from Middle Row Farm – where there were some 1,000 Herdwick sheep to care for, as well as a small herd of Friesian cows and a few chickens and ducks. Joss spent most daylight hours outdoors, without human company. That's not to say that he was solitary: on the contrary, he was well known and liked throughout and beyond his valley, and could often be found enjoying an evening pint and a game of darts at the Wastwater inn. But by day he worked much as his father and grandfather had worked, alone, immersed in the lives of the animals around him and the passage of the seasons over the hills. Everything he has done should, I believe, be considered in the context of his relationship with his environment.

To a cynical, urban mind, records such as Joss's can seem pointless. What does it matter, ultimately, whether someone takes nineteen hours or ninety hours to visit all the waters of the Lake District? What is the point of extending upwards the numbers of peaks one can climb in a single day? One might just as well get excited about how long it takes to touch all the railings around

Hyde Park, or how many times one can bang one's head against a brick wall.

But the man who is truly at home in the mountains sees more deeply than that. He can see that our selves can never be entirely divorced from our surroundings; and that the man who is lucky enough to live among beautiful hills, and who enters into an intimate relationship with them, is also deeply in touch with himself. Joss chose to pit himself heroically against the mountains not just because they were there, but because his heart was there too; and also because, in his fellow mountain-lovers and fell-runners, he found companions whom he could respect and love. Striving to achieve great things on the fells wasn't just an amusing diversion from his life; it was his life.

Which made it rather depressing when, also in 1977, his back took another turn for the worse. He had to take four weeks off work; eventually, the doctors told him that four more discs in his back had deteriorated beyond repair, and that there was nothing more they could do for him. This was when the wheelchair was mentioned: if he carried on with full-time farming, they suggested, he might end up spending the rest of his life in one.

Reluctantly, he looked around for other work and in 1978 found a position training apprentices at what was then Winscale (now Sellafield) atomic plant. The plant was still being developed then, and thousands of local people worked there; indeed, it was the only major employer in a deeply economically depressed area. It was also an undemanding employer, known locally as 'the holiday camp'. Perhaps that's why, having sold his cattle, Joss decided to keep his 1,000 Herdwicks 'as a hobby'. The result was that, in effect, he hadn't so much given up his job as taken on a second job in addition to the first. And, of course, he carried on running.

It doesn't seem to have done him much harm. At any rate, he was still in fairly good shape when, eight years later, he embarked on what was arguably the most staggering of all his epic achievements.

Lovers of the Lake District will know that the late Alfred

Wainwright published seven volumes of his *Pictorial Guide to the Lakeland Fells*, covering a total of 214 peaks over an area of some 500 square miles. It was Chris Bland, Billy's cousin, who first had the idea of linking all seven volumes into some kind of continuous run. There are fit walkers who have devoted half-lifetimes to bagging all the 'Wainwright tops', in the same way that some people bag Monros; Chris thought he could do a book a day. In fact, he never managed to set aside enough time to put his grand design into practice, although he did complete a slightly reduced course – 192 of the 214 peaks – and raised enough money in sponsorship in the process to give Borrowdale's church a new roof. Then, in 1985, Alan Heaton – the same one who did the BG in 1960 – worked out an easier way of doing it, covering all 214 peaks but linking them in the most convenient way, rather than according to the cruder divisions of the books. He tried it, and completed the course – starting and finishing at Keswick Moot Hall – in 9 days, 16 hours and 42 minutes. Joss was impressed – and decided that he could do better.

If this kind of thing excites you at all, I urge you to obtain a copy of Joss's own account of his attempt. Called *Joss Naylor MBE Was Here*, it is a little pamphlet of about 8,000 words that describes how, in June 1986, a fifty-year-old man set out to climb all 214 Wainwrights – covering a distance equivalent to nearly fifteen London Marathons and climbing up and down more than four Everests' worth of mountain – within a single week. In it, you will read how the first four days of that week saw a freak heatwave which caused at least one local death from heat exhaustion. You will read how Joss's physical condition gradually deteriorated as he pushed himself mercilessly in the heat: swollen feet, swollen hands; throat and tongue so swollen that he could barely drink, let alone eat or talk; both ankles eventually rubbed through by ill-fitting shoes until the ligaments were showing. You will read how he nonetheless had enough spare energy for a diversion on the third day to rescue a lamb trapped in a mudhole – and enough high spirits to end most days by sharing a laugh and a can of Mackeson's. You will read how he averaged three hours' sleep a night, mainly on a mattress in the back of an old van. And you will read of the most extraordinarily devoted support from, by my count, some three dozen friends, admirers and family members, including two who had started off on an innocent evening training run and ended up staying out all night – by which time they were, of course, miles from their homes and workplaces. (Joss's legend is full of such tales of devotion. Ten years later, a scarcely less ambitious venture inspired one of his Sellafield colleagues to offer his services as a pacer, even though he could only make himself available by calling in sick at work. He pleaded an injured toe. At the end of his stint, the malingerer found himself in the embarrassing position of handing over pacing duties to his own foreman. 'I felt the toe needed some exercise,' he explained.)

You will also discover, if you read between the lines of the pamphlet, one of the most stirring stories of pig-headed endurance in the annals of human adventure. You won't, of course, find any reference to the fact that ordinary human beings – even hardy young fell-runners – are regularly reduced to whimpering surrender by challenges only a quarter as destructive. Nor will you actually be told what it was *like*: that is, how with each advancing stage of exhaustion the battering of sharp rock on bruised joint became more intolerable, while energy and morale leaked ever more quickly from jellied muscles. But even Joss, who plays down his own heroism until it is scarcely visible, cannot disguise the fact that, by the second day, he was in difficulties; or that, by the third, he was more than ready to chuck it all in; or that, thereafter, there was nothing to keep him going but the bloodiest obduracy, and an almost religious refusal to surrender to pain.

'We had to drag from ourselves not only our accumulated fitness and basic strength,' he writes in one uncharacteristically emotive passage, 'we had to reach even deeper into ourselves when natural physical abilities had been drained, deeper than I had ever had to reach even in the most serious mountain conditions. I just do not have the words to describe the discomfort, the physical pain, the frustration, and the worry we all had to suffer.'

Finally, however, you will read how that same fifty-year-old staggered back to Keswick Moot Hall, half-dead with agony and exhaustion but with all 214 peaks behind him – seven days, one hour and 25 minutes after he started. The total time elapsed from the first peak to the 214th was 6 days, 23 hours and 11 minutes. You can decide for yourself whether or not his original objective was achieved. For Joss, and for those who witnessed this triumph, the original objective had long since given way to a far greater one: to endure; to strive, and not to yield – no matter how overwhelming the pressure to do so; to keep driving on, defiantly, cheerfully, uncomplainingly, in the face of all reason and sanity; to scorn pain and exhaustion as pernicious impostors; and to prove that an indomitable human will is as mighty a force as any in nature.

I love this little pamphlet. It is artlessly written, yet bears comparison with many a more literary travelogue. I always think of it in the same emotional breath as John Clare's *Journey Out Of Essex*, in which the Northamptonshire poet describes his escape from an Epping lunatic asylum in 1841 and his subsequent 95-mile journey home – walking for four days and nights without food, shelter, map, money or even sanity, just a dogged determination to keep putting one foot in front of the other until he was reunited with his home and his imaginary wife. And, just as I am always moved by the final entry in Clare's journal ('July 24 1841: Returned home out of Essex and found no Mary – her and her family are nothing to me now though she herself was once the dearest of all – "and how can I forget" '), so the closing lines of *Joss Naylor MBE Was Here* have a permanent place in my mental book of quotations: 'I'm not a great one for words, it's been very difficult for me to get this account of my run down on paper. To find words to express my gratitude to those who took part is beyond me. Those who know me well will sense what I want to say; I don't show my feelings but I do feel things deep inside me; I'm a man for doing, not saying. Others might one day put more polish on this story, but one thing I can say with certainty: "It will be a very lucky man who is able to make the bonds of friendship that have been my good luck ... Happy days".'

It will certainly be a lucky man who can find as much peace in his retirement as Joss has found. He lives today less than 2 miles from the farm where he was born, and from the farm where he spent most of his working life. For the past five years he has been 'retired', which means that his son, Paul, runs Bowderdale Farm, while Joss just keeps a few sheep as a hobby. This, naturally, requires him to spend much of each day up a mountain.

His new home, which I visited on a day when rain hammered down so fiercely you could scarcely stand upright in it, is warm, comfortable, immaculate. Only the glittering trophy cabinet gives any clue that this is the residence of a great fellsman and shepherd, rather than, say, a suburban commuter. But Joss himself is unmistakably an athlete: brown, lithe, bright-eyed, with the kind of relaxed animal confidence one often encounters in elite sportsmen. He is sixty-eight now, and his face looks leathery and lined enough to suggest, in a certain light, a chicken, with a startled crest of wiry hair above. But my overwhelming impression, as he lounges back with his arse in one armchair and his feet in another, is of rude, almost boyish health.

Retirement, he says, is 'all right, because I always find something to do every day, like. You know, I work all day, no bother, dig ditches, build walls, chase sheep all day. I've still got me dogs, so I usually go up round the tops, like. I've been very lucky, really.' He has his wife, and his children nearby, and more close, lifelong friends in the area than most of us can hope for when our rootless lives begin to wind down. You see him from time to time at fell-running events, usually in the background, watching with a sheepdog's quiet alertness. He rarely goes long without some old friend or other coming over to greet him – while younger runners glance and whisper, awed to see a legend in the flesh. If the event is within 15 miles or so of Wasdale as the crow flies, it's more likely than not that he'll have got there on foot.

He still runs, too: more slowly than before, but confidently enough to complete the Duddon Valley and the Mountain Trial, about halfway down the field. It's only a few years since, aged sixty, he attempted to scale sixty local 2,500-footers in thirty-six hours. He'd damaged his back – yet another accident – a couple of weeks earlier, and spent much of the attempt in agonising spasms. Nonetheless, he completed the course in 36 hours 57 minutes, and raised over £20,000 for multiple sclerosis research in the process. He won't rule out a similar stunt when he's seventy: 'Oh yes, I ought to, I ought to: seventy at seventy. I'll get my knee injected up.'

There are shadows in his life as well. Only one of his three siblings is still alive. (His brother, Michael, still lives at their birthplace, Middle Row.) He himself had a nasty episode in 1992, when he accidentally inhaled some sheep-dip, causing him to feel 'real low' for the best part of three years; at one point, he feared it might 'drag me right down'. Meanwhile, the circulation problems in his legs have become so bad that he is proposing to spend future winters in Spain, in a little house he has built there, to avoid the shooting pains that would otherwise result every time the Wasdale winter sinks below 10 degrees Centigrade. It's hard to imagine a less likely expatriate. 'I don't worry about dying,' he said once. 'But I'm going to miss these hills.'

The other irritant in his life is the fact that his epoch-breaking Lakeland twenty-four-hour record no longer stands. On a fine June day in 1988, Mark McDermott, an IT worker from Poynton, Cheshire, achieved a round of seventy-six peaks in 23 hours 26 minutes. Mark is demonstrably an outstanding athlete, who has subsequently, among other things, climbed Everest without oxygen. From Joss's perspective, however, he was a complete unknown. And whereas fell-running champions are traditionally delighted to hand over their laurels to younger runners – and indeed actively encourage the breaking of their records – Joss found this particular breakage hard to accept. Eight years later, I was working at the *Independent on Sunday* when we published an interview with Joss. Reading the article on proof, I excised a quoted remark by Joss that struck me as libellous. The comment that remained was oblique, but sufficiently bitter in flavour to prompt Mark to write to the paper pointing out: 'I was accompanied at all times during my run by some of the foremost members of the fell-running community, numbering twenty-odd people in all.' Which, I should add, he was.

Today, Joss is more accepting of McDermott's achievement, and of that of Mark Hartell (another Macclesfield Harrier), who, supported by McDermott, raised the record by a further peak in 1997: 'Aye, they're strong lads, very strong,' says Joss, running an anxious hand through his hair. 'Yes, they worked hard at it.' Yet he still seems reluctant to accept that they could have outdone him in terms of pure stamina, preferring to attribute their success to better planning. 'Of course, they put it through a computer,' he explains. 'You know, computerised it.'

This is a bit silly – and yet not entirely baseless. McDermott and Hartell attacked the challenge with the weapons of the modern world: meticulous preparation and ruthless focus. McDermott, who has a doctorate in mathematics, spent countless hours analysing Joss's 1975 route and schedule, calculating possible improvements; and he did indeed end up putting it all on a spreadsheet, which, as he says today, 'isn't exactly rocket science' but does allow you to adjust the figures more quickly; Hartell did much the same when he refined the schedule further for his attempt. In each case, the computer's role was negligible: it was the men themselves who were making the calculations, which were based on exhaustive on-the-ground analysis of the route itself and their own ability to run on it. (Hartell reckons that, by the time he set his record, he had been over every peak on the course eight times – at record pace.) In this they were following the philosophy of their friend and pacer Martin Stone, the Cambridge-born, London-educated Dark Peak runner who set a series of astonishing twenty-four-hour records in the 1980s. Stone was famous for spending hours 'devising and tuning' his schedules, test-running every part of his route at record pace and then going over it all again with his calculator. 'People used schedules before,' says

Stone, 'but we raised it to a fine art. By the time I started a record attempt, I always had complete confidence that, if I stuck to the schedule, it could be done.'

McDermott and Hartell were also, self-evidently, able and experienced fell-runners, who had already done fast BGs. (Hartell would later run the second-fastest BG ever, beating Stuart Bland's time by two minutes.) And both trained obsessively for their record attempts. Yet it's not entirely spurious to argue that it was the thoroughness and intelligence of their preparation, and their precise definition of their objectives, that gave them their edge. As Stone points out, 'Joss just went out to do the most he could possibly do. I don't think he himself really knew how many it would be. He just went out at top pace and carried on until he ran out of time – I'm sure he would have looped back earlier if he'd needed to. And he moved the whole thing up by a huge quantum. The two Marks had a much narrower target: they just had to nibble away, replicating the existing record and adding one or two. So they could practise doing the route at exactly the right pace.' This isn't meant as a criticism. Stone still rates Hartell and McDermott as two of the very greatest fell-runners ever. So do I; not least because their approach – trying to make the impossible possible by dint of remorseless logic and determination – was precisely the approach that I had hoped would enable me to conquer the BG.

Neither interloper knew the Lakeland fells so profoundly as Joss did, although each had made himself intimately familiar with the route. Nor did either of them really have the resources to implement his plan if the elements were against him. (Bad weather forced Mark Hartell to abort two attempts, in 1993 and 1994.) Perhaps that makes their records in some way less historic than, say, Joss's extraordinary foul-weather run in 1972. Yet you could also consider the determination with which Hartell twice came back for more, or the single-mindedness with which McDermott shrugged off the Lakeland consensus that his attempt was doomed, and argue that both men displayed a pig-headedness of precisely the same heroic kind that we admire in Iron Joss.

Perhaps what bothers Joss is the idea that two relative Southerners – 'computer programmers from Cheshire', as McDermott puts it – could have stolen such an intensely local record. This is not, ultimately, very reasonable. Should Cumbrians be debarred from seeking to realise their dreams in the South? Yet he's not the only one to have felt uncomfortable about relatively well-heeled outsiders sticking their fingers into what had hitherto been a fairly private Lake District pie. There were hostile whisperings in the Borrowdale valley, too, for a while, and Mark McDermott, especially, was worried that he might have been trampling on local sensibilities. 'Afterwards,' recalls McDermott today, 'we all went for a slap-up breakfast at a posh hotel above Keswick – and I remember thinking: "What will folk think?" ' To which the answer is that different folk think different things, and that some thoughts do them more credit than others. I can understand that Joss and his admirers might have found his successors' achievements hard to accept; I hope that Joss, at least, has now found it in himself to accept them; and I suspect he probably has.

What's undeniable is that, generally, Joss is known for his generous spirit. He is fulsome in his praise of rivals and successors from nearer home – such as the Blands – suggesting, for example, that 'if the likes of Gavin Bland would get the time to do what they [McDermott and Hartell] would do, he'd do it faster, because he's got the legs to do it'. He is also known for his generosity towards less gifted fell-runners. Ross Brewster, the cheerful journalist who helped found Keswick Athletic Club in the early 1970s, echoes many middle-of-the-pack runners when he recalls running the Ennerdale one year, 'and Joss had done it in about two-and-a-half hours and I had done it in about seven, and yet there he was at the line, waiting. And he never said what he'd done – he always enquired how you'd done. Joss is a great local as well as a great runner. There's never been any sense of arrogance or self-importance to him.' 'When any local lad beat him,' adds Ken Ledward, 'he appeared as happy as if he'd won himself.'

Nor is Joss usually averse to expressing admiration for athletes from further afield – he is, for example, a great fan of the current crop of Kenyan distance runners. 'They're the best runners there are. They've got a hell of a lot of stamina, and their legs have that kind of elasticated muscle. Marvellous. If our lads think they can beat the Kenyans, they've got another think coming, because they've been too softly brought up, like. But if you've had a hard childhood, like the Kenyans have, that's good training. Their stamina gets laid down in childhood.'

The one sport he can't stand is football. He had a couple of brushes with hooliganism in the 1960s and was disgusted with what he saw. 'What sort of people are they? It makes you sick. They're all brave when they've someone to stand behind.' He has scarcely more time for the players. The pampered prima donnas of the modern Premiership can earn more from their sport in a day than Joss has earned in forty years of top-level fell-running. And yet, he says, 'They're not playing to their potential half the time. A lot of these top players need their arses kicked. I just can't understand how they can take so much out of the sport and put so little in.'

Does he never wish he had converted his sporting gifts into even moderate amounts of wealth – by running on the roads, say, or on the track? He shrugs. 'I just hadn't the time, like. I had too much work to do at home. I'd have had to get somebody else to do my work.'

I can't help wondering, in any case, whether a few million pounds in the bank would have added much to Joss's quality of life. He isn't rich, yet his life is remarkably free from material want. He seems more concerned with what he can give away than with what he can get. Most of his epic runs were performed to raise money for good causes; in several cases, it was the desire to raise money that prompted him to conceive the challenge. And the fund-raising habit persists. The pictures on his walls include several by Mary and by their daughter Gillian, one of which – by Mary, of Joss running – is sold in print form to raise money for charity; profits from *Joss Naylor MBE Was Here* are given away too (to buy safety equipment for the FRA); he also gives regular talks in local hospitals. 'Some of the old ones you see there, it makes you so sad to see them . . .'

It's not that many years since Joss, visiting hospital as a patient rather than a celebrity, was shown off to a group of students by his consultant. 'He said, "Take a good look at this one, because you don't get a specimen like this more than one time in 200,000."' This may well have been correct. But what makes Joss unique isn't the quality of his muscle fibres or his pulse rate or his power-to-weight ratio. It's his spirit. For those who know him, his fell-running records are neither here nor there, except in so far as, having been carved out in defiance of pain and injury, they symbolise the man's integrity. What they'll miss about him when he's gone is the quiet, selfless, cheerful inner strength that has prevented him from indulging in either self-aggrandisement or self-pity, though he's had more reason than most to indulge in both. That is what puts fire in your veins when you see Joss Naylor at a fell race: the sense that here is living reminder that a man can, if he chooses, be more than the sum of his appetites and fears. And that, I think, is the real reason why a man whose most spectacular gift in life is an essentially unnecessary ability to keep going indefinitely over mountainous terrain is so widely loved and hero-worshipped. As Ross Brewster puts it: 'He isn't just a strong runner. He's a strong man – a good man with a real affinity for the fells.'

Joss is a legend, not because he ran further or longer than anyone else, but because he did so without ever complaining, or losing his sense of humour, or losing his interest in matters beyond his sport. Accounts of days on the fells with Joss always involve lots of chatting – about views, nature, family life, the way of the world. He finished his '60 at 60' enthusing about 'the may in blossom and the Lake District like a looking-glass'; on the Wainwrights round it was a 'mighty red stag' that caught his imagination – so much so that he 'tripped over watching it'. 'He's a quiet man,' says Pete Walkington. 'He's not a great raconteur or anything. But he's good company, especially on the fells.' 'Many people think of Joss as only being a hard physical person,' says Ken Ledward. 'But I have jogged with him through the night and into the dawn and heard him eulogise on the weather, the views, the birds – and always as a true countryman.'

Interviewed about his sport, Joss is as likely as not to start talking about whatever else is on his mind at that moment: the shortcomings of the National Trust, the advance of tourism into Wasdale, the marvels of the high-tech equipment he has just seen installed (thanks to his fund-raising) at a local hospital. He rarely talks specifically about the sport itself; he'd rather talk about the laughs he was having with his companions, or what the view was like.

And his secret? 'He's a natural,' says Neil Shuttleworth, 'who happens to live right by England's biggest mountains.' 'He chose his parents correctly,' says Pete Walkington. 'It's in his genes. Plus he'd sleep on anything, eat anything, and he weighed nothing.' 'Bloody-mindedness,' says Ken Ledward. 'There's nothing suits Joss better than to be told: "That's impossible – nobody can do that."' 'He has very, very strong will power,' says Mary Naylor. 'He just will not give in. He's not so good when he's got a cold, though.'

But is there any physical aspect of his lifestyle or training regime that an aspiring fell-runner might usefully imitate? Joss is happy to offer what advice he can, but it's not very remarkable. He trained as much as he could but less than he wanted, and owes most of his stamina to a combination of genetic good luck and an active job. He has thrived on the devoted support of his family and friends. He weighs next to nothing: 9 stone, which on a man of 5 feet 11 inches is skeletal. (I'm an inch taller, relatively fit, and 4 stone heavier.) Yet he has never dieted; on the contrary: 'I'll eat owt.' (One Southern journalist briefly misinterpreted this to mean that he ate only at restaurants.) 'He just eats what we eat,' confirms Mary, 'although he used to eat huge quantities of cake.' Nor is he averse to the occasional drink: 'Tha wants to get plenty a Guinness and cider down thee,' he once advised a young runner. Running has never been a chore for Joss; nor – crucially for the legend – has it been a science.

He has always moved over the fells with great natural economy, partly because of his confident, controlled descending and partly because of a gift for 'reading' hillsides and finding the best lines. He also believes that it is important to understand the stones underfoot: 'You've got to read them, like when you're building a wall. You've got to tell which are loose and which you can count on. You've got to treat them with respect. If you step on one and it's loose, you're on your back.' Which makes obvious sense but is not, ultimately, very helpful; especially if you've never made a dry stone wall yourself.

Oh yes, and one other thing: 'You've got to be able to switch off. If you thought about it, you'd lie down.'

20

Scenes from a fell-running year: July

It's uphill-only racing at the European Mountain Running Championships at Monte Bondone in northern Italy. Britain's men can manage only eighth place; but Angela Mudge wins individual silver, thirteen seconds behind the Belgian favourite, and – with Lou Sharp twenty-fourth and Helene Diamantides thirty-fourth – the British women win the team bronze, behind Italy and the Czech Republic. Lou describes herself as 'really chuffed' with her performance, which has confirmed her as a runner of real class. A few weeks later, she wins the 16-mile Holme Moss race, near Huddersfield, and so bags herself the English championship; now it's all down to next month's Brecon Beacons race to see if she can retain her British title. Meanwhile, she's still looking for a new home.

At the more rugged end of the fell-running spectrum, there's a good turnout for the Wasdale: sixty-eight starters to race 25 miles over unrelentingly mountainous terrain, with 8,000 feet of ascent, on a course that takes in Whin Rigg, Seatallan, Pillar, Great Gable, Esk Hause, Scafell Pike and Lingmell. But only twenty-six of the runners are under forty. Rob Jebb, whose smiling face is becoming hard to avoid at this year's most prestigious prize-giving ceremonies, is first of fifty-three finishers.

In Scotland, there's a record field of eighty for the North Cape Dollar hill race in Kinross. Borrowdale's Phil Davies wins comfortably, and wins the Scottish Hill Runners Championship in the process. Carnethy's Jill Tait does likewise among the women. The course has been changed slightly, following problems with aggressive buzzards the previous year; this time, more than a third of the field are stung by wasps. Afterwards, there's a vociferous campaign to revert to the buzzards next year. Meanwhile, there are only twenty-six starters for the British Hill Running Championship at Alva – once the biggest event in the professional calendar and described by Fred Reeves as the toughest course he ever ran on: 'It's straight up and down and it's a terror. There's steep rocks and bracken and even cliff-faces with cracks you have to climb down. You should have seen Tommy go down that.' Dan Whitehead of Cosmic Hillbashers wins the BOFRA-organised event in 20 minutes 49 seconds – more than two-and-a-half minutes outside Kenny Stuart's 1981 record. Helen Sedgwick, fourteenth overall, is first of three women in the field.

In Wales, the International Snowdon Race is won by Tim Davies for the second year running. His time of 1 hour 5 minutes 57 seconds is nearly a minute-and-a-half faster than his nearest rival's – and three-and-a-half minutes slower than Kenny Stuart's 1985 record. Most runners are competing for their clubs, but the top couple of dozen wear national vests. England win both team prizes, but there is, as ever, a strong showing from the Italians, with Silvio Gatti and Massimiliano Zanaboni taking fifth and seventh place respectively. Italians have been competing in – and often winning – the Snowdon race for nearly twenty-five years now, and the relationship between the two nations' runners is now so warm that Llanberis is to be twinned with Morbegno (whose mayor acts as race starter). This is a fitting farewell tribute to Ken Jones, the local man who created the race and is now, twenty-seven years later, stepping down as race organiser.

There are also some impressive ultra-endurance performances this month. In Scotland, John Fleetwood of Kendal completes the year's only successful Charlie Ramsay round – and only the thirty-first ever. Problems with his knees, and with deteriorating grip on his old fell shoes, slow him down, and only a desperate final slither down Ben Nevis gets him back within twenty-four hours – with just seven minutes to spare. Martin White of Winchester, the first of three people to complete the Paddy Buckley round this year, cuts it even finer, with a suicidal finishing sprint down Cnicht proving just enough to get him back in 23 hours 54 minutes. In Colorado, meanwhile, Mark Hartell is pipped at the post – by a mere forty-seven minutes – after leading for much of the Hardrock 100. His time – 28 hours 49 minutes 10 seconds – would have been quicker if he hadn't spent most of the last 25 miles being sick. 'I was desperately disappointed to be passed by the favourite on the final section, but I still finished nearly two hours faster than the last time, and I know that I could get the record. So that's another trip I will have to do again.'

Other July highlights include the Kentmere (where Tim Austin, finally recovered from his virus, comes third); the Blisco Dash in Langdale; the Lyke Wake race – a 40-mile slog across what used to be Cleveland which you can, if you like, run while singing the ancient Lyke Wake Dirge ('When thoo frae hence away art passed/Ivvery neet an' all;/To Whinny-moor thoo cooms at last,/An' Christ tak up thy saul'); the Inter-Counties Fell Running Championship on Ingleborough (won by Rob Jebb and Lou Sharp); the Five Tops Hill Race in Moray (where seventy-year-old Bill Gauld comes twenty-fourth out of thirty-seven runners); Ambleside Sports (where Nick Sharp wins the guides race by over a minute); and, of course, Skiddaw.

Keswick's big Sunday is cool, grey and dry: perfect conditions, they say, for a record attempt. Walkers who struggle to get to the top of Skiddaw and back in a single day may struggle to comprehend the thought that Kenny Stuart once completed the round trip in 1 hour 2 minutes 18 seconds. So do many fell-runners. In the nineteen years since Kenny set the record, no one has got within a minute of it; most Skiddaw race winners can scarcely break 1 hour 5 minutes. But with so many top runners in today's field, and with the added advantage of the improved path, who knows what might happen?

All morning, there's been feverish activity in Fitz Park, as Allan Buckley and assorted helpers have transformed the long, white, wooden cricket pavilion into a combined registration centre, changing room, bar and catering base. Outside, volunteers have been taping off the start area on the grassy knoll behind; taking down the fence on the narrow path by the tourist car park a third of the way up; planting flags to mark the section of Jenkin Hill where runners are allowed to leave the path; and, in a few cases, trudging up to the very summit, hoping that they have brought with them enough food and clothing to sustain them there for a long, largely motionless morning acting as marshalls.

'It's not my favourite race,' confides Pete Richards, hurriedly hoovering the Dunsford breakfast room before rushing upstairs to change for the race. 'It always gives me blisters. But it's a nice atmosphere. I'm planning to enjoy it today. At least I can run it.'

Pat Richards is not so lucky: a thigh injury sustained nearly two months earlier is still giving her trouble, and she has decided to marshall instead. Her patch is the tourist car park, and the path from it that leads to and up Jenkin Hill. 'It's more complicated than usual,' she explains, 'because they're making everyone stick to the path' – except for the flagged section higher up where runners can take the direct, pathless route on the descent. More work for the marshalls; but good news for latter-day Kenny Stuarts with ambitions to run a three-minute off-road mile.

Back down at sea level, Fitz Park is filling rapidly with people who look as though they might fit exactly that description. Lean, muscular and tanned, they bound around the park in warm-up routines that most people would take for flat-out sprints. They also rush backwards and forwards, collecting and discarding kit and performing idiosyncratic rituals with their shoelaces and bumbags; and, occasionally, making last-minute purchases from Pete Bland, the Kendal sportswear supplier who, as usual, is here with his van.

Then, as 12.30 p.m. approaches, they begin to settle around the start. A marshall checks our kit as we enter the taped starting area, within which most runners cluster into colour-coded swarms according to their clubs: Borrowdale in purple, Bingley in blue-and-white, Clayton-le-Moors in white with an orange-and-black band, Keswick in brilliant yellow-and-green. There's Gavin Bland, looking pale and drawn; there's Ian Holmes, stern and focused; there's Rob Jebb, laughing as usual; there's Wendy Dodds, stretching methodically. Everyone who's anyone – apart from the select few who, like Lou Sharp, are competing in Europe today – seems to be there. And everyone seems to be talking to more or less everyone else. The

Keswick runners are chatting nervously about the race: the prospect of blisters; the anticipated cavalry charge towards the bottleneck on the corner; the fact that no one will admit to having done any recent training at all. 'It's not like it's anything to be ashamed of,' remarks someone. But Mark Denham-Smith and Nimrod Lockwood, Keswick's two best hopes, have gone quiet. This is their home turf, and anything less than a very good run from either will be a big disappointment. Nearby, I hear someone ask Ian Holmes if he thinks the record can be broken. 'No chance,' he says.

Then Allan Buckley, looking remarkably relaxed in shorts and yellow T-shirt, calls us into line, says a few words about the path and the flagged section, and introduces the official starter, the Mayor of Keswick, who tries in vain to prevent the starting bell he hands her from emitting an unintended tinkle. By the time she has rung it properly, we have already started: 365 of us, stampeding down 100 yards of grassy slope, dodging trees and legs. Within a minute we have slowed abruptly to filter through the 'bottleneck' path; and then, out in the lane, we settle into our preferred paces for the race proper.

This is much as you would expect. Uphill for the first half; downhill for the second. Some fell-runners speak disparagingly of Skiddaw: too boring; no navigational challenges; no really rough ground. Others like it, for much the same reasons. Both groups have a point. This is the first time I've done it as a race, but I know it well; it's the first peak on the Bob Graham route. On this occasion, however, the uphill seems to last for ever, and, although I have resolved to run the entire way, on the steepest part of Jenkin Hill I realise that, after overtaking fairly regularly up to this point, I am no longer catching up the people in front of me, who have switched to a fast walk. I'm reluctant to change tactics: once you start breaking mental resolutions, it's hard to stop, and there's a danger of losing the will to race altogether. But eventually a fast-walker overtakes me, and I bow to the inevitable. I lean forward, lengthen my stride, place my hands on my knees to spread the weight, and walk for all I'm worth, making each stride count. By the time we've reached the top of the steep bit – and can resume running – I've overtaken three more people.

Skiddaw has its faults as a race, but it's hard to imagine another that gives the middle-of-the-field competitors such a fabulous view of the elite runners at the front. Once you're past Jenkin Hill, the slope becomes slightly flatter and, with the summit soon more or less straight ahead, you can theoretically see most of the way to the top from a long way off. In practice, of course, the summit is usually smothered in cloud; but today, although there are grey wisps blowing about, there is all the visibility you could ask for. The top itself is a giant heap of boulders and scree, enclosed by a fence. You always think you're at the summit when you reach that fence, but the giant heap is steeper and longer than it seems, taking anything from five to ten minutes when you're running up. This can be rather dispiriting.

Not today, though. About forty-five minutes into the race, I'm halfway along the section of easy path that immediately precedes the summit heap, when I notice a runner coming towards me. No, not 'coming' – flying. When I first see him he is probably 300 metres away; by the time I have worked out what he is, he is passing me. This is the race leader – Simon Bailey of Staffordshire Moorlands – already heading for home. I swear I can feel the rush of wind as he passes. But by now there are two, three, four other runners following him, skimming across the boulders; again, they seem to reach me much sooner than they ought to, like cars travelling too fast on a road you are trying to cross. Ian Holmes, who appears to be in seventh or eighth place, is moving fastest of all.

By now, I have reached the beginnings of the summit scree myself, and runners are pouring back over the skyline in dozens. The slate-grey sky and the traces of wet cloud, tossed about like birds in a storm, lend an apocalyptic air to the scene; the boulders could be blasted ruins, the figures galloping across them Valkyrie. They have flung all caution to the winds – they can afford to, for the slope is easy at this stage – and their recklessness feels wildly heroic. It's also mesmerising, with each choosing a slightly different route through the rocks, diverging and converging according to some not-quite-perceptible logic, as raindrops run down a windowpane.

Inspired, I press on to the summit with renewed enthusiasm, and soon I too am flying back down. It's hard to imagine a more thrilling mountain experience (although presumably this is the kind of kick people get from skiing). My speed is manageable, but only just. There is no possible way of controlling my momentum, except by accelerating, like a motorcyclist taking a corner. The giant summit heap is gone in a minute, giving way to the relatively smooth and stable path. Then it gets faster. At the lower end of the path I'm off down the flagged, pathless section on the steepest bit of Jenkin Hill, and the needle falls off my mental speedometer. This is insane. Impulses make it from my brain to my feet only in the nick of time – and even that requires extreme mental effort. I cannot even imagine what it would feel like to run faster than this. My footfalls come in such impossibly quick succession that there is no time to replace the air that each impact drives from my lungs. The temptation to stop for breath grows harder to resist, but, of course, there is no way of stopping. Anyway, I have overtaken at least a dozen blurs of colour that I think must be runners. I'm enjoying this.

Shortly afterwards, the slope flattens out for a bit and, idiotically, I twist my ankle on the slowest moment of the descent. I hop and curse, then limp angrily for the final couple of miles, losing most of the places I have gained. But I still finish in two minutes under an hour-and-a-half – and just inside the first half of the field. Even as the pain boils in my ankle, I cannot suppress my satisfaction. I don't care what anyone says: that was fun. And I bet Ernest Dalzell felt the same.

From then on, the day takes on a quieter tone. Runners continue to trickle in for the best part of an hour after me (the day's fastest and slowest times are 1 hour 3 minutes 11 seconds and 2 hours 23 minutes 28 seconds). Having done so, they drift back to the pavilion, where they don't so much buzz as hum gently. The pent-up nervous energy of the morning has evaporated. People sit on the grass now, or on the wooden benches under the verandah; others queue patiently for the sandwiches, tea and biscuits on offer inside – and devour them gratefully. Some manage to shower and change; others slip into tracksuits, or stay as they are. There is less colour-coding than before, partly for obvious reasons and partly because people are mixing more, catching up with old friends. The race itself, with such minimal scope for navigational triumphs and disasters, has provided relatively few talking-points, but there are plenty of past and future events to discuss. It's a gentle English scene, more suggestive of cricket than of rough mountain exertions. But then, what could be more conducive to a mellow frame of mind than the knowledge that a flat-out dash up and down one of England's biggest mountains is behind you?

Ian Holmes, who came second after picking up eight places on the descent, is sitting on a wooden bench with a cup of tea. He spends a long time talking to a red-faced Scotsman, who quizzes him in minute detail about his lifestyle and racing plans. 'Who was that?' I ask afterwards. 'No idea,' says Holmes. 'Just someone who likes fell-running, I suppose.'

Stephen Fletcher is attending to the needs of Alison Wyeth, once British 1,500-metres champion, now a blazered development officer for UK Athletics and the Amateur Athletic Association of England. She's been invited as part of a general bridge-building exercise: fell-running comes under her 'development' brief, but she's never seen a fell race before. Her goodwill could prove invaluable for future grant applications. Someone else, meanwhile, is filming the entire proceedings: the resulting video will form part of the FRA's World Trophy bid presentation. I don't know if perfect settings and idyllic atmospheres are the kind of thing that either UK Athletics or the World Mountain Running Association is interested in, but it's hard to believe that anyone could observe all this and not be deeply impressed.

Wendy Dodds is talking to a group of fellow veterans, apparently discussing her next 'proper' challenge. Mark Denham-Smith and Nimrod Lockwood (twenty-eighth and forty-seventh respectively) are looking pensive together. Pete Richards (300th) is talking to Pat. Rob Jebb is having a laugh with his Bingley mates. Kenny Stuart, who is due to present the prizes, is sipping a pint of beer on the pavilion verandah. You could put him on the television and not one viewer in 100,000 would recognise him. Yet here he seems to bask in a glow of celebrity, like a latter-day George Best, dispensing friendly words to a stream of admirers – while never entirely letting down his guard. Allan Buckley is standing by the table with the prizes on it. You can tell from the dazed but satisfied look on his face that he knows he's in the home straight now.

If you didn't know they were prizes, you might not guess: just a few bottles and some envelopes containing vouchers from Pete Bland Sports. Occasionally, such envelopes contain cheques, although I don't think any of these do. I still find it baffling that anyone can ever have believed that it mattered much either way; or that so many people can have got so worked up about professionalism and amateurism when the inducements at issue were – and are – so modest. It's hard to imagine a sport less tainted by market forces: the overwhelming impression here is of selfless volunteer labour, and of runners who race for love, not money. Each of them, remember, has paid £4 simply to enter the race, and few will have spent much less than £10 on petrol and parking. If material reward is what you're after, it's hard to think of a less effective way of using your energy.

But if your idea of satisfaction is to sit contentedly on the grass of what *Wisden Cricketers' Almanac* has called 'the loveliest cricket ground in Britain', gazing up at the mountain behind while reflecting on a race well run on its slopes, and listening as you do so to the wind in the leaves, the click of cup on saucer and the friendly murmur of a few hundred like-minded people who can't quite summon the energy to go home yet, then this must be one of the best possible ways of spending a summer Sunday. You can feel all the social and sporting history swimming around you, and it feels good.

As I leave, Ian Holmes is talking to Kenny Stuart. I wish I had a camera: it strikes me as a precious image – two great athletes saluting one another, each radiating respect, like Bobby Moore and Pelé at the 1970 World Cup.

They are talking, not unnaturally, about Kenny's record.

'Someone'll break it one of these days,' says Kenny.

'Not in your lifetime,' says Ian.

21

Risk and responsibility

PETE BLAND IS A TALL, SERIOUS-LOOKING MAN, sixty-three years old, with white hair and glasses that make him look like a teacher. He has a slightly vague manner which, combined with a hint of a stoop, might be taken to suggest absent-mindedness. In fact, the proprietor of Kendal's most famous sports shop is one of the most astute operators in fell-running.

His CV includes ten years as manager of the England mountain-running team (from 1990 to 2000, during which time Martin Jones was twice world mountain running champion) and twenty-four years – and counting – as membership secretary of the FRA. He's also spent most of the past three decades as the sport's most successful purveyor of specialist equipment.

He was still a leading runner, having recently switched from professional to amateur, and earning his living at Kendal's K Shoes factory when, in 1974, he had his first big business idea. A few runners had begun to use a new kind of fell-running shoe, designed by the great Norman Walsh of Bolton. Hitherto, the only purpose-made footwear had been heavyweight and expensive, more like golf shoes than running shoes, with metal studs and kangaroo-skin and snakeskin uppers. The top runners had their shoes made to measure by mail order – from Fosters in Bolton, where Walsh spent much of his career. Others made do with various compromises, not excluding football boots. Then Walsh, who set up on his own in 1961, began making a lighter fell-running shoe, with a rubber 'ripple' sole that combined a certain amount of shock-absorption with a certain amount of grip on wet grass and rock.

Pete Bland and a friend, Alan Evans, heard about this. 'So we went down to see Norman Walsh and met him in his tiny workshop and told him who we were and we wanted to buy a dozen pairs of shoes off him and sell them at races. So he gave us a bit of a discount and we went off with these shoes in the back of my car.'

The enterprise prospered, and within seven years Bland was running his own business in the premises he still occupies today. Pete Bland Sports is a poky-looking establishment on a grimy bend at the eastern end of the main road into Kendal. But to fell-runners it's a mecca, in the same way that, say, London's Thomas a' Becket gym has traditionally been a mecca for boxers: a repository of expertise, history and authority. In the shop itself, you'll find not just sports kit but books, videos, fixture information, memorabilia; indeed, you might be lucky enough to be served there by the great Jon Broxap, a former youth-hostel warden and pioneer of ultra-distance fell-running who would probably have dominated the sport in the 1980s if Billy Bland and Kenny Stuart hadn't been around (and who in 1988 set the all-time Scottish twenty-four-hour record of twenty-nine Monros). On the shop's website, there's almost as much information and advice on offer as there is kit. And you'll rarely find a big race north of the Pennines at which Pete and his red van aren't parked somewhere near the start, with a selection of kit laid out in boxes on the ground and selected famous and not-so-famous runners exchanging news and memories nearby. (Further south, the van is more likely to belong to Tony Hulme, proprietor of the considerably newer Running Bear shop and kit range.)

But Pete Bland's role in the story of fell-running is more significant than that. In 1985, he perfected and patented a kind of sole that has yet to be bettered for running on mountains. It's a flat, smooth rubber layer with nearly sixty small studs on it, each in the shape of a square pyramid about 1.5 centimetres tall, strategically laid out in evenly spaced but staggered rows over the length of the sole. For the fell-runner, this provides the advantages of metal studs (good grip on sloping or slippery turf) without the disadvantages (weight, plus a tendency to bend and break), with the additional advantage of a surprising amount of grip on rock (because the softish studs 'drag' like tyre treads). The design proved an instant success. Pete went into partnership with Norman Walsh and began to produce and sell 'PBs', which combined this new sole with the suede and nylon uppers that were already a feature of Walsh's other shoes. Novice fell-runners assumed that PB stood for 'personal best'; insiders knew better. Either way, PBs were what serious fell-runners more or less unanimously took to wearing, although imitators soon followed. Even today, despite numerous refinements and substantially more competition (and despite Walsh shoes generally being referred to as 'Walshes' rather than 'PBs'), most fell-runners wear footwear that is recognisably modelled on the PB.

'No one has even come close' stated an early advertisement for PB Walshes, cashing in on the fact that Kenny Stuart used them with a full-page photograph of Kenny in action. It was a fair assessment of both athlete and product. Another such photograph hangs in Pete Bland Sports. Depicting Kenny narrowly ahead of John Wild on a steep ascent in the Welsh 1,000 Metre Peaks race of 1983, it formed the basis of another, earlier advertisement. Stuart wore (pre-PB) Walshes; Wild wore Reeboks. 'We never forget that the competition is always on our tail – we intend to keep them there' said the slogan.

A few feet away, there's another famous photograph. It shows a young runner leaping wildly in the air, arms flailing, with an expression of joy on his face so wild it makes the hairs on the back of your neck stand up. The scene is Ambleside, 1968, and the young man is Pete Bland. Thirteen years earlier, as a fourteen-year-old, he had been all but crippled in a motorcycle accident that left him with a double compound fracture just below the left knee. The doctors had said he would never run again. But he did, and, after years of desperately slow rehabilitation, he eventually began to compete at the highest level. He spent the 1960s snatching at the vests of Teasdale and Harrison, with getting on for a dozen top-three placings at Grasmere and Ambleside. But a major prize always eluded him – until that day, when, incredibly, the erstwhile write-off and also-ran didn't just win but won easily. 'It was one of those days – they don't come often in your career – but it was like being in a dream. I had no pain. I just felt so comfortable and easy. I couldn't believe that I won by such a long way. I was miles in front at the finish, and I just had no pain. It was like floating on clouds.' You can see it in his eyes in the photograph, and you can see it in his eyes as he recounts it. And, when you see it, you can understand why people love this sport.

Most sports administrators have a moment or two of youthful competitive glory to treasure in later life. Pete Bland has, in addition, a searing and ineradicable memory from his behind-the-scenes experiences. It is not a happy one.

In addition to all his other desk jobs, Pete organises races. He is responsible for the Senior Guides Race at Grasmere and the aforementioned Rydal Round at Ambleside, and, further east, the Kentmere Horseshoe. He's been running the Kentmere – administratively – for nearly thirty years. It's a circuit of around 12 miles over a ring of rolling fells south of Haweswater – Black Stones, Kentmere Pike, The Knowe, High Street, Ill Bell, Buck Crag, Ewe Crags. Generally, it's a green and pleasant route, but, like anywhere else, it's exposed to the extremes of local weather. Colin Donnelly won the 1980 race in knee-deep snow. And on Easter Sunday 1994 – the twentieth running of the race – the weather won a terrible victory.

It was raining hard at the start, and, higher up, the rain turned to snow. By halfway there was a blizzard raging, with blowing spindrift creating what were described as 'near white-out conditions'. Seventy-eight of the 253 competitors failed to finish, cutting back to the safety of lower ground via various escape routes. One never made it back. Judith Taylor, a forty-five-year-old mother of two who ran for Clayton-le-Moors Harriers, was found dead by Patterdale Mountain Rescue several hours after the finish. She was an experienced runner, with good navigational skills, and had been well-equipped with protective clothing. Nonetheless, she had died of hypothermia. 'She got lost, and wandered around for a long time, and basically just laid down and died,' says Pete. She wasn't found until 8 p.m. that evening near The Knott below High Street, some way off the race route.

She was widely mourned, and was commemorated in print by her husband, Philip, with whom she had been planning to do the Bob Graham a few months later. *Judith's Round*, published in aid of Kendal Mountain Rescue, combines memories of Judith with an account of Philip's endeavours to fulfil his half of their joint commitment to complete the round. If you want to know whether or not he succeeded, you will have to track down and buy a copy.

Pete Bland, meanwhile, was almost crushed by regret. 'It was a hard cross to bear. She wasn't just a competitor: she was a friend and a customer. Unfortunately, there was nothing anybody could do about it. The rules were in place; the checkpoints were all marshalled; she was carrying the right gear and everything.'

At the inquest, it was suggested by the coroner that Pete had been at fault for not cancelling the race – a suggestion that makes less sense the longer you examine it. Should a fell race be called off whenever there is a possibility of severe weather? If so, half the fell races ever run have arguably been reckless. And if the weather deteriorates suddenly after the start, does a mid-race abandonment – inevitably a somewhat chaotic process – reduce the risk or add to it? Pete pointed out that his main concern had been for the safety of his marshalls – who, being motionless at their checkpoints, are more exposed to cold than runners moving at speed; and that they were happy to continue. He could also point to the fact that he had offered to refund the entrance fees of any competitors who didn't fancy running in what were clearly going to be fairly harsh conditions; and to the fact that, whatever he had done, and whatever the weather, there would always be an element of risk to life and limb in that kind of fell race.

But the fact remained that a much-loved wife and mother was dead. Shrugging off such tragedies as part of life's cruel tapestry is not something that comes naturally to the modern world – people like someone to blame.

'A lot of people spoke up for me at the inquest, including her husband,' says Pete. 'But I had a traumatic time from the press. I had twenty phone calls on the Monday morning after it happened, from different newspapers all wanting the story. The *Daily Express* reporter came on, and wanted a story. I told him to speak to the police, but they hadn't given him what he wanted, so he said: "You're the race organiser, and people are going to point the finger at you, because it's your fault that this lady's died." So I just said eff off and put the phone down. But that upset me – that made me feel really bad.'

Pete Bland wasn't the first race organiser to experience such trauma. As far as I am aware, six competitors have died in British fell races in the past seventy years. Little is recorded about the first two: Phil Altman of Hallamshire Harriers, who died on Bleaklow at Marsden Edale in 1930s; and John Rix of Surrey, who died in the 1957 Ben Nevis race. Both died of exposure. The only other thing I know about Altman's death is that that race was subsequently discontinued, although it was revived in a different form forty years later. Rix was found sheltering behind a boulder about halfway down the mountain, having wandered off course and lost his shoes. He died while being stretchered down.

The death of Ted Pepper in the 1978 Three Peaks provoked more soul-searching. Pepper ran cross-country for Blackheath Harriers and had no experience of racing on wilder terrain. He got lost coming off Ingleborough and was not found for eighteen hours, by which time he had died from hypothermia. Safety regulations for this and other races were subsequently tightened – a process that continued when, three years later, Bob English of Keswick died in the Ennerdale race. Unlike Pepper, English was a hardened fell-runner. A voluntary National Park warden, he had completed the Bob Graham the previous year. He died on a foul day, with strong winds, driving rain and mist down to 500 feet, conditions that prompted sixty-four other competitors to retire. He was well equipped, but he went off course after the final checkpoint on Crag Fell, after which he must have fallen. He was found unconscious above Anglers Crag with serious head injuries and suffering from hypothermia; he died in hospital.

The common threads of such deaths are obvious enough: severe weather, disorientation, exposure. How they might have been prevented is more obscure. English's death led to the publication of a twenty-four-page booklet on safety by the Cumberland Fell Runners Association, organisers of the Ennerdale and forerunners of the FRA, which was adopted by the FRA in 1982. Its recommendations range from insisting that all runners carry full body cover, map, compass and whistle to requiring the race organisers to be aware of the rough whereabouts of all competitors at all times. They form the basis of the sport's safety regulations today. They could not, however, render the sport risk-free.

In 1991, at the Welsh Water Reservoir Relay in the Brecon Beacons, another mild-looking morning turned into a vicious afternoon, and another life was lost. Carol Matthews, a forty-one-year-old mother of two, was running for Penarth & Dinas Runners in her first-ever fell-race. The course was described in the fixture list as 'marked', but the bad visibility led to several runners going astray on the 6-mile leg from Neuadd Reservoir to Pencelli. Matthews was one of them. She was not well clad, and, although she strayed only about half a mile from the route, she never found a way back. Her body was found the next morning.

The aftermath was bitter. The organising club, Mynyddwyr de Cymru, spent more than a year under the shadow of a threatened compensation claim from the Matthews family, while the race organiser, John Brooks, was aggressively cross-examined at the inquest. No damages were paid, but several lessons were learnt: that it is unwise to describe a course as 'marked' unless you are absolutely certain that the markings are foolproof and weatherproof; that it is unwise to assume that runners will carry adequate protective clothing and safety equipment unless explicitly required to do so; and that the only surefire way for race organisers to avoid being blamed for future casualties was to refrain from organising races.

Fellow administrators were aghast to hear Brooks being asked questions such as 'Who took the minutes at the pre-race organisers' meetings?' – and to see his bill for legal representation race into the thousands. One can understand the Matthews family's need to get to the bottom of their shocking loss; but, as the FRA's general secretary, Mike Rose, pointed out at the time, all that John Brooks and his helpers had done was 'work diligently to organise an enjoyable and safe event for their fellow runners, with no thought of personal profit'. If putting on a race meant exposing oneself to the risk of being blamed and held liable for any mishap that terrain and elements could inflict, why, asked Rose, would anyone bother?

A decade later, the world has moved on, and the question is more pertinent than ever. As Pete Bland puts it, 'Every man and his dog wants to sue,' while the mountains remain as unsafe as they have always been. As recently as 2002, I ran in the Borrowdale race and on the ascent from the Langstrath valley to Bessyboot was scarcely 50 yards away from an incident in which a runner was struck on the chest by a large falling boulder, dislodged by one of scores of runners further up the hill. The victim required hospital treatment for broken ribs and a punctured lung; it didn't take much imagination to realise that, had the boulder bounced a few inches higher, it could have killed him. Subsequent issues of the *Fellrunner* have seen impassioned correspondence on this incident. One correspondent argued that the ascent in question – a steep, wooded, muddy, bouldery slope that churns up easily under the feet of 200 competitors – is fundamentally unsafe, and that the organisers should consider themselves lucky not to be the object of a lawsuit. The magazine's editor, Dave Jones, felt moved to present an immediate counterblast, arguing that to remove fell-running's inherent dangers would leave the sport unrecognisable. 'A large portion of the appeal of our sport lies in its freedom, and that includes the freedom to make mistakes, some of which might result in nothing and some of which, in the way of things, might result in injury . . . I suspect that the majority of fell-runners would have it no other way.'

I have no doubt that he is right. But the preferences of most fell-runners are neither here nor there in the age of no-win-no-fee and Claims Direct. What matters is the likely view of a jury ('most of whom,' as another correspondent put it, 'will probably be simply incredulous at what we get up to at weekends'); and, even more so, the likely view of the insurance companies – because, of course, no one in their right mind would organise a fell race without insurance, and insurance companies hate risk.

'The climate's changed a lot in the past few years,' says Jones, a big, cheerful ex-headmaster from Greater Manchester who drifted into (unpaid) magazine-editing because, like most of the sport's administrators, he 'wanted to put something back'. These days, he says, 'a lot of new people are coming into the sport, and some of the attitudes they're bringing in are more the attitudes of athletes who are used to being treated like thoroughbreds. It's a different mindset. They don't think: if I'm going out in the hills in filthy weather, what do I need to take? They see that as someone else's responsibility. That's wrong.'

Traditionally, the FRA has shunned publicity, in order to discourage any troublesome influx of naïve outsiders. But the recent growth of international mountain-running competitions has created opposite pressures: for fresh athletic blood from track and road, and for the kind of profile and membership base that can generate funds for international campaigns. As a result, it is no longer safe to assume that, in any given race, most competitors will have a solid grounding in mountaincraft. In some races, the naïve outsiders may be in the majority. Can ruinous litigation be far behind?

The FRA places its faith in the idea that, as long as competitors are not forced to take a particular 'dangerous' route – that is, as long as the route choice from A to B is left to each runner's discretion – then the race organisers cannot be blamed if competitors put themselves at risk by choosing a route that turns out to be dangerous. But this presupposes that, in a sport of this nature, there are *any* safe routes.

Meanwhile, a surprising number of born-and-bred fell-runners express a deep ideological aversion to any rules, about safety or anything else. 'When I came to amateur fell-running,' one reinstated professional told me, 'a big part of what attracted me was the freedom of the hills. We don't want to be told what to do. We want to be responsible for ourselves.'

For some, this means deliberately flouting safety regulations – by, for example, refusing to carry full body cover and emergency equipment even when the organiser's rules explicitly require them. Others take pleasure in looking for loopholes. 'When it says you have to carry map and compass,' one old rebel told me, 'it doesn't say you have to be able to use them. But a map's no use to me. I never take my glasses – they steam up – so I can't read it. I'm not breaking any rules, though. Come to think of it, it doesn't usually say *what* map you have to carry. Maybe you could just take a page of the London *A–Z*.'

On a slightly less childish level, it's instructive to note the outrage that ensued when, for example, the 1980 Ben Nevis race was cancelled because of 'dangerous' weather conditions higher up. Runners such as Billy Bland – who had been training for the event all year, was in the best form of his life and had made a significant sacrifice of time and money to get to the event – were apoplectic with rage; Premiership footballers have been known to accept adverse penalty decisions with better grace. A hard core of nine competitors ran to the top and back anyway, and insisted that the conditions had been innocuous. Others doubted their word. Either way, you can understand the runners' frustration – and imagine the opprobrium that would have been heaped on the organisers' heads if the race had gone ahead and someone had died.

Tormented on one hand by those who expect to be cosseted and on the other by those who refuse to be cosseted, organisers are in an unenviable position. The wiser runners realise this – including Billy Bland, whose wife's involvement with the Borrowdale has taught him more about the administrators' perspective in the decades since that Ben disappointment. 'I was furious with the organisers,' he says today. 'As far as I was concerned there was nothing wrong with that day. But I think now I know a bit more from Ann's point of view, so I wouldn't slag them off completely. I didn't think it was a bad day, but I guess they weren't thinking of me.'

Ann Bland, meanwhile, has rerouted the start of the Borrowdale to avoid that 'dangerous' climb up Bessyboot. You can understand why, and no doubt the FRA will be relieved. But those who run in the mountains in the hope of escaping the stifling grip that litigators and insurers exercise over the rest of our lives may feel a stab of regret – and wonder where it will all end.

Organising fell races, like organising anything, tends to be a thankless task. Trevor Batchelor organised races for BOFRA, week in, week out, for twelve years, from 1982 to 1994, and, he says, 'Every single week, there was always someone, somewhere, who was going to have a go at you. "I wasn't ninth, I was tenth . . .", "You spelt my name wrong in the results . . ." – that sort of thing. Sometimes I despaired.' Nonetheless, he felt sufficient devotion to his sport to keep races happening, and enriched thousands of lives by doing so.

Today, every fell race that happens does so as a result of similar public-spiritedness on the part of some private individual or other. Some of these individuals strike me as positively saintly: Dave and Eileen Woodhead, for example, who every year organise eight or nine senior races (and nearly as many junior ones) in the Keighley area; or (also in West Yorkshire) Allan Greenwood, who organises around a dozen – some of which I have mentioned already – around Ogden Water, Mytholmroyd and Wadsworth. (The numbers are vague because both have a propensity to lay on extra events on the spur of the moment, often in aid of a good cause.)

Greenwood, a printer from Cleckheaton, also likes to lend a hand to other organisers – 'when I'm feeling daft enough to stand on top of a hill in the rain' – and, when he can, to run in races himself. For his impending forty-second birthday, he's hoping to fit in a quick Bob Graham. How does he manage it? 'Er, basically, I never, ever stop – I'm always doing something.' He's been doing this for a dozen years, essentially because 'it gives you such a feeling of satisfaction – having a little idea in your head and then working it all out and having people come up to you afterwards and say what a great time they had.' And who keeps the minutes of his pre-race meetings? He laughs. 'We don't have meetings. We just get a bag of flags out of the car and say: right lads, here we go.'

Perhaps there are people who would consider Greenwood the

kind of person from whom society needs protecting. No doubt they would feel the same about the Woodheads, whose races (the oldest of which has been going for twenty years) are famous less for their severity than for their jolly family atmosphere, with prizes for everyone (a bottle of beer at the New Year's Eve Auld Lang Syne race; maltloaf at the Stanbury Splash; Easter eggs at the Bunny Run series) and prize-givings that, according to Dave, 'ought to be as memorable as the race itself'. Once a leading runner himself ('I won a few races, but I was never in the Ian Holmes class'), Dave was goaded into the administrative side 'after someone said, "If you think you can do better, go and organise a race yourself." ' It's generally accepted that he's become pretty good at it, and consistently large fields are testament to the popularity of his inclusive philosophy, which holds that 'if it wasn't for all the people behind Ian Holmes, Ian Holmes wouldn't be a winner'. He's particularly proud of his 'quarry races' for children – as he says: 'children give so much back'; somehow I doubt, though, that these strictly comply with European Playground Safety Standards.

Does he worry at all about the threat of litigation? 'Yes, it obviously does worry us. But . . .' He tails off. 'The weather isn't a problem for our races, because they're fairly short, and they all start from quite a high point, so you can tell at the start what the conditions are going to be like on the course. But these days, with this American thing of no-win, no-fee, you never know. We've had someone break an ankle, and they were fine about it, which is what you'd expect. Most fell-runners are down-to-earth people, and they take responsibility for what they choose do. But you can never tell who'll come along next.'

Such concerns have caused the Fellrunners' Association to recommend that, for long races over more exposed terrain, organisers should provide an alternative 'bad weather route' on lower ground. Is this a helpful idea – or just an example of the kind of backside-covering that litigation culture encourages? Selwyn Wright, a former FRA chairman who organises the notoriously tough Three Shires race over 12 mountainous miles around Langdale, Cumbria, recently announced that he was not prepared to organise such a route for his race. His reasons are worth examining. 'If you make it the organiser's responsibility to make the race as safe as possible,' he explains, 'then you take individual responsibility away from the person on the hill. I don't want people to think that, if the weather's bad, they shouldn't worry. I *want* them to worry, and to take responsibility for themselves – which is what most fell-runners currently do. I attended the inquests of both Judith Taylor and Carol Matthews, so of course I'm concerned about safety. But I don't want people to come along to the Three Shires race who think that I'll take all the responsibility away from them. I'd sooner let them know the dangers, and that if they don't have the right equipment and the right attitude, they're better off not coming. The last thing we want is an influx of people who think it's *safe* to do fell-running.'

This strikes me as a fairly persuasive argument; but, as we've already seen, what people like me think is neither here nor there. What matter are the opinions of coroners, lawyers and jurors whose empathy for the sport might be no deeper than Lord Hutton's empathy for journalism. And, as Wright concedes, 'in the event of a tragedy, the person who's doing the race – who might see things exactly as we see them – isn't the one who's going to sue. Their dependents might take a completely different attitude.'

In which case, what should organisers like Wright do? Make sure they're on the right side of the law – or on the right side of their conscience? It's the kind of dilemma that most of us prefer to leave to someone else.

Dave Jones organises a couple of races himself: one of them a gentle 8-miler from his local pub and the other a trans-Pennine relay involving up to a dozen clubs between Sheffield and Manchester. Neither could be described as logistically simple: there's parking to be arranged, and traffic police and mountain rescue to be organised, and time-keeping, and toilets, and marshalls (half a dozen even for the smaller of the two), and route definition, and FRA approval to be sought (in order to get the benefit of their insurance), and landowners' permission for access, and prizes and prize-giving, plus answers to any number of questions and quarrels generated by the inevitable cock-ups and confusions on the day. Even without the risk of being held responsible for any accidents in the course of the race, these are the kind of burdens for which most people consider life too short. And for someone like Jones – who is already producing a quarterly magazine in his free time, serving on the FRA committee and, in the latter capacity, advising less experienced organisers on how to make their races work – there is an obvious temptation to knock it all on the head. He mutters darkly about the prospect of insurers providing 'tick lists' and says: 'If anyone started saying that one of my races needed a formal "risk assessment", then maybe that would be the time to stop.' If similar broodings are running through the heads of even a few dozen of the two or three hundred people in Britain who currently organise races, then the future of the sport may be less healthy than it seems. But presumably the law would consider that a good thing.

In fact, where there are obvious steps that organisers can take to reduce the likelihood of competitors coming to harm, they generally need no encouragement to take them. Pete Bland, for example, moved the Kentmere race from April to July shortly after Judith Taylor's death. 'A lot of people have said that they don't like it in July,' he says, 'and you don't get nearly as big fields as you used to. But I have the peace of mind that if someone gets lost it's not too cold. I think that a lot of the legislation that's coming from the government with reference to extreme sports is over the top, but that's the world we live in. Meanwhile, the one thing I will never, ever do is organise another fell race in winter.'

But some people *want* to race in winter. For some, fair-weather fell-running provides insufficient challenge and escape. As Selwyn Wright puts it, 'I know there's a risk, but then isn't that why we all head for the fells anyway?' What does the future hold for this kind of fell-runner? There is, presumably, nothing that anyone can do to stop me if I decide that I want to try and join that elite handful (including Wright) who have completed the Bob Graham in winter – despite the obvious risks of falls, injuries and exposure exacerbated by exhaustion. But if I made such an attempt and came to grief, where would that leave the Bob Graham 24 Hour Club, whose officials have been known to honour winter rounds with special commendations (reserving the highest praise for those conducted within a fortnight of the shortest day)? Could they be held liable for my injuries, on the grounds that they had encouraged me? And what about the countless injuries and illnesses that have been sustained, over the years, in the course of thousands of unsuccessful summer attempts? I find it all too easy to envisage a lawsuit – and the consequent destruction of the Bob Graham 24 Hour Club and much else besides.

I am sure I am not the only fell-runner to have noticed a report in the *Sunday Telegraph* on 17 August 2003, headlined 'HSE Has No Head For Heights'. The report (subsequently repeated, with embellishments, in other papers) claimed that the Health and Safety Executive – interpreting the EU's 'Working at Heights' directive 2001/45 – was laying down rules that will extend to the rockface safety regulations originally designed for building sites, including the requirement that notices be erected to warn mountain-users when they are about to cross 'fragile or brittle surfaces' such as snowfields and icy rock. Reading between the lines of the report, one realises that the regulations must apply only to mountain 'workplaces' – that is, places where licensed instructors teach 'adventure' activities such as climbing and caving. But how long will it be before licensed adventures are the only kind permitted?

The same newspaper reported the following year that GCSE geography field trips will increasingly be replaced by simulated 'virtual trips' – 'because of fears that real outdoor trips could be too dangerous'. Britain's second largest teaching union, the NAS/UWT, had advised its members to refuse to take children on such trips, on the grounds that 'society no longer appears to accept the concept of a genuine accident'. Does this surprise you? I doubt it. But the implications are depressing. It becomes easier by the year to envisage a future in which treacherous surfaces are deemed as unacceptable on mountains as on pavements. It's rather harder to see how this will make Britain a better place.

There is one other death that deserves a mention in this chapter.

In March 2003, Chris Bland, Billy's cousin, hanged himself in a Borrowdale car park. He was sixty-two years old, and left behind a wife, three children and scores of friends and admirers – all devastated. He had lived and worked all his life in the Borrowdale valley, mostly as a stonemason, and was known as a rock of the community. He was a church warden, a local cricketer, a co-begetter of Keswick Athletic Club, the co-creator of the Borrowdale race, an orienteer, an energetic fund-raiser, and a man who spoke up for local people at, for example, planning inquiries. He was, by common consent, a good man, more concerned with what he could give than with what he could take. Some might have felt overshadowed by all that superior athletic talent in the family, but Chris – who once came seventh in the Keswick club championship with six Blands ahead of him – wasn't that kind of person. Beyond being able to earn his keep, live in Borrowdale and enjoy the freedom of his local fells, he asked little for himself. Neil Shuttleworth, a former Keswick runner who wrote a tribute to him in the *Fellrunner*, remembers him as 'decent, kind and honourable'; Ross Brewster as 'such a relaxed, easy-going chap'; Dave Spedding as 'a gentleman and one who stood up for the people of the valley'; Miles Jessop as 'a wonderful man and a terrible loss'.

As far as anyone could tell, Chris had been suffering from depression since the foot-and-mouth crisis of 2001 put an end to his orienteering activities and prevented him from gathering stone for his work. It's an all-too-familiar Cumbrian story. Even when the immediate crisis was over, the damage – the sense of shattered certainties – remained. A man with enough native optimism to have repeatedly attempted the all-but-impossible – starting an athletic club, creating an epic race on his own back doorstep, running all the Wainwrights in a week – was left without hope. 'He thought everything was going down the pan,' his widow told the inquest. His sister-in-law added that he had told her that he felt he could not work properly, and that he was letting his wife and family down.

And so Chris Bland, co-creator of the Borrowdale race, inspiration behind the Wainwrights round, organiser and instigator of countless initiatives that have enriched life on and around the Borrowdale fells and a hero to hundreds of fell-runners both local and otherwise, took his own life because he considered himself a failure.

I feel uncomfortable intruding even this far into so very personal a tragedy. I have done so for two reasons. Firstly, because so many people in the fell-running community seem so profoundly shaken and saddened by it. And, secondly, because it reminds us that there are other risks in life apart from the various hazards one encounters in the mountains – and that one of those risks is the loss of one's dreams.

22

Lost and found

I'M LYING IN A PUDDLE IN A FIELD IN SCOTLAND, an icy wind screaming overhead. I'm caked from head to foot in sweat and mud, despite having spent five minutes in a freezing river, fully clothed, trying to rinse the worst of it off – followed by quarter of an hour standing in the wind, arms spread like a cormorant's wings, trying to get vaguely dry. The nearest hot tap is probably 20 miles away. But at least Lewis and I have managed to get our tiny tent up; and, although liquid mud from the waterlogged field is already seeping through the door, we're a great deal warmer and drier than we have been all day. We're also not running, which, to be honest, is all that really matters. Instead, we're lying in the tent, sharing an ex-fruitcake that has been battered back into its constituent parts, and washing it down with some minestrone Cup-o'-Soup from a shared mug that still carries the flavour of that morning's tea. It is, by some distance, the most delicious meal I have ever tasted.

We are sharing the field with some 350 other pairs, all of whom have spent the day roaming one of Scotland's most notoriously wet mountain ranges on possibly the wettest day of a two-month local wet spell that we're told has been the wettest for half a century. The range in question is the Trossachs, and we're halfway through the Lowe Alpine Mountain Marathon (universally known as the LAMM), a two-day event which began that morning at a flooded campsite near Brig o' Turk.

The object of the exercise, as with all mountain marathons, is to navigate our way to a series of obscure and distant checkpoints as quickly as possible, while carrying with us all our needs for a night in the open (including compulsory cooking gear). The following day, we will set out in search of a new series of checkpoints, equally obscure and distant; after which we should end up back at the original campsite (whose location was first revealed to us only thirty-six hours ago) and – assuming we're not too late for the coach back to Glasgow – will be able to go home.

There are several problems with this programme. First: the checkpoints, details of which are given to us a few minutes before the start, are tiny objects the size and colour of traffic cones, the only clues to whose location are six-figure grid references and bald descriptions such as 'stream junction' or 'south facing re-entrant'. (A re-entrant, I'm told – after several decades of mountain enjoyment in which I have never encountered the term – is a kind of crease in a hillside: the concave opposite of a spur.) Second: the entire range is immersed in dense cloud, from which rain is cascading so heavily that it's sometimes hard to keep your eyes open. You can't even spot a large mountain 100 metres in front of you, let alone a small dent therein. Third: there's no point in following other competitors. There are six different courses, according to standard, and scores of different starting times. So it's highly unlikely that any given pair you spot will be looking for the same thing that you're looking for. Fourth: everything is so waterlogged that parts of the landscape have changed beyond recognition, with raging rivers where the map records only dry re-entrants and small lakes where the map records nothing. Fifth: at one early river crossing I was almost swept away by the torrent, and, lunging to save myself, broke my compass on a rock. Sixth: most of my map has disintegrated in the rain. (As a mountain-marathon novice, I didn't realise that I'd need an extra-large map case to house the organisers' specially printed map.) Seventh: with no sun, and identical grey cloud and watery grass wherever one looks, I have completely lost my sense of direction. Eighth: the ground is so waterlogged that I keep slipping over – a problem exacerbated by the fact that, expecting damp rock rather than sodden grass, I've opted to wear flat-soled ankle-boots rather than studded shoes. Ninth: I can't keep up with my partner.

Everything else would be tolerable without this last problem. Lewis, a Welsh-born computer expert from Cambridge, with whom I teamed up twenty-four hours earlier after my original partner dropped out with a sprained ankle, is a brilliant orienteer, on whose better judgment I'm happy to sponge. He's also ten years younger than me and far fitter. Two months ago, we both ran the London Marathon. My time was 3 hours 15 minutes; his was 2 hours 45 minutes. His sensible, sustainable pace is my unsustainable surge. And a whole day of surging desperately in his wake – interspersed with half-a-dozen falls per hour and twice as many narrow escapes – has led me into hitherto unimagined depths of miserable exhaustion.

Three thoughts have sustained me so far. First: the obvious point that giving up is out of the question. I haven't the first idea where we are, but I know that it's nowhere near civilisation. The alternative to continuing is death – or at least a shameful mountain-rescue call-out. Second: there are more than 700 other people doing this, some of them female and some a decade or more older than me – they can't all be super-human. Third: nothing goes on for ever, and somewhere in my rucksack, along with food, stove, cooking utensils and spare clothing, is a sleeping bag that may well still be dry.

Now, lying in my puddle and savouring the subtle nuances of minestrone-and-fruitcake, I'm toying with the idea of extracting that sleeping bag from its plastic bag when Lewis, who doesn't know me well, says, rather seriously: 'Can I ask you a question?'

'Of course,' I say.

'Are you enjoying this?'

'Absolutely,' I say. 'Best thing I ever tasted.'

'No, not this. *Today*. Have you enjoyed today?'

I think deeply. I think back to our 5 a.m. wake-up call from a lone, demented bagpiper, and to the cheerful chaos of the campsite that morning, awash with mud and midges, with 700 campers slooshing amiably about in search of breakfast, Portaloos and last-minute items of kit. Yes, I enjoyed that. It's a curious thing about fell-running that, at any event you go to, you can speak to any stranger you bump into and they'll always have a friendly word to share. (The only other group of people of whom I'd say the same are motorcyclists.) I also enjoyed our long, scenic journey – more than an hour by coach and steamboat – from Brig o' Turk to the race starting point, deep in the mountains at the far end of Loch Katrine. And now, at this new campsite, equally waterlogged and amiable, with a circle of grey-green mountains rising peacefully into the encircling cloud banks, I once again feel happy to be where I am. I tell this to Lewis, but he is unconvinced.

'What about the bit in between?'

I think again. Enjoyment? Did I enjoy being winded by too quick a scramble up the mudslide of the first hill? Did I enjoy that half-hour we wasted, wandering in increasingly frustrated circles while the rain switched from heavy to torrential, trying to locate the first checkpoint at the top of that same hill? Did I enjoy all those falls, or my growing desperation as, with each succeeding hour, my struggle to keep up with the pace grew more hopeless? Did I enjoy arriving at the sixth and most distant checkpoint half-dead with exhaustion and realising that there were not two more legs to go (as I'd been imagining for the past hour) but three? No, I tell Lewis; no, I can't honestly say that I do remember a great deal of enjoyment.

'So why do you do it, then?'

It's a good question, which doesn't apply only to mountain marathons, but I struggle to answer it. Instead, I contemplate the hundreds of evidently happy campers around me and ask myself – as I've asked myself at many fell-running events – if they are somehow different from me. Am I the only one who feels the cold? The only one whose feet and joints get sore? The only one who dislikes feeling sick with extreme exhaustion? Years of discreet enquiries suggest not.

Yes, there are a few superheroes who appear to be immune to physical discomfort. An obvious example is the organiser of this event, Martin Stone, who, not content with becoming the first person to complete all three of the great British twenty-four-hour rounds, also insisted on doing them all solo and unsupported, and did two of them – the Bob Graham and the Paddy Buckley – in the depths of winter. He told me once about how, during his winter BG, he got stuck on the frozen side of Bowfell, 'unable to go up or down', and how, on another occasion, he was almost literally blown off the Helvellyn ridge, when a violent blizzard appeared from nowhere and the ground was so icy that even lying down on it wasn't enough to guarantee stability. Just listening was enough to put me off winter fell-running for life. Yet he seems to regard those experiences as among the happiest of his life.

But most fell-runners I know feel – and dislike – the sport's pains. Those who persist see them as the price that must be paid for the compensatory pleasures. These include the scenery (doesn't apply on days with zero visibility), the conversation (doesn't apply on days when you can't keep up), the joy of being outdoors in the wilderness (doesn't apply in foul weather), the joy of making full use of your physical powers (doesn't apply when you're having an off-day), and the joy – which applies all the more when the other pleasures don't – of it all being over, and of being able to share your relief with like-minded people.

It's possible that, not having grown up in the mountains, I may be more sensitive to the pains than some, in the same way that there are some London gym-bunnies who would feel physically traumatised by what I would consider an entirely unremarkable winter training run across muddy Northamptonshire fields; and I suppose it must be a *bit* easier if you're a few stone lighter and a decade younger. But we're all made of the same flesh and blood. And although it's tempting, looking around at the others in the field, to conclude that I am the only person here who has found today a physically distressing experience, subsequent enquiries – and a fairly large drop-out rate for the second day – suggest otherwise.

I can see no sign, however, that anyone is unhappy about the lack of hot baths and comfortable beds. This seems perverse. If ever there was a day that demanded hot baths and comfortable beds at the end of it – not to mention hot meals and plentiful beer – this is it. But there's something about the lack of mod cons that adds to the appeal of the event; and which is, presumably, part of the reason why people do it.

Christopher Brasher, taking part in the Karrimor International Mountain Marathon in 1972, tried to extract from his fellow competitors some explanation of why they did it – but could extract nothing more helpful than: 'Oh, come on, Chris, you know why.' Later, writing in his *Observer* column, he speculated thus: 'Perhaps it is escape from the pressure of life, but really it is more than this: it is proof that, sophisticated man though you may be, you can still go out with all your worldly needs on your back and survive in the wild places of Britain. That knowledge is great freedom.'

That seems to put it pretty well, but, more than thirty years later, it doesn't tell the whole story. We are richer now, but also more overworked, more deeply in thrall to the addictions of getting and spending. We have more possessions, and they tyrannise us. Each new mod con must be shopped for, maintained, insured, upgraded; each new *thing* must be stored, kept track of, kept secure, tidied; and the whole package is paid for in overwork, time-poverty, round-the-clock availability and round-the-clock insecurity. We have more, and we have less.

In such a world, freedom is both more precious and more elusive than ever. And one of the few surefire ways of liberating ourselves from the tyranny of the consumer society is to put ourselves beyond its reach. This is one of the attractions of all long days in the hills: you escape from all those *things*. It's also an attraction of many forms of adventure racing, and of that small number of elaborate challenges (for example, the Scottish Island Peaks, the Three Peaks Yacht Race) that combine fell-running with yachting. But it seems to me to be a particular attraction of mountain-marathon-running, because, whereas as some of the more exotic events carry their own temptations to consumerism (better boats, better bikes, better kayaks), with mountain-marathon-running the whole point is to carry as little equipment as possible. Success depends on what you have in your head and your heart; the less you have in your backpack the better.

To reach the end of a long, hard day and realise that you have no more chores awaiting you than to crawl into a lightweight tent and extract food from Bag A and sleeping bag from Bag B is to feel a stifling grip, of whose pressure you might not previously have been fully conscious, dramatically releasing your neck and shoulders. There is nothing to distract you from the once-simple business of being human, eating and talking and resting beneath the stars. And if the price of this escape is a night without beds, electricity and running water, who cares? You just have to think positively – which, sustained for a whole weekend, is in itself a hugely refreshing experience.

None of which is either here or there when, as darkness falls, Martin Stone addresses us all. It has, he tells us, been an exceptionally and unexpectedly hard day. Some people have dropped out already, and arrangements are in place to get them back to the Event Centre tomorrow. If any of us feels unable to continue, we should contact him now, and similar arrangements will be made for us. Alternatively, we may prefer to switch down to the Novice Course (the easiest of the six) for the second day, so that we can 'enjoy' our return journey without subjecting ourselves to intolerable strain.

It's a tricky moment. The thought of not having to subject myself to a repeat of today's tortures is impossibly tempting, consumer society or no consumer society. Just imagine: a gentle walk, or, better still, a lift in some kind of vehicle, and then straight into a warm, dry coach . . .

Lewis looks at me in a concerned way: 'What do you reckon?' Before I can reply, he adds, sympathetically: 'It's OK by me if you want to stop.'

'Pull out!' scream my damp, aching bones. 'I'll be fine,' I mutter half-heartedly, and wait for him to insist that I won't.

He doesn't.

Ah well. It's a catastrophic blow to my immediate yearnings, but I can't help suspecting that it would have hurt more to admit defeat. At least now I can soothe my aches with the balm of self-congratulation. I'll just have to get back to the positive thinking.

And, when I do, it's surprising how good it feels. Rain, mountains, wind – so what? It beats going shopping.

Shortly afterwards, trying hard to think not of tomorrow but simply of the warmth of my sleeping bag and the amazing softness of the waterlogged earth, I sink into the sweetest of sleeps.

An instant later – or, more exactly, at 5 a.m. the next morning – I'm woken from dreams of sofas and central heating by that same deranged piper, playing (I'm subsequently told) '10 Battalion the HLI Crossing the Rhine' and 'Pipe Major Donald Maclean of Lewis'. Every trace of positive thinking has vanished with the night. My bones ache; my joints ache; even my brain feels cold and damp. All I can think of – and on sober reflection, I have to say that it's not a bad rule of thumb – is that you should never trust a fell-running event that involves bagpipes.

Lewis, who was snoring when I dropped off the night before, is utterly silent and still. He does not even seem to be breathing. Is he dead, I wonder? I'm ashamed to confess that part of me feels disappointed when he finally stirs and stretches. So we *will* have to run today, after all. Oh well, back to the positive thinking.

This is soon sorely tested, for a reason that has been preying on my mind ever since we arrived. Take 700 runners and put them in a field overnight, and the one thing you can be certain of is that, before they start running again, they will all want to evacuate their bowels. Put them in a field miles from the nearest drainage, and you have a problem. Solution: trench latrines. So: about a minute's walk from the main camping area there are two large canvas windbreaks, one marked 'Ladies' and the other marked 'Gents'. Behind each windbreak is a trench, each about the length of a cricket pitch but only a quarter of the width, and each about 6 feet deep. Into these, all 700 of us must, to put it plainly, shit.

For the first few dozen, who presumably sneaked over while the bagpiper was still warming up, this may have been an only moderately unpleasant experience. For those of us who have been putting it off until the last minute before the final 7 a.m. start, it is altogether more challenging. By now, the trench behind the 'Gents' sign has been squatted over and shat in by well over 500 men. The stench is indescribable; there's a serious danger of passing out. Worse, the ground is so waterlogged that the sides have been collapsing under the weight of the squatters, leaving latecomers with an awkward choice between falling short or falling in. Rumour has it that one man already *has* fallen in, although I cannot confirm this. One version of the rumour insists that he is still in there.

I won't trouble you with more detail. Just take it from me that this is one of the less enjoyable aspects of escaping the shackles of consumerism. Then again, once it's over, it's over, and you can reimmerse yourself with fresh enthusiasm in the pleasures of being in the wilderness. And, by comparison, the prospect of any further ordeals that the wilderness has in store for you seems – for the time being – mild.

In fact, our second day of wet-weather orienteering is in some ways more painful than the first. My legs seem to lose the will to live more or less immediately. The rain seems heavier, the cloud denser, the checkpoints harder to find and further apart. And although today's map has yet to disintegrate, that's only because it's in the bottom of my rucksack. I still have only the vaguest idea of where we are – and Lewis is still just a shadowy figure in the mist ahead.

Yet one thing I do know: we are on the way home. As the hours pass, this thought sustains a small flame of hope. This cannot, I remind myself, go on for ever.

Nor does it. Towards the end of the morning, the rain stops. Then, slowly, the cloud begins to vanish. Around noon, I become aware of that most glorious of mountain sensations: the sun on my back, drying out first my clothes, then my skin, then my bones. I'm still knackered, but the hope is burning more strongly within.

To boost me further, the waterlogged grass gives way to a series of long slopes of deep heather in which my ankle boots come into their own. Where others are picking their way more tentatively than before, I can relax and stretch out. Suddenly we are overtaking people; in fact, after flying down one long downhill, I have to wait for Lewis to catch up. And before long there's only –

by the most pessimistic calculation – a couple of hours to go. (I'm not sure what this calculation can have been based on, given my ignorance of our whereabouts, but such straws are useful to cling to even when fallacious.)

Eventually, we are near enough – and the views are clear enough – for me to be able to see where we're going. It's a doubly morale-boosting sight, both because it proves that the end is within reach and because the loch-spotted valley below is stunningly beautiful – as is the sweet scent of drying heather all around us. My legs, fillipped, come back to life, and our final half-hour is, though I say it myself, pretty good. We overtake about fifteen pairs – not all of them doing the same course as us – and at some points it's me who is making the pace. This is partly attributable to a pig-headed desire on my part to prove to Lewis and myself that I'm not yet a spent force. It's also because I'm anxious not to miss the early coach back to Glasgow, whose departure time is getting ominously close. (Most competitors have other transport arrangements, but for the handful of us who are returning to the South there are some tight connections to be made.)

Our final position – fifty-fifth out of a hundred in the B class – is not impressive in objective terms. It has, for example, taken us several hours longer than it took the winners of the far longer Elite course. But I take great pride in the fact that we not only kept going but actually gained half-a-dozen places on the second day.

I also take great satisfaction from the fact that, after an attempted wash in a muddy water trough, a quick change into dry clothing, some frenzied packing and a final heavily-laden sprint, we catch the bus, which, in turn, makes it to Glasgow with minutes to spare. Within two hours of crossing the finish line, I'm on a cheap easyJet flight back to the Midlands. I stink. I'm stiffening up agonisingly. I'm gorging myself on one of the most unappealing-looking decomposed pasties that can ever have been considered for human consumption – and I can't look much better myself. But I'm glowing with pride. I've exposed myself to one of the toughest wilderness experiences imaginable, and I've survived.

I am, of course, deceiving myself. In fact, this is nothing like the toughest wilderness experience I could have tried. Even within British fell-running, there are harder tests: the KIMM, which takes place in winter, or the Great Lakeland Three-Day Mountain Marathon, or one of the aforementioned yacht-and-run or adventure races. There's also any number of self-tailored trials – solo unsupported extensions of the Ramsay round, and so forth. And there's the wider world, right the way up to Arctic exploration and the Himalayas, where a few British fell-runners do sometimes test themselves.

But that's not what I mean. The satisfaction of an event such as the LAMM lies not in the toughness of its tests (which vary according to which level you choose) but in their purity. You have to find your way, perfectly, in an environment in which your natural reaction would be to get lost; you have to keep yourself alive and well in an environment in which your natural reaction would be to succumb to exhaustion and hypothermia; and you have to use whatever athletic abilities you possess to the full, when your natural reaction is to feel sorry for yourself. It is, in other words, a test of self-reliance, mountaincraft and survival skills.

In this respect, mountain marathons have much in common with what many top fell-runners consider to be their sport's supreme test: the Mountain Trial. This is an orienteering event of between 15 and 25 miles that is held in a different part of the Lake District each year, usually in September. Unlike conventional orienteering, it is not just about navigation: it is an all-round trial of your ability to move quickly, safely and accurately through rough mountains. The navigation is deliberately hard, with competitors repeatedly faced with difficult but crucial route dilemmas, over terrain where it is all too easy to get lost or injured and where bad weather – which historically is more likely than not – can be devastatingly debilitating.

The quality of the competition means that, to stand a chance of winning, you must do everything at extraordinary speed; but anyone who finishes at all is considered to have acquitted themselves with honour, because the real point of the event – like that of the LAMM – is to test self-sufficiency in the wilderness. A list of the top Mountain Triallists of the past fifty years reads like a hall of fame of amateur fell-running, from Joe Hand, Ted Dance and George Brass to Mike Davies, Joss Naylor and Billy and Gavin Bland; and, among the women, Ros Coats, Sue Parkin and Angela Brand-Barker. But there's as much sense of history in the list of regular also-rans: Fred Bagley, Stanley Bradshaw, Chris Brasher, Jon Broxap, Mike Cudahy, the Heaton brothers, Ken Ledward, Martin Stone, Hugh Symonds, Harry Walker, Pete Walkington, Miriam Rosen, Wendy Dodds. Not all of these were great athletes in the sense that, say, Kenny Stuart was. But they are the British men and women who, more than any others, were at home in the mountains in the second half of the twentieth century. No matter how hostile and remote the terrain in which you were to put any one of them, they could look after themselves.

It's interesting that the event on which the Mountain Trial community looks back with greatest pride is the 1962 contest, in which the weather was so atrocious that all but one of the runners (who included Joss Naylor, Eric Beard, Alan Heaton and Joe Hand) failed to finish. Some of the pride relates to George Brass, the indomitable winner who hobbled home after 6 hours 50 minutes with only one surviving shoe; but most of it relates to the fact that, as A. Harry Griffin wrote in the *Lancaster Evening Post* at the time, '37 of the 38 competitors decided at one stage or another ... that to stick it out any longer would be to court disaster – and they had to make the difficult decision at a point where they had sufficient reserves to get back to base'.

What an inquest or insurance company would have made of it had anyone come to grief hardly bears thinking about. The combination of gales, deluge, mist and cold was unquestionably life-threatening. There were reports of competitors being forced to 'cling to rocks or fall prone to stop themselves being blown into steep gorges'. But no one considered his safety to be anyone's responsibility but his own. And, as Griffin went on to observe: 'The fact that only one man finished the whole course is not nearly so important as the fact that 38 runners knew exactly their own capabilities under the most trying conditions they are ever likely to experience. Thirty-eight mountain men went off into the unknown with their maps and compasses and returned safely, having tested themselves to the utmost. Some were lost for a time, but all extricated themselves.'

I don't pretend for a minute that my own feeble adventures bear comparison to those of the great Mountain Triallists, let alone to Brass's. But I suspect that my post-LAMM sense of satisfaction may be partly attributable to a feeling that I am beginning to share in their world. I, too, have been through an ordeal which a less self-sufficient person might have found intolerable. I have come close to my limits, without being reckless enough to exceed them. I have shrugged off the counsels of despair from my feebler, urban self. And I have come through the ordeal without disgracing myself.

After leaving the airport – still less than four hours after the finish – I find myself stuck in a motorway tailback on the final stretch back to Northamptonshire. I drum my dashboard in frustration and worry that my rickety old Renault may be about to overheat. Better book it in for a service in the morning – except that I won't have time before rushing off to work. Damn. Maybe it's time to cut my losses and get something slightly newer – except that I haven't any money, and, even if I had, I'd need it for repairs to the house; and, of course, for our impending family holiday, for which I really must find time to start packing soon.

Then I pause for a moment and think. How quickly and completely I have been re-entangled in the tentacles of the consumer society: the constant hurrying, the striving with crowds, the possessions clamouring for attention, the anxieties and deadlines and timetables . . . I think myself back to the peace of the previous evening: to the comfort of that muddy puddle, the deep calm of that well-earned rest, and the sense of freedom I felt on contemplating the wild, windy, moonlit void above us. And, for a moment, I feel the grip loosening on my shoulders again.

I must not forget this, I say to myself. In fact – and I don't think I've ever said this so soon after a painful fell-running event – I must do this more often.

23

Scenes from a fell-running year: August

For some, August is synonymous with short races: Grasmere and Burnsall (of which more later); and many other straight-up-and-down dashes that have descended from the old shepherds' meets. BOFRA has more than a quarter of its calendar crammed into this month, with events at Grassington, Hawkswick, Gargrave, Malham, Hebden and Reeth (all in North Yorkshire). If daredevil descents are your thing, this is the time and place to see them.

But there are also some of the great long races this month, from the Seven Sevens in the Mourne Mountains to the Brecon Beacons in Wales – which also happens to be the culminating event in the British Championships. On a 'scorching' hot day, Lou Sharp holds on grimly over the 19-mile course to come second to Sally Newman. It's just enough to ensure that she – and not Newman – wins the championship. She's both delighted and somewhat surprised to have done so well in such an emotionally draining year: 'I just turned up and did what I always did . . . I had no idea really how I would do, as my mind was not really focused.' Among the men, Rob Jebb, Nick Sharp and Ian Holmes all start the race with a chance of the championship, with Jebb ahead on points. Ian Holmes struggles with the heat and hard ground, and can manage only eleventh place. 'It was bone dry,' he reports, 'and I got really sore feet. I just couldn't keep going at the end.' Nick Sharp wins, with a powerful final mile, and for a few tantalising minutes is leading the championship. Then Rob Jebb trots home in fourth place – just enough to win him the title by a single point.

There are no such dramas in the Borrowdale race, but there's a fine day for what some regard as the most perfect of the classic races, and 203 runners complete the notoriously strength-sapping 17-mile course. Simon Booth is first of four Borrowdale runners in the first five, but his time, 2 hours 49 minutes 12 seconds, is quarter of an hour outside Billy Bland's 1981 record. The slowest finishers take twice as long. Mark Hartell is seventh, Gavin Bland eighth. Dave Spedding (twenty-first overall) is first Over-50 veteran, Nicola Davies (twenty-eighth) is first lady.

The knees-up in the marquee afterwards is, as usual, high-spirited, but it doesn't get out of hand. In previous years, over-refreshed fell-runners have repeatedly found it necessary to express their post-race exuberance by trying to climb the marquee poles – a practice that does little for the well-being of the marquee and which led on one occasion to the lower parts of the poles being draped in protective barbed wire. This year, however, according to a relieved Miles Jessop, 'It was all perfectly civilised. They were a great credit to themselves.' Or perhaps they were just tired.

In America, Scotland's Angela Mudge (whose victories at Slieve Bernagh and Stuc a Croin were her only attempts at British championship races this year) becomes the first European ever to win the famous Pikes Peak marathon in Colorado, where she's been doing altitude training. She's three minutes ahead of the next woman, and fourth overall – which is a couple of places better than Joss Naylor managed when a group of admirers flew him over in 1975. Back in Scotland, an exceptionally good year for broom and gorse produces a dazzling display of yellow blossom for the Tap o' Noth Hill Race in Aberdeenshire, and a scarcely less dazzling display of scratched and bloody legs at the finish. In Northumberland, there's an altercation between some fell-runners and some trail-hounds during the Falstone Falcon race. In Wales, at the Waun Fach race, near Talgarth, Powys, ten competitors are barred, on a glorious summer day, for refusing to carry full protective body cover. A distressed organiser refunds their entry fees – and they run the race 'informally' anyway. In Cumbria, on Joss Naylor's doorstep, Tim Austin sets a new record in the 4-mile Lingmell Dash, while a bit further south there's some impressive young talent in action at the FRA junior championships, held in conjunction with the 14-mile Sedbergh Hills race.

And in Whinlatter Forest, near Keswick, little noticed by anyone outside the elite, there are the World Trophy trials, with six male and four female senior places up for grabs for next month's championships in Alaska. On a blazing hot day, the contestants include Tim Austin, Simon Booth and Simon Bailey – and Andi Jones, a twenty-five-year-old design teacher from Didsbury who is visiting Keswick on holiday. A top-class road-runner, Jones has never run in a fell race before, but a friend persuades him to enter. Austin can manage only tenth; Jones is 'amazed' to win by a huge distance – which tells you something about him, or about the quality of the competition, or about the fact that the difference between road-running and the international version of mountain-racing is smaller than you might expect.

24

Hallowed turf

EVERY AUGUST, ON THE FIRST SATURDAY after the first Sunday after St Wilfrid's Day, a small crowd gathers outside the Red Lion pub in the West Yorkshire village of Burnsall, shortly before 7 a.m. The faces – up to a dozen – change from year to year, but there are diehard regulars among them. They are generally an unathletic-looking bunch, dressed with varying degrees of prudence, with an age range that has been known to embrace toddlers and pensioners. Most are locals – gentry rather than labourers – but there's usually a guest or two as well, or perhaps the odd baggy-eyed tourist recruited in the pub the night before. One or more should be carrying a flagpole and a flag.

When the clock strikes seven, they head for the hill: that is, for Burnsall and Thorpe Fell, a round, heathery peak of just over 500 metres, a little to the west of the village. Up they plod: along the lane past the village green, up the farm track, across the fields, generally stopping to admire the view of the Dales from the top of the highest field before crossing a stone wall and continuing through deep heather to the felltop. Actually, it isn't the top: it's a large stone cairn a mile or so short of the true summit, and some 70 metres lower. But to all intents and purposes it is the top – especially today.

The walkers generally reach this 'top' at around 7.30 a.m., whereupon they pass round a small flask of whisky and begin to dismantle the top of the cairn. After a while, they make a hole in which they can insert the flagpole, then rebuild the cairn around it to make it secure. The flag is unfurled, in an atmosphere that veers between solemnity and hilarity. Later in the day, it will be the key item of furniture in Burnsall Feast Sports, an athletic festival with roots in Elizabethan times. But by then the walkers will have long since returned to village-green level. In fact, they're usually installed in the Red Lion by 8.15 a.m.

'Tradition insists that we all have a glass of beer after our mammoth exertions,' according to Christopher Fitton, the oldest of the diehards. 'In truth, I'm doubtful whether any of us enjoys it. But by God, that's never stopped us.'

Tradition insists on a lot at Burnsall. It insists that the sports day begins with a brass band marching from the church gate to the village green, led by the president of the Sports, Leonard Horton, who has been on the committee since 1948. It insists that the same family is always responsible for erecting the flag on the cairn – the Fittons and their friends and relations have been doing so since the 1930s. It insists that the festival is blessed by the local vicar; that the main entertainments, apart from the fell race, are limited to such old-fashioned fare as wheelbarrow races, Punch and Judy shows and egg-throwing contests; that any funds raised go to the same causes (church, village hall, village green); and that the day concludes with a mass singing of the hymn 'Jesus Shall Reign'.

And it insists that the race which is the highlight of the day is also the highlight of the British fell-running calendar.

There's certainly a case to be made, if not for it being the best, then at least for it being the most steeped in legend. The race (as opposed to the festival) goes back to the mid-nineteenth century, reputedly to a bet struck in the Red Lion in, depending on whom you believe, 1847, 1865 or 1870; you may remember an earlier mention of Thomas 'Weston' Young, the man who won that bet by running naked up to the (then flagless) flag cairn and back. Thereafter, serious runners were drawn to contest the same course, and we know that by 1882 – when Nathan Newbould lost a shoe at the start, kicked the other off mid-race and won barefoot against Trevor Batchelor's great-uncle, Harry Nixon – the best professionals of the north were racing at Burnsall on Feast day. They continued to do so until 1931, after which the event became amateur, as it has remained since (although since 1980 a parallel professional event, now organised by BOFRA, has been run over the same course a few weeks after the Feast).

It's a gentle race by fell-running standards: less than 2 miles, with 900 feet of ascent, and runnable throughout. Perhaps for that very reason, it's hugely prestigious. It's a place where, for once, the thoroughbred athletes have the advantage over the mountain goats, and can give of their very best. And, of course, if you run a course like that fast enough, it isn't easy at all.

The most famous running, to which I have alluded before, was in 1910, although that was not at the Feast itself. Two years earlier, Tommy Metcalfe, a doctor's servant from Hawes, had won the Feast race in an astonishing 14 minutes 23 seconds – more than a minute faster than any previous winner. Some refused to accept the time as genuine, blaming a faulty stopwatch. Subsequent races did little to clarify the matter: Metcalfe was under the weather when he won the 1909 race in 15 minutes 27 seconds; in 1910, the course was waterlogged on Feast day, yielding a winning time of 16 minutes 5 seconds. So the village postmaster and the landlord of the Red Lion organised a special race, which they hoped would settle the argument once and for all. Instead, it started a new one.

Conditions were perfect: the turf springy, the rocks dry, the heather newly burned; and, as a further inducement to speed, a £5 prize was on offer. Seven leading runners contested the race, including Tommy Metcalfe himself – and Ernest Dalzell, the twenty-six-year-old Ormathwaite gamekeeper and Lakeland hero who had recently recorded his sixth successive victory at Grasmere. Dalzell had cycled down from Keswick the evening before – a journey that today takes two hours by car. Nonetheless, he had enough energy left on race day for a performance of miraculous verve. Two seconds behind at the summit, he launched into a sensationally fast descent that had spectators gasping in disbelief and commentators (some of whom were quoted in Chapter 3) grasping in vain for adequate superlatives.

The result was a winning time of 12 minutes 59.8 seconds – of which only 2 minutes 42 seconds had been spent on coming down. Some observers, including the race starter, refused to believe the stopwatch, insisting that it must have been out by a whole minute. More than sixty years later, they were still arguing.

Every sport has its defining legends – the Matthews final, or Obolensky's try. For fell-running, it is 'Dalzell's race': a moment of impossible perfection when a fearless athlete overcame not just his rivals but the laws of gravity and common sense. If everyone who claimed to have been there really had been there, they would have had to flatten half of the Yorkshire Dales to make room for them. But the important thing, from Burnsall's point of view, was that everyone in the sport got to hear about it – and that every subsequent running of the race has carried with it the tantalising possibility that maybe, just maybe, someone might come up with a performance of comparable magic.

Generations of subsequent runners – including some of the best athletes of their day – took up the challenge. Among them were Jack James (the last professional winner); T. P. 'Pat' Campbell, the Olympic steeplechaser; and Derek Ibbotson, the one-time world mile record-holder. None got near Dalzell's time. (Those three had ten wins between them; the fastest was just under two minutes slower than Dalzell – a huge margin for such a short race.)

Then, in 1953, the professionals had a go. Bill Teasdale and his sort were, of course, entirely unwelcome in the race proper, but a series of accidents that summer led to a rare chance for him to measure himself against an amateur yardstick. Teasdale had been running in the nearby Kilnsey Crag race, where one of his pursuers had dislodged a rock that struck him on the head. He went to Grassington for treatment, got lost on his way back – and ended up in Burnsall. Naturally, he inspected the famous course, and soon found himself talking to some locals. The upshot was another 'special' race a few weeks later. There were fifteen runners this time, all professionals, contesting an £8 prize, with a further £5 on offer for anyone who broke the record. Teasdale won easily, but to the disappointment of his admirers could only manage a time of 14 minutes 7 seconds – twenty-three seconds faster than anyone other than Dalzell had ever run, but still more than a minute slower than the record. Some argued that this only proved the impossibility of Dalzell's alleged time; others felt that Teasdale had handicapped himself by choosing the shortest and steepest route up the fell, rather than the curved ascent favoured by course specialists. Or perhaps there really had been (as one who saw the 1910 race suggested) 'something inhuman' about Dalzell's victory.

The arguments continued for a further twenty years. Athletes of the calibre of David Humphreys, Dave Cannon and Mike Short won the race but not the record. Then, on a cool, dry June day in 1977, a third 'special' race was held, to mark the Queen's Silver Jubilee. Twenty-five professionals turned out to run for the £50 prize. The main contenders were Fred Reeves and Tommy Sedgwick – then at the height of their powers – with a youthful Kenny Stuart also in the field. Reeves, running in lighter and better kit than anyone could have imagined in 1910 (or in 1953, for that matter), reached the top in 8 minutes 55 seconds, considerably faster than Dalzell, after which, realising that history was within reach, 'I almost flogged myself to death.' The result was a brisk but not mind-boggling descent, an easy victory – and a new record of 12 minutes 47.2 seconds. Sixty years after being killed in battle, Ernest Dalzell had been defeated.

Two months later, Dalzell's record was broken again, when Ricky Wilde ran 12 minutes 50.2 seconds in the amateur event. The second- and third-placed runners were also inside Dalzell's time that day. Six years after that, in 1983, John Wild set a new amateur record of 12 minutes 48 seconds. Two subsequent winners – Andy Peace (twice) and Steve Hawkins – have also run sub-12:59 times. All of which tells you something about the unbreakability of unbreakable records.

It also tells you something about Burnsall's obsession with tradition. Strictly speaking, Dalzell's record is now no more relevant to the event than Roger Bannister's is to the Olympics; yet, two-and-a-half decades after Reeves, no report or public statement about the event is considered complete without Dalzell's name being mentioned. (Nor, for that matter, is the interior design of either of Burnsall's two pubs.) Without its past, Burnsall would be just an inaccessible village with an unremarkable summer show, fighting for the attention of a public spoilt for leisure choice. With it, it's a heritage attraction.

'I've seen three village sports go to the wall recently,' says Leonard Horton, a retired businessman who masterminds the Sports from his home in the neighbouring village of Embsay. 'But Burnsall has a history. Of course we're proud of our tradition. I've seen every Burnsall race since 1928. Why would we want to change anything?'

A rather gruff, jowly man of eighty-one, rarely seen without blazer and MCC tie (but with a kinder heart than this description implies), Horton has served on the Burnsall Sports committee for fifty-six years, including a decade as chairman and president. In an age when all organisations from charities to churches pursue the chimera of modernisation, he is stubbornly – some would say pig-headedly – old-fashioned. 'I run my committee exactly as my forebears ran it. If it worked before, that's how we'll carry on doing it. There's many newcomers today who don't appreciate that, but if someone suggests something new, you think: no, I don't want that. Sometimes people say that they'd like to change something. I ask them: "How long have you been here? Five years?"'

A clergyman who was new to the job once had the temerity to suggest that perhaps he might skip that year's blessing, owing to other commitments. Horton, who once stood for Parliament as a Conservative, was unimpressed. 'I told him: "I'm used to having a parson open his diary on 1 January and the first thing he puts in it is Burnsall feast." "Well ..." he said. I said, "No 'Wells' – that's how it's got to be."'

Not everyone in the area appreciates this approach – indeed, it wouldn't surprise me if Horton's years of service were ultimately rewarded by a modernisers' putsch – but for many its inflexibility is part of the occasion's charm. Recent event programmes have included an entertaining account by Christopher Fitton of his family's seventy-year spell of duty as erectors of the flag in the cairn. ('The flag is, and always was, the great problem. No one can ever find it ... Sometimes there is a pole but no flag, and sometimes there is a flag but no pole. We take whatever bit or bits we can find.') Another local family, the Smiths, held the secretaryship of the Sports committee for more than ninety years. And in 2003 a minor variation in the positioning of the brass band was deemed sufficiently remarkable to be noted in the *Craven Herald*, whose reporter felt that the bandsmen had been 'a touch further away from the river bank and, if memory serves me right, facing away from the bank rather than towards it'.

Yet for those of us up on the fellside, warming up on a grey afternoon while the first junior race threads past us up and down the lower fields, there's nothing in sight that's noticeably different from any other fell race. There's the same range of cars in the car park (mostly small, sporty, grubby and overcrowded), the same scent of Vaseline and Deep Heat, the same air of gathering tension, the same sounds of car stereos and banter. There's even many of the same faces – Ian Holmes, Rob Jebb, Andy Peace, Rob Hope – although it's hard to be certain which of the other wiry, bounding figures are fell-runners and which are taking part in that controversial innovation, the 10-mile road race.

'There's not so many this year,' says the man taking entries for the fell race at the side of the green. 'People are doing the 10-mile road race instead.' Which may be true – at one point, road-race entries are outstripping fell-race entries by two to one – but the field for the fell race could hardly be described as thin. Dalzell had just six men to beat when he set his record; I have seventy-nine – plus thirteen women.

From the green below, the commentator's voice can be heard hinting at dodgy thumb-work in the egg-and-spoon race. Higher up, dozens of us are trying to distinguish the old Burnsall hands from the novices, with a view to working out precisely which route we should be studying. Ideally, in a race this short, you want a fairly good idea of your downhill route before you start. But the various individuals and groups I consult seem more doubtful of the details than I am. Eventually, I stroll back down behind a plump girl of twelve or thirteen who is walking the course with her father, presumably with a view to running in a junior race. He seems concerned that she might sprain an ankle on the rough ground. 'If I do,' she says helpfully, 'I'll just sort of walk and limp.' I wish I knew if she's entering to please him, or if he's letting her enter to please her. But I daresay they're thinking equally patronising thoughts about me.

The race kicks off at 5 p.m. The afternoon's mugginess has cooled, and I'm standing in the lane, yards from the spot where Dalzell began his race of races. The old stone buildings and the green and the bridge over the River Wharfe must look much the same as they did to him; yet the sense of history is somehow underwhelming. There's a drab hum of bouncy castles in the background and a glimpse of grubby ice-cream van between the trees. And there's a certain twenty-first-century pushiness about the crowd of contestants, jostling and jibing and ignoring the starter's pleas for quiet.

Tourists in baggy shorts and humorous T-shirts are outnumbered roughly two-to-one by club runners in dazzling synthetic singlets. The former wear thick-soled trainers, the latter Walshes. 'I'm feeling so fit I'll stuff you all,' announces a good-humoured voice, in an accent you couldn't put a place to. For some reason this makes me think of H. Mortimer Batten's description of contestants in pre-war events in the programme for the 1949 Feast Sports: 'The spartan spirit of the youths of that time, generally improperly clothed and improperly trained for such an event, was illustrated by the frequency with which the runners had to be carried down and revived on the village green.' How many spartan spirits are present today, I wonder?

In fact, hardiness is of less use in this race than a devil-may-care attitude: partly to speed you on the descent and partly to impel you to a mad sprint at the very beginning. The alternative, for those who, like me, prefer to use the first few hundred metres of a race to settle into a rhythm, is to find yourself boxed in behind fifty or more runners with more self-confidence than ability, all of whom have to be painstakingly overtaken. This becomes particularly frustrating once you have crossed the wall to the upper fell, after which the narrowest of paths cuts through knee-high heather towards the cairn. Stay on the path and you're limited to the pace of whoever happens to be in front of you. Move off it to overtake, and you realise why everyone else is sticking to the path.

Coming down, by comparison, is a doddle. At least, it's a doddle to overtake a dozen or more of the plodders who have been slowing my climb. Accelerating to Dalzell speed is a different matter. It's not that I don't dare to – there's enough heather and turf around to make this feel considerably safer than most descents. It's just that I don't see how you can move your feet fast enough, with the heather clinging each time you pick them up and the rocks and ruts totally concealed when you want to put them down. Even if you could bring yourself to disengage your brain, surely you would fall flat on your face?

The quickest route down involves climbing over the wall, which is around waist height from above but nearer head height from below. Other runners' testimonies have led me to believe that this is an obstacle that should be leaped at full speed – a daunting prospect, but one that I have been steeling myself to attempt. Yet my momentum is nothing like enough to get me airborne. Without consciously chickening out, I find myself not so much flying over it as scrambling and flopping. Could a better runner do it better? Presumably. But I have no idea how the momentum would be generated – unless he or she was running (as Dalzell did) when the heather had been burnt back to its roots.

Below the wall, the rutted turf seems smooth as a running track by comparison, and the rest of the descent cannot take me much more than a minute. My great reckless bounds do something to relieve the frustrations of the first three-quarters of the race, but little to improve my time of just over twenty minutes. The fact that fifty-six people finish behind me is of limited consolation. Ten minutes after the end I am cursing myself for not having done the uphill half faster – and specifically for not having overtaken for all I was worth through the heather approaching the cairn. But that, I think, is what always happens with short fell races – at the time, lungs bursting, I was cursing myself for doing it at all. No doubt Pudsey & Bramley's Rob Hope, winner for the second year in succession (in 13 minutes 51 seconds), is similarly berating himself.

At around 6 p.m., the prizes are presented by Miss Rachel Daggett, local spinster and long-term member of the Village Green Committee. The crowds are evaporating by then. There weren't that many in the first place: perhaps three or four thousand, compared with a pre-foot-and-mouth peak of around 5,000; Burnsall is too inaccessible to take more – and, perhaps, too staid. Later, as our traffic jams jostle their dreary way back through the thin lanes towards Skipton and Grassington, it occurs to me that, for the locals left behind, the best part of the day is probably just beginning – a long summer's evening in which the bouncy castles and the public-address system are silent, and the exhaust fumes drift away, and the sun sinks behind the fell, and contemplative types who have brought their drinks out on to the bridge can watch the shadows deepen on the green and hear the river rippling beneath them and reflect that, if you catch them in the right light, Burnsall and its fells must look almost exactly as they did on that day of wonder in 1910.

I, meanwhile, am thinking about the future – and, specifically, about tomorrow, when another fell race steeped in legend will be taking place.

On the face of it, the Senior Guides Race at Grasmere has much in common with the Burnsall race. They're around the same distance, with roughly the same ascent and the same simple there-and-back, in-full-view-of-the-spectators format. The best runners – but only the very best – can complete each course in just under thirteen minutes; a couple – Teasdale and Reeves – have held records for both simultaneously. Like Burnsall, the Guides Race is part of a wider sporting festival. And, this year, those festivals are both being held on the same bank-holiday weekend.

Yet their souls are quite different. Burnsall, for a start, is in Yorkshire, whereas Grasmere is in Cumbria. Burnsall, whatever its origins, is recognisable today as a northern relation of a Home Counties village fête; Grasmere, a descendant of the old Grasmere sheep fair, is rooted in a rougher heritage. Burnsall's best-loved heroes (Dalzell and Reeves notwithstanding) are the clean-limbed young amateurs who drove from far and wide to test themselves on its sheltered slopes between 1932 and 1992: Pat Campbell, Dave Hodgson, David Humphreys, Peter Watson, Dave Cannon, Martin Weeks, Ricky Wilde, John Wild – men who, generally speaking, earned white-collar livings as bank officials, engineers, technicians and the like. Grasmere's hall of fame is a less well-bred place, whose inhabitants are as likely to be wrestlers or sprinters or even hounds as fell-runners, and few of whom, before the 1970s, were ever in a position to drive themselves anywhere. The great Grasmere fell-racers have tended to be poorly paid outdoor workers – shepherds, farmworkers, gamekeepers, quarrymen, gardeners, woodcutters, or even, in some cases, guides (such as George Woolcock of Langdale) – who would have laughed at the idea of amateurism. You certainly wouldn't find anyone being booed here for being a professional.

From its earliest days, Grasmere has been closer in spirit to horse-racing than the Olympics. Its aristocratic patrons – notably 'Lordy' Lonsdale – were generally enthusiasts of the turf as well, and there seems to have been a fairly widespread consensus among participants and spectators that one of the prime purposes of the Sports was the pursuit of prize money and gambling winnings.

In 1946, the first Sports after the war, Grasmere drew 10,000 spectators, reflecting the fact that, in those parts, that was about as good as public entertainment got. It also drew thirty-seven bookmakers. Most of their business, then as now, related to the hound trails and the wrestling; but the guides races have had their fare share of money wagered on them as well (and their fair share of sharp practices), ever since 1878, when John Greenop – the future verger of St Oswald's Church, Grasmere – issued his famous challenge to race any man in the world on the course for £100; four years later, Greenop retired, whereupon the local great and good, including four colonels and an earl, presented him with 10 guineas and a certificate 'in recognition for honestly contesting the guides race and for refusing the betting fraternity's tempting offers'. Such offers and such patronage can be assumed to be in the background of much of Grasmere's folk history.

The bookies are still there today: half a dozen of them, anyway. I don't suppose many people notice them. There's too much else going on: not just the hounds and the wrestlers (female ones as well, now) but also acrobats, mountain-bike racing, tug-of-war, a mini-climbing wall, face-painting, cyclo-cross, a dog show – and around fifty stands selling and promoting wares from binoculars, camping equipment and garden furniture to magnotherapy, henna tattoos and 'eco-yurt' (don't ask).

Most of this is anything but traditional, but it doesn't seem to matter. Unlike Leonard Horton, Dr Chris Lane, show director for the past fourteen years, believes that '"*We have always done things this way*" prevents progress and dilutes content.' That's why he got rid of the grass-track running and cycling races, which were popular with traditionalists but not with the wider public. (These can still be seen at Ambleside, a few weeks earlier and a few miles further south.) And that, presumably, is why the current show looks so brash and modern and, to my untrained eye, dazzlingly successful.

The spectacle is spread over half a mile or more of wide, flat fields along the west side of the A591. There are too many parked cars to count, but attendance is said to be approaching 10,000. Yet the central area – with two large arenas, a wrestling ring, a pavilion and a beer tent – seems large enough to accommodate us all without discomfort. On the opposite side of the road, the bottom field of the most hallowed slope in fell-running is bright with banners advertising Jennings Bitter and Sarah Nelson's Grasmere Shortbread – two of the sponsors that Dr Lane has persuaded to put up some of the £30,000 cost of running the show. Somehow I can't imagine a similar sight at Burnsall.

Mind you, I don't suppose half the people present even know what a guides race is, let alone that such a race is about to take place. But for those who are interested – which is still a fair number – it doesn't matter. There's plenty of history in the air, despite the modern glitz. Here, after all, is Pete Bland, who raced here against Teasdale, Harrison, Reeves, Sedgwick and Stuart, chatting by his van as usual. Here, too, is Kenny Stuart, pint in hand, basking in a pleasing glow of low-level adulation and reflecting on his two daughters' equally pleasing victories in the Under-14s and Under-17s Guides Races. And there is Helen Sedgwick, warming up for the Senior Guides Race – which is, of course, mixed these days. As Tommy's daughter, she's a minor celebrity when she comes to Grasmere. Pete Bland singles her out for a special cheer in his pre-race address on the PA system.

The names of Sedgwick and Reeves are, I think, the most evocative you'll hear here; their story is perhaps Grasmere's defining legend. Their memory is revered for many reasons. There was, for a start, something compelling about the balance of their rivalry: Fred's thoroughbred athleticism against Tommy's sheer pluck; Fred's ups against Tommy's downs; tall, dark Fred against stocky, fair Tommy; Fred's initial ascendancy, his unexpected overthrow by Tommy, and Fred's eventual glorious restoration. Sporting dramas are rarely so well constructed; and this one was given extra resonance by the quiet nobility of both main players, neither of whom was ever heard to make an excuse or to react to defeat with anything other than fearless self-examination.

Reeves won easily in 1969; in 1970, he was leading by 100 yards at the top, was overtaken by Sedgwick on the descent, and then regained the lead on a desperate final run-in; 1971 saw a similar pattern, with Sedgwick clawing back more than 200 yards on the descent, only to lose it in the final field. Sedgwick went away to work on his climbing and general running skills, and in 1972 he was only 20 yards behind at the top – close enough to open up a commanding lead on the descent. In 1973 he won it again, breaking Bill Teasdale's long-standing course record. So Fred went away to work on his descending skills. For seven weeks in the summer of 1974, Fred visited the course every Wednesday evening, after finishing his work as a draughtsman for Burlington Slate. Each time, he would walk up and run down – three times each evening. By his twenty-first descent, his feet were gaining in confidence. His twenty-second was on race day itself, when, after leading to the top as usual, he amazed onlookers – and regained his crown – with a descent almost as suicidal as Tommy's. And so it continued: Reeves, Sedgwick, Reeves, Reeves, Reeves. By the end of the sequence, the course record had been lowered to 12 minutes 21.6 seconds – nearly half a minute faster than it had been when the rivalry started.

It probably helped that Tommy's flowing blond locks were so brilliantly visible to spectators during his daredevil descents; it probably helped, too, that all this took place when professional running was struggling for survival and respectability. Reeves and Sedgwick made guides racing *matter* again.

But what also mattered was the sense of joy the two communicated as they pushed each other through the pain barrier to new heights. 'Looking back through my Grasmere album of pictures,' Reeves once recalled, 'I see that in almost every one where Tommy and I are together, we are always smiling.' Actually, there's one well-known picture of them, arms on each other's shoulders after the finish, in which both look as though they're about to be sick, while a St John's Ambulance man looks on anxiously. But the general thrust is valid, and no one doubted Fred when he added: 'He's a great friend to have. People refer to it as "my" record, but I prefer to think of it as "our" record.'

And now here I am, standing on the same starting line that they used and looking up at the slope where all that heroism took place: two steep fields beyond the road, leading up to a dry stone wall, behind which is a sea of bracken and, up on the skyline, a clump of conifers, to the left of which two serrated ridges lead to the two grey teeth of Butter Crags, each with its own flag – after which the runners complete the third side of the triangle by sprinting down diagonally in a straight line from the left-hand flag to the bottom of the first field, then stagger back across the road into the arena.

Unlike Fred Reeves, I've never even walked the course. But I've no plans to break any records, and, even if I had, I think I may have rather blown them by running at Burnsall yesterday: my legs feel as heavy as two sacks of wet socks. I think there are only six others who are doing this double. Five of them – Rob Hope, Rob Jebb, Ian Holmes, Andy Peace and Gary Devine – were the first five home at Burnsall. I don't imagine that it will be very different today, although Ian Holmes complains about heaviness in his legs too.

Apart from that, there's a slight lack of big names in the field. Keswick and Borrowdale have only three contestants between them. Many modern fell-runners, it seems, don't train for events this short any more, and I don't think Grasmere can claim any longer to be the sport's undisputedly supreme prize. It isn't a 'counter' in either the British or the English fell-running championships this year, and it hasn't been for some time.

Yet there's no shortage of contestants: ninety in all, ranging, as at Burnsall, from serious fell-racers to foolhardy tourists who want to see what it's like. Reeves and Sedgwick never had to cope with this. I must be careful not to make the same mistake as yesterday. But nor must I disregard the advice that Kenny Stuart has just given me, which is: 'Don't go off like a hare at the gun. Those first two fields are steeper than they look, and you don't want to go into oxygen debt before the wall. If you do, you won't get a chance to recover.' And Kenny, whose 1985 record in the amateur version of this race was an incomprehensible 12 minutes 1 second, ought to know.

Then the gun goes, and ninety hares stampede for the road. It's all I can do not to get trampled. Up the fields it's not too bad, if you can find space in front of you. There's a bottleneck at the half-gap in the wall – which I suspect is rather easier to climb through than it used to be. Bill Teasdale, who is just 5 foot 3 inches, complained of having had to negotiate a wall 'as high as my ceiling' and lost the 1951 race to Stan Edmondson after his attempt to climb it went wrong. I, on the other hand, am through it soon enough and, still feeling fairly good, jogging up through the bracken. It's very steep here, and some people ahead have slowed to a walk. Even Fred Reeves used to walk the odd bit: 'I didn't like to, but in certain places it was quicker.' Personally, I'd be happier with a bit more running. It feels like another Burnsall traffic jam – so I try a few thoroughly debilitating overtaking manoeuvres. Then the track widens out to a wider track, known by some as the 'road', and I remember Kenny's other piece of advice: 'You'll have plenty of time and space to overtake on the road.' He's right. If only I had plenty of energy as well.

Actually, I could keep this up for a fair bit longer, despite the loud rasping of my breathing (part of a bizarre chorus that makes this section of the field sound like a flock of sick geese). The tricky thing is finding any extra speed for overtaking – and, which worries me more, keeping something in reserve for the descent. The two things everyone agrees on about Grasmere are that it's steep, difficult and dangerous on the way down – far trickier than Burnsall – and that the easiest and safest way to negotiate the descent is to attack it vigorously.

Nonetheless, I don't want to get to the finish and feel that I haven't given it my best shot, so I push on as hard as I can, up to the skyline, round the first crag and flag (Stan Edmondson claimed to know a good short cut here, but I'm damned if I can see it), then across the top on loose, uneven rock towards the second, higher flag. The last few metres are more of a scramble than a run, but finally I'm there. Now it's all downhill.

Several people, including Fred Reeves, have confessed to finding the immediate drop from Butter Crag quite frightening; I expect I'd feel the same, but I'm too busy scrambling down the mini-cliff to examine my emotions. I wonder if this is the drop at the bottom of which, according to Grasmere legend, Charlie 'Boss' Turnbull used to lay himself a thick bed of bracken the day before the race, so that he could leap down on to it during his descent. (On one occasion, he noticed in mid-leap that an opponent had removed it.) Bill Smith, who's generally right, insists that this didn't happen at Grasmere at all, but at Coniston Gullies; but you never know. Anyway, I'm happy to get down by more conventional means. In fact, I don't really feel in that much hurry to begin my planned fearless sprint. That last push to the top has left me catching desperately for breath – if I could just ease off for a bit and fill the void in my lungs I'd feel a lot happier about getting stuck in. Yet even I can see that, in a race this short, easing off would be a bit defeatist.

A crashing and grunting behind me restores my sense of

urgency. If I don't get going, I'll be overtaken. What was Tommy Sedgwick's tip? 'Brakes off, brain off.' Oh well: you're only middle-aged once. I lengthen my stride into purposeful leaps, and am soon gathering alarming momentum.

The trouble is, it's all done at a slant, with your right foot considerably lower than your left. You can't really relax into it. The other trouble is that, halfway down, there's a boggy area, which, I now recall, I have heard mentioned before. Unfortunately, I recall it too late. My feet shoot from beneath me, and I slide the next 20 metres or so on my back. Painful, but quick.

Back on my feet, I feel the gradient gradually decreasing, and my confidence grows. I even manage to overtake someone. Next comes the wall. There's a gate through it on the way down, and while I know that Bill Teasdale had to vault it, this time it's open. We just have to get through the gap without hitting the sides. I remember Fred Reeves's description of being overtaken by Tom Sedgwick just before a similar gap: 'He was out of control . . . If he'd missed it he'd have gone straight through the wall like something out of a Yogi Bear cartoon.' Come to think of it, I think Teasdale once had an accident around here – something about being brought down by another runner and ending up with stud-marks all down his back. Oh well, can't stop now. The wall rushes up to me, and – yes! – I'm through it and out into the lower fields.

I'm flying now: still gasping for oxygen, but resigned to the idea that the best way to get any is to reach the finish as soon as possible. The fields flash by like scenery through a train window. Best of all, there's a couple of slow-moving runners in the lower field. I'm past them in seconds and, amazingly, I hear roars of approval from the crowd on the other side of the road. It's like playing football at Wembley – although it's possible, I suppose, that the roars aren't intended for me.

I finish in thirty-eighth place, in a disappointing 19 minutes 51 seconds. Ian Holmes, the winner, is wandering around, shirtless, smiling and chatting and looking as fresh as if he'd been no further than the beer tent. It's his third Grasmere triumph, but his first for five years. 'It means a lot,' he grins. 'It's still the one that matters, isn't it?' His time, 13 minutes 35 seconds, is unspectacular, but not bad considering the heavy legs. Now he's talking about running at Hebden Sports, back in the Yorkshire Dales, the next day, subject to some blisters clearing up. 'You can win some good prize money there,' he explains; he's already won £150 for this. Rob Hope, Rob Jebb, Andy Peace and Gary Devine fill four of the next six places (and win £230 between them); Nick Sharp and Nick Fish, both of Ambleside, are the others in the first seven. None of them looks the least bit knackered.

Ten minutes later, some runners are still picking their way down, shaken by the unexpected severity of the challenge. 'It's the worst thing I've ever done,' says one first-timer, a Londoner. 'I don't want to see hills again.'

But I'm feeling more positive. Who cares that I only came thirty-eighth? Who cares that I was a minute slower than Helen Sedgwick? Who cares that I have grazes all down my back and my thighs, or that my legs have stiffened up so much that I'm already waddling like a pensioner – or, for that matter, that my car keys seem to have fallen out of my pocket somewhere on the fellside? At the age of forty-three, I've run in the most famous fell race there is, and I've finished in one piece.

25

A dying art

IT IS A CURIOUS COMMENTARY ON OUR TIMES that fell-running, for all its vigour and recklessness, is, by and large, an old man's sport. In the 2003 Three Peaks race, there were more over-sixties than under-thirties, and the number of eighteen-to-twenty-five-year-olds didn't reach double figures. The organisers calculate that the average age of entrants is increasing by six months each year. Out of 500 entries in the 2003 Ben Nevis race, 300 were from over-forties. There were fifty over-forties out of eighty-six finishers in the Grasmere Senior Guides Race; forty-six out of eighty in the Burnsall race; forty-two out of sixty-eight in the Wasdale race. Trevor Batchelor, meanwhile, reckons that in most senior BOFRA races 50 per cent of the field are over forty – whereas 'when I was running you weren't allowed to run at Ambleside if you were over forty'.

There are all sorts of reasons for this: the old are fitter and healthier than ever before, and fell-running enthusiasts – whose sport carries relatively little risk of overuse injury – have tended to stay fitter and healthier than most. Stamina tends to improve with age anyway. So, for many of us, does technique, as experience refines our feet's mastery of rough ground. Mark Hartell says that, at thirty-nine, 'I feel my age in terms of having to stretch a bit more, but in terms of speed I seem to be getting faster. It's amazing.' And when Wendy Dodds, just turned fifty-one, recently did an extended BG of fifty-three peaks, it took her less time than her original BG, twenty-three years earlier – 'and it felt far easier – I just sailed through it'. (It would have been fifty at fifty but for foot-and-mouth; then it was going to be fifty-one at fifty-one, but she added two more 'just for fun'.)

Many of the veterans running on the hills today are not there instead of younger runners: they are there as well as them, in many cases tagging along behind while the prizes are contested between a dozen or two serious young athletes – which is about how many would have been contesting the prizes thirty or forty years ago.

Yet mention the words 'age profile' to anyone involved in administering the sport – at the FRA, at BOFRA, or just in connection with individual races – and they will tell you that they are worried about the lack of young people coming into the sport. No one minds the veterans filling up the back of the fields; but they worry when the older competitors start to win – as in the 2003 Turnslack fell race in Lancashire, where the first three finishers had a combined age of over 140. And they worry that so many winning times are so far adrift of records set fifteen or twenty years ago. (Just study the records for Ben Nevis, Snowdon and Borrowdale.) There are several good youth training schemes, and several highly promising youngsters, but it's hard to get many of them to stick at it when they hit their twenties. And so the sport as a whole grows slowly more decrepit.

Actually, you can speak to anyone involved in administering just about any sport and they will tell you much the same thing. The twenty-first-century young emerge from unprecedentedly sedentary schooldays to be confronted with an unprecedentedly diverse choice of leisure activities: from Game Boys and couch-potatoeing to hang-gliding, sky-diving, triathlon – and white-water-rafting at the far end of a long-haul flight. Even for the fit, fearless and tiny minority who would be prepared even to consider the possibility of running up and down a wet mountain, an awful lot of alternative pursuits compete for their time, most of them marketed as being a good deal more glamorous than fell-running.

Does it matter? I can't pretend to be among those who particularly care. If young people don't want to run in the mountains, that's their loss. All the more room for me – and all the more years in which I can run in races and achieve vaguely respectable placings. I can see why parents hope that their children will get their thrills on the fells rather than in less wholesome ways;

but what parents hope and what parents get are rarely the same thing. And I can understand why those who organise national squads would like to reverse the trend: no young runners means no young talent, which means fewer medals at future world cups. But I've never really seen winning medals as being a major part of what fell-running is about.

Yet there is another level at which the ageing of the sport does bother me. This is a problem not so much of age as of mortality: the passing-away of an old way of thinking. Perhaps it's coincidence, but as I write this, the sport seems overshadowed by death. I have already mentioned the loss of Chris Brasher, Mike Rose and Chris Bland. I should add that of Stan Edmondson, who died in 2003 at the age of seventy-four. One of Bill Teasdale's great rivals, he was also a pillar of the Borrowdale community – and an unsung pioneer of mountain rescue in the area. Countless walkers have been directed by guidebooks to take the path up to Scafell Pike that goes 'past Stan Edmondson's farm' in Seathwaite, without having the least idea who he was. Now he is gone, taking a slice of history with him. And then there was George MacFarlane, the imperturbable modern-languages lecturer from Fort William who organised the Ben Nevis race for as long as anyone could remember; he too died recently, at the end of 2002, breaking a link with the past that Scottish hill-running had come to take for granted.

Other founding fathers of the sport are still with us, but they can be under no illusions as to which end of their lifespan they now inhabit. A. Harry Griffin, first president of the Lake District Mountain Trial Association, author of the *Lancaster Evening Post* article that inspired the first serious attempts to emulate Bob Graham, and inspiration for countless long days in the hills, recently announced that he was no longer strong enough to walk in his beloved mountains. Ken Jones, father of the Snowdon race, has stepped down, plagued by ill health, after nearly three decades of organising it. Alf Case, founder chairman of the FRA and founder secretary – forty years ago – of the Three Peaks Race Association, no longer takes an active role in the sport; he is seventy-four.

Leonard Horton, guardian of the Burnsall flame, is in his eighties; Stanley Bradshaw, pioneer of too many long-distance amateur adventures to list, is in his nineties. And then there's Fred Rogerson, eighty-three as I write, still turning out to encourage BG attempts but noticeably and increasingly frail.

It would be morbid – and premature – to mourn the passing of this generation. Yet the people mentioned above all knew a world that has vanished, and for that I envy them. They grew up in a Britain I will never know: a Britain whose wild places really were wild. As Douglas Croft, Case's successor as Three Peaks secretary (now also retired himself), points out: 'When Fred Bagley and Alf Case and Stan Bradshaw ran that first Three Peaks race in 1954, it was largely unkempt wilderness. People had hardly been on the fells for several decades. Many of the footpaths were overgrown, there were bogs you could fall into – only farmers and sheep ever went there. Now it's more like a motorway.'

Nor is that all. There were no mobile phones to use in emergencies then, no Global Positioning Systems, no lightweight Gore-Tex coats, no foil survival blankets, no energy bars and isotonic-drink pouches and freeze-dried food sachets. To get lost or injured in the mountains was both easier and more serious than it is today; to survive was a greater achievement. Simply to provide support for a long-distance fell-running adventure could involve driving for hours in a rickety car over badly made roads, or shivering in a car park in a not-entirely-waterproof anorak, with a view to administering not much more than tea, sandwiches and thick woollen blankets. And to be an active participant in such an adventure was to do something seriously bold.

That's not to say that the likes of Mark Hartell aren't bold; or that the likes of Ian Holmes aren't serious. Spend an hour with Hartell, for example, and hear him talk over a pint about the trials of the Alaskan Iditarod ('The snow was so deep I was reduced to a crawl') or the magic of Scottish yacht-and-run races ('You're cold and wet and stiff [in your boat], but when you see the next mountain rising out of the sea at dawn, you couldn't possibly want to be anywhere else') and you realise that you are in the presence of as extreme and romantic an adventurer as ever ran up a mountain. Nor is there anything inherently objectionable – except to the most dogmatic traditionalist – about most of fell-running's modern manifestations: wider participation, greater international competition, better equipment, more scientific planning, and so on.

But somehow, somewhere, for most of us, a little romance has been lost. The great challenges have been partly tamed by familiarity, while we ourselves have grown more sophisticated but no hardier. We have more choices; we can drive ourselves to more fell races in more places and in less time; we can equip and prepare ourselves more scientifically; and we can communicate far more quickly and constructively with a far greater number of like-minded souls. But we will never quite know the thrilling simplicity of those pioneering expeditions, when peace and the freedom to roam Britain's wild places were still recently won luxuries.

I was struck by such thoughts when I witnessed the launch of the Lake District Mountain Trial Assocation's fiftieth-anniversary booklet, *50 Years Running*, at the 2002 Borrowdale race. All the great Mountain Triallists were there: Stanley Bradshaw, Joe Hand, John Nettleton, Maurice Collett, Joss Naylor and more. And, as they lined up to have their photograph taken, I suddenly found myself imagining that I was looking at a group of elderly First World War veterans: all that youthful strength and courage, shrunk by the years into frailty.

I was struck by similar thoughts when I first visited Fred Rogerson at his home a few years earlier, at around the time of his retirement. I was expecting – in my sophisticated, modern way – to meet a bit of a weirdo. In a sense, I was right. But the quiet certainties of his life put me to shame.

His house, which he built himself on the side of a hill near Lindeth, is small, neat and light. It's also a Bob Graham shrine. There are photographs, certificates, books (including a leather-bound, hand-typed edition of his 1978 work, *History and Records of Notable Fell Walks Within the Lake District*); and charts on which he has calculated precise schedules for people attempting both the Bob Graham and more exacting records. There are bits of the original cut-and-pasted artwork from which the BG membership certificate was printed. There is also a cupboard full of large ring binders containing reports and peak-by-peak times of all successful attempts at the Bob Graham round since 1932, as well as less detailed records of unsuccessful attempts.

My first patronising thought was: 'Typescripts! Ring binders! Scissors and paste! What century is he living in?' My second was: 'How sad for a life to have been so dominated by a single obscure obsession – he's worse than me.' But Rogerson is wiser than that. He is, for a start, wise enough to recognise that what matters about such material is not its form but its content.

He is too modest to say how effusively many of the reports express gratitude for his help. But it is clear that such gratitude means a lot to him. 'My late wife and I used to keep all the reports that came in until the winter months,' he says, 'and without a word of a lie they were nectar. It's always nice when someone says thank you. It's all the reward I've ever wanted.' And when I read some of them myself – and, some time later, saw the choking emotion with which hundreds of members honoured his retirement as club chairman by presenting him with a whole volume of personal tributes – I realised, humbly, how much richer than most his life has in fact been.

A builder by trade, he has also worked as a tutor at a local youth centre, and in the 1960s he helped form the Lake District's first orienteering club. He has also been an active committee member for the Lake District Mountain Trial Association and a vice-president of Clayton-le-Moors Harriers. But his Bob Graham years have, he says, been 'the most pleasurable of my life. It was a pipe dream that materialised. To actually be in at the grass roots – to conceive an idea and see it materialise – I can't put it into words, the satisfaction. And I don't care what sport you do or where you go; you'll never find camaraderie like you get on the fells.'

This is something he feels strongly about: the tradition that, on the fells, everyone counts equally. 'We don't know the vocation of members, and we never will, as long as I'm alive. People put on fell boots and like attire and come into the Lakeland fells to get away from their work. I can't name the vocations of more than five of our members, and I've no wish to. People come from every walk of life: shepherd, factory hand, opera singer, men of the cloth . . .' In a world obsessed with status and fame, such common sense is deeply refreshing. But then much about Fred Rogerson is refreshing.

'He's got a passion that's quite incredible,' says Selwyn Wright. 'For someone who's not even done it himself to be so passionate really builds people up – it makes you think that what you've done must be quite important.' Which is, when you think about it, an extraordinary gift to have given to more than 1,200 people.

At times, Rogerson seems old and tired, especially when he recalls the sad death eight years ago of Margaret, his beloved wife of fifty-four years. But talk of heroics on the fells puts the fire back into his eyes. Ask him about Billy Bland's split times, or Joss Naylor's greatest achievements, and he enthuses as if he had only just discovered the sport. 'I don't think you'll find a finer group of people anywhere.'

It takes slightly more probing to make him admit that his obsession has been responsible, directly and indirectly, for the raising of hundreds of thousands of pounds for charity. Most of this has come in the form of sponsorship raised by individual contenders. But the Bob Graham 24 Hour Club also regularly donates its surplus funds to two local Outward Bound Trusts for handicapped people. 'These two bodies have people going through them who but for their disabilities would be doing what our members have done,' is Rogerson's modest explanation.

But his most remarkable contribution is to have made possible literally millions of person-hours of happiness and satisfaction. As Jean Dawes put it, shortly after becoming the first woman to complete the round in 1977: 'Fred Rogerson has a lot to answer for, encouraging us in these mad but beautiful days on the fells. But he has given us all some moments in our life which are unforgettable.'

He is not, and never has been, a fashionable figure. His sights and his profile have rarely been raised beyond the hills he grew up in; and the struggles in which he has involved himself – between man and mountain, man and the elements, man and himself – have been private ones. Yet his peculiar obsession has led him, over nearly forty years, to a long series of private acts of kindness and encouragement to ordinary individuals. As a result, the world is a better place.

Multiply his story half-a-dozen times – because it has much in common with those of Alf Case, George MacFarlane, Mike Rose, Ken Jones and several others – and you realise what a heavy load of unsung heroism is slipping away. There are new heroes to take their place, of course: mainly baby-boomers such as Dave Woodhead, Martin Stone and Allan Greenwood. But, as Douglas Croft points out, 'The pool of recruits is drying up. In the past, runners used to get to forty or so and then they'd retire and become officials and organisers. But now no one's retiring any more. They all still want to race – right up to their fifties and sixties.'

I can't blame them for doing so. But they – we – can hardly complain if the future shape of the sport is then determined by modern off-comers with a quite different vision of what fell-running is for. Perhaps the golden age of the sport – the age of adventure – is simply over.

26

Scenes from a fell-running year: September

The hills grow colder, the air damper, the ground heavier, and the thoughts of ordinary fell-runners drift naturally towards endurance – which there's plenty of opportunity to test this month. Typical September challenges include the Yorkshireman Off-Road Marathon – the classic 26.3-mile distance in the often boggy heart of the Pennines; the Three Shires – 12 rough miles around Little Langdale, won by Tom Austin in torrential rain; and the Stretton Skyline, a deceptively exposed 18-mile tour of the Shropshire highlands.

But the most famous of all is the Lake District Mountain Trial. There's an unusually strong field for this year's Trial, which is just as well, because although the weather is calm, the course, which starts from Little Langdale, is unusually rough. The ninety-eight runners who complete the main men's event visit Wrynose Fell, Hellgill, Great End, Rough Crag (on Scafell), Slight Side, Yeastyrigg Gill, Cold Pike and Greenburn Reservoir. A further thirty-one fail to finish. Mark Hayman of Dark Peak wins comfortably ahead of Borrowdale's Jim Davies; with Andrew Schofield, Mark Seddon, Ifor Powell and Mark McDermott among the also-rans. The biggest cheer is for the fifty-seventh finisher, Joss Naylor, who trots in just over two hours after the winner, not noticeably more distressed than if he had been out rounding up his sheep. That's more than can be said for the runner from Surrey who has to be carried off the fells by the Langdale and Ambleside Mountain Rescue Team after falling and breaking his collar bone. Generally, though, the day is considered a great success. In the women's event (run separately),

Keswick's Liz Cowell and Angela Brand-Barker come first and second respectively. Wendy Dodds is ninth, forty-eight minutes behind. And a further eighty competitors – including such distinguished veterans as Selwyn Wright, Ken Ledward, Harry Blenkinsop and Alan Heaton – take part in a separate Short Trial. The winner, Boff Whalley of Pudsey & Bramley, is better known as guitarist in the pop group Chumbawumba; his fellow band member, Danbert Nobacon (the one who emptied an ice bucket over John Prescott at the Brit Awards), is also a fell-runner, though not quite such a good one.

Elsewhere, there are plenty of other classic events to choose from: the Stanage Struggle, Thieveley Pike, the Two Breweries, the Grisedale Horseshoe, the three-day Isle of Wight Fell Series, the Scafell Pike race (won by Ambleside's Nick Fish by an astounding six-minute margin), and the Ben Nevis, to which we'll be returning later. There's an entertaining inter-club relay, too, between Keswick, Cumberland Fell Runners and Helm Hill. (In the veterans' team, I have the ambiguous privilege of partnering Chris Knox, one of the sport's great descenders. He gains us several places by leading us the 'short' way off Lonscale – that is, down a vertical cliff; I am relieved and somewhat surprised to finish the short cut both alive and only 100 metres or so behind Chris.)

But for many of the elite – and for many leading lights in the FRA – the only action that matters this month is taking place in Girdwood, Alaska, where 250 athletes, representing twenty-seven nations, are competing for the 19th World Mountain Running Trophy. The course on Mount Alyeska, near Anchorage, is not nearly as rough underfoot as a classic Lakeland or Scottish race; World Trophy courses rarely are. Some British purists disapprove. Ian Holmes generally prefers to stay in Britain for the Ben Nevis; conversely, taking part in something so hazardous and debilitating as the Ben race will pretty much guarantee you deselection from your country's World Trophy team. Much of the Mount Alyeska course is on a hard-packed gravel ski path, and when there's a heavy snowfall before the senior men's race, officials sweep most of it away. But there's no denying the steepness of some of the slopes, and it is, if nothing else, a good test of leg and lung power. Andi Jones confirms the promise of his unexpected trial win to take fourth place, while Tim Davies comes fifth for Wales. England's Simon Bailey (eleventh) is next Briton home, helping England to team silver. Italy's Marco De Gasperi wins individual gold – in almost exactly half the time of the Slovakian who finishes last – and the Italians also win team gold. As they usually do.

Lou Sharp comes a disappointing thirty-third in the women's event, which is run in the aftermath of a blizzard. 'I don't know why,' she says. 'I just ran an absolutely terrible race. Sometimes you do.' Keswick's other world-class runner, Angela Brand-Barker, comes twenty-fifth for Wales. But Angela Mudge wins silver, and, with Tracey Brindley in third, Scotland win the team gold. And England's junior women win silver, thanks to a magnificent performance by seventeen-year-old Karrie Hawitt, who wins the individual gold. Hawitt, from Runcorn, has done much of her training on a dry ski slope. Her admirers are convinced that she has a brilliant future, but seem undecided as to whether it lies on the fells, in cross-country, or on the track.

What everyone does agree on, though, is that none of the credit for England's successes should go to Sport England, whose lack of support is particularly frustrating in the light of the contrast with Sportscotland. Angela Mudge spent two months preparing for the event by training at altitude in Colorado; Tracey Brindley did some of her training in the Austrian Alps. Both were funded by Sportscotland, who also paid the Scottish team's travel costs. The FRA, by contrast, had to finance the England team from their own funds, and in the end could contribute only £400 towards the £900 cost of each runner's trip. Several top runners, including Martin Cox and John Brown (ranked sixth and ninth respectively on the World Mountain Running Association's Grand Prix circuit), were absent; and many of those who did go were in two minds about whether they could afford it.

If you take the view that international medals and glory are what fell-running is about, then you could argue that this is a disgrace. Or you could argue that, if poverty is the consequence of staying largely below the sports bureaucrats' radar, that's a price worth paying for remaining in the less achievement-focused world of sport for sport's sake. Fell-running is – or should be – its own reward.

But that's not much comfort to Keswick, who learn with some bitterness – and surprise – that the 2005 World Mountain Running Trophy will be staged by Wellington in New Zealand. Keswick get the consolation of hosting the World Masters (i.e. veterans) Trophy, and there's always the 2007 main event to bid for. But, as Dave Hodgson, financial controller for the past two bids, puts it: 'Some of us have put an awful lot of time and work into the last two bids, and been knocked back twice. I'm not sure how many of us are up for going through all that again.'

27

Highland things

HALFWAY THROUGH SATURDAY MORNING, on 6 September 1997, the British Isles grew quiet. It was a profound, disorienting silence: the kind in which Sunday afternoons used to be immersed half a century ago.

The funeral of Diana, Princess of Wales was about to begin, and the nation was united in real or pretended grief. Those who cared wept or choked back tears, gathered round televisions and along the streets of central London. Those who didn't care lowered their heads and eyes. Shops closed, sporting events were cancelled; football administrators who considered carrying on as normal were abruptly set right by an illogically self-righteous press.

Around noon, after the service and following a minute of formal, official silence, the half-muffled bells of Westminster Abbey began to toll, desolately, through tens of millions of television sets; then the quiet fell again like leaves.

The quiet dragged on into the afternoon, as the television cameras followed the princess's coffin on its slow, dismal journey from London to Althorp.

Then, at 2 p.m., in Western Scotland, there was a loud horn blast in Fort William, followed by a loud cheer. The sound signalled the start of the sixty-fourth Ben Nevis race and the climax of a week of bitter controversy. Many in north-west Scotland felt that the race should have been cancelled, as the Braemar Highland Games had been; many others disagreed. The race committee had agonised for days before voting eight to one to go ahead; the dissenting member had faxed a two-page complaint to the local media, who had responded with predictable hysteria.

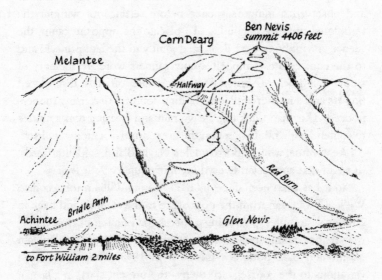

The committee's defence was that the funeral was over by the time of the race. Their real reasoning was that hundreds of athletes had invested huge quantities of time and effort in preparations for the event, while some had built their whole year around it. They knew from bitter experience how ferociously a cancellation would be resented. Some of them still remembered the howls of protest and excoriation that followed the decision (on mountain-rescue advice) to cancel the 1980 race. They had no wish to repeat the experience.

A few of them might have added, but didn't, that they hadn't really cared that much about the late princess anyway; and that, in so far as they felt bereaved, it was in connection with the recent death of Eddie Campbell, a local hero who had completed forty-four consecutive Ben Nevis races. There were certainly people in the fell-running community who felt that way, and some of them began discreetly to make their feelings known.

To placate the objectors, the 381 runners wore black ribbons and observed a minute's silence before setting out without the traditional pre-race bagpiping. To placate the opposite camp, the silence and ribbons were dedicated jointly to the late princess and to the equally late Campbell. Many runners wore 'In memory of Eddie Campbell' T-shirts. At the summit, officials had placed flowers and a memorial plaque, but it's doubtful that many runners noticed. They had thick fog, heavy rain and freezing temperatures to contend with, not to mention the great brute of a mountain itself. As the eventual winner, Borrowdale's Gavin Bland, said afterwards: 'It never gets any easier. Everything moves under your feet.'

So it has been ever since, in 1895, a Fort William tobacconist, William Swan, ran from the post office to the summit and back in 2 hours 41 minutes, provoking a succession of attempts to beat his record that culminated in the first formal race (won by William Macdonald in 2 hours 18 minutes) in 1899. There have been variations to the course since then – the present start, in Claggan Park, was first used in 1971. And there have been periods – 1905–36, 1940–41, 1945–50 – when there has been no race at all. But the basic idea has remained the same: to run up and down Britain's biggest mountain as quickly as possible. So has the basic problem: that the mountain in question never gets any smaller or easier.

Ben Nevis isn't just Britain's biggest mountain. It's one of the steepest and rockiest, with a reputation for Arctic conditions at the top. Fort William, meanwhile, is at sea level, so you have to climb all 1,343 metres of it. That's half as far again as the typical ascent of Snowdon or Scafell Pike – at high speed. And going up, as we all know, is the easy bit. Even Kenny Stuart, the record-holder, hated it. 'It's just so unforgiving,' he told me once. 'It used to take ages for my body to recover.'

Which is not an encouraging thought as, six years after Diana's burial, I find myself shivering on a damp Fort William playing field with 378 other runners, ringed by spectators and marquees. Gangs of wet clouds loiter above. But the chill in the air is as nothing to the icy dread in my blood.

In a few minutes' time, I too must race to the top of the Ben – currently hidden in the biggest, meanest cloud – and, for good measure, back again. Fit walkers take seven hours for such a journey; Kenny Stuart took 1 hour 25 minutes.

The runners around me – bantering in mainly Highland accents – seem devoid of fear and body fat. I, by contrast, am a nervous, almost-middle-aged, 13-stone Southerner. I'm reasonably fit at the moment, but it has dawned on me with awful certainty that, here and now, 'reasonably fit' won't do.

I've been spending much of the morning reading about Eddie Campbell, perhaps the only man ever to have lived who might have contemplated calling Joss Naylor a softie. The idea of this reading was to fill me with inspiration, but it seems to have had the opposite effect. A Fort William taxi driver, Eddie is thought to have run up and down Ben Nevis more than 800 times in his life. He generally did so in the same battered pair of Green Flash plimsolls, the same red bandana, and the same faded pale-blue vest. He never used a compass, and once turned down the offer of a basic navigational aid with the words 'A map? That would be as much use to me as a copy of the *Oban Times*.' But he knew the Lochaber hills as no one else did, and I have only heard of one instance – during an early attempt at the Ramsay round, which he helped to pioneer – of his getting lost.

Like Naylor, Campbell inspired extraordinary devotion in those who knew him, devotion which he generally exploited by persuading his admirers to join him on mad expeditions in the hills. If he ever felt any discomfort from wind, rain, snow or exhaustion, he never gave the slightest sign of it. 'Let it howl' was his slogan. His only dietary need appeared to be for boiled sweets. He once suffered an attack of cramp during a marathon and spent the rest of the race running backwards. In photographs, he is generally recognisable by his great Old Testament beard, and by his tendency to be running through deep snow without very many clothes on.

For many years he was also a leading shinty referee, but he had no time for athletic officialdom. In 1976, he 'organised' the first

Lairig Ghru race (28 miles from Braemar to Aviemore – with no obvious way of getting back) by inviting a dozen runners to Braemar and saying: 'Thanks for turning up, lads. Now, this is the start, and we're going to run through the Lairig to Coylumbridge, turn left and finish at Aviemore police station. It's about 27 miles. Ready? Go!' In later years, the Scottish AAA refused him a race permit, to which he responded by inviting 'the cream of Lochaber AA' to accompany him on 'an unofficial run over this famous pass'. He later formalised the race by creating a flyer, boasting that the race offered 'NO PERMIT – NO OFFICIALS ... Nothing will be organised. NOTHING. There will be nobody to blame ... Be sensible and DO NOT COME ...' He was also a great advocate for the widely disapproved-of Three Peaks record (Ben Nevis, Scafell and Snowdon, linked by car), for which he held the record for a while.

As with many fell-running heroes, there's a temptation to dismiss Eddie Campbell as a mere eccentric; but, as with Joss Naylor and Fred Rogerson, such patronising thoughts would be misguided. He was a man of few words, who nonetheless emanated courage, good nature and anarchic exuberance. As one friend put it, he 'had the happy knack of leaving you feeling specially privileged when you beat him or he beat you.' In fact, everyone who knew him seems to agree that, simply by his quiet, rock-like presence, he made the world feel like a better place, and imparted strength to those around him.

When the 1980 Ben Race was cancelled, Eddie, then forty-seven, led a party of nine disgruntled entrants on an unofficial run to the top and back. They returned insisting – in defiance of all reason – that conditions were 'flat calm'. His twenty-five sub-two-hour Ben races owed much to his fearless descending and to his matchless knowledge of the mountain. In a memorial pamphlet produced by his admirers on his death, several top runners report having had near-identical experiences in the Ben race: on the way down, they passed Eddie still going up. 'Ah!' they thought, 'I'm going to beat the famous Eddie Campbell.' They pressed on with renewed confidence, only to reach the finish and find that Eddie was already there, laughing quietly.

Perhaps, if I latch on to one or more of the fifty-eight runners in today's race who belong, as he did, to the local Lochaber club, I'll be able to find one of his secret short cuts. Failing that, I'll just have to remember the advice he gave about the race shortly before his death: 'It's not a long, slow run. You have to be fast. There is a knack to it, especially coming down, and a lot of runners find the descent hurts more than they thought it would.'

Which isn't really much comfort, I reflect, as a kilted bagpiper strikes up and leads us towards the starting line. (Bloody bagpipes again! When will I learn?) We follow him meekly – like cattle, I think, or soldiers about to go over the top. Why don't we simply refuse to budge?

An apocalyptic starting horn blasts away my self-pity. Off we charge. Round the playing field; up the lane; it's a mile uphill before we even reach the mountain. 'I'd love to keep chatting, Brian,' says a voice. 'But I'm knackered.'

The lane gives way to a wide stone path, still uphill. (Well, it's hardly going to be downhill, is it?) A flaw emerges in my canny race plan: how do I find a Lochaber runner with whom I can keep up? I glance at my watch: ten minutes of running, and I'm hanging on grimly.

The Ben Race is often subtitled 'the ultimate test of athletic endurance'. This is debatable in these days of multi-discipline and ultra-distance events. But it is, unquestionably, tough. In 1942, the leading runner collapsed 100 yards from the line; it was the second time someone had collapsed in three races. (There was also a runner who collapsed in 1903; he remained unconscious for ten hours.) In 1957, as previously mentioned, John Rix died, after getting lost in bad weather. Dozens more have been mountain-rescued (eighteen in 1988 alone), or rushed from the finishing line to hospital (this happened to Billy Bland once, after a fall); several (including Hugh Symonds) have temporarily lost their eyesight in freezing summit winds. Countless others have limped down too slowly to count as finishers.

I suppose that's why I'm doing it, when I'm old enough to know better. You can't say you've 'done' fell-running if you haven't attempted one of the biggest and hardest races of all. Few sporting challenges have such an aura, and few arouse such passionate devotion. Places in the race are usually all taken by April – there's a limit of 500, which generally whittles down by about 20 per cent in the course of the summer – and many people come back again and again. Prior to today, thirty-seven people have received plaques for completing the race twenty-one times or more. Four out of five runners in today's event have done it before.

I'll be amazed if I finish once. The stony path is steep and uneven but runnable, with bends that we cut off by scrambling up near-vertical muddy banks. After 2 miles of this, about 450 metres up, we cross the stream known as the Red Burn and begin a mile-long stretch of brutally steep ascent that takes us to about 1,250 metres. There's a path, but there's no time to follow its extravagant zigs and zags. Instead, we climb straight up scree so loose that you slide down half a pace for every two paces up. You can run it if you like, but it's quicker – though not easier – to go at a fast walk, bent forward with hands on knees. Either way, it seems to go on for ever.

The runners are well strung out now, right up to the skyline. Their bowed figures look like slaves on the side of some hellish South American mine. Occasional gaggles of supporters and tourists shout support; otherwise the only sound is the rasping of lungs and scree. From time to time, I force myself to overtake, but my legs are running out of fuel. On a normal mountain, we'd be at the top by now.

As it is, the scree slope gives way only to a mile-long sloping summit plateau. The gradient is gentler, the ground rougher, with loose boulders as far as the eye can see – which up here is only about 50 metres. (These, I'm told later, are 'ideal' conditions: cool but not life-threatening.) We can run properly now, but I'm alarmed to find myself tripping and stumbling. My legs have taken on a life of their own – I'm starting to bonk, and I'm not even halfway. I eat some chocolate from my compulsory emergency kit in the hope of fending off collapse.

A sudden crashing distracts me, as the leading runner flies out of the cloud. It's Rob Jebb, on his way back down already. He's gone within seconds, but more soon follow: Simon Booth, Ian Holmes, and others I don't recognise. It's a thrilling sight, but also demoralising; especially as, with each passing minute, the number of returning runners increases. I try not to notice the women and old men among them.

At last, from deep in the swirling mist, the summit appears. I hand my tag to a marshal after eighty-eight minutes. Yes, the winner could be finished by now, but hundreds are still behind me. I turn and head for home on a surge of restored morale.

There's only one tolerable way to run down a mountain like this, and that's quickly. George MacFarlane, the recently deceased race organiser, used to speak of the need for 'stamina for the climb and courage for the descent'. Or, as Pete Bland, here with his van as usual, advised me earlier: 'When you turn at the top, disengage your brain.' Positive thinking brings my jellied legs under some kind of control, and soon I'm running like the wind. This is almost enjoyable.

The slope steepens. My brain tries to re-engage. You could break every bone in your body if you crashed at full speed on this stuff. Then again, you could die of exhaustion and boredom if you did it all slowly. I force myself to accelerate, trip, get up (mildly cut), overtake half-a-dozen people and, surprisingly soon, emerge beneath the cloud. The Red Burn is visible far below, and, impossibly far beyond, some specks that must be Fort William. Still thousands of feet to go, and my legs are reverting to jelly.

I'm moving too fast to give any thought to subtle Campbell short cuts. I'm just vaguely following the people below, while trying to resist the temptation to drift to the right, where the slope is gentler but slower. Eventually, the scree gives way to an even steeper stretch of muddy, bouldery grass; what's needed here is not so much running as leaping. I leap, hobble, slip and hop. Both calves have cramp, and seize up painfully each time I stumble. Before long I can hardly stand, let alone run. I'm reminded of an expression Joss Naylor once used, describing a rough patch he'd had: 'My feet – I couldn't guide 'em. Didn't belong to us.' I get down one particularly steep and slippery section by sliding on my bottom, an effective manoeuvre that earns me a set of gouges such as I haven't seen since I was beaten at boarding school.

'That's cheating,' says a female voice, and a young woman who doesn't look out of breath at all bounds nimbly past me.

Every fell race has its tortures, but most have compensations: undulations, views, stretches of kind, grassy slope where you can relax and run; or simply the fact that any given up or down is over within a tolerable time. The Ben Race just goes on and on: the same relentless stones, the same merciless gradient. I noted this on the way up and I note it again, bitterly, on the way down. Even Billy Bland, who won in 1978, noted it: 'It's a 4,000-foot drop – you just can't train for that. I led at the bridge [about three-quarters of the way down] about five times after 1978, but I never won again. My bloody legs used to go.' And so, emphatically, have mine.

What keeps you going in such circumstances is the thought that, if you don't, you'll have to stay on the mountainside indefinitely. Better to get down as quickly as possible. Eventually I do, swaying and shaking and covered in mud, grit and blood. I later calculate that my descent from summit to road has taken a shade under forty minutes – every second of which was devoted to the same relentless downhill movements. The long descent from Scafell to Wasdale Head, which has reduced many a Bob Graham contender's legs to jelly, takes just twenty-six minutes.

Even having reached the road, there's still another undulating mile to go. Everyone warns that this will be torture: 'I always used to start staggering like a drunk as soon as I hit it,' remembers Dave Cannon, who won the race in 1971, 1972, 1974, 1975 and 1976. So it proves with me (the staggering, not the winning). The only consolation is that the runners ahead of me are now swaying drunkenly as well, and I manage to pick a couple of them off. Then, to my horror, they make us do a lap of the playing field at the end.

Eventually I slump over the finishing line. My time, 2 hours 15 minutes 24 seconds, would have won the 1942 race. Today, I'm 183rd (or twelfth woman – if I was a woman). The winner, Rob Jebb, was nearly forty-six minutes faster. But twenty-eight Lochaber runners are among the 196 competitors who either finish behind me or fail to finish within the three-and-a-half-hour limit; and Ian Holmes, I later discover, had a similar experience to mine: 'My legs went to pieces on the descent. It's because I couldn't get any tea last night – I could only find a burger in Glasgow.' (It didn't stop him coming fourth, though.) I suppose I should feel pleased. Instead, for hours after, there is only one thought in my head: that I am never, ever going to do that again.

Later on, at the prize-giving, friendly voice after friendly voice tells me the opposite: 'You'll be back. Next year. Just you wait.'

One of these voices belongs to Donald Cameron, Lochaber AC president, who is delighted to meet a Keswick runner because, having just announced the organisers' intention to invite Kenny Stuart and Pauline Howarth to next year's race to celebrate the twentieth anniversary of their still-unbroken records, he would appreciate any advice on how he might get in touch with them. I ask about the implications of the £1,000 prize he's just announced for anyone who can break either record. What if half-a-dozen people do so? 'Oh,' he says, 'we'd be surprised if anyone got near them. We think our money's safe.'

Another friendly voice belongs to a delicate-looking man with snow-white hair who reveals that he has just completed his thirty-third Ben race. It turns out that this is Jimmy Jardine, close friend of Eddie Campbell and something of a legend in his own right – thirty years ago, he won a downhill-only race from the summit of Ben Nevis in 23 minutes 30 seconds, beating Campbell by four minutes. Jimmy is a driving examiner whose training, in his prime, consisted of a 20-mile cycle ride to work, a 5-mile run at lunchtime, and a 20-mile ride back. His lunchtime run was complicated by his employers' insistence that he should never leave or enter the building except in his work clothes. He used to change in an allotment and run carrying his work-clothes in a bin-liner. (Jardine's employers weren't alone in their lack of sympathy for the sport. When the World Mountain Running Trophy was held in Edinburgh in 1995, Tommy Murray couldn't even get the day off from his employers at Inverclyde District Council; instead, he had to begin an evening shift within hours of winning the silver medal.) Before that, Jimmy worked as a lorry-driver for Peebleshire County Council, and was in the habit of parking his vehicle at likely-looking mountain lay-bys and disappearing into the hills for training runs. Since he rarely had a map, this was a high-risk strategy. He once came back down into the wrong valley, and realised that he did not have the faintest idea where his lorry was.

It seems odd that so soft-spoken and frail-looking a person could have run in the mountains at all, let alone built up a reputation as one of the hardiest men ever to do so. As so often in this sport, however, the strength lies within. It turns out that Jimmy's success as a fell-runner owes much to his uninhibited descents – he once came down such an impossibly steep cliff in the Creag Dubh hill race in Newtonmore that he had to jump down into the upper branches of a tree in order to climb to the bottom. He attributes this fearlessness to a previous sporting passion for motorbike scrambling, which involved pretty much flying down hills with the occasional halfway bounce. 'I just applied the same [approach] to running.' His best time for the Ben is a very respectable 1 hour 39 minutes, but times and results aren't really his thing, he says. He subscribes to an older philosophy of hill-running that sees the point of the sport as being 'to compete yourself against the hill'. He misses the sport's earlier, gentler days – 'When I first did the Ben, you'd get people like Peter Hall and Mike Davies going at it hammer-and-tongs, but they'd still open gates for each other, or exchange sweets' – and he's been known to speak disparagingly of 'English lads who want changing facilities and better prizes'. For him, anyone who puts winning before the joy and beauty of hill-running is missing the point.

Now retired and living in Avoch, overlooking the Moray Firth, Jimmy has more or less given up racing, preferring to run simply for pleasure: 'If I do go to a race, I'll just be blethering on at the back with my cronies. I'm not interested in where I finish.' He's recently been working on a photographic book about Ben Nevis, a project that requires regular visits here ('It's a long way, but my pensioner pass gets me there for free') and innumerable hours wandering the mountain's great grey slopes. 'It's a lovely mountain, and there's always more to discover.' As for the Ben race itself, that's the one event he won't miss for anything – and he doesn't think I should, either. 'You mustn't stop after just the one,' he insists, in a persuasive, musical voice. 'It's such a lovely race. Such a beautiful mountain. And the people are so friendly.'

I can't deny that it's a warm atmosphere; nor that, as the memory of the ordeal recedes, a strange euphoria creeps over me. Many bottles of Glen Nevis whisky have been distributed to prize-winners, and the Bingley table – where Rob Jebb, Ian Holmes and Andy Peace are celebrating the team prize as well as Jebb's individual one – is one of several lively-sounding groups.

Meanwhile, I keep hearing mysterious phrases such as 'Grey Corries' and 'Cuillin ridge' and 'Cairngorm four-thousanders' and 'Scottish islands peaks', and I'm beginning to realise that there's a whole world of Scottish mountain-running about which I know hardly anything. Perhaps now is the time to start exploring it – or at least to drink my way into the subject.

Word has it that the post-race celebrations can get a bit wild: one champion of years gone by narrowly avoided arrest after starring in an impromptu nude motorcade through Fort William, and on another occasion the police broke up a mass streak. But that was many years ago, when fell-runners in general were younger. By the time one beer has slipped down, all I can think of is sleep; and I can see that I am not the only one. The alleged tradition of a 'hairiest arse' competition appears to have been discontinued, and although some of the Lochaber contingent manage to find somewhere to go dancing, most people are drifting bedwards by 10 p.m. I don't blame them.

By next morning, all I can think of is that I can't move. By the afternoon, I am wondering if I will ever be able to walk normally again. Only about three days later do I begin to think of my first Ben race as I should do: as pleasure – the kind of thing that anyone, given the chance, should do at least once before they die. Who knows, maybe I *will* try it again? Now that I know the course, I could pace myself properly, train properly, maybe break two hours . . .

Which is, of course, precisely the kind of folly that Eddie Campbell used to inspire.

28

Scenes from a fell-running year: October

The English Championship culminates with the Langdale Horseshoe, a difficult, old-fashioned fell race of 14 miles over rough and often confusing ground. Rob Jebb needs to win to add the English title to his British one; he also needs to beat Ian Holmes by several places. Holmes can just concentrate on beating Jebb. Thick cloud on the tops adds interest to the situation, and most runners spend at least part of the race lost.

Gavin Bland doesn't. He knows these hills as most of us know our back gardens, and he gallops to a comfortable victory in 2 hours 4 minutes 24 seconds. Ian Holmes is second, five seconds ahead of Rob Jebb, which means that Holmes, not Jebb, is this year's English champion. But no one seems too bothered – what's a title between friends? – and there's widespread pleasure at Bland's return to form.

But there's no lack of competitive spirit at the month's big relay events: the British Fell & Hill Running Relay Championships at Church Stretton in Shropshire (won by Pudsey & Bramley); and, a couple of weeks earlier, the Ian Hodgson Mountain Relay. For many people, the Ian Hodgson is one of the highlights of the year. They love the four-leg, 25-mile course in the hills around Glenridding, east of Helvellyn. They enjoy the chance to run as teams. And they like the sense that, now that the championships and the international season are over, the whole fell-running community is turning out for the year's last big event. Borrowdale, with Gavin Bland and Mark Roberts running the final leg, win comfortably ahead of Ambleside and some sixty other men's teams. Keswick win the ladies' prize, thanks to a record-breaking third leg by Lou Sharp and Angela Brand-Barker. 'I love these two relays more than any other events in the calendar,' says Lou. 'I love being part of a team.' Afterwards, people linger and chat for a long time, enjoying the refreshment tent and the balmy afternoon, before beginning what in some cases will be a very long journey home.

A similar spirit pervades the sixteenth Reunion Dinner and Dance of the Bob Graham 24 Hour Club the following weekend. It's meant to be biennial, but foot-and-mouth led to the cancellation of the 2001 event. So nearly 200 members pack into the Shap Wells Hotel, on the bleak moors north of Kendal, to eat roast beef, renew old friendships, see thirty-eight certificates awarded to new members (Keswick's Mark Denham-Smith among them), and dance the night away to the music of the celebrated fell-runners' ceilidh band, Striding Edge.

Elsewhere, there are big turnouts for the Woodheads' Withins Skyline race on Haworth Moor and for Allan Greenwood's Race You To The Summit race in Lancashire. (The Summit in question is a pub.) A runner needs an overnight hospital stay after a fall in the Brontë Way race on the Yorkshire/Lancashire border. In Shropshire, Mercia's Andy Davies wins the 50-mile Long Mynd Hike in driving rain, icy wind and, after nightfall, heavy frost. (The only people who reach the finishing line in daylight are the tail-enders, who are still at it at daybreak.) Ian Holmes makes his traditional autumn visit to Italy for the Trofeo Vanoni in Morbegno – sister to the Snowdon race. He doesn't win anything, but that's not the point: it's just something he likes to do at this time of year – another chance to renew old fell-running friendships. In the early 1990s, he spent three years living in the Italian mountains and used to keep fit by racing a chair-lift on a 1,500-foot, 2.5-mile ascent.

At the Screes race in Nether Wasdale, Tim Austin is leading by a minute at the summit – then fractures his foot on the steep, rough descent. 'I thought at first it was just one of those sprains where you can run it off. So I tried, but I soon realised that that wasn't going to happen.' As it happens, there are soon several members of Wasdale mountain rescue team hurrying down the mountainside after him: the race is held in aid of the team, whose members, in turn, like to support it. But Tim is content to make his way down at a hobble, eventually finishing 'last – by about forty minutes'. It turns out that he has badly damaged a number of tendons and ligaments, and snapped a bone in his foot. Estimated healing time: six months.

Further north, that same weekend sees the father of all mountain marathons, the thirty-five-year-old Karrimor International (the KIMM), This year's event is held in the Scottish Borders, near Langholm, and, despite good conditions underfoot and clear weather, it proves to be one of the toughest for some time. On the A and B courses, there's a drop-out rate of around 50 per cent – even after the second day's course is shortened in mid-race. 'If I'd known it was this hard, I would have done Everest first,' says one competitor, Robert Pollhammer of Munich. A below-freezing campsite does little to repair battered morale overnight. But Morgan Donnelly and Steve Birkinshaw – both toughened by a few recent weeks of sleepless nights with new-born sons – seem to relish the hardship, and they win the Elite class for the second year running. Birkinshaw then reveals that he will shortly be heading for Namibia, to take part in the BBC challenge programme *SAS Desert: Are You Tough Enough?* (Fell-running clubs are constantly approached with invitations to their members to take part in such programmes, and Birkinshaw will not be the only fell-runner to take part in this one.)

For Mark Hartell, the KIMM brings yet another second place, this time with his regular mountain-marathon partner, Mark Seddon. But he isn't disappointed. After a slowish start, the pair put in the Elite class's fastest overall time for the second day, and Mark finishes in such high spirits that he makes a life-changing decision. Next morning, he goes into work and resigns from his job with Xansa, the multinational IT and consultancy giant: from now on, he's going to work as a freelance – something he's wanted to do for ages. He applied for voluntary redundancy a year ago but was turned down, 'and, because of the financial situation, didn't have the confidence to go it alone. One year later, I found that confidence . . . I had a great run, then went into the office and finally chucked in the job. It was such a huge weight lifted from my shoulders.'

29

A talent to endure

TOUGHNESS COMES IN MANY FORMS: from brute physical strength to quiet inner stoicism. However you define it, it is close to the essence of fell-running. All great fell-runners have it, even ostensibly delicate ones such as Kenny Stuart. A few have it to a degree that verges on lunacy – Joss Naylor and Eddie Campbell being the obvious examples – and are hero-worshipped as a result; not because they are incomparable athletes but because their defiantly indestructible spirit epitomises the aspirations of their sport.

Who will be the next such legend – the next iron man of the mountains? It's difficult to say. There are several people who have run further and faster in hostile places: Mark McDermott, Jon Broxap, Martin Stone, Mark Hartell. No doubt there will be more. There have, furthermore, been fell-runners of comparable durability: Ian Holmes, for example, who has spent more than a decade at the top, or Colin Donnelly, who was British fell-running champion in 1987, 1988 and 1989, yet was still running well enough in 2002 to be British over-40s champion. And there have even been a few with the same gloriously imprudent ambition – such as Hugh Symonds, who in 1990 ran all 303 3,000-foot mountains in Britain and Ireland in a continuous ninety-seven-day traverse. (I recommend his book on this adventure, *Running High*.)

All the above-mentioned are spectacularly hard men: if I described all their achievements this book would be half as long again. But I don't think that any of them can be said to have developed quite the same aura of legend as that which surrounded

Joss and Eddie. Their fellow fell-runners admire them, but they do not think of them as being a species apart.

There is, however, one other runner whose mere name is enough to provoke mutterings of 'not quite human' among followers of mountain heroism. She is not a man. She is a physiotherapist of Greek descent who came to Britain in 1982, lived at various times in Durham, Coventry, Glasgow and Ambleside, and now lives in Harrogate, North Yorkshire. She is beautiful and sophisticated, with a serene, playful charm that has cast a spell over more than one leading male fell-runner. Her name is Helene Diamantides.

Her early biography shows few traces of the Joss Naylor template. She was born in 1964, in Guisborough, North Yorkshire, but spent the first six years of her life in Ghana, where her Greek father was working as an accountant. The family later moved (via London) to Athens, where Helene and her younger sister were educated.

Helene didn't shine academically, but her sporting talents were prodigious. Her early enthusiasms were for riding, gymnastics, swimming and, in her teens, pentathlon, in which she competed internationally. She slipped into running accidentally, as a way of avoiding volleyball. She was obviously gifted – 'In a different country, the times I was doing on the track would probably have led to considerable pressure to stick at it' – but her parents insisted that she should never allow the lure of medals and records to blind her to sport's true purpose: pleasure. 'Yes, dear, but did you *enjoy* it?' would be their response to news of her latest triumph. She remembers once 'getting really worked up before a race, and my mother said, "Right. I'm not going to let you do it. There's no point in doing it if it's going to make you miserable." I've never forgotten that.'

When she was sixteen, a teacher persuaded her to try a marathon – on the original Olympic course. It took her just over four hours. 'I absolutely hated it. I thought I was going to die. I thought: "I'm never, ever going to do long-distance running again."' Which just goes to show how little we know about ourselves.

She moved to Britain when she was seventeen, in 1982, to study at a college in Durham for an education degree (in ecological studies and PE teaching, specialising in children with learning difficulties). For a year or so she was miserable and lonely ('I wasn't a beer-swilling party animal, and although I seemed English, I knew nothing at all about all the music and television programmes and things that everyone else was talking about'); then she discovered the running club at Durham University and, through it, a subset of fell-runners who made regular weekend journeys to the Lake District. Suddenly, she felt she belonged. ('I hadn't even realised that you could walk in the hills before.') She ran her first fell race – the Fairfield Horseshoe – in 1984, turning up on the starting line in heavy walking boots, 'carrying a map on a string'. She struggled on the ascents but 'really came into my own going down'. After that, she was hooked. She joined Dark Peak, the Sheffield club whose members included not just her Durham friend Alison Wright – who in 1985 became, at nineteen, the youngest woman ever to complete the Bob Graham round – but also such giants of the contemporary fell-running scene as Martin Stone, to whom she became close. She began to race regularly, 'lying through my teeth' about her age to secure a place in that year's Three Peaks. She didn't win anything, but it was obvious that she was taking to the sport like a natural.

Over the next couple of years she competed in a widening range of events, including the White Peak challenge, a fairly tough 35-mile yomp through Derbyshire which she won with Alison Wright, and the Karrimor International Mountain Marathon, in which they won the A class. Eyebrows began to be raised at her rapid and apparently effortless progress. She also qualified as a teacher, and, in 1986, moved to Hinckley, near Coventry, for her first school position. Neither the place nor the job gave her much pleasure, but she escaped through regular expeditions to the mountains of Cumbria and Wales.

In 1987, she did her first Bob Graham, in 'about twenty-two hours'. She didn't give it much thought. 'Everybody was doing it then: it was just something you did. I didn't recce it or anything. But I knew most of the mountains by then. It was hard, but I enjoyed it.'

That autumn, Diamantides's restless spirit took the upper hand. She took a term off and went with Alison Wright to Nepal to attempt to break the record (set by the famous Crane brothers in 1983) for running from Everest Base Camp to Kathmandu. They weren't sure how realistic this was: the three-week trek to the start would have done for most people. But they were confident that they would at least finish: 'I can keep going for ever, and so can Alison.' As it was, the 167-mile route – including 32,000 feet of ascent, 46,000 feet of descent and, on this occasion, a total of eight hours' sleep – took them 3 days 10 hours 8 minutes: some twenty-four hours faster than the record. A team of pursuing Sherpas finished twelve hours behind.

More eyebrows were raised, especially among those who understood the sport best. The following January, a fell-running enthusiast from Perth paid for Helene to fly to Africa to compete in the 31-kilometre Mount Cameroon race. The deal was that she would pay him back if she won any prize money. She did. 'I've never felt so responsible in all my life. I ran my heart out – and I won.' She also took thirty-five minutes off the women's record, coming sixtieth overall in a time of 5 hours 9 minutes 41 seconds. The same year she ran (and won) the famous Mount Kinabalu race in Borneo, and came third in the 100-mile Hoggar 'Super Marathon' in Algeria, adding to her haul of prize money. She gave up the teaching job – 'With hindsight, I never really wanted to teach' – and used her accumulated winnings to spend an unsettled period living with a godmother in Stockport while running 'semi-professionally'.

It didn't feel right. 'It took the pleasure out of it. I enjoy running too much to do it as a job. I kept worrying: what will happen if I sprain my ankle training?' So she looked around for a more conventional way of earning a living and, figuring that she might as well do it in a congenial location, focused her search on the Lake District. In due course she found a job there with a management training company: 'you know, using challenges in the outdoors to make teams work better'. She moved to Kendal, joined Ambleside AC – 'one of the nicest bunches of people I've ever met' – and discovered proper training. 'Before that, I'd just gone for lots of long runs. Now my training began to have a structure.'

Her speed on the fells improved accordingly, as became clear when, on a hot June Saturday in 1988, she did her second Bob Graham. This time, she did it solo and unsupported. 'That was one of my favourite experiences of all. It was all so peaceful. Not easy: these things are never easy. If you don't cry going up Red Pike you're not trying. But I never really had a bad patch. Everything felt right – even the slices of cold pizza I ate on the way. I only told about two people I was doing it.' It took her 20 hours 17 minutes – a new women's record.

Work proved more troublesome. 'I was awful at it – I was twenty-three, twenty-four, and I was telling managers how to manage. They pretty soon made me redundant – which was a kind way of putting it.' A period of unemployment followed, punctuated by supply teaching and various odd jobs, including a stint as a labourer. If this got her down, it didn't seem to affect the blithe confidence of her running. Perhaps the mountains seemed uncomplicated by comparison.

In 1989, she decided to run all three of Britain's classic twenty-four-hour rounds in a single summer. No one, male or female, had ever done this before. Twenty-four-hour rounds take a lot out of you. Most people reckon that you need two or three months of recovery before your mental and physical resources are fully replenished. It's also complicated to plan these things logistically. But Helene couldn't see what all the fuss was about.

She began with the Paddy Buckley round, a 61-mile, forty-seven-peak circuit of Snowdonia, on 3 June. Her time, 20 hours 8 minutes, beat the existing men's record by two hours. On the car journey home, with her then boyfriend, fellow Ambleside runner Mark Rigby, she announced that she intended to go for the 'treble'. She'd been toying with the idea since the previous summer, but no one believed she was serious. She was now.

It then transpired that another runner – Adrian Belton, whose Welsh record she had just broken – was also planning to do all three rounds that summer. Just over a month later, she was in the Highlands for the Ramsay round, which she completed in 20 hours 24 minutes, looking, according to Mark Rigby, 'as fresh as if she'd just been to the hairdresser's'. She was only the sixth person to complete the Ramsay successfully (even now, only thirty-one people have done so), and she beat Jon Broxap's 1987 record by more than an hour. Adrian Belton, whose own treble attempt was now in progress, erased Helene's time from the record books eighteen days later. But she remains in the Ramsay hall of fame as one of only two women ever to have completed the round in less than twenty-four hours. (The other, Jane Meeks, who did it in 2000, took 23 hours 59 minutes 10 seconds.)

The following month, just seventy-one days after her Paddy Buckley, Diamantides and Belton teamed up to complete their treble together. This time they did the Bob Graham in 19 hours 11 minutes, which from Helene's point of view was another record – the BG women's record, beaten by more than an hour. Apart from two 'quite sore knees' she was none the worse for the two-and-a-half-month exercise, which she had knocked off with less fuss than some people make about going for a jog in the park. She admits, though: 'I haven't been able to eat rice pudding since.' Understandably, she was voted Long-Distance Fell-runner of the Year for 1989. But the truth was, she was still only starting out.

In 1990, she won a series of major races, notably at Wasdale, where she was not only first woman by a huge distance but came thirteenth overall – a performance that was described in the *Fellrunner* as 'the greatest ever' by a woman. Then her father died, from a stroke; a traumatic episode whose one redeeming feature was that it finally revealed to her what she wanted to do. 'I saw the physiotherapists who were working with him, and I thought: "Why didn't anyone tell me that this job existed? This is what I want to do."'

She subsequently retrained – for four years, in Glasgow – and has been working as a physiotherapist ever since (although not with stroke victims). Meanwhile, the mountains still beckoned. She missed much of 1991 through injury, but still managed to equal Pauline Stuart's 1984 record for the Borrowdale. Then, in 1992, she faced her biggest challenge yet.

The Dragon's Back was supposed to become a regular race. In fact, 1992 was the only year it happened. Perhaps that was just as well. It was almost too perfect – and too extreme. The organiser, Ian Waddell, who devised the event to raise funds for a rehabilitation centre, persuaded the petrol company Jet to sponsor it, and the Parachute Regiment to provide logistical back-up. As a result, he was able to lay on a race of breathtaking ambition and simplicity. Contestants, in teams of two, had to race from one end of Wales to the other, in five one-day stages, taking in pretty much every major peak in the principality, with overnight camps organised by the marines. You can see it on any map of Wales: a great winding, mountainous spine, 220 miles long. What you cannot sense is quite how wild and trackless much of it is, or quite how appalling it would be actually to have to run it all yourself.

I have compressed so many accounts of high-speed mountain achievements into these pages that the hills themselves seem to have shrunk. The words 'she climbed a mountain' no longer evoke much sense of struggle; the heroes and heroines of this book climb mountains without batting eyelids. 'She climbed a mountain' – what, just the one? 'She climbed a dozen mountains' – yes, and what did she do after that? But the reality is unaltered: every mountain is big, difficult and dangerous; to run over large numbers of them requires extraordinary – sometimes super-human – stamina and boldness.

To get a sense of what Diamantides did that September, in partnership with Martin Stone, you need to imagine yourself there, standing in the rain at Conwy Castle on the north coast and contemplating the coming ordeal. Somewhere to the south of you should be Conwy Mountain and the Carneddaus, but all you can see are wet foothills and low cloud. You are cold already, but you know that this is as nothing to the chill you will feel on the high ground. You are about to spend the best part of a week on that high ground, immersed in cloud, with most of your waking hours devoted to climbing and descending as fast as your body will allow, while knowing all the time that if you stop concentrating on your map and compass for a moment you will be lost. Does your heart sink? If not, think about it again until it does.

Helene's heart sank. She was in better shape for the challenge than most of us could possibly imagine being in ourselves: a few months earlier, she had set a record that still stands (3 hours 45 minutes 10 seconds) in the Lairig Ghru race, Eddie Campbell's famous 28-mile creation; a few weeks later, she would set another record that still stands (2 hours 23 minutes 25 seconds) in the Langdale Horseshoe. Even so, she was beset by doubts. 'I felt really unfit,' she wrote later, 'and desperately afraid of what I'd entered.'

Nonetheless, there she is, one of fifty-five competitors who line up in the rain for the start shortly after dawn on 21 September 1992. Among her rivals are three teams of paratroopers, and some of the best ultra-runners in the world, including Germany's Stefan Schlett, who recently ran 3,000 miles across the United States, and Sweden's Rune Larsson, who once ran 162 miles in twenty-four hours. Larsson accounts for the odd number: he refuses to take a partner because he doesn't want to be held back.

It doesn't take long for the mountains to put him right. The first day involves a 'mere' eight summits, scattered through 36 miles or so of the Carneddaus, the Glyders and Snowdon. But the going is extremely steep, and, navigationally, it's a nightmare. Team after team gets lost in the mist, and times for that day's leg range from seven hours to fifteen. Rune Larsson suffers more than most. 'I was lost in the mist in a strange country and felt very alone,' he tells the *Independent*'s Rob Howard afterwards. 'Then I was trapped on a rockface, frightened and thinking of my seven-month-old son. So my desire for competition changed to a basic will to survive, and winning became less important.'

Diamantides and Stone are first home, and appear to be enjoying themselves.

On the second day, many spirits are broken by the sheer

roughness of the ground in the Rhinogs. Diamantides and Stone seem more confident than most about the best lines to take – she reconnoitred the course a few weeks earlier, while he is an unrivalled mountain navigator. Some rivals try to latch on; a few fast descents down rocky gulleys leave them floundering in the mist. At one point, Diamantides and Stone split up to confuse their pursuers, then regroup at an agreed rendezvous. But another British pairing, Mark McDermott and Adrian Belton, who between them hold every major British twenty-four-hour record, are also moving strongly, and are first to reach that night's camp. It's clear that no one can afford to ease off.

By day three, the weather is arting to clear, but Diamantides and Stone are paying the price of their fast start. A long, rough, hilly day, taking in 'Cadair Idris and Pumlumon and all the scenic country in between', leaves them shattered. They regain the lead, but only by nineteen minutes. Ten teams have already dropped out; but McDermott and Belton are still in there, along with six paratroopers and such ultra-distance specialists as Mike Cudahy, Stefan Schlett and Adrian Crane (whose Himalayan record Diamantides broke five years earlier).

Day four is worse. The endless tussock grass of the Elan Valley tortures the runners all day. There simply isn't a pain-free way of running, or even walking, on this stuff. More or less every step involves a slip or a stumble; it's impossible to get a rhythm going. Even the toughest feet eventually succumb to blisters here, and even the toughest calves are eventually reduced to water.

Eventually, as Diamantides' subsequent account in the *Fellrunner* puts it: 'I keeled over into a bog and didn't get up again. Martin force-fed me chocolate, took my rucksack and spoke very roughly to me. It worked, and I continued to move forwards. But not very fast. And certainly not with a rucksack.'

By the time they crawl into camp, they are back in second place – but only by five minutes. They might still win, if they can only rekindle their ambition and confidence.

It's a big 'if'. The final day is the longest: 48 miles. That's an awfully long way to run through wet mountains at the best of times.

Imagine trying to do so when you're so stiff and footsore that you've barely been able to get dressed. And then imagine forcing yourself not only to keep putting one foot in front of the other, but to do so all day at your fastest possible pace. Only the very greatest athletes can voluntarily expose themselves to such agonies.

This time, it is Stone's body that rebels. He can keep going on the rough terrain, but not fast enough. The chance of victory slips away. But Diamantides won't take second for an answer. This time, she carries his rucksack. It's just enough to turn things around. Gradually, their pace picks up. As they do so, their hopes and morale revive. McDermott and Belton, meanwhile, are struggling: Belton is having problems with his shins, and they are reduced to what McDermott calls 'a walk/hop'. Diamantides and Stone regain the lead; McDermott and Belton can only 'watch helplessly' as they go past. Then, for the first time, Diamantides and Stone get badly lost. By the time they realise their mistake, they are well off course; and, by the time they have regained their bearings, they are behind again. So they do it all again. 'It was quite funny,' recalls McDermott today, 'when Helene and Martin came past us again, all het up.' It probably didn't seem quite so funny at the time.

When the pair stagger up the final cruel slope and into Carreg Cennen Castle – 8 hours 18 minutes after they started that morning – they have regained a substantial lead. Stone collapses tearfully on the line. Diamantides seems relatively fresh.

McDermott and Belton hobble in thirty-two minutes later, utterly exhausted. Belton is later diagnosed with a stress fracture. For the victors, meanwhile, the magnitude of their achievement is sinking in. 'I've always wanted to win a race outright,' Helene enthuses. 'At last I've done it.' Actually, it's the first time any woman has won outright a fell race involving men. And Helene has done it on perhaps the toughest course ever, against the toughest opposition imaginable. 'It was fantastic,' says Stone. 'And enjoyable, too, apart from the bad patches – it's wonderful to journey through the hills like that towards a distant destination. But it was brilliant to win it with a mixed team, especially when there were so many other strong teams competing.' Twelve of those teams have dropped out. Diamantides and Stone have completed the 220 miles in 38 hours and 38 minutes. The six paras who finish take thirteen hours longer. We talk of athletes rewriting the record books; Diamantides has rewritten the physiology books.

In the past, pretty much every female fell-runner of note had to fight not only against gravity and the elements, but also, to some extent or other, against male prejudice. That prejudice has declined since the Scottish Amateur Athletic Association barred Kathleen Connochie from competing in the Ben Nevis race in 1955. (The sixteen-year-old Fort William girl ran anyway, starting two minutes after the twenty-seven male runners and beating three of them.) Significant numbers of fell races began to admit women, by popular female demand, in the mid-1970s: the Edale Skyline was one of the first, in 1974. The first official women-only race was at Pendle in 1977, a year that also saw Jean Dawes, a thirty-six-year-old insurance clerk from Windermere, become (on her second attempt) the first female member of the Bob Graham 24 Hour Club. In 1978, women were finally allowed to run at Ben Nevis and in the Mountain Trial (Ros Coats, of Lochaber, was first female finisher in both), and in the KIMM elite course (Ros Coats and Anne-Marie Grindley were first female team). The following year saw Ros Coats win the first British fell-racing championship for women, Wendy Dodds and Janet Sutcliffe become the first women to complete the Manx Mountain Marathon, and Anne-Marie Grindley complete an impressively extended Bob Graham of fifty-eight peaks. That was also the first year that women were allowed to compete in the Three Peaks.

Even that didn't entirely dispel the view that women are too delicate to withstand the rigours of serious fell-running. In 1979, Veronique Marot, the French-born Yorkshirewoman who held the British women's marathon record from 1989 to 2002, was forbidden to run in the Ennerdale Horseshoe. No woman had run in it before, and the organisers felt that the course (which two years later would claim the life of Bob English) was too severe for any but the hardest men. Marot, who had only taken up running the previous year, ran anyway, unofficially, and finished in a highly respectable time of around five hours, ahead of many of the men.

Since then, the tide has been one way (although it was not until 1986 that a woman, Ellen Bailey of Keighley, competed in a BOFRA championship). There are still men who privately regard it as an intolerable slur on their honour ever to be overtaken by a woman; they usually grow out of it, painfully. And there are occasional arguments about whether or not there should be separate starts for the two genders. But no one has seriously questioned women's capacity to race on the fells.

But nor – until Diamantides – did anyone seriously consider the possibility that, one day, women would eclipse men altogether. Today, that possibility can no longer be entirely dismissed – at least as far as the great ultra-distance records are concerned. Physiologically, there is evidence to suggest that women have a higher tolerance for pain than men, and that their higher fat-to-weight ratios may be advantageous in events that require you to burn off fat for energy. (It's interesting that Diamantides, in common with many leading female fell-runners, does not have the kind of skeletal figure that we associate with elite female distance runners on the track.) The female body may also be more efficient in the way that it converts those larger fat reserves into energy. Women's lower centre of gravity may give them better balance – useful for running downhill. And it has been suggested that women sweat less wastefully, which could make a significant difference in a long contest on a hot day. In most races, men can compensate for these disadvantages through superior muscle power and size; but the greater the distance, the more the scales tip towards women.

But is a woman inherently a better long-distance mountain-racing machine than a man – in the same way that she is, probably, a better cross-Channel swimming machine? That's an altogether more contentious proposition. Men have a higher red-blood-cell count, more blood, bigger lungs, more testosterone, a higher power-to-weight ratio, and, generally, longer legs. And all the significant ultra-distance fell records are still held by men. Then again, this could be attributable to the fact that only a tiny minority of women ever get round to fell-running. (Many may be presumed to feel uncomfortable with the sport's macho image; it is, as Diamantides once put it, 'difficult to look elegant when you're covered in mud and there's blood running down your shins'.)

The evidence of other endurance events – marathon-running, for example – neither proves nor disproves the hypothesis that women are better equipped. You can point to the fact that Paula Radcliffe is minutes faster than all but a couple of male British runners currently competing; or to the fact that she is minutes slower than the few dozen elite men around the world whose times hover around the world-record mark. Which fact defines her? And which is attributable to her gender? There is no way of telling.

In the same way, it is impossible to determine whether Diamantides has achieved what she has despite her gender or because of it. To do that, we have to wait until there are as many women taking up fell-running as there are men; a state of affairs which is still a long way off.

Wendy Dodds, who wrote an interesting article on this subject in a recent issue of the *Fellrunner* (and who was a member of the only all-female team to finish the Dragon's Back), reckons that, in terms of physical strength, women generally fall short of men by about 20 per cent. But that's before you take into account the psychological components of ultra-endurance: what if men are comparably disadvantaged in terms of mental strength?

Diamantides believes that 'the ultras are the one area where women are less disadvantaged. I can never see women equalling men in short events: the power-to-weight ratio isn't there. But over the bigger distances, who knows?'

In statistical terms, there's good reason to believe that Diamantides is just a forerunner, with a slowly growing army of mountain superwomen coming up behind her. Her records for Borrowdale and Wasdale have already been beaten (although around a dozen of her other major race records still stand). Two of her ultra records have fallen, too, thanks to Anne Stentiford of Macclesfield Harriers, who in 1991 did a 19-hour-1-minute Paddy

Buckley round (supported by Diamantides) and in 1994 did a sixty-two-peak Bob Graham extension that included a split time of 18 hours 49 minutes for the basic forty-two peaks. Sarah Rowell, the former Olympic marathon-runner, has won a mixed ultra-distance event outright. And four-times British champion Angela Mudge has achieved far more than Diamantides ever has in terms of championship races and international competition; indeed, if current trends continue, the number of British men capable of beating Mudge will soon be measured in single figures. Perhaps that's stretching it a bit; but given that it's scarcely twenty-five years since women were considered incapable of competing in tough fell races at all, it would be foolish to rule out the possibility.

Diamantides does not believe in ruling things out. Her two great heroes are Roger Bannister, conqueror of the four-minute mile, and Stylianos Kyriakides, the impoverished Greek runner who, in 1946, wanting to draw the world's attention to the catastrophe of his country's civil war, sold his family's few possessions, bought a one-way ticket to America and, against all the odds, won the Boston Marathon. (He subsequently became involved with her primary school in Athens, although she never met him.) 'They both believed that they *could*,' she says, 'when everyone else said it was impossible.'

So it is with Diamantides. The secret of success in ultra-distance running is, she believes, as much mental as physical. 'There are a lot of mind games, which I enjoy. In the really long races, there's nothing much you can do about what everyone else does, but there's an awful lot you can do to sort yourself out. It's partly about knowing your limitations, and having the confidence to say, hold on, we've got to ease back for a bit.'

The Dragon's Back, she remembers, 'was brilliant. It was tough, and there were some really bloody painful days. It was incredibly competitive: you know, we led, we lost it, we led, we lost it, someone else was in front with two hours to go. But we won. A lot of it was tactical: you could maximise the advantage of knowing how to look after yourself. It really suited me.'

She was only twenty-seven at the time, and some of her

admirers imagined that she would spend the next decade on similar challenges, setting ever more outrageous records at the furthest frontiers of ultra-distance fell-running. Instead, she has spent much of the past dozen years or so channelling her talent into a series of quite different events. There was, for example, a phase of doing ultra-distance track- and road-running, during which she twice helped Britain to a 100-kilometre bronze in the European Championships. 'I didn't enjoy it that much, but it meant a lot to wear my country's vest.' She also ran (just a few days after competing in the World Mountain Running Trophy) in the World 100-kilometre Championships, as a member of a British women's team that came fourth. And she competed in the Western States 100 Miles race in the United States. 'I came second. Afterwards, I said: right, that's it. I'm glad I've done that, but that's enough.'

She has also devoted a lot of time to the international adventure-race circuit, competing in such multi-discipline events as the Scottish Island Peaks (in which she and Angela Mudge set a women's record that still stands, in 1996) and the Western Isles Challenge (which she won outright – against strong male opposition – in 2000), or, further afield, the Australian Three Peaks Race (which she won in 1998) and the Kaweka Challenge in New Zealand (where she set a record that still stands, in 1999). Such events typically involve two, three or four very long mountain races in as many days, interspersed with periods of cycling or kayaking or, if you're lucky, stretches of 'rest' in the bottom of a racing yacht in which the rest of your team are ferrying you to the next destination. Helene has compared this last experience to 'sitting in a bidet and having buckets of water thrown over you'. It's clear, though, that her talent for enduring and shrugging off discomfort has made her a natural at the sport.

More recently, she's become mildly disillusioned with it. 'I hadn't realised how big the money thing was in adventure racing. But it is. If you have better equipment, you'll perform better. That's why I love hill-running. It's just: "Off you go – if you're good enough, you'll be there." Everyone has the same kit, the same challenge ahead of them.'

Instead, therefore, she has focused on the more modern, high-speed end of the fell-running spectrum, running for both Scotland and Great Britain in a succession of major international tournaments. She's had less success than Mudge, who won gold in the 2000 World Mountain Running Trophy and silver in 2003: Helene's best World Trophy position to date has been seventeenth. That's not to be sneezed at, though, especially in a runner who was once dismissed by a bitchy rival as a 'carthorse' (a jibe that still sharpens her motivation). But the truth is, the relatively short championship distances aren't ideal for her. Nor, I suspect, are the relatively tame environments.

For her, as for the adventurous spirits who pioneered amateur fell-running in Britain in the 1960s and 1970s, wilderness is the whole point of the experience, not just an inconvenient by-product. That's why she hasn't given up the longer, simpler events, such as the KIMM, in which she and Angela Mudge achieved the highest-ever Elite class placing by an all-female team – sixth – in 1999. The fact that she has also chosen to test herself in disciplines less tailor-made for her particular strengths is a testament both to her versatility and to her courage.

Some say that she would have made a more indelible mark in the record books if she had stuck to running impossibly long distances in the mountains. To which she responds: 'What are records? That's not what fell-running is about. I can't even remember the times I've done, or when I did them. They don't matter.' What do matter are the adventures she has had, and her stock of memories of what she calls 'journey runs' – that is, runs 'where you're seeing something new'. The fact that many of these have involved ultra-distance challenges is incidental. Like Kenny Stuart, she didn't want easy triumphs. She wanted to explore the limits of her potential. 'I never want to be in a position of thinking: "Damn, I wish I'd tried that."'

I think that's why, for me, and for many, she remains the great pioneering figurehead of women's fell-running. (Martin Stone calls her 'the most outstanding long-distance runner this country has ever produced, in terms of all-round ability in the hills'.) Never mind the championships and the records (all that sweat and adrenaline, all that cold and pain and brilliant wilderness, reduced to a list of numbers and dates). What makes a fell-running hero or heroine is attitude; and Diamantides' attitude makes her a worthy successor to the tradition of Naylor, Bland and Campbell. Her itinerant life story to date may have little in common with theirs, but they would understand her approach to the mountains and to 'impossible' challenges. There's a cheerful casualness about the way she has exposed herself to discomfort and danger, a blithely positive cast of mind that verges on the heroic. And if there is also something peculiarly feminine about her talent to endure, then so much the better for the legend.

When we say that she was the first person to prove that women could not only compete with men on the fells but might also, in some circumstances, be stronger, it is to her mental strength, as much as to her phenomenal athletic abilities, that we are referring. And when we look ahead for the next Helene Diamantides, what we seek is not so much the talent to break records as the stoicism to withstand, gracefully, the worst that exhaustion and wild mountains can inflict.

Meanwhile, the story of the current Helene Diamantides is not yet over. In 2000, she went to Australia as physio to the British Paralympic team, and stayed in Tasmania, racing and working, for a couple of years afterwards. Her running career had a setback in 2001, when she ruptured an Achilles tendon while doing a cartwheel on the beach, but she seems to be fully recovered. In 2003, she won the island's 82-kilometre Cradle Mountain race, breaking the course record in the process.

By then, however, she had replanted her roots in Britain, having decided to settle down here with her partner, Jonathan Whitaker, a runner who works as a forensic scientist in Wetherby and Birmingham. That, she says, was 'the most frightening thing I've ever done – and the most important'. The couple are based in one of the greener parts of Harrogate, where her physiotherapy practice appears to be thriving. She isn't sure what her next athletic challenge will be, but plans to keep pushing herself 'for as long as I can. I have got very crunchy knees. But I made a decision some time ago to do as much as possible while I could. And so I will.'

As I write this, however, she is preparing for a challenge that neither Naylor nor Campbell nor Bland ever had to confront: motherhood. It will, she agrees, put her in a good position to pronounce on a theory that has often been advanced by male fell-runners: that doing one of the great twenty-four-hour rounds is comparable as a physical ordeal to childbirth. There are obvious similarities: the duration, the systemic physical stress, and the aforementioned quirk whereby you can never remember the pain vividly enough to deter you from putting yourself through the ordeal again. But I've never heard of a female fell-runner who subscribed to it. 'I'm pretty sure,' says Diamantides, 'that childbirth will be worse.' And while there is evidence to suggest that having babies can aid long-distance athletes by increasing their red-blood-cell count, she inclines more towards the view that 'if it does help you, it's because it teaches you what real pain is'.

By the time you read this, she will know the answer. But I'm happy to leave her there, poised on the threshold of a new journey, both daunting and thrilling, in which she will once again explore from a feminine perspective the mysteries of human endurance.

Before I leave, though, it seems perverse not to seek her advice on how an ordinary bloke might best prepare himself to endure the great ordeals of the fells. The tips trip off the tongue, with a fluency that suggests she has also witnessed a few failures in her time. 'Find out what's involved. Find out what your strengths and your weaknesses are. Face up to your problems – there's no substitute for knowing yourself. Also: learn to navigate. Sort out which pair of shorts don't chafe and what food you can keep down. Do your homework. There's no such thing as good luck. Good luck comes to those who are best prepared. Above all, if you're not going to enjoy it, don't bother. It's an awful long way, and an awful long time to be miserable.'

30

Scenes from a fell-running year: November

For elite runners, the year's real business is done; for the rest of us, it's also-running as usual. There are fewer races to choose from, but there's a welcome return of elbow room in those that we do choose, now that the summer cavalry charges are over. There's also a special kind of satisfaction to be had from long winter slogs in which mountaincraft can be as important as speed and even finishing last can leave you with a glow of righteous pride.

At the Dunnerdale, a steep 5-mile circuit near Broughton Mills in Cumbria, spectators are astounded to see John Atkinson, the champion guides-racer of the late 1980s and early 1990s, sprinting away from Gavin Bland to win. Atkinson, a health and safety manager at Burlington Slate (Fred Reeves's old employer) in Kirkby-in-Furness, was generally agreed to have retired from running. It doesn't seem to have slowed him down. In Wales, a similarly rejuvenated Colin Donnelly – fourteen years after his third British championship – wins the 11-mile Penmaenmawr race in Conwy, beating a field of nearly 200 at the age of forty-four.

At the 21-mile Tour of Pendle in Lancashire, some old-timers are heard to grumble at the fine weather. Traditionally, there's a chance on this complex, eleven-checkpoint route for hill-wise plodders to steal a few places on faster but navigationally challenged rivals. As it is, Borrowdale's Andrew Schofield – who is both hill-wise and fleet of foot – is comfortably the first of 116 finishers.

Elsewhere, Ian Holmes beats 168 rivals at the Shepherd's Skyline in West Yorkshire. Simon Bailey wins the Roaches in Staffordshire on a day of plentiful mud and mist. Slight confusion about the start time – because of the clocks going back – doesn't prevent eighty people from enjoying the Meall a' Bhuachaille in Inverness-shire. And Billy Burns, former World Trophy bronze medallist, international marathon-runner and another notable English absentee in Alaska, wins the Kirkbymoor fell race in Cumbria.

In Kendal, meanwhile, the great and good of the fell-running world descend on the Castle Green Hotel for the FRA's annual dinner and dance. Rob Jebb and Ian Holmes collect trophies for the British and English championships respectively. Lou Sharp gets two, one for each of her women's titles. Ambleside – and Nick Sharp – win the men's team title; Bingley the women's. Not for the first time this season, the Bingley boys and girls celebrate with an enthusiasm that makes you wonder how on earth they manage to run so well.

There are also a couple of awards for Wendy Dodds: the English Over-50s women's championship and the women's Lakeland Classics Trophy – both for the second year running. The Lakeland Classics is a parallel championship, designed to encourage the survival of the great long-distance fell races, such as the Ennerdale and the Dockray-Helvellyn, both of which would have been counters for the trophy had they taken place this year. The others in the series are the Duddon Valley, the Wasdale, the Borrowdale, the Three Shires and the Langdale. All fall into one or other of two categories: Long and Super-Long. It's a big boost for the organisers that the FRA have allowed them to present their prizes at this dinner; so too is the general consensus at the dinner that this is an important cause. The Lakeland Classics are events that still do what amateur fell races have always been supposed to do: test resilience, resourcefulness and self-reliance as well as speed. Even completing the requisite four races out of six is a test of durability. Only thirty-four runners managed to do so this year – of whom only twelve were under forty. One of these was Mark Hartell, aged thirty-nine, who came third overall. Another was Rob Jebb, winner of the men's trophy, who further delights the assembled long-distance enthusiasts with a short speech declaring that races of this kind are at the heart of the sport. Everyone should resolve to compete in at least one next year, he tells them, and they should 'take along a friend'.

Wendy Dodds agrees: 'I enjoy long races that test your strength and endurance. I would find it sad if they just gradually disappeared. For the Wasdale and the Borrowdale,' she adds, 'I was just pleased to be running – I didn't expect to win the series overall.' But it has, she concedes, been a 'most pleasing' season, 'considering it was based on a small amount of training'.

Ian Holmes, whose career total of four British and five English championships, four Ben Nevis wins, three Grasmeres and countless records across the whole spectrum of distances gives him a reasonable claim to be considered the most successful all-round fell-runner ever, seems similarly satisfied with his year. 'Aye, it wasn't a bad season,' he says. 'It was a pity to miss out on the British, but I was pleased to get the English. It's hard to train as much as I used to – having a family gives you a new perspective. So I'm grateful for what I can get. But I've had a good time. And I won Grasmere – I hadn't done that for a few years.'

Lou Sharp (who after two months sleeping in a camper-van has finally found somewhere to live) looks back with mixed feelings on a year with more ups and downs than a medium-length fell race. 'I was pretty emotionally drained and going through a major life trauma. Running kept me sane, really. But I was surprised that I did so well with my running as my mind was on other things.' She's a bit disappointed about Keswick Ladies losing their title – 'We just had too many people who couldn't run in key championship races' – but delighted to end the year as she began it, as British champion. And, she adds, 'It was nice to get in the World Trophy team. Even if I was rubbish.'

What with Angela Brand-Barker winning the Welsh championship (again) and Duncan Overton winning the men's Over-50s title, it hasn't been a bad year for Keswick. Even Mark Denham-Smith's sixteenth place in the men's championship is not to be scorned: that's better than anyone from Dark Peak, Clayton-le-Moors or Cumberland Fell Runners could manage, and only three of the Borrowdale men were ahead of him. 'Yes, I was pleased,' says Mark. 'But I think I could do better.'

Tim Austin has had a more obviously disappointing year:

'Basically, I missed half the season.' Yet he's conscious that what he did do, he did well. 'Yes, I had some good results.' If he could steer clear of illness and injury, who knows what he might achieve?

For Mark Hartell, meanwhile, a year with few spectacular successes in terms of results has proved unexpectedly fulfilling. 'I think 2003 was an off year or a consolidation year,' he says. 'I had other challenges: separation, financial settlement, access to my daughter. But then I think: "Well, not too bad for all that." Now I have to convince myself that I have plenty left in me – maybe even that the best is yet to come. But I will only get there with focus.'

31

Sub-twenty-four

A COUPLE OF WEEKS BEFORE MY FOURTH ATTEMPT at the BG, it dawned on me that I could succeed. I was on the outskirts of Plymouth, running on the roadside with a 60-pound rucksack on my back, 2 or 3 miles into an entirely uphill slog of nearly 10 miles to Clare's parents' house on the edge of Dartmoor.

We had come down to stay with them for ten days. Clare and the children had arrived a few days earlier while I was away working. (There's nothing like the arrival of a second child to make you more impatient to begin an extended stay with your parents.) Running from the station with an entire holiday's worth of luggage on my back (including extra books for ballast) was the first item in my final burst of intensive BG preparations; and, within fifteen minutes or so, I was starting to feel sorry for myself. Runners often do. The more you learn about your limits, the more devastating are the moments when you realise that you have exceeded them. The pain – mental as much as physical – hits you like a kick in the stomach, leaving a dull, debilitating ache. 'Oh God,' you moan, 'what have I done? How can I possibly keep this up for another minute, let alone another hour?' Becoming a good runner is partly about learning to control and subdue such moments; but even the very best can 'blow up' if they misjudge their pace – and then they, too, can be swamped by self-pity.

I, meanwhile, was not so much blowing up as dissolving. It was blastingly hot; my load and my legs felt like lead; sweat was splashing from my T-shirt; and my minimalist breakfast was a distant, shrinking memory. 'Oh God,' I said to myself. Why hadn't

I listened to Clare when she said this was a stupid idea? How far would I have to struggle on – or what excuse would I have to come up with – before I could telephone and ask to be collected without losing too much face?

Then my brain stopped in its tracks. Abruptly, everything was clear, as if a curtain had been opened.

If you stop now, said a voice in my head, *you will never, ever stand the remotest chance of finishing the BG. All your training will have been wasted. All those years of obsession will have been so much self-deception. Stop now, and you might as well call off the attempt and save wasting any more of everyone's time. Never mind all the training you already have in the bank, or all the training that you're still planning to do. This is the only moment that matters. Fail now, and you will always fail. Stick to it, and – well, you won't necessarily succeed, but you'll be in with a chance. Sticking with this is the basic, entry-level qualification. You won't in a million years get round if you can't live with this.* 'This' being the level of pain I was feeling, and my general sense of dauntedness.

It was the dauntedness that was the real barrier – the feeling, which I've mentioned before, of *'Do I not like this?'* Living with pain is relatively simple: you just have to learn to detach yourself from it. Dread is a more awkward co-habitee – especially that particular kind of dread that involves knowing how much physical distress you're in and fearing how much worse it will get if you stick with your current plans. To tame that, you must consciously will your distress to be extended and redoubled – a mental trick that it is hard for a normal person to perform.

But that is what people like Billy Bland and Joss Naylor do: they put their bodies on the line, not in ignorance but in conscious courage; not shrinking from distress but willing it. Could I do the same? Well, why not? I was a man, no less than they were. And my lack of their great athletic gifts made it all the more foolhardy to imagine that I could dispense with their mental strengths as well.

So I made a deal with myself: *do this without stopping and you will do the BG.* I knew this was nonsense, as such deals always are. I also knew it was true. To surrender now would be to surrender always. If I wished to have anything more to do with fell-running, there was only one option. Keep going. Keep going, whatever happens, however long it takes, however much it hurts; keep going or die trying. All moments are contained in this moment. Master this moment and anything is possible.

It was a foolish discourse, really; and, recounted now, it seems ridiculous. But there was one undeniable truth in it: if I couldn't complete this, I certainly wouldn't be able to complete forty-two peaks in twenty-four hours a fortnight later. To believe any different would be the grossest self-deception. And that was my breakthrough. I realised that, although I had never been an habitual surrenderer – runners rarely are – I had not yet entirely shed my capacity to self-deceive. And that, if I chose, I could now do so.

I chose.

I kept going. Up the hill I plodded, mile after mile, lane after lane. My feet burnt in my shoes. My shoulders were rubbed raw by the weight of my pack through my drenched T-shirt. My dry lungs heaved until I thought they would split. My dry brain throbbed until I thought my head would burst. I had never imagined that there could be so much continuous uphill gradient in such a limited space. My legs flopped so limply I thought I would fall to the ground. But I knew – and had known, since about the fifth mile – that there was no question of my doing anything but continue. And this confidence created a layer of mental peace over the physical pain. Whatever I was feeling, whatever I might feel, I was stronger than those feelings, because I chose to be.

From then on, the whole question of the BG seemed simple. I reached the house. I bathed my wounds. I recovered. I played and parented and did other holiday things and also ran twice a day on the steep and plentiful hills. I finalised the logistics of the coming attempt. And I kept reminding myself that, if I wanted to succeed, all I had to do was choose.

One such choice could be made there and then. I mentioned many chapters ago that there is a point in the BG circuit, between Scafell Pike and Scafell, where the quickest route is via an exposed climb known as Broad Stand. I think I also mentioned (didn't I?) that I am terrified of heights and that each time I passed that way the prospect of climbing Broad Stand filled me with a dread that verged on – and in some cases spilled into – panic. What I didn't mention – because at the time I had hardly dared mention it even to myself – was that for my second and third attempts I didn't even use Broad Stand, but instead used a detour, via Lord's Rake, that takes ten or fifteen minutes longer.

Most walkers use this detour (or another that goes around the other side, via Fox's Tarn), and many successful BG rounders have done so too. They argue, as I did, that if the prospect of a terrifying climb appals you, the dread and panic will take so much out of you that it's at least equivalent to an extra fifteen minutes of running and climbing. Perhaps they are right. Perhaps I was, too. Or perhaps I was deceiving myself.

Perhaps? Of course I was deceiving myself. Other runners might have enough skill and stamina in hand to be able to throw away fifteen minutes; I, patently, didn't. If I chose nonetheless to do so, then, clearly, I didn't really want to succeed. And, now that I thought about it, I realised that, on those earlier attempts, perhaps I hadn't really wanted to succeed.

That sounds absurd. It isn't. I don't mean that all those months of training weren't fuelled by a fierce desire to complete the round, or that I hadn't wanted to succeed when I set out on my attempts, or even during their opening hours. They were, and I had. But as the hours passed, and the pain and exhaustion accumulated, so the consequences of continued success had invariably begun to seem less attractive. Dragging myself up Steel Fell, say, with eight hours of running in my joints and real and metaphorical clouds looming ahead, I had inevitably become aware of a disheartening calculation: that success – that is, keeping going to the end – meant another sixteen hours of the same and worse; whereas failure – that is, falling so far behind that I could reasonably call it off – could see me back in a warm bath within eight hours or less. That calculation wasn't in itself enough to make me choose failure. But it took the intensity out of my desire to succeed.

Which was logical; but not quite as logical as to focus honestly on that calculation before my next attempt started: to contemplate those extra hours of pain with the same clarity as I would in the attempt itself; to summon up as much memory as possible of the worst moments of misery and dread; to feel the self-pity in advance – and then to ask myself, do I want this or not?

And did I? I had to repeat the process several times before I could answer in a way that was neither self-deceiving nor defeatist. But after a certain amount of mental readjustment I reached a firm conclusion. I didn't want to give up on the BG without another attempt. I didn't want to fail again. Therefore I wanted to succeed. Therefore I must want success and all that that entailed: that is, misery, pain, exhaustion, cold, extended for a full twenty-four hours rather than a mere fifteen or sixteen; and, of course, a climb over Broad Stand. 'But . . . but . . .' stammered my weaker self – to be silenced by the withering question: 'Do you want to get round or not?'

From then on – bizarrely, given my record – I never seriously considered the possibility of failure. I gave no further thought to the terrors of Broad Stand: my decision to do it was non-negotiable, so what was the point in worrying? I completed my remaining days of training conscientiously but not manically. I put the finishing touches to the logistics thoroughly but not neurotically. And whereas with the past two attempts my body's memory of previous ordeals had made me feel positively sick with nerves the day before, on this occasion I felt strangely calm. What was there to worry about? My destiny was in my own hands.

I had fewer supporters on this occasion than for previous attempts. I'd only decided a few weeks earlier to do it, more or less on the spur of the moment, and it was too late for many people – including Gawain and Charlie – to change their arrangements. But I wasn't bothered about who else was involved. This time, I was going to rely on only one person: me.

The day of the attempt dawned in the usual way – which is to say, it didn't dawn, but midnight came, and Clare shook me awake from the briefest and deepest of sleeps. An hour later I had shrugged off my nocturnal feebleness and was starting off yet again with Charles up the black slopes of Skiddaw.

What followed was curiously straightforward. I tried to remain half-asleep for as long as possible, saving any passion or adrenaline for much later. The night was cloudy but not impenetrable. I felt neither happy nor unhappy: I was simply doing a job.

We went off course coming down off Skiddaw, running down the bumpy, bouldered turf with more speed than care and attention and ending up on the south side of Hare Crag. Many attempts have foundered on precisely this mistake, which leaves you with a sea of ditches and heather to wade through in order to get back on course. Miraculously, we found ourselves on the one tiny sheep-trod-turned-path that threads firmly through it. We could never have found it deliberately. Now that we were on it, it was easier than having stayed on the correct route.

The night lasted longer than usual. It was mid-August – late for a BG attempt. Our feet froze in the pre-dawn chill coming up Blencathra, and it was still dark when we came down the other side. This made it hard to go flat out on the descent, which cost a few minutes. I wasn't bothered. I knew that everything was going to be all right.

I didn't stop for a break at Threlkeld: why postpone what has to be done? Instead, I ploughed on, not talking much, eating and drinking as much as I could without being sick, focusing dispassionately on my task as if I were a machine. I remembered an account by one of Mark Hartell's supporters for his seventy-seven-peak record, according to which 'he could quote bearings from memory, foresee and warn of possible navigational errors ... relentlessly clawing back minutes from the schedule'. That, I resolved, should be my model.

There was no glorious dawn. Clouds clung to most of the peaks on the Helvellyn ridge. But there was always just enough visibility for my immediate purposes. Each time I saw a great grey cushion smothering one of the peaks ahead, I reassured myself with the thought that it would be gone by the time I got there. And so it generally was.

To say that everything went right would be to oversimplify. There was something about my state of mind that made it right. On a few occasions, we were completely immersed in thick cloud. Instead of becoming despondent, I welcomed the chance to stay cool and hydrated. When the cloud broke, I welcomed the fact that I could see.

I'm not superstitious, nor do I believe in Providence. Yet somehow I convinced myself that, in some obscure way, it had been divinely ordained that I would succeed – or, rather, that there would be nothing to prevent me from succeeding if I chose to do so. On previous attempts, I had always believed – without framing it in those words – that the outcome lay in the lap of the gods. This time it lay in my own hands.

Halfway up Steel Fell, I took my first rest. I was more or less exactly on schedule, and earned myself a bit of slack by getting back to my feet after just ten minutes rather than the alotted twenty. Just as the certainty of failure had banished all strength from my legs on my previous attempt, so my conviction that this time I was destined to succeed now banished most of the pain. Visualising this moment in advance – plodding the last impossibly steep 50 metres to the crest of Steel Fell – I had imagined myself trying to dredge reserves of morale from the depths of a sea of exhaustion and despondency. In fact, I felt quite fresh. Or, rather, since I fully intended to keep going for nearly sixteen hours more, I wasn't really in the business of feeling anything at all.

On I went, eating up the peaks – and that's about all I can tell you about it, really. There was nothing beautiful or magical about it: my mind was too full of bearings and times, too busy concentrating on what I had to do. But I do remember seeing the whole Scafell massif buried in cloud as we came off the Langdale Pikes, and knowing that the cloud would be gone by the time we got there – and being right.

I also remember reaching Scafell Pike and realising that I hadn't yet spent a single moment dreading the approach of Broad Stand. That couldn't be right. Tackling a scary climb without first working myself up into a fever of terror had always been an impossibility for me. I needed to start panicking fast. Then I stopped myself. The decision to make the climb was non-negotiable. What was the point of feeling fear?

Minutes later, I was down at the base of Broad Stand, Charles (who had rejoined us from Wasdale) helping me with a rope, me looking upwards, feeling nothing at all, and resolved to continue feeling nothing at all. Minutes after that I was up and over it, resting on the allegedly flat (but actually steeply sloping) slab of rock just above it, while Charles helped guide his brother, Richard, up to join us. I wasn't absolutely without apprehension: otherwise I wouldn't have been tucked so tightly into the furthest corner from the edge. But the apprehension was theoretical: I felt nothing. No thoughts entered my head about the chasm below, or about how easy it would be to overbalance or slip and tumble hopelessly into the void – or, if they did, I was detached from them, and dismissed them before they could register.

Perhaps you need to have some personal experience of vertigo to realise how remarkable this was. I have subdued my fear of heights before and since – in the sense of forcing myself to do something that I didn't really fancy doing. But only then has the fear been entirely absent.

And once we were all up and moving safely over the top of Scafell, a wave of euphoria burst on me that carried me for hours to come. I had gained fifteen minutes – quarter an hour of, as it were, the casino's time. I had had a few minutes' rest in the process. I was within forty unproblematic minutes of Wasdale Head and was still more or less on schedule – which meant that success, for the first time, was a serious possibility. Best of all, I had stopped lying to myself, and I had confronted and beaten Broad Stand. If I could do that, I could do anything.

And so I did. Down I sped on that long, long descent to Wasdale that had reduced me to despair the first time I had tried it, five years earlier. This time I skipped down it joyfully, skidding down the scree channel lower down with whoops of enthusiasm and sliding on my back down the steep grassy field below it for the sheer fun of it. Straight through the campsite without a break, up most of Yewbarrow while still warm, a short break, then off on the long, relentless slog towards Red Pike, Steeple and Pillar – once again, there wasn't a great deal to report. The clouds continued to recede just in time. The sun must have receded too, although I don't recall a sunset. I had, in any case, no time for admiring views. All my thoughts were focused on the job in hand, and on the outcome that I had chosen for myself.

Then, suddenly, after nearly eighteen hours, something went wrong. I'm not sure what or why – perhaps it was the sudden sense of enveloping darkness, or perhaps my blood-sugar level had dipped below a crucial threshold. But on the way down from Pillar to Kirk Fell, a wave of pathetic exhaustion overwhelmed me. The world seemed to wobble. My feet seemed to shake each time I picked them up. Fingers of cramp began to explore my calves. My pacers seemed to be finding it hard to slow down to my pace. My head felt too heavy to keep upright.

I stumbled on, down through Black Sail Pass and up towards Kirk Fell. But a crack of doubt had appeared in my mental foundations. What if it all went wrong again? What if I was destined never to succeed? I could remember no trace of the euphoria and confidence of the previous few hours. All I could think about was the fact that I was using every watt of my will power just to keep going to the top of this slope.

The pacers began to show signs of concern, but said nothing to encourage my gathering defeatism. I tried to refuel with dried apricots, then motivated myself with the promise that I would rest for two minutes halfway up that climb. I did so; the minutes had gone before I had stopped panting. I plodded on, wavering and staggering, luring myself with another promise, of a break halfway up Great Gable. This part of the circuit is, by general consent, one of the hardest patches of any clockwise round, with three of the biggest peaks of all – Pillar, Kirk Fell and Great Gable – in quick succession. After that, it gets easier; but knowing that it will do so doesn't make the patch any less painful. The sheer quantity of ascent and descent consumes your morale as voraciously as it consumes your strength.

A third of the way up Great Gable, I flung myself to the ground. 'Two minutes,' I muttered to Charles.

I fumbled with some apricots, and tried to drink between my gulps of air.

'Come on then,' said Charles, after what seemed like ten seconds.

'Five minutes,' I mumbled.

Charles looked at his watch. 'You're losing a lot of time. You really can't afford to lose any more.'

I could hear the tension in his voice, but there was nothing I could do. 'Got to have five minutes,' I insisted.

A few minutes later, I was still slumped on the ground. Someone was whispering a few yards away. Then Charles spoke again. I can't remember exactly what he said, except that both his tone and his wording were curiously formal – something like: 'It would be a great pity not to make the most of this opportunity.' The furious subtext was clear: *get up, or I'll kill you*. Which was fair enough.

I rolled over, in a state of mind indistinguishable from that in which you roll over on a Monday morning, poised between getting up for work and going back to sleep. Which would I choose? Throw off the duvet – or burrow down deeper? At some point I had to choose – but both options had obvious drawbacks. Meanwhile, sleep was winning. I realised that the choice could be postponed no longer. All moments were contained within this moment. All the hopes and struggles and exertions of the past five years boiled down to this minute. Did I choose failure or success?

I staggered to my feet without a word, without further thought. Onwards and upwards, swaying from side to side. Never mind how slowly, never mind how painfully. I had made my choice now, just as I had on those Devon lanes. There were no other options: just one foot in front of the other until the end.

It was growing dark, and I had no sense of where the summit was, but my heart grew steadily lighter. The shadow of failure had passed. Sooner or later, the top would come; eventually, it did. From then on I knew it could be done. I had dropped about forty minutes on the twenty-three-hour schedule, but that still left me twenty minutes in hand for the twenty-four hours. There was no catching up to be done, no more major mountains to be climbed, just six straightforward peaks that seemed to become less daunting with each passing minute.

By Honister Pass, the night was pitch-black, and the cramp was resuming its attacks, but there was no question of giving up. I stopped for five minutes on the way up Dale Head to drink some hot Bovril while two lucky volunteers – Clare and Baer, I think – each massaged a thigh. 'He's a tough old bugger,' I heard someone say. 'Who'd have thought he'd still be going now?' There's nothing like a remark of that sort to put a bit of fire back into your legs. Hadn't thought I could do it, had they? Well, they'd soon be thinking again – just as Billy Bland was in 1988, a couple of weeks after dismissing Mark McDermott's attempt on Joss Naylor's seventy-two-peak record with the words: 'Yon lad's living in cloud-cuckoo-land.'

Then I was off again, trudging up into the darkness, unsteadily trying to stuff a banana into my mouth and congratulating myself on having stolen another ten minutes from the Rogerson schedule (which allows for a fifteen-minute break at this point). All we had to do was keep going and not get lost.

The latter wasn't as easy as it sounds, with no hint of starlight or moonlight penetrating the clouds. We knocked off Dale Head, Hindscarth and Robinson easily enough, with a fresh wave of euphoria refuelling my legs when I realised that all forty-two peaks were now behind me. But the rocky descent from Robinson was tricky, and at the bottom we became confused in the nocturnal blackness and for a moment had no idea at all of how to find the road.

The panic passed; the farm track revealed itself. Soon I was where I had dreamed of being for five years, trotting down the lane past Newlands Chapel with more than an hour in which to get to Keswick and no possibility of getting lost. (You can take the runner out of the South, but you can't take the South out of the runner: despite all the wonders of the mountains, there's something reassuring about a road.)

This time, the euphoria relaxed me, to the point where I almost fell asleep on my feet. I slowed down, walking stretches that I could have run and running, when I did run, at little more than a shuffle. There was no point in pushing myself, and I certainly didn't want to risk blowing up. In any case, I wanted to sit back and enjoy the moment.

A 6-mile run through Cumbrian lanes at midnight may not constitute everyone's idea of relaxation and idle pleasure, but I find it hard to imagine a more overwhelming contentment. The night was peaceful, framed by deep shadows of trees and farm buildings and curiously curved mountains. Newlands Chapel slept among the trees on our left. The warm air tasted clean and sweet, with a gentle breeze carrying past us occasional mysterious sounds, of night birds and sheep and other unspecified creatures. Friends surrounded me, chatting desultorily as people do at the end of a long, happy summer evening. In my sleepy way, I felt as if I was running on air: not swiftly, but softly, in a painless, patient rhythm that I could have kept up all night.

I was still somewhat detached, both from my feelings and from my surroundings. But my cocoon of purpose was beginning to peel away in the blackness of the August night. There was no longer much need to focus on the job in hand; instead, I could allow myself to enjoy a small glow of self-congratulation at a hard job well done. And as the high hedges of Portinscale on the south-west edge of Keswick signalled that we were within a mile of the finish, all the years of disappointment and frustration and shame and anxiety and pain resolved themselves simultaneously. I could feel their weight lifting from my shoulders – and realised with amazement quite how heavy they had been. Every step brought me nearer to the moment I had been longing for, and yet I felt no impatience to get there. It was done now. I had conquered the mountains. Or, rather, I had conquered myself.

I scarcely remember the final moment. I touched the railings of the Moot Hall at twenty-eight minutes past midnight – 23 hours 28 minutes after I started. Some drunks were shouting abuse from a hotel window. Someone took a dark, impossibly blurred photograph, which I still have, showing me slumped by a wheely bin outside the Moot Hall, wrapped in a foil blanket, eyes red from the flash, with my two-year-old daughter, Isobel, blinking in bemusement in her grandfather's arms. Someone else produced a bottle of champagne and some plastic cups. One of the pacers, Matt, a fell-running novice who had doggedly accompanied me all the way from Wasdale, drank his and was instantly sick. I had a couple of sips and nearly did the same. And then, disoriented by the unaccustomed absence of disappointment, we hurried off to bed.

The next day, I was surprised to experience no trace of the aches and bruises and stiffness that had plagued me for weeks after each of my previous three attempts. I was conscious, however, of a profound, peaceful weariness. For the best part of a week afterwards, I slept for about ten hours a night, and it was an effort to keep my eyes open through the days in between. The lethargy didn't entirely pass for a month or more.

I'm told this was a normal reaction to the unnatural ordeal I had put my body through. But I know that it was something else as well. It was a symptom of the deep peace of mind that comes when one finally unburdens oneself of a major load of unfinished business.

32

Scenes from a fell-running year: December

A wet, windy December makes for a quiet end to the year. Most of the action, if you don't count the Keswick AC annual dinner at the Swinside Inn, is concentrated in a few days around Christmas, and the spirit is more festive than ferocious. After the Cardington Cracker in Shropshire and the Hexhamshire Hobble in Northumberland towards the beginning of the month, there's the 50-mile Calderdale Way relay in West Yorkshire (where Clayton-le-Moors win the ladies' prize with a team consisting largely of over-fifties, Wendy Dodds among them). And then it's into Christmas week: the Stoop in West Yorkshire on the twenty-first and, on Boxing Day, the Turkey Trot in the Mourne Mountains and the Whinberry Naze Dash at Rawtenstall, Lancashire. The following day, there's the Guisborough Woods in North Yorkshire.

For many of us, such events are scarcely distinguishable from the training runs they interrupt. The alternatives – a warm pub; a warm hearth; a warm bed – are equally tempting in each case. The post-running rituals – slowly defrosting feet beneath cold taps, or laboriously purging shoes and clothes of stitch-rotting, drain-blocking mud – are equally time-consuming. And there's the same paradoxical experience whereby, the more wild and unwelcoming the mountains grow, the more liberating it feels to run in them.

Meanwhile, it's a good time for dreaming – because fell-running is above all about making unlikely dreams come true. For Lou Sharp, that means thinking about a third successive British title ('Well, I'll give it a go') and perhaps too about another shot at the World Trophy: 'I'd like to get into the England team again, and maybe do a bit better than last time.' Ian Holmes won't rule out an unprecedented fifth British championship. 'What I'd really like, though, would be to win a fifth Ben race. But I'm not expecting to break Kenny's record.' Allan Greenwood is thinking about his Bob Graham; Tim Austin is hoping to be running again by early March, in time for the new championship season; Mark Croasdale is dreaming of a final glorious triumph over his equine rivals; Mark Denham-Smith is wondering if he can get into the British top ten.

Wendy Dodds is looking forward to earning a special commemorative plaque by running that twenty-first Three Peaks race; after which – who knows? – perhaps she could do twenty-one more. 'I don't fell-run primarily to get faster and beat other people,' she explains. 'I'm a mountain person rather than an athlete. I'll be happy if I'm still able to go out in twenty years' time and run in the hills.'

As for Mark Hartell, he's looking forward to a future of unbounded striving: 'I'm still finding new running challenges, and I also find races that I would love to do again, so the list keeps growing. In the first half of this year I scaled back a bit: I think you need to have stability and a good base from which to perform. But later on I started to reach out again, and I am very optimistic and excited about the year or two ahead.' One day, he admits, 'I might run out of running challenges. But I want to build a successful business, build a house, restore an old sports car, climb some big mountains, relearn the piano . . . I will never run out of some sort of challenge.'

Which is a curiously uplifting thought to dwell on as the fell-running year comes to its traditional close: in West Yorkshire, where 375 people gather on Penistone Hill on New Year's Eve for the tenth Briscoe Breweries Auld Lang Syne race. There's an icy gale blowing, and the boggy uplands of Haworth Moor are frozen more or less solid. But it's hard to imagine a happier bunch of 375 people. Dave Woodhead, the organiser, is for some reason wearing a cabbage on his head; the official starter – Ian Holmes's four-year-old son, Louie – is wearing a Batman costume. Everyone is convinced they're wearing the wrong shoes (trainers grip better on sheet ice; fell shoes grip better on everything else); but no one intends to do anything about it. Nothing entirely makes sense, and no one particularly cares.

Ian Holmes has won the race every time it's been run; he even won it when it wasn't run, in 1996, when bad weather forced a cancellation but – in the time-honoured way – a bunch of diehards ran it anyway. No one seriously expects to beat him today – or, if they do, they're not admitting to it. Most of us are more interested in staying upright than in winning. There's ice at the road crossing; ice on every puddle in the stony track that weaves through the frozen heather; great sheets of ice on the climb up to Top o' Stairs; and whole miniature lakes of ice in the boggy ground along the Oxenhope Stoop skyline. Ian Holmes, it emerges, is wearing trainers; the Walsh-wearing majority trust to luck, and to the fact that, three times out of four, the ice cracks as we land on it, resulting in a cold foot but a firm grip. The rest of the time, we pretend we're skating.

The cold air burns our lungs as the pace picks up in the second half of the race, but I, at any rate, welcome it. Every now and then, I raise my eyes to the sleeping Pennines in front, frost-white against a pale grey sky. How privileged I am to be able to run through such hills, in such an atmosphere – even if, by some standards, I'm not going very fast.

By the time I finish – and there are more than 200 behind me – Ian Holmes has been back for fifteen minutes and is changed and on his way to the pub. I don't think anyone begrudges him his victory, or the ease of it. We've all done what we set out to do: survived a bracing winter run in some beautiful hills. The fact that we've also run shoulder-to-shoulder – notionally – with one of the greatest athletes of our age is a bonus; as is the fact that we've each been given a bottle of Auld Lang Syne beer. Whatever indulgences New Year's Eve has in store for us, we can reasonably argue that we've earned them. And, indeed, no one can blame us if we now seek shelter from the biting wind in the Old Sun pub – where, at a warm, crowded prize-giving, Ian Holmes is awarded what looks like his weight in beer – before hurrying away to get home before the snow starts.

By nightfall, the Pennines are blanketed in snow. There will be some hazardous driving to be done by anyone with plans to run in the nearby Giant's Tooth race on New Year's Day. But there's no point in worrying now. We can think about that next year.

33

Over the hill

SOMETIMES I FEEL ASHAMED of how much of my life has been devoted to fell-running. I add up all the thousands of hours spent not just running but training, travelling, preparing – and all the thousands of pounds squandered on petrol, accommodation, kit, maps, sports drinks, sports doctors, osteopaths, chiropractors, acupuncturists – and I wonder what madness can have possessed me. Were there really no better ways to spend all that time and money? No more constructive channels into which to pour my energy?

Of course there were. There were also more destructive ones. Who knows how much nastier a person – how much weaker and more wound-up – I would have been without fell-running? The alternative uses I could have found for my strength, stamina and will power would have been as likely to make the world a worse place as a better one. We don't always give ourselves enough credit for doing no harm – and running with like-minded friends in wildernesses that most people consider too bleak and distant to have anything to do with is about as harmless a diversion as it's possible to imagine.

In any case, I know that, from another perspective, the remarkable thing about me is how *little* of my life I have devoted to fell-running. Some people reading this book will be appalled that a Southern yuppie who has been running on the fells for scarcely a decade-and-a-half – and has run fewer races in his lifetime than some people would in a season – should set himself up as an authority on the subject. Some will also be appalled – as I am too – at how much I have left out. What? No mention of the

World Trophy triumphs of the 1990s? No mention of Martin Jones and Carol Greenwood and Sarah Rowell and Keith Anderson and Mark Kinch? No chapter on Jeff Norman or Harry Walker or Mike Short or Colin Donnelly? And what about the other great fell-running clubs: Dark Peak, Clayton-le-Moors, Eryri, Carnethy and so on? Sorry, I just ran out of space.

Yet I don't apologise for my outsider's perspective, nor for the fact that my first-hand knowledge of fell-racing has been gained largely from the back half of the field. Great sports are about much more than the rarefied activities of their elites. Their souls come from the mediocre majorities who know how difficult the achievements of the superstars really are. Think what football would be without all those millions whose visceral understanding of the game's skills and difficulties is derived only from park kickabouts. The knowledge and passion of the also-rans are what give meaning to the activities of the elite. If the elite aren't interested in our perspective, they should be.

That's not to diminish their achievements. The best fell-runners are, as Chris Brasher once observed, 'athletes of real world class – if their sport lent itself to being held in a stadium surrounded by television cameras then they would be known the world over.' But it doesn't: not just because of the difficulties of getting mountains in stadia or cameras on mountains, but because the essence of the sport is largely invisible. Watched through a television camera, a top fell-runner racing down a rough hillside looks more ungainly than spectacular. You cannot simultaneously see his movements and the details of the ground that make them so erratic; and nor, unless you are there, can you sense the momentum that makes them so dangerous. Even in video footage of international races, where the courses are smoother and the gait is therefore more graceful, there's something missing: you cannot see the gravity. Watch the world's best mountain-runners racing neck and neck up a steep hill and you'll probably ask yourself why they are being so lackadaisical. They know how close they are to breaking point; but it doesn't show. The real action is internal.

It's the same with the great ultra-distance challenges. Mike

Cudahy, who accomplished quite a few such challenges himself, put it well: 'If few can grasp the almost super-human ability needed to cover 26 miles at under five minutes per mile, and if one must actually be there to appreciate the astonishing speed of the top-class sprinter, who can be expected to comprehend the endeavour and the endurance hidden within the painful shuffle of the ultra-runner? (Look, Mummy, joggers!)'

I suppose that's what this book is for. My fell-running achievements are negligible; so, by some standards, is my experience as a fell-running spectator. But at least I have some idea of what the sport and its struggles feel like from the inside.

And although I am faintly ashamed that it took me so long to get the Bob Graham done, I don't regret it. Many members have breezed round it: either because they are more gifted athletes than I am, or because they have been 'carried' round by a highly experienced team of supporters, or simply because everything went right for them first time round. In a marginally different life, something similar might have happened to me. I don't think that life would have been a happier one. The satisfaction I have gained from completing the BG has derived precisely from the fact that it was, for me, so impossibly difficult; and from the total immersion in the subject that I was forced to undergo in order to achieve it. When Fred Rogerson finally presented me with my certificate at the BG dinner, and shook my hand and quietly said 'Well done' – it meant something.

And when I occasionally return to the route (for no club member should lightly refuse a request for help from a new aspirant) I continue to be surprised by the friendly glow of recognition it gives me. Some of this relates to thoughts of fell-running heroes: the sense of being in Bill Teasdale's patch as one leaps through the tangled heather of Great Calva, or of approaching Joss Naylor's as one skids down from the cloud on Scafell. But most of it is more personal: look, there's that little hole in the turf that becomes a pool when it's wet . . . there's that rusty old iron gatepost that doesn't seem to be anywhere near any trace of a fence . . . and isn't that the rock where Charlie sat and ate Mars bars after he sprained his ankle? It feels like coming home; and, in a sense, it is. These are not just mountains: they are also a kind of communal garden, rich in many people's memories, in which I have earned a share.

I may briefly have deluded myself that my BG membership certificate in some way entitled me to consider myself the equal of the fell-running elite. I soon realised my mistake – in athletic terms, at least. But in human terms I have yet to meet a fell-running legend who has treated me – or even, I think, considered me – as anything other than an equal. And that is the other reason why I am glad that the BG detained me for so long. If it hadn't, I might never have felt the urge to dig deeper into a sport that had hitherto passed me by, as it passes most people by; in which case I would never have been drawn into one of the most generous-spirited communities imaginable.

There's a code of honour among fell-runners which places one's obligations to one's fellow runners firmly above one's obligations to oneself. Not all of them live by it – but a surprisingly large proportion do. I think this is because, almost by definition, fell-runners are people who are ambitious neither for prestige nor for profit. Instead, they are motivated by a thirst for joy: the joy of being totally absorbed, as our ancestors were, in wild environments; the joy of throwing off the straitjackets of caution and civilisation; the joy of finding and pushing back limits; and, occasionally, the joy of doing things that one had thought impossible.

For a brief period after my BG success, I found it hard to let go. Many people do. When Hugh Symonds got to the end of his continuous traverse of the British 3,000-footers he was so reluctant to stop that he went over to Ireland and did all the 3,000-footers there as well. So it was with me. Having developed the physical and psychological tools to complete an overwhelmingly difficult fell-running challenge, I felt almost irresistibly tempted to find other such challenges on which to use them. There are plenty to choose from: adventure races, the Scottish and Welsh rounds, the great overseas challenges; or, on more familiar territory, bigger and better variations on the original BG theme. As I write, there are thirteen people who have done Rogerson-approved '50 at 50' rounds (i.e. fifty peaks at the age of fifty), twelve who have done fifty-five or more (including three who did so at the age of fifty-five), nine who have done winter rounds (a far harder proposition than those two short words suggest) and one who has done two rounds in forty-eight hours. There was no danger of my doing any of that, or of my climbing Everest (as Mark McDermott did) or attempting to win the world's most elite 100-mile races (as Mark Hartell did). But surely there must be some such further peak I could aim for – perhaps even one that no one else had done before? For a moment I found myself wishing away whole decades of my life, with a view to reaching a conveniently 'virgin' age that could be matched to an achievable number of peaks. Then I came to my senses, and moved on.

The pleasure I get from fell-running these days has as much to do with memory as with participation. The journey up to the Lakes never gets shorter; the journey back down gets more painful with each passing year. Inevitably, I head for the hills less than I used to. And if I make any use of the aforementioned physical and psychological tools, it is in other areas of life. But I hope it will be at least a decade before I can't get to the top of Skiddaw and back without walking; and a few decades more before I finally hang up my Walshes for good.

By then, I imagine that fell-running will be a far more marginal sport than it is today. It won't have ceased to exist altogether: they can't stop us going into the mountains – can they? – or impose a speed limit on us when we do. Yet somehow it is hard to imagine very many young people being capable of running in the mountains in twenty years' time. When Jean Dawes, the first female member of the Bob Graham 24 Hour Club, was a child growing up in Troutbeck, she and her friends used to disappear into the Lakeland hills to play for whole days at a time. When Ken Jones started the Snowdon race in 1976, children as young as six were sent scampering up to the halfway point, unaccompanied, in a junior preliminary before the main event. When Wendy Dodds was five, she was left by herself halfway up Striding Edge (in winter) and told to wait while the rest of the family proceeded to the top of Helvellyn and back. What parents today would contemplate such shocking neglect? And what children, consequently, will grow up with the kind of fearless self-reliance that is second nature to Dawes, Dodds and their ilk?

It is possible to consider the future of fell-running and be overwhelmed with melancholy. In a certain frame of mind, I see Billy Bland and Joss Naylor slipping into the same isolated obscurity as Bill Teasdale; Fred Rogerson and Roger Ingham scorned as foolish old men; Kenny Stuart tormented by memories of his lost powers; marriage after marriage falling by the wayside; Mark Hartell consumed by ever more far-fetched obsessions; and all the others, with their dodgy knees and their incomprehensible tales of derring-do, fading away like old soldiers, unheard and irrelevant.

There is a simple cure for such negative thoughts. You put on your Walshes and your Ron Hills and you head for the mountains; ideally with friends or, failing that, alone. If it's cold and wet, and your fitness isn't all that it should be, so much the better. You sniff the damp air, as a dog does; feel your shoes soften as the moisture penetrates them; and feel the breeze grow fresher as you begin to climb. Before long, you are breathing hard; a little later, you slip into the familiar rhythm and begin to focus less on what it feels like than on where you are going and how you can use your wits to deal with whatever the fells have in store for you. When you eventually get round to examining your feelings again – which might not be for some time – you realise that your anxieties have slipped unnoticed from your shoulders. And you stride forward into the unknown with new hope in your heart.

34

The view from here

SCAFELL PIKE. AN EARLY AFTERNOON IN AUGUST. It's as hot as a crowded tube train, and yet somehow strands of thin cloud, carefully arranged, obscure all but the sharp rocks in front of me.

My left ankle is a giant bruise, and I'm half-mad with thirst, but I daren't slow down for fear of losing touch with the pair of runners in front, perhaps 20 or 30 yards away. Once that happens, it's back to the map and compass, and everything will take twice as long. On the other hand, we've been running for nearly two hours already and, frankly, I've had enough.

It's no good even thinking about that. Once you start feeling sorry for yourself, you're finished. Or, rather, you're anything but finished, because you still have to get home, and the distances don't get any shorter when you give up. They just take longer.

On this occasion – the Borrowdale Fell Race – I reckon we've done about 8 out of the 17 miles, with Great Gable and Dale Head the only significant summits still to climb after this on the way back to Rosthwaite. Funny how long it takes, though, on a day like this. I'm less fit than I was in my Bob Graham days, and I'm beginning to discover just how much less.

Funny, too, how the heat drains the strength from your legs. Funny how we haven't passed any streams recently. Funny how the very best runners are already probably 3 or 4 miles ahead. And funny how, every time I get lost in my thoughts, the next time I look the pair in front are even further away.

We reach the summit, then plunge down northwards, suppressing every impulse of common sense to run freely across the slanting moonscape. It hurts, but then by this stage it hurts if you walk, too. And, the faster you run on this kind of terrain, the less likely you are to damage an ankle. Conversely, you're more likely to fall off a cliff. But there's no time to think about that. Too busy looking at the rocks.

Some walkers coming the other way glance at us indifferently: half the field will have passed them by now. Nonetheless, one of them – a middle-aged man with a thin, intelligent face – catches my eye and seems to mouth a single, incredulous word: 'Why?'

It's a good question, but, of course, there's no time to think about that either. Take your mind off these rocks for more than a fraction of a second and you'll be flat on your face or worse. And any fractions of a second you *can* spare are desperately needed for keeping an eye on the pair of runners ahead – who have now all but vanished into the mist.

'When you get to the scree on the Corridor Route,' the race organiser announced to us at the start, 'remember, it's very wet at the moment, and it's *dangerous*.' Which is a pity, because (a) I hate all forms of mountain-related danger, and (b) the scree on the Corridor Route is, I think, exactly where we're now headed.

Oddly enough, despite years of fell-running in these parts, I've never previously used this route. I suspect I haven't missed much. True, it's a brilliantly direct way to get from just below the summit of Scafell Pike to the Sty Head saddle by the lower slopes of Great Gable. But it's slippery and narrow and uncomfortably steep, and I'm pretty sure there's a ghastly drop somewhere to my left.

Then we get to the scree slopes, and my spirits rise. Yes, the 'path' heads almost vertically down. Yes, it's a long, long way to the bottom. And yes, if you once lost control it would be difficult to stop. But the stones are nice and small, and, in this stormy heat, they're not so much slippery as sticky. Never mind dangerous; this is the kind of stuff you can really let go on. You just whack your feet in and it yields like soft mud, making it twice as fast as a solid path and half as painful. I lengthen my stride and, for the first time in miles, run for the fun of it.

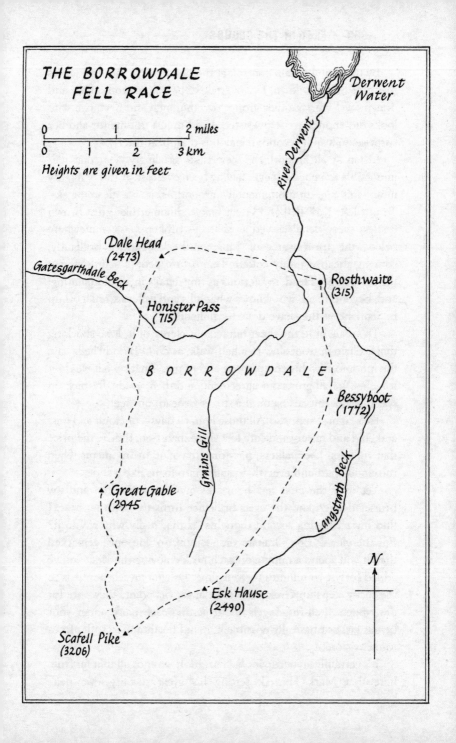

By the time I regain control, at the point where the path leaves the scree halfway down, I've overtaken the pair in front of me and drawn level with another group: two thin men and a woman who looks old enough to be my sister. And I'm just in time for another surprise: in a split second, the clouds disappear utterly.

Instantly, all around, the view is so dazzlingly clear that it is impossible to imagine it ever having been overcast. A rim of mighty mountains juts up monumentally around us, into a gleaming sky. To our left, Kirk Fell and Great Gable shimmer like great brown castles, every detail carved as sharp as broken glass; somewhere below, the fresh water of Lingmell Beck sparkles brilliantly; straight ahead, gaudily coloured miniature people scuttle across the grass at Sty Head, mysterious as tiny details in an old painting; and, beyond them, who knows what hills and valleys stretch off up to Scotland as they have done for millennia.

The scale of it, the sheer miraculous clarity of it, is so shocking that the trio in front slow to a half-walk, as do I. 'Bloody hell,' says the hindmost, to his companions and to me. 'That's what we do it for, eh?' We all grunt our agreement; and then, gradually, pick up speed again, refocusing on the stones beneath our feet.

He's right, I suppose. All those hours – days – of cloud and mist and cold and misery and sore feet and exhaustion: they're the price that runners, like walkers, pay for a few glorious moments when the clouds part and everything snaps into focus like a slide.

Yet over the next few hours, as my muscles stiffen and my bruises deepen and the clear brilliance turns to torturing heat, I find myself having second thoughts. Is that really why we do it? For the views? Bob Graham didn't think so. He once remarked that, if you spend a minute on each peak enjoying the view, you've added forty-two minutes to your time. Driving myself onwards to the rocky steps up Great Gable, I can see his point. Views are for daytrippers. Fell-running is about getting each peak under your belt as fast as physically possible. Or am I beginning to suffer from tunnel vision?

It's certainly an occupational hazard. It was not all that far from here that Mark Hartell, setting his great seventy-seven-peak twenty-four-hour record in 1997, bumped into some long-lost friends from his university days a decade earlier. Not only did he not stop; he didn't even slow down. And just as well: he completed the round with just thirteen minutes to spare.

But that was a special occasion. Fell-runners who entirely forget (as many from time to time do) how to see their sport in terms other than times and records and finishing positions are, clearly, missing the point. We run in the mountains – and not round a track or on a treadmill – because it is a more beautiful, uplifting, liberating experience. That's not to endorse the conventional modern cult of the view, which holds that areas of outstanding natural beauty exist only to be looked at, preferably from approved viewpoints and picnic areas. Rather, it's to share the more perceptive analysis of natural beauty expressed (for some reason) by Oscar Wilde. 'It seems to me that we all look at Nature too much, and live with her too little,' he wrote in *De Profundis*. 'I discern great sanity in the Greek attitude. They never chattered about sunsets, or discussed whether the shadows on the lawn were really mauve or not. But they saw that the sea was for the swimmer, and the sand for the feet of the runner. They loved the trees for the shadow that they cast, and the forest for its silence at noon . . .'

In the same way, if you're not cold, or wet, or lost, or exhausted, or bruised by rocks or covered in mud, you're not really experiencing the mountains properly. The point is not the exertion involved: it's the degree of involvement, or immersion, in the landscape. You need to *feel* it, to interact with it; to be *in* it, not just looking from the outside. You need to lose yourself – for it is then that you are most human.

These last thoughts occur to me about half an hour later, as I come careering down over the boulders on the far side of Great Gable, causing a party of walkers to look at me with what seems like astonished disapproval – as if there were something irresponsible about moving so quickly. I'm reminded of the old lady in the public swimming pool who tuts and sighs every time a passer-by is thoughtless enough to splash. What does she think a swimming pool is for? And what do these people think a mountain is for?

For some reason the grumbling of the loose boulders makes me think of Billy Bland's description of a moment in this same race, on this same slope, twenty years earlier. He was leading narrowly from John Wild, the year Wild won one of his British championships, and 'he were sitting on me all way round, and coming up Gable he were still with us. I was beginning to get concerned. I thought, "If I can't get rid of him off Gable, it's a bit kinder ground after that, he'll beat me." Anyway, for last quarter of Gable I think he was suffering a bit, but he stuck to us – he was as hard as nails, was John; I was soft next to him. Then we left Gable, and I put on a spurt, and he fell on a stone, a few hundred yards off Gable, heading for Windy Gap. I just shouted: "You all right, John?" "Aye." Anyway, it were misty as well, so I thought: "This is my kind of weather – down into Windy Gap and away." John ended up down in Gatescarth, because he lost his guide. It was a big kick to beat him, because he was a lot better runner than me. But some days you get your reward. But if he'd have said "No", I'd have turned round.'

That's what a mountain is for: stretching your limits on, not pussyfooting around. Down into Windy Gap and away. A sense of history, of running in the footsteps of the great, brings life back to my tired legs as I hobble and leap down that same bouldery slope. A sea of cloud is descending as I reach Windy Gap, and several of the runners in front – half a dozen are in sight now – seem confused. I don't share their uncertainty. It's the BG route for the next couple of miles, and I could do it in my sleep. I strike out confidently for Green Gable, Brandreth and Grey Knotts, and smile smugly as several of them ignore my lead and head off in different directions. I call to a couple of the nearest to set them right. It's not as if I'm racing to win.

Smugness keeps the spring in my step on the way down from Grey Knotts to Honister. There's a clever zigzag you can take that allows you to do the whole descent on soft turf at a runnable gradient. You'd never discover this from map-reading: it's two sides of a triangle rather than one. But the direct route is too steep and rocky to be negotiated at speed, while exhaustive tests (by me,

Charles and Gawain) have shown that the long way is both quicker and easier.

After Honister, though, my strength drains away. The ascent to Dale Head should be easy: not too long, not too steep, nice springy turf, with an obvious path by an obvious fence. Yet today it seems to go on for ever. Once again, a pair of runners ahead pulls away into the mist. Once again, I try not to think about what I am feeling. Instead, I think about something Kenny Stuart told me about this same stretch of this same race.

He, of course, was leading; but John Wild – again – was pressing him hard. 'It was a hot summer's day, and I was starting to get cramp. You set off from Honister, and it drags and drags, and I was knackered and I had to keep stopping with cramp. But I could see him coming up behind me, and because *he* wasn't getting any faster, that was the only thing that got me back home. He was knackered – so maybe it was worth keeping going. And eventually I got back to coming through the quarries, and I recovered again.'

Once again, I look to history to reinvigorate me. This time, it doesn't work. Kenny was a great champion. I'm not. I'm knackered, and I stay knackered. But I do keep going, and the top does eventually come, as tops generally do. This one, unfortunately, is succeeded by half a mile or so of particularly agonising descent, tussocky, bouldery and littered with hidden holes. It's too steep to be taken slowly, too wildly uneven to be taken at speed by anyone but a lunatic. My only comfort is that, below, I can see some other runners staggering leglessly and, from time to time, slowing almost to a rest. Maybe it *is* worth keeping going. Growling audibly, I force myself into a series of aggressive leaps and slithers, and by the time I have reached the slate quarries I have caught them up.

'Whose bloody idea was this?' says one.

'Yours,' says his friend. I hope the grumpiness is feigned.

I weave my way to the front of the group, and fall into conversation with the one who is moving best. He's a fellow Southerner, running his first fell race – and, he insists, his last. 'I've done most things,' he wheezes, 'marathons, triathlons and all that stuff. Someone told me I couldn't come to Borrowdale without trying this. Well, I've tried it now, and I'm not bloody trying it again.'

'Same here,' I say. But, even as I say it, I know that I probably will try it again. I'm trembling with pain and exhaustion, but I've just enough positive spirit left to reflect that, if I don't like this, I shouldn't be doing it; and that, if we don't look for the pleasure in our more challenging moments, we won't find it. Sod it, I think: I *will* enjoy this.

So I do. Stretching my stride, skipping from loose slate to loose slate, I leave my companion behind in an instant. Soon the quarry gives way to a long stretch of one of those perfect grassy fields that it seems churlish to cross by any means other than running at 100 miles per hour. It's smooth, springy, even-cambered and steep without being too steep. Given that I'm still not entirely sure I ever want to run another fell race in my life, I might as well do this one justice; so I call to mind some of the countless zoological metaphors that I have encountered during my researches: Ernest Dalzell displaying 'the speed of a Helvellyn fox and the sure-footedness of a Martindale deer', Bill Teasdale 'the agility and sure-footedness of a mountain goat', Joss Naylor 'the quiet agility of a cougar' – and down I fly like a wild beast, leaping and bouncing, joyfully, madly, hanging in the air longer than nature intended, my whole being singing with physical alertness. I just hope there aren't any nasty surprises hidden round the corner where the path disappears through the gate below.

There aren't. The path begins to level out, and soon – after a wade through a cold ford that reduces my legs irretrievably to jelly – I'm dragging myself over the final few hundred metres of lane. It can't be more than a quarter of a mile to the finish, but it seems to go on for ever. Do I really have to do this? My legs are entirely dead. Would it really matter if I stopped here?

But I know I'd regret it if I did, so I plod leadenly on, distracting myself with the memory of that last field, and with the thought that, whatever troubles I may have been carrying around in my head before the race, I have now entirely forgotten what they were. This thought is rather refreshing. Whatever physical pains it has involved, this ordeal has utterly absorbed me, forcing my brain to focus on the kind of concerns for which it evolved – navigation, survival, balance, digging deep – rather than on the fretful urban anxieties to which it has become habituated. Reconnecting with your inner animal, I suppose you could call it; and it feels good. Especially when, blissfully, I catch sight of the finish.

I limp into the final field just in time to hear an old fell-running joke on the PA system – 'Let's hear it for the real men who can stay on their feet for five hours' – before collapsing over the line in 105th place. The fact that nearly a hundred others are either slower or have given up altogether doesn't alter the fact that I haven't performed well; or that some people finished more than two hours ago. But, frankly, I don't care. I've had a long, hard run, and now it's over. And, as Joe Hands famously told a journalist after winning an early Mountain Trial, 'Ah feel better noo ah've stopped.'

After ten minutes on my back, I get up. There's nowhere to shower or change, and nothing to drink but the contents of a shared dustbin of saliva-flecked orange squash. Yet somehow or other I need to make myself feel human again before hurrying off to another appointment.

So I hobble down the lane to a stony track which leads in turn to a little knee-deep ford behind a field, crossed by stepping stones and hung about with old green trees. And here, for fully fifteen minutes, I lie down in the cool stream. Never have I felt such comfort: the smooth stones beneath, the gentle massaging of the current, the feel and scent and taste of the sweetest fresh water. But the view, too, seems supernaturally perfect: dappled, liquid shadows in the foreground, and, visible through a gap in the leaves, a line of green mountains shining beneath a clear blue sky. This, I tell myself, is England at its best. And I am immersed in it.

Back in the field, some hours later, the registration tent becomes a party marquee, with a bar and a band and, it seems, the whole of Borrowdale youth, out for a wild time. (Have the local shops run out of bras?) Dehydrated runners are beginning to reassemble, too, and there's already a rising buzz of hilarity. I'd like to stay to see some pole-climbing, but we're here as a family, and children aren't allowed after 9 p.m. So we wander off quietly, drinking in the cool of the evening, before heading back to the house we are staying in near Penrith.

Clare drives, fearing that I might fall asleep; so I gaze peacefully out of the window as we wind through Borrowdale's shadowy lanes. Through the trees on our left, I catch sight of Derwent Water, impossibly delicate and beautiful, like a watercolour accidentally smudged into perfection. For the second time that day, I find myself seeing the Lake District as Wordsworth or Turner – or, for that matter, an ordinary tourist – might have seen it: liquid, luminous, tranquil as eternity. The evening light is so soft it feels like moonlight; the lake is a melting glass of mauves and greys; the mountains behind are green and still; and the air is sweet with the smell of fresh water.

The sense of sublimity is so overpowering that I seem to be dissolving. And the thought for some reason slips into my head that, when it is my turn to die, there might be worse ways to prepare than to gaze once more on a sight like this, as Mike Rose gazed on Jura. Perhaps, I muse (and the thought is a happier, less morbid one than it sounds), one or more of my children might consider taking me to Keswick in my last days, and, depending on their fitness and mine, leading me or wheeling me on one final expedition into the mountains. There would, of course, be no question of moving at speed; nor, presumably, of going very far. Yet I suspect that the draining-away of life might nonetheless feel better if offset by a farewell gaze at the splendours of these Lakeland hills: perhaps a Helvellyn sunrise, or the enchanted tapestry of the Newlands valley spread out below Dale Head.

And though I may have lost the power of speech by then, my escorts can reasonably assume that, as I gaze, my head will be full of thoughts of fell-running joy and glory: of Ernest Dalzell, careering down Burnsall in defiance of the laws of physics; of Joss Naylor, hurrying invincibly through endless scorched rock fields; of Fred and Margaret Rogerson waiting in car parks on stormy nights with hot drinks and blankets; of Charlie and Gawain, giggling in hopeless despair at their and my navigational ineptitude; of Pete Bland, trance-eyed with delight on the Ambleside finishing line; of my own unreal finest hour, trotting through moonlit Newlands lanes to complete my Bob Graham round; and of Kenny Stuart, dancing like an angel on the points of needle-sharp rocks, light and sure-footed as the rest of us are in dreams.

Epilogue: 2021

Authors reread their published works at their peril. Flaws leap out at you with merciless clarity, and after a few hundred pages you're liable to feel a crushing sense of failure. Nonetheless, in recent months I have revisited this book repeatedly.

There were several reasons for this. One was an escapist urge, in the shadow of the Covid-19 pandemic, to revisit happier times. Another was practical: in late 2020, I recorded an audio edition, for Isis Publishing, which required me to read the whole book out loud. But Aurum's 2021 reprint – the edition you are now reading – has prompted a more searching re-examination. Is *Feet in the Clouds* still fit for purpose? Or has it failed the test of time?

The book is full of facts that are now out of date. It is full, too, of assumptions and observations about the world that seem less perceptive now than when I wrote them. Every chapter could be substantially improved with the benefit of hindsight. To take one very small example: halfway down page 4, you'll find the dismissive assertion that 'Feelings are for girls'. It barely seems necessary, in 2021, to point out what's wrong with that. I'm embarrassed to have written it. Even in 2004, it was crass. A male runner who suggested that a woman couldn't match a man for inner steel merely made himself look stupid, especially if he himself was an ageing plodder of obviously limited toughness, and even more so today, in the era of Jasmin Paris and Nicky Spinks. So why does that sentence still appear in this new edition?

The answer is: partly *because* it makes me look stupid. Back in the 1990s, when that particular internal monologue was taking place, that was how I and male runners of my generation tended to talk among ourselves; it never occurred to us that anyone might be offended. We didn't mean it literally. We all knew women who could out-run us on the fells, and we all knew women who were far less likely than us to wilt in other areas of life. But this was the language with which we were used to motivating one another; the sporting language we had grown up with – 'Man up!'; 'Grow a pair!'; 'Come on, you big girl's blouse . . .', and so on. Excising that four-word sentence from this new edition would, at a stroke, make me appear less patronizing, sexist and dinosaur-like than I really was. I would be falsifying the record to make myself look better. So I have left those four words unchanged and, as a result, continue to look stupid.

It is only a slight comfort to remind myself that there was also a practical objection to changing that sentence. If I started rewriting the past, where would I stop? So, with some anxiety, I have allowed nearly all of the book's superseded facts to remain uncorrected. Dates, times, distances, record-holders: I've left them all as they were in April 2004. There is one major exception: the length of the Bob Graham Round. Measurements with GPS systems and modern mapping software suggest that the traditional figure of 72 miles, accepted for decades and quoted in all previous editions of *Feet in the Clouds*, may be an overestimate, with the true distance probably being nearer 66 miles, always assuming that you never deviate from the optimum route. The Round is so central to my story that it seems perverse to stick to a key measurement that I know to be inaccurate. Hence the revised figure used in this edition.

For the rest, however, I have upheld my rash policy of standing by what I wrote, even when it is no longer true. I realize that this, too, makes me look stupid, yet somehow it feels healthy to accept and embrace that. Time makes fools of all of us, and writers of contemporary non-fiction more than most. We think we are depicting the world as it is, only to find that our published writings describe the world as it used to be, long ago. *Feet in the Clouds* may not yet qualify as ancient history, but it is starting to show its age. The whole ethos of fell-running has evolved since 2004, while the boundaries of what's possible on the fells have shifted considerably.

Hence this Epilogue, to acknowledge that the sport celebrated in this book is no longer quite as I described it.

The summer of 2020 alone saw a once-in-a-lifetime spell of record-breaking on the British fells. There isn't space here to list all the new 'fastest known times' (as they're now called), let alone to describe their setting. (Read Ally Beaven's book, *Broken*, for the astonishing full story.) Yet *Feet in the Clouds* feels naked without any reference to them at all, so here are a few highlights. In July 2020, the 268-mile Pennine Way record, set by Mike Hartley thirty-one years earlier, was broken twice in a week, first by John Kelly (64 hours 46 minutes) and then by Damian Hall (61 hours 35 minutes 15 seconds). That same summer, Ian Stewart became the first person to complete a continuous run of all fifty-eight Cairngorms Munros, in 5 days 22 hours; Finlay Wild ran Ramsay's Round, solo and unsupported, in 14 hours 42 minutes 40 seconds; Paul O'Callaghan became the first person to do a double Wicklow Round, in 46 hours 20 minutes; and Sabrina Verjee, an Ambleside vet, became the first woman to complete a continuous round of the Wainwrights, in 6 days 17 hours 51 minutes (although she didn't claim this as an official record, having received some physical assistance from her supporters).

More dramatically, from the perspective of this book's themes, Kim Collison, a professional running coach from Mungrisdale, pushed the Lakeland 24-hour record up to seventy-eight peaks (twenty-three years after Mark Hartell's seventy-seven-peak record); Beth Pascall, a paediatrician from Derbyshire, cut the women's Bob Graham record to 14 hours 34 minutes; and, in October, George Foster, a teacher, coach and running guide from North Yorkshire, ran the BG in 13 hours 44 minutes – 9 minutes faster than Billy Bland's legendary 1982 time.

The assumption was that people had benefited from that year's unprecedented lockdown: more training, more focus, fewer distractions. But the grand old records had been tumbling even before the Covid-19 pandemic began. Foster's achievement would have made more headlines had Billy's epic mark not been erased from the record books already, by Kilian Jornet, the Catalan full-time athlete and celebrity, whose 2018 time of 12 hours 52 minutes seems unlikely to be surpassed for a while. Billy, whose record had stood for thirty-six years, congratulated Jornet warmly at the finish.

In 2019, meanwhile, Paul Tierney set a Wainwright's Round record of 6 days 6 hours 5 minutes (7 hours faster than the time with which Steve Birkinshaw first broke Joss Naylor's record in 2014). That was also the year in which Jasmin Paris – another vet, based in Edinburgh – became the first woman to win the Montane Spine Race (the Pennine Way in the depths of winter), in 3 days 11 hours 12 minutes – 12 hours faster than the men's record. Paris's other jaw-dropping achievements included, at that point, a women's BG record of 15 hours 24 minutes, set in 2016, which knocked more than two and a half hours off the record set the previous year by Nicky Spinks, a West Yorkshire cattle farmer. But Spinks, just a few weeks later, reclaimed her place in the record books by becoming only the second person to complete a sub-48-hour back-to-back double BG, with a time – 45 hours 30 minutes – more than an hour faster than Roger Baumeister's pioneering double in 1979.

Those are just a few of the more sensational headlines, selected from the past seven years rather than the past seventeen. There are plenty more, but the general point should already be clear. The epic fell-running achievements of the twentieth century, which seemed unsurpassable when I described them in this book, have mostly been surpassed, often by spectacular margins, in the early decades of the twenty-first century. That's partly because the most daunting challenges have been tamed by repeated conquest, just as Everest and the four-minute mile were tamed. It also reflects a more important truth: life goes on. Oceans of rainwater have flowed under Cumbria's stone bridges since 2004, and the fells via which most of it descended remain gloriously unchanged. The world, however, has remade itself.

Those superseded records are arguably the least of *Feet in the Clouds*'s anachronisms. The real issue is that fell-running itself has changed.

When I first wrote this book, the informed consensus (as discussed in Chapter 25) was that the sport was dying. In one sense, sadly, it has continued to do so. Time has been picking off its grand old witnesses, including Fred Rogerson, who died in 2010; Bill Smith, who died out on the fells in 2011; and Pete Bland, who died in 2020 of Covid-19. All three were much mourned by a fell-running community that recognized that part of itself had died with them.

Yet the sport itself has survived, or perhaps even been reborn. Membership of the Fell Runners' Association now stands at around 7,500, up by almost half since 2004; the Bob Graham 24-hour Club has grown similarly: as I write this, the number of people who have completed the Round stands at 2,384. (I was 1,023rd.) At the same time, there has been a huge rise in the popularity – and profitability – of adventure-racing, trail-running and, in particular, ultra-running. Kit shops, magazines and coaching and guiding services have thrived on the trend; adventure-running memoirs have become an established and occasionally best-selling literary genre; and the internet is awash with videos, blogs, websites and social media accounts from which outsiders can absorb the basics of the sport without going anywhere near a mountain.

Fell-running has felt the effects in many ways. Today's champions and record-breakers are very different – superficially, at least – from the heroes of *Feet in the Clouds*. They have kit sponsors and websites and share their adventures on social media. On the fells, they benefit from technological advances that even visionaries such as Mark Hartell and Mark McDermott could barely have imagined in the 1990s. And, of course, it's not just the record-breakers. There's a whole new generation of fell-runners who are accustomed to using a whole new generation of kit: lightweight packs; thermals and waterproofs that you barely notice you're wearing; lighter, grippier fell shoes that also provide cushioning and support; hydration packs, soft flasks, energy gels and drinks calibrated with ultra-runners in mind; lightweight walking poles; tiny but brilliant head-torches; heart-rate monitors; trackers; and, in many cases, all-but-infallible GPS watches.

It would be mean-spirited to argue that any of this detracts from the spectacular achievements of recent years: athletes have always sought the best available kit. But it does make it all the more impressive that a handful of the records mentioned in this book – for Grasmere, the Three Peaks, Borrowdale, Ben Nevis, Snowdon – remain, even now, unbroken. Perhaps I underestimated the extent to which I was writing about a golden age of the sport.

Meanwhile, those leaps-and-bounds advances in mountain-running technology are symptomatic of a wider alteration in the sport's character. Fell-running has been dragged into the twenty-first century. You can still find no-frills races where the greatest luxuries are a dustbin of orange squash, a nearby stream to wash in, and a picnic table for the prizes. But more and more frequently, events share the values of the mainstream running industry, where people expect goody-bags and changing facilities, and bad experiences provoke complaints, and the organizers are seen as service-providers rather than kind souls who are doing the rest of us a favour.

Traditionalists regret this. In a column for *The Fellrunner* a few years ago, former FRA chairman Graham Breeze spoke for many when he wrote of his yearning for 'the values of an era before we had football crowds turning up to compete in fell races, forum requests for Garmin routes, demands for race results before the last competitor has finished and, from the narcissists, "Are there any photographs?"'

I share his nostalgia. In recent decades, the profoundly natural and inherently low-cost activity of running has increasingly been packaged and sold back to us as a consumer product, implicitly out-of-reach to those without the disposable income to pay for it. It's not for me to judge those who choose to buy into this conceit. But I can't help feeling that it misses the point of fell-running.

Of course you can partially tame the wild if you throw enough cash at it. Just look at the queues of moneyed mountaineers on Everest, kidding themselves that paying £30,000 to be shepherded to the top is comparable to the insane heroism of Hillary, Tenzing, Mallory or Irvine. But it isn't. For mastering the mountains to mean something, you have to use inner resources, not financial ones – hence the Bob Graham 24 Hour Club's announcement in 2020 that it would 'no longer accept applications for membership where paid-for or professional guided services have been used'.

Then there are the crowds. Race organizers who worry about not having enough competitors are now vastly outnumbered by those wrestling with the problem of having too many. Enter the Senior Guides Race at Grasmere and you could easily find yourself up against twice as many rivals as I faced in the crowded race described in Chapter 24, and ten times as many as Reeves and Sedgwick typically ran against. If there aren't one or two among them whose lack of experience or ability makes them a nuisance to everyone else, consider yourself lucky. And that's before you consider the simple equation that twice as many runners means twice as much erosion.

There are some who say that all these developments are my fault, and that without *Feet in the Clouds* fell-running would still be the unspoilt, niche pursuit it used to be. I rarely hear this charge without examining my conscience. On balance, however, my conscience is clear.

It's true that this book reached a far wider audience than I or anyone else anticipated. It has sold in the tens of thousands rather than the expected hundreds, spawned countless media articles, been generously recommended on physical and online runners' grapevines, and provoked a surprisingly persistent stream of letters thanking me for the book, asking my advice on fell-running matters, asking for support on BG attempts (although I'm getting a bit slow for that), seeking feedback on unpublished fell-running memoirs; and, gratifyingly often, sharing priceless nuggets of fell-running lore or experience that they had previously thought no one was interested in. All this suggests that *Feet in the Clouds* may have helped to release a collective enthusiasm that was already there.

But to blame the overcrowding and commercialization that have sometimes accompanied this enthusiasm on 'the *Feet in the Clouds* effect' seems absurd and unfair. Yes, numbers on the fells are up. Numbers are up everywhere. The UK is a more crowded country – by 8 million people – than in 2004. We are also a more modern country: more mobile, more connected, more materialistic and, in many cases, more focused on the pursuit (and sharing) of thrilling adventures and fulfilling experiences. None of this has anything to do with me; and you have only to read *Feet in the Clouds* to find proof that there were problems with crowds, and complaints about incomers, back when I was still writing the book.

People have been urging the exclusion of outsiders and newcomers from the fells for generations. William Wordsworth campaigned in 1844 against the Kendal and Windermere railway, arguing that the line would open up the Lake District to the masses. He was correct but also, self-evidently, wrong: had the fells not gradually been made more generally accessible – by transport, by access legislation, by bank holidays, by the National Trust – a great social injustice would have been perpetuated, and the culture of fell-running as I have described it would barely have existed.

I'd also argue that the ultra-traditionalist 'keep-the-sport-secret' approach is counter-productive. The argument that people should be allowed to take responsibility for their own welfare in the mountains holds good only if there are people who are *capable* of looking after themselves in a hostile mountain environment. Every expert in such matters was a newcomer once, and if a new generation is to learn the necessary skills and attitudes, novices need encouragement.

Meanwhile, if those who are in a position to do so don't talk and write about what fell-running is really about, then the incomers who inevitably drift into the sport will arrive with the wrong mindset, and the rest of the world will regard it, them and their detractors with incomprehension and, occasionally, hostility.

Readers with medium-length memories may recall a weekend of fell-running headlines in October 2008, when hundreds of fell-runners were widely reported to be 'missing' in the fells around Borrowdale after 'biblical' storms disrupted the Original Mountain Marathon. What the excited media largely neglected to point out was that the runners in question were experienced, well-equipped navigators who had been expecting bad weather and had come with the express intention of spending the night on a mountainside. They were only 'missing' in the sense that the police – who persuaded the organizers to cancel the event after it had started – could not say precisely where they were. The runners could.

I wrote about the controversy for *The Independent* and, before doing so, spoke to many of those who had taken part. None had felt themselves to be lost, in trouble or let down by the organizers. Yet mine was, I think, the only article in the national press that did not imply (or state) that the organizers had been culpably reckless in letting the event go ahead.

This underlined, for me, one of the points made in Chapter 21: that there is a philosophical gulf between the way those of us who love fell-running see the world and the way 'normal' people see it. If this gulf is widening, the consequences can be deeply unpleasant for those who find themselves on the wrong side of 'normal' opinion – as the organizers of the 2008 OMM will attest. I find it hard to understand how, in such a climate, a book that attempts to explain the mindset of fell-runners to a wider audience can be a bad thing.

I'd also argue that the gulf between old and new may be smaller than it seems. Authors like me can romanticize the sport as much as we like, but we can't magic away the difficulties and discomforts of running in the mountains, and newcomers who don't feel a genuine calling to be fell-runners are unlikely to stick with the sport for long. At the elite level, meanwhile, the epic fell-running feats of the early twenty-first-century seem grounded in precisely the same admirable qualities – mountain-craft, resourcefulness, courage, positivity, bloody-minded resilience – that made possible those famous twentieth-century achievements that I have chronicled in *Feet in the Clouds*.

If I were writing this book afresh today, it would alter the tone very little if I added a chapter about Nicky Spinks, whose fitness and resilience, like Joss Naylor's, owe much to the rigours of her life as a farmer; or if there was another about Jasmin Paris, whose mid-race pauses to express milk for her baby while she was winning the Montane Spine Race seem to echo Joss's diversions from his record attempts to help lambs in distress. The old order may be changing, but fell-running's special soul continues to express itself, in subtly altered ways. Even Kilian Jornet, for all his professionalism, shares some of Billy Bland's mountain-goat-like qualities and, like Billy, seems more at home on a rough scree-slope than in the bright lights of a busy city.

I cannot agree with those hard-core traditionalists who reject modernity in all its forms. Nor do I believe that the fell-running should embrace uncritically the shallow, self-centred values of the twenty-first-century consumer-runner. The sport I have tried to celebrate in *Feet in the Clouds* is a sport in the broadest sense: not just a set of challenges and records but a culture whose appeal has a lot to do with the fact that it is rooted in untamed places and in traditional, local, community values. There's a place in it for science and technology, and a place for ferocious competitiveness and individual ambition, just as there has always been. But it isn't, or shouldn't be, an exclusive or a selfish sport; and nor, by implication, should it be a materialistic one.

Perhaps I've become an old fogey, but for me fell-running's great gift is to re-introduce us to parts of ourselves that neither thrive on material possessions nor wither in their absence. Seventeen years ago, its attractions included the escape it offered from a culture of suffocating affluence; today it's as likely to offer solace in an age of economic hardship. In each case, it isn't about money or the things that money can buy. It is about more essential forms of enrichment. Fell-running humbles you; you are a feeble nothing relative to the might of nature. But your struggles with the mountains empower you, too, by reawakening dormant instincts for freedom and survival. And sometimes, if you keep going, they can bring you to the most thrilling discovery of all: that you have the courage to do much, much more than you ever thought possible. Can any of us really claim the right to block others from seeking such rewards?

If *Feet in the Clouds* has stimulated new interest in fell-running, I have no regrets. To thrive in the future, the sport needs new enthusiasts, to nurture and cherish it as this book's heroes have done. Each new generation will love it in a slightly different way. If the love is genuine, it will include respect as well as desire. The challenge for the older generation is to pass on their values to the new. The challenge for the incomers is to listen.

Richard Askwith, Northamptonshire, February 2021

Acknowledgments

I am indebted to so many people that it would be invidious to single out anyone – apart from my family – for special thanks. Pretty much everyone who is mentioned by name in this book has helped me; so have many who are not. I am grateful to them all.

I would, however, like to acknowledge some of the written sources I have used – not least so that those who find the subject interesting can find further reading.

Chief among these is Bill Smith's wonderful *Stud Marks on the Summits*, privately published in 1985 and long since out of print. *Stud Marks* is a definitive sporting history in a way that this book can never be; it is also an object lesson in authoritative historical writing. Without that as my introduction, my work would have been immeasurably harder. And I am all the more indebted to Bill because he has also been kind enough to give me time and advice.

The rest of fell-running literature – at least until the beginning of 2004 – can be listed pretty much in its entirety. Most, unfortunately, are either out of print or, at best, hard to obtain. Unless otherwise stated, they are privately published. Roy Lomas's encyclopaedic *Grasmere Sports: The First 150 Years* (2002) is expensive, but packed with fascinating historical detail and old photographs. *See the Conquering Hero Comes*, by Michael Miller and Denis Bland (1973), focuses more specifically on the Grasmere Guides Race, while *Our Traditional Lakeland Sports*, by Marjorie Blackburn (Ambleside Sports Association, 2000), tells you most things you could want to know about Ambleside Sports.

Further south, Rob Grillo's *Staying the Distance* (1999) and Peter Watson's *Rivington Pike* (Walsh, 2001) will tell you about the history of fell-running in Keighley and Horwich respectively. And there are valuable profiles of several leading fell champions in Neil Shuttleworth's *The Best of British* (1990) and Rex Woods's *Grasmere's Giants of Today* (1975).

42 Peaks, by Roger Smith (Bob Graham 24 Hour Club, 1982 and

1992), should be the first port of call for anyone interested in the BG. For a fuller picture, it's worth trying to obtain Fred Rogerson's monumental *History and Records of Notable Fell Walks Within the Lake District* (1978), while A. Harry Griffin's *Inside the Real Lakeland* (Guardian Press, 1961) has an interesting chapter on the subject.

Hugh Symonds's *Running High* (Hayloft, 1991, reissued 2004) and Mike Cudahy's *Wild Trails to Far Horizons* (Unwin Hyman, 1989) give vivid personal accounts of historic fell-running exploits from the perspective of the great athletes who performed them, as does Joss Naylor's pamphlet, *Joss Naylor MBE Was Here* (KLETS, Braithwaite). *Eddie Campbell: An Appreciation* (1998) does what it says on the cover; as does *Fifty Years Running: A History of the Mountain Trial* (LDMTA, 2002).

Suse Coon's *Race You to the Top* (1989) and Hugh Dan MacLennan's *The Ben Race* (Ben Nevis Race Association, 1994) cover Scottish hill-running, while *The History of Welsh Athletics*, by John Collins, Alan and Brenda Currie, Mike Walters and Clive Williams (Dragon Sports Books, 2002), has a good chapter on the origins of the sport in Wales.

Fell and Hill Running, by Norman Matthews and Dennis Quinlan (BAF, 1996), and *Off-Road Running*, by Sarah Rowell (Crowood, 2002), are good practical introductions. PWT Productions, Striding Edge and Zanzibar Films have all made useful videos.

And that, apart from various tangentially connected academic papers, is about it. (Talking of which, several members of the British Society of Sports Historians – notably John Bale, Tony Collins, Lynne Duval, Jeffrey Hill, Martin Johnes – have been kind enough to help me.) I should, however, express special thanks to Fred Rogerson, Leonard Horton, Roger Ingham, Trevor Batchelor and Neil Shuttleworth, for sharing the contents of their memories and their archives with me; to Dalesman Publishing, for letting me trawl through their archives; and to the staff of Ambleside, Kendal, Keswick and Skipton public libraries and of the Armitt Library and the PA and Colindale newspaper libraries. I have also derived much pleasure and information from immersing myself in some excellent periodicals, especially the *Fellrunner* (with special thanks to Jon Broxap and Paul Condron for letting me study their collections, and to Dave Jones, the current editor, for his time and advice); Dave Woodhead's late lamented *Up & Down* magazine (with special thanks to Dave for digging out old copies); and Keswick Athletic Club's *Pacemaker* newsletter (with special thanks to Dave Spedding for lending me all his back issues). My fellow members of Keswick have, I should add, been overwhelmingly kind and helpful; I am particularly grateful to Pete

Richards for his time, enthusiasm and kindness, which extended to drawing my attention to various errors in my manuscript – a service also performed, no less generously or valuably, by Selwyn Wright.

I should also thank Graham Coster, who first suggested that a book such as this should be written; and Brie Burkeman, who first suggested that I should write it. Above all, though, my thanks are due to Clare, Isobel and Edward, for their patience and encouragement; to my father and sister; and to the great mass of ordinary fell-runners, friends and strangers, whose collective generosity in pretty much all matters has done wonders for my faith in human nature.